© TOPOGRÁF Kft. 2003

ROHÁLY – MÉSZÁROS – NAGYMAROSY

TERRA
BENEDICTA
2003

Lukács János úrnak

a Corvin lánc birtokosának

őszinte barátsággal

Rohály Gábor

Budapest 2004. febr. 25.

For dr. Josef Schuller M.W.

TERRA BENEDICTA

THE LAND OF HUNGARIAN
WINE -TOKAJ AND BEYOND

GÁBOR ROHÁLY

GABRIELLA MÉSZÁROS

ANDRÁS NAGYMAROSY

BORKOLLÉGIUM

AKO PUBLISHING
2003

Edited by
GÁBOR ROHÁLY

Written by
GABRIELLA MÉSZÁROS
ANDRÁS NAGYMAROSY
GÁBOR ROHÁLY
LAJOS SZOLLÁR
SÁNDOR TÓTH

Translated from the Hungarian by
PÉTER LENGYEL

English translation checked and corrected by
ROBERT HODGSON, BSc

Design and typography
ROZINA PALOTÁS

Layout
QVIRT GRAFIKAI MŰHELY:
GYÖRGY MAURER • ÁDÁM MOLNÁR

Maps
EDE-ANDRÁS MOLNÁR
TOPO-GRÁF LTD.

Photos
TIBOR DÉKÁNY • ZOLTÁN KOMÁROMI
ATTILA MÉSZÁROS • GÁBOR ROHÁLY • ZOLTÁN SZABÓ

Published with the generous support of
Hungary's Ministry of Foreign Affairs

Printed by
DÜRER NYOMDA KFT., GYULA
managing director András Megyik

Published by
AKÓ KIADÓ

ISBN:
963 210 6628

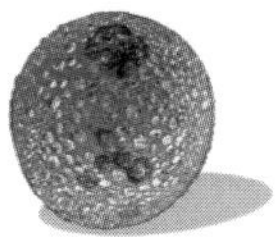

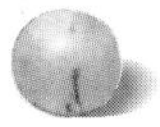

Introduction

Terra benedicta – Blessed land. This characterization of Tokaj, uttered by Pope Benedict XIV, is a good place to start from in an attempt to introduce the grape-growing and winemaking of the country. The Carpathian Basin is perfectly endowed with fertile land for agriculture, and the rich flavor of fruits and produce grown in the best ecosystems within this larger region has won universal admiration. Although hardly a match for the world's wine superpowers in size, the regions of Hungary offer wines of a diversity and personality that can rival selections from even the greatest of wine producing countries. Hungary has it all, from crisp sparkling to fruity but full-bodied dry whites, to intriguing Kadarka or velvety Cabernet—not to mention Tokaji, that miracle of a sweet wine.

In presenting this book, we aim to fill a gap by providing much-needed up-to-date information about this little-known country and its wines. It has also been our intention to dispel misconceptions and fallacies, such as the picture of a peasant drinking Tokaji Aszú *from the bottle* on the cover of a French book on Tokaj… What nonsense! This flies in the face of everything ever written about Tokaji, by such authors as Andersen, Balzac, Böll, Brentano, Browning, Casanova, Diderot, Dumas, Flaubert, France, Goethe, Ibsen, Körner, Lenau, Mickievicz, Montesquieu, Neruda, Swift, Tolstoy, and Voltaire.

While we have attempted to supply basic reliable information, it was never our goal to write a treatise of scholarly and scientific precision, in which every detail—say, the list of vineyards in a particular "appellation"–is infallibly accurate, complete and true both historically and with regard to the present state of affairs.

The new challenges facing Hungary since the collapse of the Communist system have now multiplied with the country's impending accession to the European Union. As the regulatory framework is in constant flux these days, much of Hungary's wine legislation tends to be rather ephemeral. Under the circumstances, even if we attempted an in-depth legal analysis, most of the regulations would no longer apply by the time this book reached the reader. A particularly volatile area is the designation of wine regions or appellations, where significant changes have occurred in every one of the past five years. We ask the reader to bear with us on this count.

In this book, we have sought to emphasize those assets of Hungarian viticulture that could help make the country's wines successful contenders in the global arena—particularly the fascinating diversity of its terroirs. The best winemakers of the country have begun to exploit the fabulous potential of this blessed land, and they certainly deserve whatever recognition we can give them on these pages. Just as auspicious are the recent developments in the wine trade of Hungary, where for a long time there was only central distribution but no trade as such to talk about.

Often the only regret with which wine professionals leave Hungary after their first visit is that they did not come earlier. We only hope that this book will provoke the reader into asking himself: "Why have I not read all this about Hungary before?"

The Publisher
Budapest,
May 2003

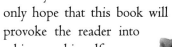

5

Foreword

Hungarians, with very good reason, have always been proud of their deep-rooted wine traditions. In the second half of the twentieth century, however, under communist rule these traditions faltered and, in some cases, all but disappeared. Now, as the wine industry emerges from this period of mass-produced, low-quality wine made from high-yielding and easily-maintained vines, Hungarian winemakers are reaching back to their past for inspiration.

It is not a question of simply trying to recreate this past. Few of the wines made sixty-five years ago would, perhaps, satisfy the increasingly sophisticated tastes of the new millenium. As economic circumstances alter, fashions change – and wine is no exception to this rule. Rather, Hungarian winemakers are rediscovering their traditional grape varieties, cultivating them increasingly in accordance with the viticultural norms that are now taken as standard almost the whole world over, and are beginning once again to make wines which reflect the individuality of these grape varieties.

Their names are wondrous to behold – and sometimes very difficult for non-Hungarians to get their tongues around: Csabagyöngye, Ezerjó, Hárslevelű, Juhfark, Kéknyelű and Leányka, not to mention modern cross varieties like Királyleányka and Cserszegi Fűszeres. However, as western tastes for the grape varieties that have been so successful over the past quarter century – most notably, Chardonnay – begin to get a bit jaded, these wines, which are increasingly to be met with beyond the borders of Hungary, present a wonderful (export) opportunity to respond to the emerging fashion for new and different tastes. And, as Hungarian wines become better known to western enthusiasts, it is natural that they will be curious to know more about them. Until now, however, the problem has been that, despite the vast literature about Hungarian wine written in Hungarian, information about it has been frustratingly inaccessible to the non-Hungarian-speaking wine lover. Happily, this situation is slowly beginning to change, and *Terra Benedicta* is a welcome addition to the increasing number of sources of information in English that are beginning to appear in print. As an enthusiast for Hungarian wines myself, it is therefore a pleasure to recommend this book to English-speaking wine lovers, whether they already know something about Hungarian wine or are coming to it for the first time. There is something to interest everyone in this information-packed volume, which deals not only with Hungarian wine in a comprehensive way but with many other associated topics.

The book's Borkollégium imprint is an assurance of the authority of its contents. The Borkollégium started in the early nineties as a group of people tasting wines together, and out of this was born *Rohály's Hungarian Wine Guide*. This is an annual pocket book first published in 1995, now available in English and German as well as Hungarian, and is edited by Gábor Rohály and Gabriella Mészáros (a husband and wife team) who also run a small wine school. Modelled on the English Wine and Spirit Education Trust, the school offers two courses and its exams qualify successful candidates to go on to do the diploma course of the Austrian Weinakademie. The Rohálys and other associates of the Borkollégium are, therefore, well qualified by their long experience of Hungarian wine to write *Terra Benedicta*.

Tokaji, with its extended history of imperial connections, is a name that conjures up for most wine lovers a romantic, and even exotic image. It is by far the internationally best-known of all Hungarian wines, as well it might be, with the curious-sounding and equally exotic Bull's Blood coming a close second. But the regions that produce these wines are only two out of a total of twenty-two appellations, making it evident that Hungary has much, much more to offer to the world of wine. Part II of the book, written by Gábor Rohály and András Nagymarosy (a professional geologist and lecturer at the Borkollégium), is a survey of each of these twenty-two wine regions. Each section provides the reader with a wealth of information about the history and traditions of the region, its climate, *terroir*, grape varieties, wine production and individual wine producers. Here the reader can find out about attractive and worthwhile wines – mainly white – coming from other regions such as those around Lake Balaton and the increasingly interesting (but least-understood) region of Somló, and the smaller number of notable reds, for example, from Villány.

Underpinning this regional survey are two other sections which deal with a miscellany of matters and put Part II of the book into its proper context. These range from chapters of quite basic importance to the understanding of Hungarian wine, including sensible advice about the conditions under which it is best tasted and appreciated, to others which throw light on less central aspects of the subject, such as its links with diplomacy. I should like to single out, as specially notable in this cornucopia of information, three chapters in particular. First, the chapter on grape varieties (by Gabriella Mészáros, who has made this subject one of her specializations); secondly, the comprehensive concise history of Hungarian wine (by Sándor Tóth, himself a distinguished winemaker working in the Balaton-felvidék region), which offers the best short account of the subject yet to appear in English; and thirdly, the substantial chapter on matching Hungarian wines with food (also by Gabriella Mészáros).

The inclusion of this chapter on Hungarian gastronomy is particularly appropriate, because wine and food are generally partners. Sadly, gastronomy was also a victim of the last half century and, even now, local cuisine flourishes more in private homes than it does in restaurants. From Sopron to Debrecen and Pécs to Tokaj, restaurants offer little to differentiate their menus from each other. Although not fully-detailed recipes, the outlines of traditional dishes given here can only tempt the reader to go out and obtain a proper Hungarian cookery book with which to experiment at home. However, national dishes are not essential to enjoying Hungarian wines, and the important thing is to follow the advice offered on the types of food that match each region's wines. Some of the recommendations will startle many readers, like drinking red Kékfrankos with *Gundel palacsinta* – the classic Hungarian dessert of warm, filled pancakes with a dark chocolate sauce. Well, try it and you will see for yourself. Elsewhere, in the sections dealing with the regions, some of the growing number of restaurants that rise above the depressing sameness of national fare are indicated, enabling the traveller to find the best and most appropriate food to accompany regional wines.

One hopes that the future for Hungarian wine, as understanding of it is increased by books like the present one, will be bright. But there is no denying that the industry is going though a testing period at the moment. No-one is quite sure what will be the long-term impact of Hungary's entry into the European Union in 2004. It will certainly offer increased opportunities for the export of the best wines, which will be good news to the readers of this book. But there may also be a rationalization of the industry as a whole, in which the wine producers who are unwilling or (financially) unable to meet the competitive standards of non-Hungarian wines, not just on the export market but domestically as well, will fade away. This shake-up will be painful, but ultimately it will be healthy for the future development of Hungarian wine. What is certain, on the other hand, is that Hungarian wine is poised to recapture the honorable place it once held in world esteem, and *Terra Benedicta* offers a sound basis for understanding the traditions on which that reputation will re-establish itself.

Alex Liddell

Contents

TERRA BENEDICTA

FIRST CHAPTER

A Concise History of Hungarian Wine
Viticultural Traditions and Cellar Practices
Places and Times
Grape Varieties
Gastronomy

A Concise History of Hungarian Wine:

from the Early Days to the Present

Wine traditions form an integral part of Hungary's national heritage. Throughout history, the prevailing situation of the vintners and the quality and of their wines have been reliable indicators of the country's political and economic fortunes.

Even before Hungarian tribes occupied their homeland in the Carpathian Basin, wine played a vital role in their lives, both as a healthful drink and as a symbol of faith in pagan rites. From those early days in the 5th century, contemporaneous travelers, records, and entries in Byzantine encyclopedias mention the extensive vineyards maintained by Hungarians, and their two principal drinks: milk and wine.

The Magyar tribes always used a libation of wine to bind pacts and treaties of consequence, with the Blesser of the Wine serving as the chief witness of the covenant. The ritual of the blood contract, consecrated by a drink of wine laced with the blood of the parties, is related by Herodotus about peoples culturally related to Hungarian tribes, while Byzantine references attribute the custom directly to the Hungarians themselves. It must have been a special celebration of this rite of blood and wine which sealed the emergence of a united Hungarian nation from a band of tribes.

Of all the languages spoken in Europe today, only two have their own words for wine that are not derived from Latin: Greek and Hungarian. Records carved in a special alphabet used by ancient Hungarians attest to an early terminology related to wine:

szőlő ("grape") = K⋀K|

bor ("wine") = ƎƊX

áldomás (blessing) = ⋀ᐸᐸƊ+⋀ᐹ

The etymology of some of the Hungarian vocabulary of grape-growing and wine-making suggests that these words were originally borrowed from peoples who tilled the native soil on which *vitis vinifera* first emerged. This means that Hungarians once lived close to the original, primeval wellspring of wine, and they certainly tapped that precious source—of both drink and culture.

TWENTY-ONE CENTURIES OF HUNGARIAN WINE

In what is Hungary today, the first archeological finds showing evidence of a culture of grapes and wine—from the Dobogó Hill near the town of Keszthely, and from Bálint Zólyomi's analysis of pollen deposits around Lake Balaton—lead us back to the Celts of the 1st century B.C. Their prehistoric viticulture provided a fertile foundation for the Romans, who conquered the land as much with the plough and the pruning knife as by the sword. They found particularly suitable conditions on the northern shore of the lake and in the Szerémség (Syrmia), an area in present-day Croatia near the Hungarian border.

The wine of this latter region was so successful that it came to present a major challenge to the wine of Italy. The rivalry reached its peak in 92 A.D., when Dominitian, yield-

9

Roman sarcophagous
from Szekszárd

Vasa diathreta

ing to pressure from the domestic wine aristocracy, banned wine production in Pannonia (as the colony west of the Danube was called) and ordered all the vines pulled up.

According to a report to Julian by Aurelius Victor, second proconsul of Pannonia, the replantation of vineyards was ordered by Probus Valerius in 282 around the Empire, including in Gaul, and on the slopes of the Mons Almus in Syrmia, where Probus himself was born. (Later the famous wine hill of the region was known as Tarcal and Olaszhegy in Hungarian; today it is called Fruska Gora and belongs to Croatia). It was from here that the revitalized culture of grapes spread to neighboring Baranya, the southernmost county of present-day Hungary, and further north to the Balatonfelvidék (Balaton Highlands) and other regions. It is for good reason that so many historic vineyards in Hungary are dedicated to patron saints like Szent Márton (St. Martin) of Roman Pannonia, or St. Quirinius who suffered martyrdom here, or St. Donatus who served in the legion of this province.

In the highlands north of Lake Balaton, there is an unbroken chain of archeological evidence for grape-growing and wine-making that extends to the Hungarian conquest of the homeland and beyond. The grape production of the land is also cited by Suidas, the 9th-century encyclopedist of Byzantium. This continuity was to last for a long time to come. No epidemic threatened the vines here until the second half of the 1800's, and the protected hillsides remained immune to destructive frosts. The grape-vine is a very hardy plant that can endure a lot of abuse except the most severe conditions. In the shade it will climb to any height up trees and shrubs to get to some light; if it is trampled or cut down it will send out new shoots from underground.

Hungarians adopted Christianity after occupying their permanent home at the end of the 9th century. This contributed greatly to the significance of wine and enlarged the area devoted to the cultivation of grapes, as the missionaries brought a number of innovations to the trade. In summary, grape growing in Hungary had a threefold foundation. Firstly, it relied on the ancient traditions Hungarians

had carried with them from the Caucasian area deep in Asia. Secondly, the local version of the Latin knowledge of wine remained very much alive in Pannonia, especially in the Balatonfelvidék. Thirdly, experience and taste were imported by Benedictine missionaries, teaching mendicants and immigrant settlers from Italy, Burgundy, Anjou, and the Rhine. This wealth of influences combined with Hungary's unique climate and diversity of soil patterns to shape the character and variety of the land's wines.

A charter signed in 1006 by St. Stephen, the first King of Hungary, makes mention of barkeepers' rights. By the end of the same century, the Council of Esztergom ruled to prohibit the clergy from operating public houses. These documents, among others, do not simply indicate a significant and well-regulated wine trade, but clearly presuppose extensive consumption in taverns outside private dwellings. Various deeds and customs duty registers from the 12th century attest to a large-scale wine industry and commerce. Merchants and barkeepers had to pay taxes, and the rules of pouring wine in public establishments were strictly enforced.

Wine production flourished during the Árpád and Anjou dynasties, until 1387, and the foreign trade of wine—by then the most important Hungarian export commodity next to gold, copper, silver, and cattle—remained undisturbed by internal strife or external power. The great reverence for wine is shown by a medieval Hungarian saying which considered the cultivation of vines to be "the queen of all tilling chores."

Well-situated vineyards were held in such high esteem that town-dwelling citizens often purchased lots in them even if they were quite a distance from home. The grape seeds from the 13th century that have been unearthed during various excavations indicate eastern and Hungarian (Pontian) varieties; in the latter group, *Furmint*, *Lisztes*, and *Balafánt* have been identified. Seeds of similar morphology indicate the early existence of varieties, such as *Bakator*, *Csomorika*, *Gohér*, *Kéknyelű*, and *Mézesfehér*, which remained highly popular in the country until the phylloxera epidemic.

Interestingly, however, no trace of red-wine grapes from this period has been found.

Various charters and royal deeds bear witness not only to a thorough knowledge of the best growing locations but also to the prevailing practice of designating and protecting these vineyards, as well as of regulating grape and wine production. The royal court sourced its wines from a dedicated region: the Kál Basin of the Balatonfelvidék. Until 1341, the subjects of the seven Kál villages here were granted exemption from all manner of taxes in return for supplying the crown with wine.

Starting from 1212, we have a string of papers documenting the dispute between the citizens of Buda and the bishopric of Veszprém over what wines had the right to the Buda appellation. In 1232 the bishop took the issue to court, where litigation continued for 140 years until, in 1372, King Louis the Great ruled the suit closed by means of an edict in favor of the clergy. Subsequently, King Matthias reversed the decree to vindicate the dwellers of the royal city.

In 1241-1242, invading Mongolian hordes decimated the population, pillaged its possessions and left the land to ruin, but the country's viticulture got back on its feet with unimaginable speed. City records show that revenues from wine in the second half of the 13th century amounted to half of the income from all other industries and trades. These funds provided a solid foundation for an accumulation of wealth.

In the 1250's, King Béla IV introduced French settlers to Hungary who wasted no time in propagating their native cultivation methods and barrel types, and were equally quick to demarcate their vineyards by hedges and barriers. Wine production had special rights and obligations attached to it; even serfs were free to buy and sell their vines. As an edict from those days declared, "He who carveth a vineyard anew from the woods shall not give tithes for 12 years...and whoever would plant fallow land shall be free from burden...for 7 years of the Lord." An estate of vines was regarded as the most precious of all possessions, whose veneration during the Middle Ages generated an abundance of records and lore. In

1302 for instance, King of Hungary Charles Robert of Anjou decided to lay siege to Buda because the city had sided with his enemies. Realizing at length that he would not take the castle by force, the king resorted to a trick and started cutting out the vines below. The defenders got so enraged that they rushed out of shelter, as Charles had expected, but were so vehement that they succeeded in driving the beleaguering troops back from the walls.

The first known mention of *promontoria*, self-governing bodies of the wine communities, dates from 1271. Court papers related to the origin of wines, in particular the Buda City Codex of Law, document the sophisticated

Transporting wine in the 1400's – detail of the main altar, Jánosrét (courtesy of the Hungarian National Gallery)

11

procedural order of the wine communities and the elaborate application of wine regulations. According to an ancient democratic tradition, "Every proprietor on the hill shall obey one law and no other in the matter of vines, be he of the estate of the nobility, of the knights, or of the serfs."

During the reign of the Árpád dynasty, the most highly reputed wine regions in Hungary were Syrmia, the Balaton area, Szekszárd, Somló, Ruszt-Sopron, Buda, and Arad. Wines from Baranya, Pozsony, the Mátra Hills, the Érmellék area, Ménes, and the Küküllő Valley attained fame under the House of Anjou.

Although records are very scarce regarding cultivation methods, we know that the "lugas" or trellis training method surfaced in the first half of the 14th century, while "planting vines by order" (that is, in rows) is first mentioned by sources from the early 1500's. The general practice, however, must have been to propagate the vines by layerage and to plant them randomly at a density of about 10,000-20,000 per *hold* of land (an ancient area measure corresponding to 0.57 hectares). Using this assumption as a starting point, however, we cannot rule out the possibility that spur pruning or staking for support were employed.

Owing to the calm political conditions, the era of the Árpád and the Anjou went down in history as the golden age of Hungarian wine. The noble drink of the land certainly played a role in eliciting words of praise for the country from such authorities as Constantine Manasses, the Byzantine chronicler, who in 1175 hailed Hungarians as "a people of independent, indomitable spirit who hold their heads high, cherish their freedom, and act as their own masters."

Under the kings from the so-called mixed dynasties (1387-1526), the production and trade of wine were among the first casualties of the social and political upheaval. The notable exception was the reign of Matthias, when the golden age of wine seemed to return for a serene spell of 32 years, not least because of the king's policy of importing new grape varieties from Burgundy and Campania. Until the 15th century, Hungarian wine was predominantly white, and red wine commanded far less respect. Now more and more vintners began planting red-wine varieties, owing in part to Matthias' campaigns in Albania and his Italian connections through his marriage to Beatrix of Naples. The first red wines in Hungary to gain renown emerged from Buda, and the town of Eger to the northeast.

Almost everywhere in medieval Hungary, precisely designated and isolated vineyards formed an indispensable part of the landscape around the towns. As in times past, the origin of the wines was protected jealously by stringent regulations.

The decades and centuries of the Turkish Occupation (1542-1683) and then the Habsburg Autocracy (1565-1867) proved disastrous for Hungarian wine. The Ottoman conquest of Buda in 1542 dealt a fatal blow to the heart of the wine trade. Vineyards in occupied territory faced oblivion in all but the vicinities of Pécs and Villány, Buda, and Kecskemét. On the peripheries of the occupied zone, vintners were beset by looting Turkish raids and atrocities committed by mostly non-Hungarian mercenaries hired to defend the fortifications on the fringes.

In 1565, the Austrian provinces erected customs barriers that proved to be insurmountable for Hungarian wine, although exemptions were granted to wines grown in the jurisdictions of three municipalities, namely Sopron, Ruszt (today Rust in Austria), and Pozsony (now part of Slovakia as Bratislava). The prohibitive tariffs left Poland as the single relatively free target for Hungarian wine exports, only periodically subjected to restrictions.

The period also saw the rise of a fad for *Aszú* or noble sweet botrytis wines, whose provenance had largely been confined to Syrmia until 1523, when that region fell to the Turkish invaders. Now Aszú wines began to emerge from a number of regions around Hungary, including the Balatonfelvidék, Ruszt, Somló, and Tokaj. In fact, it was at about this time that Tokaj took over the role of Syrmia, or "the wine hill of Tarcal" as it was called back then, and catapulted its sweet wine to world fame through "the gates of Poland." In the early centuries, both Syrmia and Transdanubian regions used the name of *főbor*, or *vinum magnum*, to refer to noble sweet wines. The first written record known to us of an Aszú wine from Tokaj is from the 1550's, even though popular lore mistakenly dates the first Aszú wine to around 1650, when the minister Máté Laczkó Szepsy famously presented Zsuzsanna Lórántffy with a sweet wine made from Purcsin grapes harvested from the Oremus vineyard near the town of Sátoraljaújhely.

Initially, the sweet wine of Tokaj-Hegyalja, or Tokaj Foothills, went by the name of Tállya, a village in the west of the region, and came to be known as Tokaji only during the time of Prince Ferenc Rákóczi II. [In this context, the *-i* suffix in Hungarian is comparable to the *-er* denoting provenance in English, as in "highland*er*."] As a good indication of the popularity of Aszú wines, the National Assembly of 1665 enacted Article 79, making it mandatory to pick aszú or botrytised grapes separately from the ones unaffected by botrytis, and waiving the tithe on aszú berries throughout the country.

As the Ottoman Turks left Hungary, it became obvious that vines had survived in better shape in the western parts—just as they had in Roman times. Nearly two-thirds of the nation's vineyards were now located in Zala (in particular in the Balatonfelvidék which was still officially part of that county), and other western counties such as Sopron, Pozsony, and Vas, as well as on the hills around Buda itself. Elsewhere in the country, vines suddenly began to conquer more land in the wake of Rákóczi's War of Independence. Starting from the early 1700's, unlicensed bar keepers and their patrons were sentenced to severe fines and pillory.

The centuries-old tradition of strictly enforcing the authenticity of wines continued unbroken in the local wine communities. This spirit also informed Articles XXXI of 1655 and CXVIII of 1723, which stipulated that "Those substituting inferior grapes, or grapes harvested from inferior sites, for their wines of excellence and selling them under such excellent name... shall be subject to forfeiting their entire stock of wines immediately..."

At a later time, Queen Maria Theresa reconfirmed the exemption from tithes for wines grown in the Hungarian Kingdom, while allowing the duty on wine shipments to Bavaria on the Danube within the territory of Hungary to be raised to a level that was twelve times the rate paid in Lower Austria. Even so, Hungarian wine remained in much higher demand, and by 1775 Hungarian wines were barred from the Danube in Austria unless the merchant undertook to export an equal quantity of Austrian wine and paid the astronomical duty.

From 1780 onward, Tokaji Aszú had to reckon with a respectable contender in the sweet wine arena: the Ménes Aszú made from Kadarka, a red wine grape. In the first half of the 19th century, Ferenc Schams argued that "To decide between Tokaj and Ménes Aszú is a matter of sheer taste. Both are magnificent gems in the crown of Hungarian Bacchus, and just as compatible as a diamond and a ruby side by side."

In 1772, Galicia, a province in the southern part of Poland was annexed to Austria, tightening the stranglehold of Habsburg duty that effectively isolated Hungarian wine from the world outside. Finding their supplies cut off, Polish buyers began to look to Bordeaux and Champagne for their wines. In Hungary, the crisis of overproduction set off by the imperial customs policy severely polarized the country's growers, most of whom switched over to mass production and were soon busy underselling one another in a crowded marketplace. The situation was depicted vividly by Count István Széchenyi, who offered these words of admonition to the country's vintners: "The quality of wine depends on its longevity, its ability to endure transportation from one place to another without damage, and on the tastes of a large and solvent clientele of consumers... Growers in the Rhine,

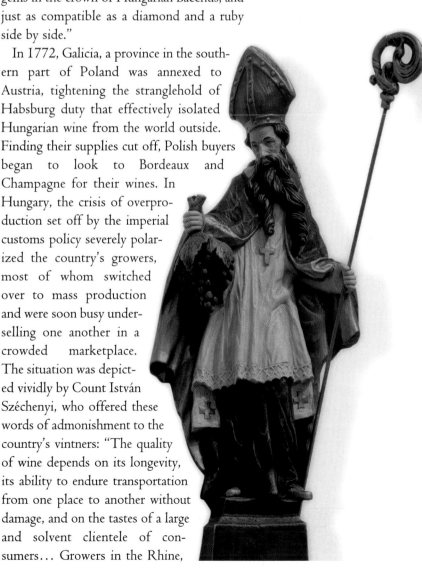

France etc... will not seek out their consumers themselves, but hire agents to find clients for them. It is this type of middleman between the Grower and the Consumer the lack of which we feel most badly... I advise all of you growers to better your wines and the roads on which you transport them... Let us not wait in indolence, as if the shackles of Habsburg duty could never slacken... Every time we do take action, we may advance our own fortunes one step forward, minuscule as that step might be..."

Some of the estate owners and the professional elite soon recognized that mass production was a dead-end street. They enlisted the help of their fellow scientists to wage war against the status quo by adapting cultivation and vinification methods already proven in the west, and by organizing the training of professionals. The leading figures of the movement, György Festetics, János Nagyváthy, Ferenc Pethe, István Széchenyi, Ferenc Schams, Lajos Mitterpacher, and József Fábián, published a number of invaluable books on these subjects.

In 1816, Vilmos Schwáb, a piano-maker in Pest, employed the first Hungarian-made crusher-stemmer, then called a "grape mill." In 1826, Jakab Goldinger, a carpenter based in Budafok, constructed the first double screw press in the country.

The first journal of enology was published by Ferenc Schams in 1836; in the same year, a committee was set up to prevent the intentional degradation of wine quality. Schams realized that recent large-scale plantations in flat areas unsuitable for quality grape production were a major part of the problem, and suggested that all new plantations be subject to the license of the county administration.

June 18, 1836, saw the foundation, on the initiative of Széchenyi, of the Hungarian National Farming Association (OMGE) which came to consider horse-breeding and wine production as its most important fields of operation. Among other objectives, the Association identified the goals "...to embrace and promote such new knowledge and inventions of utility as may have been borne out by experience... To master the obstacles

hindering the development of agriculture, and to find ways and means to foster the prosperity thereof... To propagate equipment facilitating farm works, and secure and support artisans skilled at making such machinery... To translate and disseminate foreign books of public interest... To assist capable youth of model conduct in gaining experience of prominent estates, domestic or foreign, by financing their costs of travel from the funds of the Association, and to publish their findings..." István Széchenyi launched the Association with these words: "We have come to know the way, and might as well make a head start. All we need to do now is proceed, proceed!" Indeed, from 1842, the OMGE saw a series of divisions specializing in viticulture and enology spring up around the country.

As the culmination of the aggressive imperial wine policy, a wine consumption tax was imposed by written order on September 20, 1850, when Habsburg absolutism had prevailed over Hungary's Revolution and War of Independence of 1848/49. Initially limited to communities numbering over 2,000 inhabitants, the edict was subsequently given universal force in 1859. A fee levied on public house and tavern owners was also introduced at this time.

Between 1850 and 1858, the autocratic Austrian administration suppressed all manifestations of independence, particularly social movements for freedom, and it practically paralyzed the OMGE as well. It was not until 1858 that the Association began to pick up some strength. Launched in that year, the *Borászati Füzetek* ("Pamphlets in Enology") has been published in Hungary to this day (except for a forced hiatus from 1945 to 1990).

In addition to the "wine artisan" guilds in the various wine regions and towns, an increasing number of growers' societies—comparable to the cooperatives of our age—emerged during this period in various locations, including in Ruszt (1842), Sopron (1846), Szekszárd (1857) and then, starting from 1866, in Bazin, around the Gellért Hill in Buda, in Pozsony, Köveskál, Szentbékkálla, Balatonfüred, Gyöngyös, Esztergom, Gödöllő, etc. A minor industrial revolution also took place as equipment drawn by horses or oxen suddenly gained currency in the vineyards, while the wineries began to use a variety of crushers, stemmers, iron presses, pumps, filters, and unsophisticated bottling devices.

The political Compromise of 1867, which created the Austro-Hungarian Monarchy but also made a few concessions to Hungarian self-determination, opened vast horizons for the production and export of Hungarian wine. The OMGE's National Department of Enology, which coordinated the operation of divisions around the country, now set about in earnest organizing wine exhibitions, contests, field trips and professional seminars. The vineyard acreage in the Hungarian Kingdom once again exceeded 400,000 hectares, making the country the world's third largest wine producer after France and Italy. The hillsides yielded excellent fiery and flavorful whites, with full-bodied reds accounting for just ten percent of the production, while the plantations on the Great Plain supplied much lighter table wines that were either white or rosé (the latter known at the time as *kástélyos*).

Owing to the professional groundwork since the early 19th century, the "Hungarian wine miracle" of explosive development and improvement happened, despite the hardship caused by the appearance of powdery mildew (1864), phylloxera (1875), and downy mildew (1881). In 1875, the Statistical Handbook of the Hungarian Empire estimated that "Beside grain cropping, grape growing and wine production undoubtedly form the most significant branch of Hungarian imperial agriculture in respect of present-day extension, the amount of capital invested, the number of the population engaged, the quantity and quality of the products themselves, as well as their fitness for export and their ability to win increasing shares of foreign markets…"

The esteem of the sector is indicated by the fact that the Ministry of Agriculture devoted one of its seven independent departments to "Viticultural Affairs." The organization and legal framework of wine production and trade were completed to high standards, enforced with increasing rigor. The endeavor to safeguard wine quality reached its peak in 1875, when the predecessor of today's National Wine Qualification Institute was founded.

In an effort to improve trade opportunities, the National Wine Department of the OMGE brought out in 1879 the first edition of a Viticultural Register, which provided a forum of representation to growers with a minimum annual output of 100 hectoliters, and hopes for more fruitful market relations. The Register listed the wines by category, complete with analytical parameters and translations in German and English. In 1884, it became a nationwide catalogue featuring the data of nearly 1.5 million hectoliters of wine.

In 1879, the administration made existing wine stocks subject to strict inspections by the Board of Customs and Excise (whose powers of supervision were suspended between 1971 and 2000).

Building on medieval traditions and an initiative dating back to 1797, regular public instruction in the field at the higher education level started in 1880. By 1890, there were no fewer than five state-run schools of viticulture nationwide, while itinerant instructors in seven districts were appointed to provide basic training. These latter organizations held regular courses in every significant wine producing settlement, and offered consultation services as well.

The fortunes of Hungarian wine were soon reversed by the phylloxera epidemic, which reached the country in 1875. The destruction visited by the root louse reached catastrophic proportions in 1890 and 1990, when it scaled back the former production of 4-5 million hectoliters to 800,000 hectoliters a year. Unsatisfied market demand for wine skyrocketed, while the extinction of vineyards left scores of thousands of growers in absolute poverty. Under the circumstances, wine forging in all its forms was an unavoidable consequence, including the manufacture of fake wines and the substitution of inferior grape material in making highly sought-after wines originally known by their terroir. In fact, the entire European Continent hit a similar slump at about this time.

Needless to say, neither the political elite nor the professional organizations thought they could afford to sit back and watch as the situation worsened from one day to the next. A series of heated debates from 1888 finally led to

15

some of Europe's most stringent and comprehensive wine regulations, adopted in 1893 by the National Assembly as Article XXIII. The legislators emphasized that "… wine counterfeiters are detrimental to the entire nation… In time, merchants come to distrust wine from such a discredited country, and will pay but very low prices if they still want to buy at all… For this reason, the man shall be punished who makes artificial wine, as shall the man who sells it or pours it at his place of business… Sanctions therefore await the counterfeiter who defrauds the state, but also those who purchase his product from him."

In 1896, Gyula Istvánffy spearheaded the establishment of the Central Research Institute of Viticulture and Enology. Ignác Darányi, the competent minister, assigned to the Institute the chief task of "conducting in-depth research using the most advanced means afforded by science, transplanting its findings onto the field of practical application so as to facilitate the setting of the entire system of viticulture on the road to progress, improvement, and perfection." The Institute became instrumental in honing curricula in viticulture and enology on all levels of education, as well as in developing the specialized consultation network and the organization of the Wine Inspectorates.

A Ministerial Decree of 1897, issued by Darányi, ordered the establishment of a five-member Wine Inspection Committee for each administrative district and borough with its own municipal law and/or a regular city council, and for each of the 10 districts of Budapest. The members of the 446 Committees protected the interests of those who suffered damage on account of counterfeit wines. They were entitled to inspect and take steps against any winery, cellar or other premises the use of which—for wine production, storage, distribution, or service—made such intervention reasonable. Along with the excise officers, there were now nearly 5000 inspectors watching over the good reputation of Hungarian wine, who ultimately succeeded in closing down all the fake wine operations in Hungary. However, artificial wine was not banned elsewhere in the Austro-Hungarian Monarchy, and the shared borders and customs union made smuggling a serious problem for Hungary. The ten-year struggle that ensued led to the triumph of the Hungarian party in 1907, when similarly strict prohibitive measures were finally introduced in the Austrian provinces as well.

On the other front, the fight against phylloxera owed a great deal to the OMGE's regional divisions and societies, which first proposed experimental stockyards and rootstock plantations in many counties, such as Zala (which then included the length of the northern shore of Lake Balaton), Veszprém, Sopron, Pozsony, Esztergom, Heves, Zemplén, Bereg, Szilágy, Arad, and Temes (most of the last four counties no longer belong to Hungary). Just outside Budapest, in Rákospalota, an OMGE property provided a home for the Phylloxera Research Station. Growers were able to obtain rootstock canes and scions from the stockyards cheaply or even free of charge, and mastered improved cultivation methods as they went about their daily work. On the initiative of the OMGE departments, regulations binding for all growers were adopted to help combat powdery and downy mildew as well.

Between 1896 and 1915, 80% of the country's vineyard acreage was replanted, thanks in no small part to the credit lines extended on extremely favorable terms by the National Central Credit Union, founded in 1896. The phylloxera had ruined tens of thousands of lives, but at the end of the day it stimulated the renewal of the sector. As the dreaded enemy turned into the most powerful driving force behind progress, the benefits of successful vineyard reconstruction came to be increasingly felt after the turn of the century.

The Hungarian state never tired of seeking ways to support growers by expanding and stabilizing export markets. 1901 marked the take-off in Budafok of the Hungarian Royal Public Cellar Master course, whose preeminent students set up the School of Itinerant Cellar Masters which functioned until 1927. Upon request, these professionals traveled anywhere fully equipped to assist with the handling of wines. The client had to bear only a part of the cost.

In 1901, Budafok was the setting of yet another opening: that of the Wine Auction Hall. The graciously designed and tastefully furnished building provided a venue four times a year for a well-advertised wine auction that offered advance tasting and guaranteed the authenticity of the wines. (The Auction Hall continued to do good service to Hungarian wine producers until its nationalization and demise in 1948.)

Soon after the turn of the century, a state-sponsored House of Hungarian Wine opened in London, Munich, Stockholm, Vienna, and Krakow, for the task of promoting Hungarian wines under the supervision of noted winemakers, who also happened to be traders and restaurateurs of excellence. Simultaneously, luxury ocean liners readying for a cruise were supplied with samples to hold what turned out to be very successful demonstrations of Hungarian wine in selected port cities around the world. The operative costs of the Wine Houses and the port-of-call wine shows were shouldered by the Hungarian state.

In 1902, the administration opened the Hungarian Royal Wine Museum in Budafok, for the purpose of not simply displaying invaluable "museum quality" wines, but also to expertly handle and monitor these old vintages. The exhibition soon attained world fame, and remained a favorite tourist destination until 1944, when it was devastated in the war.

In 1920, Hungary, with its mutilated territory, found itself in the grips of duty constraints over again. In the aftermath of World War I, the country had lost the majority of its wine markets and one third of its vineyard acreage. At first the government attempted to help the troubled growers by developing a network of public cellars, but a series of negative experiences convinced it to turn most of these over to the cooperatives for use. Wine regulations were also reformed at this time.

The National Department of Viticulture, an agency reporting to the OMGE, raised the idea of going independent at the First National Congress of Viticulture of 1899 in Szeged. The thorough preparations were rewarded three years later, when the Second Congress, held in Pozsony, announced the establishment of an autonomous organization by the name of National Alliance of Hungarian Wine Growers. Over the years, the Alliance modified its name twice and had increased the already impressive initial membership of 1200 to tens of thousands by 1936, but its goals, esteem, and significance remained essentially unchanged.

From the mid-1930's, the fortune of commerce smiled on Hungarian wine one more time, notwithstanding the general austerity of the era. In order to mitigate their vulnerability and better exploit the improving market opportunities, the country's growers in 1936 founded MASzOBSz (the National Cooperative of Hungarian Grape Growers for Wine Sales), MEGA (the Sales Association of Hungarian Hillside Growers), the National Alliance of Wine Communities and Growers and, on a cooperative basis, the Hungarian Tank Car and Wine Distribution Rt. By 1937, these various organizations possessed 22 wine processing facilities and cellars throughout the country's 11 official wine regions.

In the 1930's, white wines accounted for 62.5% of the total production, followed by *siller* (rosé) at 27% and red (10.5%). In terms of the quality distribution, a scant 0.02% of the total output was Aszú (sweet botrytis wine), 9.6% excellent wine branded by the name of its place of origin, 48.48% geographically identified *pecsenyebor* (comparable to today's quality wine category), and finally 41.9% inferior table wine. 95.4% of the growers had less than one hectare—specifically, 0.23 ha on average—but collectively they owned 63% of the country's vineyards. Estates of 1-5 ha (averaging 2.1 ha per owner) accounted for just 3.9% of all the estates but 22% of the total acreage. Even larger properties (9 ha per owner on average) represented 0.7% and 15% of the number of estates and the total vineyard acreage, respectively. Remarkably, 85% of the country's 7 million-hectoliter wine storage capacity was controlled by the estate owners themselves.

The enduring success and business potential of Hungarian wine during this period could be illustrated by the fact that in 1943 a wine wholesaler posted the highest net income of all the private entrepreneurs in the country. It

was also around this time that Hungarian wine trade attained its highest standards of organization, operation, and sheer proficiency.

THE LAST 50 YEARS

In spite of the affliction caused by the war and the occupation, the period between 1938 and 1948 proved to be one of vigorous development for Hungarian wine. A major milestone on this road to improvement was set down by Viktor Kosinszky, who became the first in Europe to complete a nationwide cadastre, or register, of vineyards. However, the incredibly fast-paced progress stopped dead in its tracks when the occupying Soviets imposed totalitarian rule on the country. The nationalization or expropriation of private property, the deportations, and the forced collectivization of the farming industry destroyed the infrastructure of Hungarian wine and ruined its markets.

Capacities were lined up for mass production, and the interests of political power quickly gained the upper hand over geographical and economic considerations, the significance of which was now increasingly denied by the single-party state. These trends were reflected faithfully not just by individual tragedies but by the major indicators of wine production as well.

From 1949 to 1959, private ownership was scaled back in the vineyards, and simply abolished in the commercial distribution of wine. The relentless severance of wine-making from grape-growing was executed shamelessly by brutal administrative means. In 1949, the communist government wound up the National Alliance of Wine Communities and Growers, and nationalized the credit unions along with every cooperative-owned winery and cellar, which it thereafter enlisted in the service of mandatory collection or, less euphemistically, requisitioning.

Between 1952 and 1965, the shortage of wine became acute, as did the slackening of traditionally rigorous and watertight wine regulations. A decidedly odd distribution organization, invested with the monopoly to collect and "distribute" wines, resorted to rather peculiar methods to fill the gaps in supply and

demand. Nothing shows the scourge and helpless position of the growers better than the fact that the exclusive grape buying agency of the state paid trivial prices even for excellent, twice-racked wines. In 1958, growers had no choice but to sell their crop at 36% of 1948 prices. By 1968, they only achieved 40% of that level, despite the gradual corrosion of the forint's buying power.

Following the banning of the wine communities in December 1948–a measure that was characteristically supplied with its "legal grounds" retroactively, by a Government Order issued in April 1949–the single-party state had nationalized, alienated, or collectivized 80,000 hectares of vines by 1961. This led to the neglect and ultimate extinction of some 60,000 hectares of plantation that were in good condition, consisted of quality varieties, typically occupied excellent sites, and had higher planting densities but were otherwise suitable for "modernization." At 2001 costs, the value of this tremendous waste can be estimated at 230-240 billion forints, or one billion US dollars.

Of the 56,000 hectares planted between 1961 and 1970, sheer political whim designated 38,000 hectares in completely unsuitable locations, where no one in their right mind had ever thought of cultivating vines before. For this reason, and also because of the lack of proper care in vineyard construction, 34,000 hectares of newly planted vines did not survive their tenth year, causing a loss of 140 billion forints at 2001 prices. In addition, misguided political decisions between 1949 and 1970 resulted in the extinction of vines in over 40,000 hectares of historic vineyards. These events transformed entire landscapes and dealt severe blows to the livelihoods of once prosperous communities, not all of which have ever recovered from them.

By the late 1960's, a crisis of overproduction in grapes had set in, and the state monopoly of buying and distribution stirred bitter discontent among the growers. From 1969 onward, cooperatives and state farms were gradually allowed to venture into wine making and sales–both pursuits previously banned by the government. These operations embarked on large-scale integration of activities, and provided a backdrop for the education of many excellent professionals in the trade. Regrettably, two out of three new wineries created in this period did not meet international standards. The unjustifiable drive to relocate the country's fulcrum of production to the Great Plain inflicted irreversible damage on several wine regions of formerly high repute.

On the whole, the country kept following the path of mass production. A decree of 1970 removed the legally binding force from the wine law that had been fine-tuned for centuries in the interest of protecting the quality and territorial identity of Hungarian wines. The steady deterioration of quality was the result of a combination of factors, including the prevalence of cash-strapped, undemanding consumers, the resulting miserably low prices, and the facelessness of the producers. Starting from the mid-1970's, nearly 60% of Hungarian wine headed east to the Soviet Union, and only 15% ended up with the more discriminating western importers. The orientation east would not have been a cause for concern in itself; the former Russian empire had been a very good traditional market for Hungarian wine. The problem was with the vast scale of production, the inferior standards, and the inevitable compromise inherent in catering to consumers who only demanded a semblance of vinous character with a certain content of alcohol and sugar. In fact, these demands were so low that some Hungarian winemakers managed to exceed them against the odds of misguided economic policy and abysmal clearing prices.

Hungarian consumers had to content themselves with just one quarter of the wine they produced. However, the ministrations of the Pricing Bureau at home prevented the sale of excellent wines at better than average prices that would have reflected their higher value. Consequently, the wineries had no choice but to waste these finer wines by blending them in to improve inferior ones. These inferior wines were then labeled under the name of the best sites and the most popular grape varieties.

Each of these circumstances contributed its

share to tarnishing the reputation of Hungarian wine. Discerning consumers switched over to other wines or liquor, and the great wine names and estates of former times quickly sank into oblivion. The true legacy of Hungarian wine only survived in the memory of conscientious professionals, in the showcase wineries maintained by a handful of well-run industrial operations, and in the daily practice of the many growers who continued cultivating the tiny parcels that the state had graciously left them.

While the better half of the wine world had to choose quality to fight off overproduction, in Hungary the mass production of wines without type or character became the order of the day. In the 1980's, new plantation on 50,000 hectares went hand in hand with cutting out 130,000 hectares of vines. The process of historic vineyards turning fallow continued without interruption, affecting

Pressing grapes at the turn of the century (Törley archives)

Harvesters (early 20th century)

some 20,000 hectares around the country. In 1982, the authorities added insult to injury when they arbitrarily "reorganized" the Research Institute of Viticulture and Enology, an internationally recognized organization of scientists since 1896, by annexing its research stations to incompetent state-owned corporations—a move motivated by petty interests rather than by any rationale. Dwindling eastern exports in the second half of the decade generated a surplus on the domestic market. This provided an incentive for improving quality, even as it put growers in a difficult position.

The great political transformations of 1990-1994 were inseparable from the all-out drive for privatization, which nevertheless had its disputable features as it often disregarded the interests of the former landowners as well as the professional and legal ramifications of owning property. Such mistakes notwithstanding, the country managed to reinstate the foundations of family enterprise, genuine co-operatives, and the wine law. As a result, a portion of Hungarian wines began to improve dramatically.

Starting in 1995, a number of harmful tendencies asserted themselves, setting off a drastic decline in the growers' fortunes and leading to insupportably low bulk buying prices for white wines, far below cost. It seemed as if the hapless growers had to shoulder the blame for every sin and blunder committed for the past 50 years.

GASTRONOMIC TRADITIONS

Hungarian dining rests on the pillars of wine, as do the culinary traditions of France, Italy, and Spain. The first record on the subject known to us was penned by Galeotto Marzio in 1484: "Hungarians have a great deal to eat and drink at their feasts, and they drink many kinds of wine. (The same habit was attributed by the historians to Galienus, Roman Emperor.) ... At the most luxurious feasts, several different types of wine are served."

Although Hungarian wine and cuisine both have a common national character, it would be a mistake to underestimate the wealth of local specifics. These days Hungarians have come

round to the ancient wisdom that places where wine consumption eclipses the use of other spirits have a much lower rate of alcoholism.

As great Hungarian wines have lately reappeared on the horizon, the best restaurants have been quick to adjust to the new situation. Most of them now offer an impressive selection of wines, and have successfully reinstated the sommelier as a requisite for any fine restaurant. The traditions of gastronomy and civilized drinking, for which the country was renowned before World War II, are now being rekindled with unexpected momentum and enthusiasm.

This recent chapter in the country's history goes to show that Hungarians have been, and will always be, able to restore the conditions of quality production and reclaim the honor of Hungarian wine, provided that the nation is free, the policy sound, and the political will strong enough to support the growers. Even today, we cannot afford to ignore the principle once articulated by Pál Teleki: "Hungary will never be suitable for producing huge quantities, and will therefore always have to concentrate on quality."

20

Viticultural Traditions and Cellar Practices

Paradoxically, the primordial Hungarian techniques of growing and making wine are employed today only by a handful of small backward growers and some of the most powerfully capitalized estates keen on resuscitating the old ways to high quality standards.

Archeological finds in Tokaj and throughout Hungary assist us in reconstructing cultivation methods undocumented in writing. As this overview is not intended to be an academic treatise on agricultural history, we will focus on the tools and practices that have partially survived or inspired procedures followed to this day. The other important thing to keep in mind is that viticultural practices in the Carpathian Basin show a very uniform picture, irrespective of geographical or present-day political boundaries. Consequently, the following account does not always apply only to Hungary as we know it today.

ON THE HILL

PLANTING AND SPACING

The road from *Vitis silvestris* to neat geometrical plantations of a single grape variety has been a long and arduous one. In the old vineyards, fruit trees, water channels and boulders of rock prevented regular rows. The custom of layerage–propagating vine by forcing a cane or long shoot underground to take root–did not do much to alleviate the sense of misshapenness in these plots. Before the phylloxera invasion, the most common propagation method consisted of placing unrooted cuttings in holes made with a wooden auger or an iron rod. Planting pits did not become necessary until rooted grafts had to be planted.

PRUNING

Training is intimately pruning-related, as the support system is always adapted to the shape of the vine stock fashioned by pruning. The ancient tool used for this operation was the pruning knife. In Tokaj, the pruning knife typically came with a hatchet element on the back of the arched blade (a few specimens were found without this part). This hatchet served to tap and scrub the stock to clean it, while the tip of the knife came in handy for cutting off thinner canes and scion roots. The lower part of the crescent-shaped blade had a sharp protrusion called the *sarok* ("heel"), which was used to remove thicker canes with a forward push. This pushing motion is important for its association with the bald-pruned head, an ancient training system that is still employed here and there in Tokaj. Its essential feature is a head that is larger than with other training systems. At one time, this type of head in Tokaj probably looked like an upended plate and measured up to 15 cm in diameter. Removing the densely spaced yearling canes from this

21

Pruning knife from the
Roman era

Broad-headed
pruning knife

Pruning knife from
Abaújvár (10th century)

Pruning knife from
the Middle Ages

head was hardly possible by an inward yank of the knife, and the pushing motion required the convenience of the sarok described above. Remarkably, this part is missing from the design in areas where the pruning knife was not used for bald-head training. In the middle of the 19th century, the pruning knife was superseded by pruning shears. Initially, this tool did not look like the modern version, since it was still expected to perform the functions of a knife. Because it made work much faster than its predecessor, it quickly gained currency without encountering any resistance. The shears also enabled an oblique cut-surface, helpful in keeping the sap away from the buds.

Horned-head training is still common in areas where vines are cultivated in the stake-support system. Badacsony and the other regions north of Lake Balaton all used to be that way, and the training system survives in a significant part of the Hajós-Baja wine region. Horned-head training basically consists in leaving two "eyes" or buds on the cane one year after planting. The following year, these will in turn produce two new canes with two buds each. In the third year, it becomes possible to fashion the four "horns." With sufficient care to prevent the loss of bearing units, this shape will then be sustainable for decades. The stock itself will be formed by the regularly but loosely spaced shoots evolving from the buds generally left on the outer side of the four horns.

TYING

The great diversity of plant fibers traditionally used to tie shoots included straw strings, the runners of certain plants, and the always handy grass, but the most common material, widely used to this day, has been raffia, the bast of the raffia palm. Raffia gained currency in the vineyards starting from the 1870's, along with rush. Kötőfű ("tie-grass") came to Tokaj from the Bodrogköz, the marshy area between the Bodrog and the Tisza at the confluence of these rivers, to become the favorite tying fiber in the 17th to 19th centuries. Instead of describing the various knots that were invented for secure tying, let us highlight the importance of not leaving long loose ends. This widely followed practice not only made the vineyards

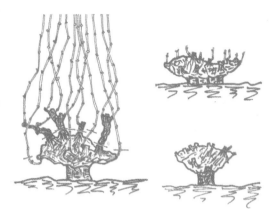

Horned-head training, with
"bald heads" on the right

look tidier; it was also a measure of frugality. Shoots were tied twice early in the summer, normally at the time the soil was hoed.

Hoeing is such a common job that it needs no explanation. While a detailed inventory of the diverse hoe types used over the centuries is better left to volumes on agricultural history, let us make special mention of the two-horned hoe, a strong implement resembling a bent fork with two tines. This was the right tool to use in Tokaj to loosen the hard-bound nyirok soil of the vineyards there.

An interesting spectacle of the hillsides was the "vine guard" or vineyard ranger, hired to protect the property and keep away animals—stray cattle, pests, and particularly birds. The vine guard kept his eye on the vineyard while lying prone on a platform built for this purpose. He was allowed to raise a foliage tent for shelter, but had to periodically tour the vineyard, generally armed with a fokos, an ancient Hungarian weapon much like a spontoon or tomahawk, and a karikás ostor, an unusually long whip also used by Magyar herdsmen. The loud crack of this whip was no doubt much appreciated by the pestilent flocks of starling. By the 20th century, makeshift cannons using food tins and carbide obtained from local miners were widely employed to shoo birds away. Another popular tool to scare off birds was the kereplő, a hand-held clapper or rattle.

HARVEST

Until about 1600, the bunches of grapes, snipped from the vine using a short-blade knife, later shears, were collected in a wooden

Horned-head training (Szekszárd)

Pruning knife from
Szekszárd (1697)

Pruning knife from
Tokaj (19th century)

Old pruning shears

Old pruning shears

(after Árpád Patay)

bucket called a *cseber*. Starting in the 17th century, in some areas this was gradually replaced by the *puttony*, a hod fitted with shoulder straps and carried on the back. (The *cseber* has remained in service though, especially since Hungarian harvesters hardly ever use woven baskets.) The *puttony*, manufactured by the local cooper, varied between 18 and 26 liters in capacity depending on the region. A charming version was the tiny *puttony* holding just 5-7 liters of grapes, made specifically for children—today more like a quaint objet d'art belonging to museums. The latter-day successor of this vessel is made of metal or plastic, and has a cornet-like flared rim that is narrower than that of examples used in Western Europe.

The first surviving record concerning the time of the harvest is from 1486, when it was held on October 18th. By and large, the harvest would take place about a month earlier until late-ripening varieties appeared. Nowadays, the starting date of the harvest that can be regarded as traditional is Simon Judah day on October 28th. Deviation from this date used to be allowed for reasons of weather or war only, as evidenced by a 19th-century document ratified by a board of estate owners.

STAKE PULLING

This was a vineyard job now consigned to oblivion, even in areas that have remained faithful to the stake-support system. The escalating cost of labor and the prevalence of cheaper sawn stakes (as opposed to the split variety) have dissuaded growers from pulling the stakes for the winter, although this has made it necessary to straighten the stakes in the springtime.

WINTER COVERING

This measure of protecting the stock against frost damage by pulling earth over it is theoretically possible in any vineyard where the stakes have not been removed for the winter. However, it really has significance in vineyards with low bald-head or horned-head training. In these plantations, earth is raked up to cover the lower part of the stock, where the buds are close to the ground and are thus particularly vulnerable to frost. Realizing that a blanket of straw or foliage would provide shelter for rodents, growers would only use the top layer of the vineyard's soil for this purpose.

IN THE CELLAR

Although stemming was not commonly performed before the advent of the 20th century, the name of an old wine type, *Szemelt*

Vines with the stake support system in Tokaj (Oremus winery)

out or pressed by stamping. Stamping was invariably a man's job, for reasons about as clear as the motivation for banning women from the cellar—a rule occasionally taken quite seriously at the time. The oldest surviving wooden presses are of the huge *bálvány* or timber-post type known across Europe. In many places, most notably in Zala County, the foundation of this press was a large vat of 2-3 m² floor space, in which workers treaded the grapes before transferring them to the basket of the press above.

The top-driven central screw press, known in Transdanubia as the *kancaprés*, had a press plate on which pressure was exerted by means of external threading, while presses fastened to the press base already employed a metal screw. The oldest press baskets had a rectangular shape; the circular basket was a much later invention. Both types often had a stone foundation, sometimes fashioned from hand-driven mills that had fallen out of use. The mash would be shaken up and repressed after maceration—even twice in places where wine quality was not the main consideration.

FILTERS AND CASKS

Hemp cloth and wickerwork were both favorite materials to make must filters. As recently as the year 2000, a wicker basket placed in the way of must flowing out of the trough was observed. The capacity and number of wooden vats and barrels depended on the size of the estate and the quantity of the harvest. These vessels were typically made from oak, but the poorer growers of the Great Plain often resorted to the wood of the locust tree for their cooperage. Elsewhere, chestnut and mulberry wood would be used as well. Casks made from mulberry wood sooner or later ended up maturing fruit brandy instead of wine.

The timing and technique of racking is vastly different for traditionally fermented dry wines and sweet ones. The former had to be racked before Christmas, while the latter could wait longer depending on the quality of the vintage and the concentration of the wine. (The sweeter the must the longer it takes to ferment.)

Rizling ("Sorted Riesling"), suggests an excellent wine made from Olaszrizling, a variety whose loosely connected berries were removed easily from the stems. The contrivance used for this task was a screen, on which the bunches were raked back and forth with a tool called the *vonó*. The berries fell through the holes, while the stems were retained on the screen surface. At small rural farms, wooden grinders were employed to crush the grapes; some of them are still in service today. Later in the 20th century mechanical crushers were introduced as well.

PRESSING

The most ancient technique of extracting the juice was sack-pressing, whereby a cloth sack would be filled with grapes and wrung

MATURATION

Apart from Tokaj, Somló, and Badacsony, Hungary's wines were hardly ever subjected to extended maturation. The last year's wine would generally be regarded as the best, presumably due to the scarcity of storage space as well as for obvious microbiological reasons. Géza Focht relates how his workers hoeing the famed Berekhát vineyard in Csopak invariably preferred to quench their thirst with the latest vintage available, as recently as the 1980's. Understandably, sweet wines received a completely different treatment, and often spent several years in casks. As for bottling, little can be said for the Hungarian wine of old, except for Tokaj, where bottled wine first cropped up in 1640.

ASZÚ

Aszú, the ancient Hungarian word designating overripe, shrivelled berries, etymologically related to *aszott* ("desiccated") and *aszalt* ("sun-dried"), probably did not imply botrytis character at first. Modern terminology nevertheless makes a clear distinction between overripe berries shrivelled due to loss of moisture (*töppedt*) and berries attacked by noble rot, called *aszú*. In the old days, the type of wine we call Aszú today was termed *aszúszőlő bor*, originally meaning "wine made from shrivelled grapes." A legend widely held until recently dated the invention of Aszú wine to around 1650, when the Protestant minister Máté Laczkó Szepsy allegedly made the first sweet wine of this type from the crop of the Oremus vineyard near the town that is called Sátoraljaújhely today. Some credit for the frequent occurrence of the word Aszú in the 19th century must be given to Badacsony and Somló. The regions of Mór (cf. Bozóky Winery today), Villány (the Gyimóthy find) and Ménes (home of the famed red Aszú in Transylvania, today part of Romania) also deserve mention as repositories of a sweet Aszú tradition. Considerations of primacy aside, botrytis-prone grape varieties like Ezerjó, Olaszrizling, and Kadarka had been well-established in these regions, taking advantage of the ideal climatic conditions. The system of grading Tokaji

Aszú by concentration, traditionally measured by the number of *puttonys* of Aszú berries macerated in a Gönc caskful (136-140 l) of base wine or must, goes back to the 1800's. Although, with the advances of chemistry, sugar and extract had been increasingly mentioned from the 1850's, these analytic parameters were not directly correlated with the *puttony* number until the end of the 19th century. If the quantity of botrytized berries added to the base wine had really been used as the sole criterion in determining the ultimate grade of an Aszú, we would have to conclude that this categorization did not originally reckon with the risk of secondary fermentation and the concomitant loss of sweetness in the wine. Indeed, sweet wines that "straighten out" are a troublesome occurrence known only too well by Tokaj growers to this day.

Places and Times

Just as the cuisine of a country or a region is often recognizable with reasonable certainty by its aromas, flavors, and favorite ingredients, so do—or should—wines wear their provenance on their sleeve. A skilled taster can quickly tell whether the wine in his glass was made from grapes grown on a plain or on the hillside, in a cooler northern region or a warm southern one. The grape variety and the method of vinification, both possible to determine by organoleptic analysis, may betray the country and the region where the wine comes from. Unless the wine is a uniform, equalized product that integrates the crop purchased from across a large area, it will bear the spirit of the land and the imprint of the hand that made it.

The better grape-growing areas of the world have been shaped for over centuries, possibly millennia. It is always the task of tradition to canonize the ground upon which wine of profitable quality and quantity can be produced. Wine regions typically encompass areas with suitable geological and climatic potential, a highly evolved viticulture, and a production of distinct, recognizable wines. In Hungary, an effective government decree—a statutory instrument invested with the same force as a law passed by the National Assembly—groups grape growing areas into greater viticultural-geographical units consisting of wine regions, which in turn may be divided into districts and wine growing areas as well as other viticultural locations. These rather convoluted categories are defined officially as follows:

Basalt tuff beds on the rim of the extinct volcano in Tihany

"*Greater viticultural-geographical unit* means one of the country's units of economic geography, which is divided into wine regions, wine growing areas, and other viticultural locations.

Wine region means a viticultural area extending across the administrative boundaries of several contiguous communes, which is characterized by similar properties of morphology, geology, and climate, as well as by plantations of a typical varietal ratio, similar methods of cultivation and training, a shared viticultural and wine-making tradition, and a production of wines with a distinct character, where at each commune the acreage classified in the wine cadastre for wine regional status is at least 7%, and the vineyard acreage actually planted is at least 4%, of the total area under agricultural cultivation.

District means a segment that can be clearly isolated within a wine region according to specific criteria. *Wine growing area (or wine area)* means a narrower growing location, site or vineyard, which typifies its region in terms of its natural potential, traditions of production and wine quality, but which nevertheless forms a clearly distinct unit within that region by virtue of the personality of its wines.

Restricted wine region means a viticultural area whose wines merit advanced protection and require special rules for the growing of grapes, and the making, handling, and distribution of its wines. (Tokaj alone is classified in this category.)

Other viticultural area means a viticultural area not belonging to any wine region or wine area but ranked by the local cadastre in the appropriate class.

Wine regions and wine areas shall comprise the land classified in the local cadastre for the communities listed as belonging to the wine region or wine area in question. The class I and class II areas of other communities shall be regarded as other viticultural areas."

The cadastre's classification categories are as follows:

a) Class I: Ideally suitable to viticulture
b) Class II: Suitable for viticulture
c) Class III: Suitable for viticulture on certain conditions
d) Class IV: Unsuitable for viticulture

In describing each wine region, the decree provides for the following categorization of grape varieties:

"*Recommended variety: A variety officially certified by an agency of the government, which defines the orientation of the given growing area's production, and especially the distinct character of its wines.*

Ancillary variety: A variety officially certified by an agency of the government, which exploits the given growing area's ecological potential well but does not play a decisive role in shaping the character of its wines.

In-situ variety: A variety no longer approved for new planting, but the existing plantations of which are nevertheless authorized for continued cultivation."

This is what the regulations say, but the savor and atmosphere of a region are of course by the wines themselves, which obey their own hierarchy of labeling rules provided by law. (See the *Appendix* for the explanation of Hungarian labeling categories.)

THE HISTORIC WINE REGIONS OF GREATER HUNGARY

The first records mentioning wine regions in Hungary date from the 18th century, but the territory of the country was not properly divided in this regard until 1833, when Ferenc Schams identified 14 wine regions. This early nomenclature did not imply legal distinctions or protected origin. In 1880, Károly Keleti redrew the country's wine map based on a fresh statistical survey, demarcating 33 wine regions that generally coincided with the administrative boundaries of the day. Working with a different system of taxonomy than Schams, Keleti did not make a rigorous distinction between quality wine regions and other growing areas, although he did introduce the category of "orchard vines" for vineyards planted in the sandy soil of the Great Plain.

"Greater Hungary," as many Hungarians still refer to the country before it lost two thirds of its territory in the wake of the Treaty of Trianon that sealed World War I, contained a great number of wine regions. Based on an 1893 survey, the Minister of Commercial Affairs appointed to the Hungarian Royal Court issued in 1897 a decree designating the country's wine regions as follows:

In a special sense, the French concept of *terroir*, in use since the 18th century, is somewhat comparable in Hungarian viticultural tradition to the *promontorium*, the strictly protected wine-hill. Like Ferenc Schams before him, the famous 19th-century poet János Arany in several poems also explicitly differentiated between "hill-grown wines" and "orchard wines" grown in the backyard or in the plain. Another case in point is the Austrian term *Weinberg*, meaning any site where high quality wine can be grown—not necessarily a slope or the side of a mountain as the literal reading would suggest, but also potentially a vineyard planted on flat land, provided that it is capable of yielding a wine of distinction. (This notion is quite independent from that of the *Bergwein*, denoting a narrow category of wines harvested from very steep slopes.) In medieval Hungary, "wine-hills" were surrounded by trenches, hedges, and gates, and the inviolability of these boundaries was strictly observed. Intimately linked with this physical demarcation was a particular system of protecting the quality and origin of wines, a right entrusted to and exercised by autonomous self-governing bodies called wine communities. This institution existed from the 13th century until 1948 and, after a hiatus of nearly half a century, was rekindled in 1994. Just as the "wine-hill" shows analogies with the French appellation system, there are some interesting parallels to be drawn between the classification of the Médoc in 1855 and an 1835 edict whereby the Zala County Council reserved first-class status strictly for the vineyards of the Tapolca Basin and the Kál Basin in the whole county. Sándor Tóth believes that Hungary's wine legislation today has yet to devise a system that will leave no loopholes in safeguarding the quality and origin of wines grown on protected wine-hills.

(g.r.)

"*1. RUSZT-SOPRON-POZSONY: Counties of Sopron, Pozsony, Moson, Vas, and Nyitra.*" The Sopron district of this renowned region remains part of Hungary. Rust and the area west of Lake Fertő belong to Austria today, where they form three districts of high repute called Neusiedlersee (Lake Fertő's name in German), Neusiedlersee-Hügelland, and Mittelburgenland. The good terroirs of Vas County that remained in Hungary, notably at Cák, are not classified with any wine region at present, while the parts annexed to Austria do belong to the wine region of Südburgenland there. The best areas of Hungary's former Pozsony County, today part of Slovakia, occupy the southern slopes of the Little Carpathians. Wine production is centered around the following communes (Slovakian names in parentheses): Pozsony (Bratislava), Pozsonyrécse (Rača), Pozsonyszentgyörgy (Sv. Jur pri Bratislave), Limbach, Bazin

(Pezinok), Modor (Modra). The village of Szakolca (Skalica, today on the Slovak-Czech border) in the Erdőntúl (Zahorie) district was at one time famed for its wines, which rather resembled Southern Moravia's wines in their style. The better growing areas of Nyitra County are located on the southern slopes of the Zobor and Tribecs Hills around the town of Nyitra (Nitra).

"*2. PEST-NÓGRÁD: the left bank of the Danube at the Royal Capital City of Budapest; the upper and lower Vácz districts and the lower, middle and upper Pest districts of Pest-Pilis-Solt-Kiskun County; and the entire territories of Nógrád, Hont, and Bars Counties.*"

These areas are not part of any wine region in present-day Hungary. Even the village of Fót near Pest, which was once famous for its wines, has abandoned viticulture altogether. However, vines are still cultivated on a larger scale in the former Hungarian county of Bars, today in Slovakia, in the vicinity of the town of Léva (Levice).

"*3. BUDA-SASHEGY: the right bank of the Danube at the Royal Capital City of Budapest and in Pest-Pilis-Solt-Kiskun County.*"

Again, these areas do not have wine regional status today, even though the wines grown outside Buda enjoyed uninterrupted fame from medieval times until the late 19th century, and constituted an important export commodity of the Austro-Hungarian Monarchy. The red wine of Sashegy, the "Eagle Hill" near the capital, used to be held in particularly high regard. The last wine from the slopes of Gellért Hill, practically in the heart of Budapest, was harvested by a professor of the nearby Technical University in the early 1900's. Wine production around the villages at the foot of the Pilis Mountains, part of the Etyek-Buda wine region today, revived in the last decade of the 20th century, and seems to be heading toward a bright future.

"*4. SOMLYÓ: four villages from Veszprém County, namely Doba, Kis-Jenő, Nagy-Szőllős, Vásárhely, as well as the Sági-hegy from Vas County.*"

Essentially, this corresponds to the wine region of Somló (note the alternate modern spelling) as we know it today.

The counties of
Greater Hungary
before World War I

"5. NESZMÉLY: the Counties of Esztergom, Komárom, Fejér, Győr, and Veszprém, except for three districts of Veszprém, namely Enying, Devecser, and Veszprém proper."

(Districts, small units of public administration below the county level, were abolished nationwide in 1977.) This comprises the modern wine regions of Ászár-Neszmély, Mór, Pannonhalma-Sokoróalja, as well as some of the Etyek-Buda region.

"6. EGER-VISONTA: all of Heves County, as well as the Borsod County villages of Andornak, Ostoros, Kis-Tálya, Noszvaj, and Szomolya."

This region is now shared by Eger and the Mátraalja.

"7. MISKOLCZ-ABAÚJ: Bodrog County except for the six villages listed in clause 6 above, as well as the Counties of Gömör, Kishont and, except for the village of Abaúj-Szántó, Abaúj-Torna county."

At one time Miskolc, now an industrial city, was considered an excellent source of wines. Today, whatever viticulture remains is relegated to the Bükkalja region southwest of the city. Gömör used to have a regional significance as a wine district, but its production waned rapidly in the 20th century.

"8. TOKAJ:

a) the Zemplén County communes of Bekecs, Bodrogkeresztúr, Bodrogkisfalud, Bodrogolaszi, Bodrogzsadány, Erdőbénye, Erdőhorváti, Golop, Józseffalva, Károlyfalva, Kistoronya, Legyesbénye, Mád, Monok, Olaszliszka, Ond, Petrahó, Rátka, Sárospatak, Sátoraljaújhely, Szegilong, Szerencs, Szőlőske, Tállya, Tarcal, Tokaj, Tolcsva, Vámosújfalu, Vágardó, Zombor—a total of 30 communes;

b) the village of Abaújszántó from Abaúj-Torna County." Village names [have been alphabetized and adjusted] for modern spelling for easier reference. Note that this list is from a historic

29

legislative document and does not fully coincide with the villages that make up the official Tokaj region today. The most obvious examples are the two villages of Kistoronya and Szőlőske, which were annexed by the Treaty of Trianon to Slovakia. These villages continue to be entitled to label their wines as Tokaj.

"9. SZEREDNYE-UNGVÁR: *Ung County.*"

An area belonging to the Ukraine, with practically no commercial production today.

"10. BEREGSZÁSZ-NAGYSZŐLŐS: *Bereg and Ugocsa Counties in their entirety, as well as the parts of Zemplén County not listed under clause 8 above.*"

Wine production around the towns of Munkács (Munkachevo) and Beregszász (Berehova), both part of the Ukraine today, lost most of its significance in the course of the 20th century.

"11. ÉRMELLÉK: *Szilágy County, and the following districts of Bihar County: Központ, Bél, Belényes, Élesd, Érmihályfalva, Magyarcséke, Margita, Szalárd, Székelyhida, Tenke, and Vaskoh; as well as the following districts of Szatmár County: Erdőd, Nagybánya, Nagysomkút, Szatmár, and Szinyérváralja.*"

Annexed to Romania in 1919, the region's wines soon fell out of repute and have been limited to local consumption ever since. The most important villages are Érmihályfalva and Érsemjén.

"12. MÉNES-MAGYARÁD: *the following 18 villages of Arad County: Radna, Paulis (Ópálos), Ménes, Gyorok, Kumin, Kovaszincz, Világos, Galsa, Muszka, Pankota, Magyarád, Agris, Aranyág, Draucz, Silingyia (Selénd), Apatelek, Boros-Jenő, and Boros-sebes.*"

Before its annexation to Romania in 1919, this region was equal to any in Hungary in terms of the quality of its wines; in fact, the red Aszú of Ménes fetched even higher prices than Tokaj. Currently half-hearted efforts are under way to resuscitate the renown of the region.

"13. VERSECZ-FEHÉRTEMPLOM: *Temes and Krassó-Szörény Counties, as well as the Alibunar district of Torontál County.*"

This region today stretches from the Banat district of Romania to Voivodina in Yugoslavia. The hub of this wine region was Versec (Vrac), producing excellent wine until the Swabian (ethnic German) residents, long noted for their reds, were deported in the aftermath of World War II.

"14. SZEGSZÁRD: *Tolna County.*"

This is now divided into two regions, Szekszárd proper [note the modern spelling] and Tolna.

"15. VILLÁNY-PÉCS: *all of Baranya County, as well as those parts of Somogy County not listed under clause 17.*"

This corresponds to the Villány-Siklós and Mecsekalja wine regions today.

"16. BADACSONY: *the Tapolcza district of Zala County and the villages of Meszes Györök and Keszthely.*"

In addition to the modern region of the same name, this comprised the western part of what is the Balaton-felvidék wine region today.

"17. BALATONMELLÉKE: *the rest of Zala County, the Veszprém, Enying, and Devecser districts of Veszprém County, as well as the Lengyeltóti, Marczali, and Tab districts of Somogy County.*"

These territories are now divided among four wine regions, namely Balatonfüred-Csopak, Balatonboglár, Balatonmelléke (known briefly from 1997 to 1999 as Zala), and the eastern section of the Balaton-felvidék.

"18. ERDÉLY-MAROS: *Alsó-Fehér, Hunyad, and Maros-Torda Counties.*"

Part of Romania today, this region was always split into two segments. While the wine production of Maros-Torda County remained strictly of local significance, the outstanding wine of the other two counties, often referred to as the "Transylvanian Foothills," attained a much wider reputation ("Erdély" is Hungarian for Transylvania). The best villages used to be Magyarigen, Borosbocsárd, Akmár, Szarakszó, Bencenc, Boroskrakkó, Csombord, Nagyenyed, and Celna. Hardly a trace of quality wine today.

"19. ERDÉLY-KÜKÜLLŐ: *the Nagyküküllő and Kisküküllő Counties.*"

(The "Great" and "Little" Küküllő are tributaries of the Maros river in the heart of Transylvania.) Part of Romania today, this region continues to supply the best Transylvanian wines—as it did in the past. The finest vineyards are located around the villages of Zsidve, Küküllővár, and Betlenszentmiklós.

"20. ERDÉLY: Beszterce-Naszód, Fogaras, Kolozs, Szeben, Szolnok-Doboka, Torda-Aranyos, and Udvarhely Counties."

Production in these parts continues on a modest local level, although some vineyards south of Beszterce (Bistrita) have been known to produce some excellent wines (e.g. from Lekence).

"21. ALFÖLD: the parts of Pest-Pilis-Solt-Kiskun County not listed under clauses 2 and 3; all of Szabolcs, Hajdú, Jász-Nagykun-Szolnok, Békés, Csongrád, Csanád, and Bács-Bodrog Counties; all of Torontál County except for the Alibunar district; Arad County except for the 18 villages listed under clause 12; the Nagy-Károly, Mátészalka, Fehérgyarmat, and Csenger districts of Szatmár County; as well as the Derecske, Berettyóújfalu, Cséffa, Mezőkeresztes, Nagyszalonta and Torda districts of Bihar County."

This vast area of the Great Plain includes three present-day wine regions in Hungary, namely the Kunság, Hajós-Vaskút, and Csongrád. A further large wine region called Nyírség, named after a district in north-eastern Hungary, existed until 1947. This region, shared by the present-day counties of Szabolcs-Szatmár-Bereg and Hajdú-Bihar, used to churn out high-alcohol mass-produced wines sourced from Nyíregyháza, Sóstó, Kisvárda, Napkor, and Debrecen.

"22. FIUME: the area of Fiume city."

This port city on the Kvarner Bay of the Adriatic, today belonging to Croatia as Rijeka, is still renowned for its red wines from the vineyards of Bakar (Buccari) and Porto Ré.

In the preamble to this extensive inventory, the decree of 1897 points out that *"The purpose of the classification into wine regions is the protection of hill-grown wines. Therefore, wines harvested within the geographical limits of the wine regions as provided in clauses 1-20 and 22 of this Decree, but from flat parts*

or vineyards planted in sand rather than on the slope of a hill or mountain, shall not be released, sold, or served under the name of the wine region but shall be labeled strictly as 'orchard wine' or 'sand-grown wine' at all times."

Although a significant part of these historic wine regions remained in Hungary after the country's territory in 1919 had shrunk to one-third of its size, the output and quality of production declined severely in the years between the two Wars, not least because of plummeting demand and stagnating wholesale markets. At the same time, the fragmentation of wine regions remaining in the country commenced. As a result of this process, the regulations by 1935 differentiated between no fewer than 18 wine regions.

Following World War II, a new cadastre survey led to the designation of 16 official wine regions in 1959. Particular interests and local lobbies exploited the opportunity of new, post-communist wine legislation in 1990 and 1997 to inflate the number of wine regions to 22—the same number the country possessed when it was three times the size it is today.

It would be important for decision-makers to realize that such a large number of designated wine regions, with wine styles not always clearly distinct and names often unpronounceable for foreigners, will surely prevent the effective promotion of the nation's wines in a European market that is opening up before our eyes. A much-needed and calculated integration into larger units would leave open the possibility to retain the current divisions on the level of districts recognized within the new units.

HUNGARIAN WINE TODAY IN NUMBERS

In 2002, Hungary had a total of 91,420* hectares of vines, divided between white and red varieties at the approximate ratio of 3 to 1. The average plantation size was a mere 0.4 ha. Data from 2000, considered a good year, gives us an idea of the country's production structure and potential. 684,440 tons of grapes were harvested around the country, with white wine grapes making up 65.37%, red wine grapes 24.63% of the total (the rest obviously being table grapes). 11.9% of the

* From the statistics of National Council of Wine Communities

31

The detailed geological built up of the individual wine regions will be discussed in the refering chapters.
This compilation shows the stratigraphic position of the dominating bedrock-types in each of them.

The geological chronology of Hungary's wine regions

crop was made into table wines, and 22.8% received a country wine classification. Quality wines, including a 2.77 % share of Bikavér, represented 53.39% of the total output, while only 5.84% earned the right to be labeled as special quality wine. This latter category featured Tokaj specialties at 1.12%, including Aszú wines, which accounted for no more than 0.26% of the country's total wine production in that year.

SUN, WIND AND RAIN

The grape-vine *Vitis vinifera* is native to the warm temperate zone. While it thrives best around the Mediterranean, it has spread to the extreme fringes of this area. Nevertheless, it is restricted in its distribution by the fact that it will not yield an appreciable crop unless it gets sufficient heat, insolation, and moisture to ripen, and is not exposed to severe winter and spring frosts.

Despite occupying latitudes between 45.5 and 48.5, close to the northern limit of wine production, Hungary still meets all these requirements. It has an average annual mean temperature of 10 °C, peaking at 11.4 °C at the cities of Szeged and Pécs in the south (affecting the wine regions of the Csongrád, Hajós-Baja, Mecsekalja, and Villány) and reaching a low of 9.5-9.9 °C at Miskolc and Sopron in the north (the wine regions of the Bükkalja, Eger, Pannonhalma-Sokoróalja, and Sopron). Consequently, the country has a relatively cool climate, and a growing season that is short compared to that of Mediterranean regions.

Era	Period	Age	Stage	Wine region	Typical rock-type
Cenozoic (0-66.5 million years)	Quaternary (0-1.8 million years)	Holocene		Tolna, South-Balaton, Aszár-Neszmély, Sokoróalja	fluviatile gravel and sand
				Kunság, Csongrád	eolic sand, resedimented (infusory) loess
		Pleistocene		Hajós-Baja, Tolna, Szekszárd, Balatonmelléke, South-Balaton, Mecsekalja, Villány, Tokaj	eolic sand, resedimented sandy loess
	Tertiary (1.8-66.5 million years)	Pliocene		Badacsony, Somló	Tapolca Basalt
		Miocene	Pannonian-Pontian	Badacsony, Somló, Tolna, Szekszárd, Sopron, Balatonmellék, Mátraalja, Mecsekalja, Villány, Tokaj	lacustrine clays and sandstone
			Sarmatian	Etyek-Buda	Tinnye Limestone
				Tokaj-Hegyalja	volcanic complex of the Tokaj-Eperjes Mts
			Badenian	Sopron	Rákos Limestone
				Mátraalja	Mátrai volcanic complex
				Eger, Bükkalja	Tar Dacitic Tuff
			Ottnangian	Mecsekalja	Szászvár Formation (gravel, sand)
				Eger, Bükkalja	Gyulakeszi Rhyolitic Tuff
		Oligocene	Egerian	Eger, Bükkalja	Eger Formation (clayey marl, sand)
				Etyek-Buda	Törökbálint and Mány Sandstones
				Mór	Csatka Formation (gravel, sand)
		Eocene		Mór	Szőc Limestone
		Paleocene			
Mesozoic (66.5-250 million years)	Cretaceous (66.5-140 million years)			Villány-Siklós	Nagyharsány Limestone
	Jurassic (140-215 million years)			Villány-Siklós	Villány and Szársomlyó Limestones
				Bükkalja	Lök Shale
	Triassic (215-250 million years)			Villány-Siklós	Siklós Limestone
				Balaton-felvidék	Upper Triassic limestones and dolomites
				Balatonfüred-Csopak	Lower and Middle Triassic limestones, marls, dolomites
Paleozoic (250-575 million years)	Permian (250-285 million years)			Mecsekalja	Kővágószőlős Sandstone
				Balatonfüred-Csopak	Balaton-felvidék Sandstone
	Carboniferous (285-360 million years)			Etyek-Buda-Velence Mts	Velence Granite
				Sopron	Sopron Gneiss

Even latitudinal position can vary in its impact depending on the altitude of the growing site above sea level, since a higher elevation will have the same effect as a greater distance from the Equator. In Hungary, vineyards typically occupy altitudes from 100 m to 300 m, generally regarded as the upper limit of profitable cultivation at this latitude. The few notable exceptions include the 513-meter tall Kopaszhegy ("Bald Hill") at Tokaj, which was densely planted with vines all the way to the top in pre-phylloxera times. Tests have shown that the sugar content of the same grape variety may drop by as much as 0.5 degrees, translating to 5-10 g/l in must, with every 100 m increase in vineyard altitude.

The amount of light or radiated energy absorbed by a vineyard depends to a great extent on the angle and aspect of the slope on which the vines are planted, while the color and structure of the soil have consequences for its temperature, heat retention, and evaporation of moisture. The incline of the slope is important, because the steeper the angle in which the rays of the sun hit the ground, the more light and heat the vineyard will absorb. Tall mountains and ranges make a vital contribution by blocking cold air which, in Hungary, typically arrives with prevailing north-westerly winds. Almost all of the country's historic wine regions evolved in the shel-

ter of mountains. For instance, Mór is protected by the Vértes Range, Eger by the Bükk Mountains, and Tokaj by the Tokaj-Eperjes Mountains. The varied morphology and terrain of growing areas in or near mountains and hills result in a diversity of microclimates, often reflected in the diverse character of the region's wines.

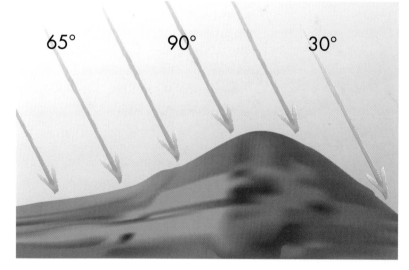

LIGHT

The grape-vine prefers a luminous intensity of 20,000-30,000 lux, and 1,800-2,000 sunshine hours from April 1st to October 31st—but certainly no fewer than 1,300 hours. In Hungary, this figure ranges from 1,250 to 1,500 hours per season, with the Kunság and

The effect of the dip of slopes upon the angle of incidence of the sun radiation

33

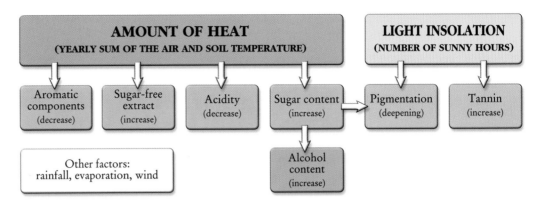

The effect of climatic factors upon the components of wine

Csongrád regions of the Great Plain being the sunniest, and the Mura River district of the Balatonmelléke region receiving the least annual insolation. Importantly, vines cannot directly utilize more than 50% of the physiologically active light coming in, as at least half the luminosity is absorbed and retained by the soil between the rows, to be ultimately utilized as energy.

Light plays a crucial role in shaping berry color, sugar, and acidity. Grapes exposed to light during ripening will have thicker skin, better color, 2-3 degrees higher sugar, and slightly (2-3‰) lower acidity than berries kept in the shade at the same temperature.

HEAT

The amount of heat available for the vine is conventionally expressed as the sum of average daily temperatures during the growing season, understood as the period consisting of days with an average temperature above 10 °C (185-200 days in Hungary). Up to a certain point, wine quality is directly proportional to the heat sum.

Excessively low temperatures can cause frost damage. Traditionally, the last day late in the spring with a possibility of frost is St. Orban's day on May 25th. Frost early in the fall before the harvest may damage the crop, while severe winter weather may freeze the vine (below –20 °C) and even its roots (below –25 °C). At the other end of the scale, temperatures over 35 °C may scorch bunches and foliage.

RAINFALL

The grape-vine is not particularly susceptible to water stress, as it lets down roots very deep into the ground where it can find the moisture it needs, even in drought-stricken years. It will thrive on 300 to 700 mm of rainfall a year. More rainfall than this can be harmful, not only because it implies more cloudy days and less sunshine, but also because rising groundwater levels may cause root rot. On the other hand, less than 300 mm of annual rain will necessitate irrigation. Average annual rainfall in Hungary ranges from 500 in the south (Kunság, Csongrád, and Hajós-Vaskút regions) to 800 mm in the west and southwest (Sopron, Pannonhalma-Sokoróalja, Balatonmelléke).

HUMIDITY

Low humidity increases evaporation, and the roots of the vine may not be able to replenish the lost moisture. Damp conditions, on the other hand, make a perfect habitat for a variety of fungal infections. For this very reason, humidity is a prized and essential climatic factor in vineyards geared for the production of grapes affected by botrytis—these days not just in Tokaj but in other areas of Hungary as well.

WIND

The grape-vine is an anemophilous plant that relies on wind as the vehicle of pollination. A good breeze in the vineyard is also essential in keeping fungal disease at bay, and in refreshing stuffy overheated air among the rows on a hot summer night. In Hungary, wind conditions are fairly normal; vineyard damage due to gales is a rare occurrence. In the middle and western parts of the country, the prevailing winds blow from the northwest.

Grape Varieties

"When Noah planted the first vine after the Flood, he opened a new chapter in universal history," writes *Béla Hamvas in his* Philosophy of Wine. *Indeed, there is hardly a plant on Earth, excepting ornamental flowers, that humans everywhere have toiled harder to grow; no crop so often planted in areas where it cannot possibly be cultivated for sheer gain. The grape vine alone has inspired man to shed so much sweat of his brow. Little wonder that it is venerated so highly, especially in places where it likes to thrive.*

There are now welcome signs that the hegemony of international varieties that has cluttered the market to oblivion—Chardonnay, Sauvignon Blanc, Cabernet Sauvignon—may be crumbling at last. The challengers are grapes typical of certain regions, such as Pinot Gris, which seems to be enjoying a renaissance, and grapes of distinct character from smaller growing areas such as Sagrantino or Primitivo from Southern Italy. "So what's the point?," you might ask. Well, it certainly feels good to be heading back to a world we can regard as normal—one in which it makes sense to talk about Somló wine that is not a Chardonnay but a Hárslevelű, or Badacsony whose true expression is Kéknyelű rather than Sauvignon Blanc, or Szekszárd conceived as

	Primary name used in Hungary	Other Hungarian name(s)	Branch	English name or translation	Other name(s)
Chardonnay		Kereklevelű	Occidentalis gallica		Chardonnay blanc, Morillon

Occurrence and Growing area in Hungary	Ubiquitous throughout the country, although in some regions cannot legally be sold as quality wine. Chardonnay began to gain more ground in Hungary during the first half of the 1980's. 2,960~3000 hectares, primarily in the Mátraalja, Balatonboglár, Etyek-Buda, Tolna, and Ászár-Neszmély.
Soil preference	While in Hungary Chardonnay is grown on all kinds of soils except fertile forest types, it performs best on clay-bearing or weathered volcanic soils rich in minerals. The variety has high lime tolerance but will yield leaner and stiffer wine on intensely calcareous soils.
Description	Medium-sized leaves barely articulated or not articulated at all. The almost perfectly regular shape must have inspired the grape's old Hungarian name *Kereklevelű* ("Round Leaf"). Open petiolar sinus; leaf base delimited by vein. Generally small cylindrical bunches, loose rather than compact, of small juicy berries that are whitish green with black speckles.
The wine	Owing its large-scale naturalization in Hungary to the international forces of wine fashion, Chardonnay here was largely confined to the stainless steel tank until the early 1990's, when experiments with small new oak began. Of the Chardonnays fermented and matured in steel, the only domestic production worthy of mention is that of the Etyek-Buda region, destined for sparkling wines. The firm but well-balanced Chardonnays grown on Etyek's calcareous soils are to this day the staple of sparkling wine manufacture based in Budafok outside the capital city.

■ THE WINE AND ITS BEST DOMESTIC GROWERS

Fermented and/or matured in barriques, the consistently best Hungarian Chardonnays have come out of the regions of Ászár-Neszmély (Hilltop Neszmély — lime bearing clay), Balatonboglár (Ottó Légli — loess bearing clay), Villány-Siklós (József Bock, Malatinszky Kúria — calcareous sedimentary clay), the Mátraalja (Mátyás Szőke — nyirok), and Eger (Tibor Gál — loess and adobe overlying volcanic rocks). The cool-climate Chardonnays, from Eger and the Mátraalja, will age well in the bottle for 5-10 years, while those grown in warmer locations tend not to stay in top shape that long. A fascinating experiment to be watched is that by Béla Fekete of Somló, whose consistently rich, mineraly, almost salty Chardonnay has proved very popular, giving the lie to the regulations that prohibit the variety to be sold as quality wine in this tiny region.

	Primary name used in Hungary	Other Hungarian name(s)	Branch	English name or translation	Other name(s)
Cserszegi Fűszeres				"Cserszeg's Spice"	
	An intraspecific Hungarian hybrid of Irsai Olivér and Tramini.				
Occurrence and growing area in Hungary	This grape, bred in 1960, has spread to a number of regions around the country, claiming the largest acreage in the Great Plain (the Kunság and Hajós-Baja) and the Mátraalja 2400 ha.				
Soil preference	Cserszegi Fűszeres likes sand and loess, but will yield more vigorous wine on calcareous soils.				
Description	Small round leaves with five lobes and a smooth shiny surface. Medium-sized shouldered bunches of incarnadine berries.				

■ THE WINE AND ITS BEST DOMESTIC GROWERS

Well-liked for its Muscat character and lively acidity, Cserszegi Fűszeres has an aroma often reminiscent of wild flowers that is never excessively perfumed or heavy. Best when drunk young, Cserszegi Fűszeres is capable of perfect balance when harvested early from calcareous soils. For years, Hilltop Neszmély's Woodcutter's White brand has been the most popular take on this grape. Equally nice if slightly heavier in style is the Cserszegi made by the Németh Winery (Zala County, Balaton-melléke region).

Kadarka instead of Cabernet. Then again, you will know what to expect from Eger or Villány, given that the established varietal structure of these regions weighs in the balance at least as much as other considerations, climatic or otherwise. And it is true that some grapes are apt to produce outstanding quality in a wide diversity of settings, due to their intrinsic qualities. After all, it was this special ability that launched Chardonnay and Cabernet Sauvignon on their campaign to conquer the world. For Hungary as a whole though, it would clearly be a mistake to settle for 10 or 15 international varieties, using them as a staple for wines without personality or distinction. For a country with this kind of potential, the road to success must lead through finding the right balance between international varieties and indigenous grapes.

THE ORIGIN OF GRAPE VARIETIES GROWN IN HUNGARY

Like other wine growing countries in Europe, Hungary for the most part relies on grapes derived from Vitis Vinifera. In the Carpathian Basin, whose homogeny of grape varieties grown is explained by its compact

	Primary name used in Hungary	Other Hungarian name(s)	Branch	English name or translation	Other name(s)
	Ezerjó		Pontian balcanica	"Thousand Blessings"	Tausendgute, Trummertraube
Occurrence and growing area in Hungary	Well-known throughout the Carpathian Basin, Ezerjó was one of the most common varieties in Hungary in the first half of the 20th century, and was widely used as a parent for various hybrids. Today, its area under cultivation has shrunk to 3,000 hectares, including 2,600 in the Kunság, 260 in Mór (where practically no other grape used to be planted), and 168 hectares in Ászár-Neszmély.				
Soil preference	As a fairly acidic grape, Ezerjó is noted for its ability to retain vigor even when planted on sand, although it yields indisputably superior quality on Mór's deeper subsoils enriched in clay, marl, and lime.				
Description	Heart-shaped, thick leaves with an intensely blistered surface and upper petioles closed or barely opened. Medium, shouldered bunches are formed by yellowish oval berries that assume a rusty hue on the sunny side when fully ripe. Thick-skinned, juicy, and tart.				

■ THE WINE AND ITS BEST DOMESTIC GROWERS

Ezerjó is said to be hard, especially when made from less than ideally ripe grapes. These wines have harsh and rough acids that will not be rounded with age. When picked fully ripe, Ezerjó makes a high-acid wine but one balanced with medium alcohol, a full body, and consummate elegance. In better years, the grape is a good sugar producer and, given the proper location, prone to shrivel and contract botrytis. If this happens, the wine made—now almost every year as in the old days—is called Móri Aszú. This sweet wine potentially has a depth of flavor on a par with the best of Tokaj, and a floral character built on a subtle tart foundation. The nicest examples from Mór have been produced by the Bozóky Winery.

uniformity as a geographical region, the majority of grapes (according to Marton's 1944 taxonomy) are of the *Pontian* branch, supplemented by smaller proportions of *occidental* and *oriental* varieties as well as their intraspecific and interspecific hybrids. Regarded as indigenous to Hungary or the Carpathian Basin, the Pontian is also known as the Black Sea group or, more specifically, as the East Central European-West Asian

set. These traditional grapes tend to have a moderately long growing season and prefer low-moisture climates. They include Ezerjó, Furmint and Kéknyelű, as well as most of the ancient Hungarian varieties that are no longer cultivated, such as Gohér, Csomorika, Kolontár, or Magyarka. The list is far from being final, and while we do not wish to take sides in a scientific debate that is still wide open, for convenience we will concede

	Primary name used in Hungary	Other Hungarian name(s)	Branch	English name or translation	Other name(s)
Furmint			Pontian balcanica		Mosler, Zapfner, Moslavac
Occurrence and Growing area in Hungary	The first mention of Furmint in Hungary dates from 1623, but the origins of the grape remain unclear. Some believe it came from Southern Italy; others point to Syrmia (today in Serbia) as its cradle. By the early 18th century, it became the leading variety in Tokaj, and began to gain ground elsewhere in the country as well. Nowadays, great Furmint apart from Tokaj is grown only in Somló. In fact, no other region has enough of it planted to mount a serious challenge. About 4300 hectares at present, with the overwhelming majority (4200 hectares) cultivated in Tokaj, plus a trickle from 24 hectares in Somló.				
Soil preference	Furmint performs best when planted on deep bound soils rich in minerals, but will thrive on weathered volcanic rock and loess as well. It positively dislikes sand and alluvial gravel.				
Description	Barely articulated leaves that are thick and waxy, with a blistered surface. Loose cylindrical bunches, varying in size depending on strain, of medium-sized, thick-skinned but juicy berries. Furmint is susceptible to frost and rot, but the latter tendency also makes it a fine substrate for botrytis. The most highly prized lots, planted 60-80 years ago with the old clones, produce small and very compact bunches. Handled separately, the wine of these old vines is much more concentrated and full-flavored than those made from Furmint planted after World War II. Of these old clones, the Madárkás, the Hólyagos and the Fehér Furmint were once considered the best.				

■ THE WINE AND ITS BEST DOMESTIC GROWERS

Furmint is a diligent acid producer, but these acids—assuming conscientious work in the vineyard—have refinement and serve as the solid foundation for the most enduring dessert wines. Because it ripens with high sugar levels, dry Furmint can be fiery wine, in Tokaj often attaining 14-15% alcohol. It has a firm nose that conveys good varietal character even at lesser concentration, and is often marked by hints of pear, quince, and clove. Made from ripe grapes, Furmint can be full-bodied but elegant, and always special whether dry or sweet. Examples grown in Somló—especially good from Imre Györgykovács, as well as from Béla Fekete and Károly Fehérvári—tend to show more restraint in their aromas and flavors, needing time and exposure to air to open out fully. These wines reach their peak at three or four years of age, and the best will remain in good shape for 10-15 years there-

that certain morphological properties do appear to support the Pontian origins of most Hungarian grape varieties.

To all intents and purposes, Hungarians have also come to regard as their own a few occidental varieties, due to their wide currency and reliable good quality. Indeed, grapes like Olaszrizling (Italian Riesling or Welschriesling), Szürkebarát (Pinot Gris) or Tramini (Gewürztraminer) have been present in the Carpathian Basin for centuries. In contrast, relatively few varieties of the oriental branch have found favor in Hungary, most of them having made deeper inroads around the Mediterranean. This is especially true for Afuz Ali and Sultanina, both table (or raisin) grapes not cultivated in Hungary. Another member of this group, Chasselas, is well-known throughout the Carpathian Basin—in

after. Furmint majors on purity of flavor and an elegance on a par with the great Rieslings of the Rhine. In addition to the mineral character imparted by volcanic soils, the variety's main asset is its distinctive acidity, which tends to appeal to seasoned vinophiles rather than to neophytes. In fact, many regard Furmint as hard wine—which it certainly is when made from unripe fruit or excessive yields. Tokaj Furmint is a little softer, but only in comparison with Somló. It often attains an acidity of 10-12 g/l, which imparts body and spine to the wine and, when coupled with appropriate sugar and/or extract, will never make the taste seem sharp. Furmint made from the fruit of vines predating the War, for instance by János Árvay or Királyudvar, is among the great dry whites of the world.

The increasing number of Tokaj growers eager to exploit the potential inherent in these old plantations also include Zoltán Demeter, Vince Gergely and, of course, István Szepsy himself. These wines need even more time to breathe than a Somló Furmint (not unlike a venerable older vintage Riesling from Bernkastler Doktor or Schloss Johannisberg). Sweet Furmint from Tokaj can be bottled as late harvest solo varietal wine or, blended with Hárslevelű or Sárga Muskotály, as Szamorodni or Aszú. An accomplished sugar producer, Furmint is largely responsible for the high residual sugar of these wines, always complemented by capable acidity and typically modest (11-12%) alcohol. The aroma of young late harvest Furmint is often defined by botrytis (citrus, orange peel, mace) accompanied by the requisite hints of pear and quince. Less powerfully marked by botrytis character, Furmint-based Aszú wines convey accents of pear, apricot, honey, black locust blossom and, when matured in American oak, chestnut, peach, and pineapple. Some sites yield Furmint with the distinct aroma and flavor of dill. As the wines mature, micro-oxidation causes significant shifts in color, bouquet, and taste, toward warmer brownish tones of walnut, hazelnut, chestnut, Turkish delight, even later chocolate, tobacco, coffee, cedar, and sandalwood. In addition to the names already mentioned, late harvest style Furmint from Tokaj is consistently excellent from Oremus, Disznókő, Pendits, and Hétszőlő.

Hungary as *Saszla*—but also as more of a table grape than a source for fine wines.

Over the centuries, Hungarian wine has been shaped by the vicissitudes of history and the foreign peoples that passed through the country or set up camp to stay for varying lengths of time. We have but a very limited record of the grapes grown here in Roman times, but it seems quite certain that Yellow Muscat, known locally as Sárga Muskotály, was one of them. During the Middle Ages, Hungarian viticulture was greatly influenced by immigrant growers from Italy, Germany, Bavaria, and Franconia, as well as merchants from Germany and Greece. In all likelihood, these settlers brought with them not just their own culture of cultivating methods, but also contributed hitherto unknown varieties to what had essentially been a white-wine diet for centuries. Kadarka (Gamza), the first red wine grape to be naturalized here, came from the Balkans via Serbian intercession. The country's occupation by the Ottoman Turks sealed the fate of Syrmia (today Fruska Gora in Serbia) which used to be regarded as the gem of all wine regions claimed by the Hungarian crown. Growers fleeing Syrmia ended up in the Tokaj Foothills much further north, where they

	Primary name used in Hungary	Other Hungarian name(s)	Branch	English name or translation	Other name(s)
Hárslevelű			Pontian balcanica	"Linden Leaf"	Lindeblättrige, Lipovina
Occurrence and Growing area in Hungary	Hárslevelű is an ancient Hungarian variety that probably emerged as a naturally fertilized seedling. Grown throughout Hungary, Hárslevelű is most popular in Tokaj, where it preceded Furmint in the 18th century, when growers began to plant it on a larger scale as a substitute for the Fejérszőlő grape. The Debrő district of the Eger region is a traditional source of fine off-dry examples. Approximately 1,300 hectares, including 850 in Tokaj, 160 in the Mátraalja, and 100 in Eger.				
Soil preference	Prefers warmer volcanic soils, but will do well on clay with weathered loess mixed in.				
Description	Large and loose cylindrical bunches often 40 cm long, with a tip sometimes split in a bifurcating dovetail shape. Thin-skinned, juicy, and round, the medium-sized berries have a greenish yellow color shaded with rusty brown on the sunny side. They are often covered by a thin veil of bloom.				

■ THE WINE AND ITS BEST DOMESTIC GROWERS

Often likened to Furmint, Hárslevelű in fact makes a softer, more aromatic wine that matures faster and is more approachable. The grape itself ripens sooner than Furmint, with subtle acids, good sugar levels, and a predisposition to hosting botrytis. Hárslevelű wines can be readily identified by their distinct aroma reminiscent of linden blossom and linden honey, often accented by hints of chestnut and clove on the nose. Grown on loess, Hárslevelű can yield particularly soft and charming wine that tends to benefit from large casks. Although a little residual sugar suits it well, it is also excellent when vinified fully dry. Remarkable exponents of the latter style are Béla Fekete and Imre Györgykovács in Somló. Further

south in Villány-Siklós, József Bock's Hárslevelű and Zoltán Polgár's Aranyhárs ("Gold Linden") rise above the average. In recent years, Tokaj has become the scene of exciting experiments with the grape in the late harvest style, spearheaded by Degenfeld, Oremus, Dereszla, and János Árvay. To date, pure varietal Hárslevelű Aszú has been produced only by Hétszőlő and Árvay, whose 1999 Hárslevelű Aszú may well stand as the silkiest sweet wine ever made anywhere. Tasted repeatedly in 2002 and 2003, this wine dazzled panelists with its flavors of chestnut and Belgian truffle. Unless we are mistaken, single vineyard pure Hárslevelű Aszú looks set to become the most highly prized dessert wine type in coming years.

	Primary name used in Hungary	Other Hungarian name(s)	Branch	English name or translation	Other name(s)
	Irsai Olivér		Intraspecific		
	An intraspecific Hungarian hybrid of Pozsonyi and Csaba Gyöngye.				
Occurrence and growing area in Hungary	Irsai Olivér used to be planted as a table grape only until the mid-1980's, when it was promoted to become a well-liked grape for white wine. Most of the 1,300 hectares devoted to it belong to the Kunság region, followed by the Mátraalja and Balatonboglár.				
Soil preference	Not a fastidious grape, Irsai Olivér seems to thrive on loose sand and bound soils equally well.				
Description	Smaller round leaves with five lobes and a thin texture. Medium-sized shouldered bunches of berries that attain a golden yellow color when fully ripe. Sensitive to frost and needs heavy pruning.				

■ THE WINE AND ITS BEST DOMESTIC GROWERS

Its delicate acids and Muscat-like aromas have made this early-ripening grape a perennial favorite that is best when drunk young. It tends to age very fast, but a little care will go a long way to preserve its freshness. As a fragrant ingredient, it is often blended with more vigorous varietals to yield an ideal wine for the summer. While Irsai Olivér can be found almost everywhere in Hungary, its characteristic softness usually makes it a safer bet for regions to the north of the country, such as Sopron, Ászár-Neszmély (Hilltop), Etyek-Buda (Nyakas), or the Mátraalja (Mátyás Szőke). Balatonboglár stands as the only region further south that has been very successful with this grape.

continued to grow rich sweet wines that were already winning high esteem in those days. Also around this time, the local selection of table grapes was enriched by varieties as tasty as their names were colorful: Genua Zamatos ("Zest of Genova"), Fehér and Kék Kecskecsöcsű (White and Blue "Goat Teat"), Kék Ökörszem ("Blue Oxeye"), Sárga Lugas ("Yellow Pergola"). 1590 saw the publication of a tome entitled *Nomenclatura*, in which the author, Balázs Szikszai Fabriczius provides a detailed account of Tokaj's grape varieties, viticul-

ture, and wine-making methods. Some sources claim that Muskotály (Muscat), Gohér and Balafánt were by then well-established in Tokaj, while Furmint and Hárslevelű, the region's decisive grapes today, had not yet made an appearance. By the end of the 18th century, a number of agricultural records and national statutes supplied meticulous inventories of grapes authorized for growing sites ranked first and second class, occasionally going so far as to ban certain varieties from specific areas. In the early 1800's, József Fábián introduced

Primary name used in Hungary	Other Hungarian name(s)	Branch	English name or translation	Other name(s)
Juhfark		Orientalis caspica	"Sheepstail"	Lämmerschwantz
An ancient Hungarian grape.				

Occurrence and growing area in Hungary	Juhfark has become synonymous with Somló, home to the overwhelming majority of the 100 hectares devoted to this grape (there are a few more lots of it in Balatonfüred-Csopak). Time was when growers planted (and confused) Juhfark with Csomorika, but things have been sorted out and the Juhfark plantations on the slopes of the Somló are clean and pure once again.
Soil preference	Most expressive on volcanic slopes, but will also thrive on calcareous soils where it makes lighter, more fragrant wine.
Description	Light green leaves with five lobes and open petioles. The elongated bunches are often curled back at the tip, which goes a long way to explain the grape's name. Greenish white berries, covered with bloom.

■ THE WINE AND ITS BEST DOMESTIC GROWERS

Regarded as the stiffest, most rustic wine of Hungary, Juhfark has a neutral aroma and taste that make it less approachable when young. Without maturation in wood it tends to be excessively harsh, even rough in its acidity. It needs plenty of air and higher than usual drinking temperature to develop in the glass, as well as at least three to four years before it reaches full maturity. By then, the initially raspy acids will have lost their edge, and a full-flavored pure wine of great elegance will have emerged. The best growers of the grape are Béla Fekete, Imre Györgykovács, and István Inhauser —all three based in Somló.

Chasselas. During the 1820's, collections were established in the Grinzing near Vienna, and then on the slopes of Sas-hegy at Buda and in Vecsés outside the city, each of which contained 675 varieties. The effort was spearheaded by Demeter Görög**, who identified no fewer than 50 varieties from Tokaj alone. In fact, many sources relate how Tokaj in this era functioned as an exporter of grape varieties to France, Italy, Germany, and Russia.

At the turn of the 18th and 19th centuries, Ferenc Schams* used his clout as the greatest viticulturist of his day to publicly denounce the chaos that characterized the country's varietal assortment, and argued for a standardized classification. A firm advocate of finding the grapes that would do best in each location, Schams decried "...the incredible carelessness informing the plantation and reconstruction of hillside vineyards around the country... Suffice it to say that most vineyards, no matter how small, have been planted with a hodgepodge of 38-40 different grapes, the good mixed indiscriminately with the inferior, where six

* Ferenc Schams eonologist 1780-1839

** Demeter Görög eonologist 1760-1833 The founder of ampelography in Hungarian language.

43

	Primary name used in Hungary	Other Hungarian name(s)	Branch	English name or translation	Other name(s)
	Kéknyelű		Pontian, balcanica	"Blue Stalk"	Blaustängler
	Widely regarded as an indigenous Hungarian variety, although some researchers claim it is identical to the Piccolit of Northern Italy. Whichever way you look at it, Kéknyelű has been present in the Carpathian Basin for centuries.				
Occurrence and Growing area in Hungary	A scant 23 hectares in Badacsony, plus negligible productions here and there in the Balaton-felvidék.				
Soil preference	As it is grown on volcanic slopes only, we have no experience of how it would perform if planted in other soils.				
Description	Moderately articulated, thick leaves with open petiolar sinuses and a smooth surface. The petiole has a bluish tint, explaining the grape's Hungarian name. The medium-sized shouldered bunches often look thinned-out due to poor berry set; the berries themselves are green and thick-skinned. Kéknyelű probably has pistillate flowers only, needing other pollinating varieties, such as Szlanka or Budai Zöld, to fertilize it.				

■ THE WINE AND ITS BEST DOMESTIC GROWERS

Kéknyelű is often described as hard wine, and it certainly has a strong acid spine. It is typically aloof on the nose and muted in its flavors. Not unlike Riesling or Juhfark, it needs time to mature and will benefit greatly from malolactic fermentation and micro-oxidation. Kéknyelű is distinguished by a tart note and, in good years of the order of 1994 or 1999 in Badacsony, a fleshy structure reminiscent of Viognier. It is a masculine wine often heralded as a true example of Magyar character next to Juhfark and Furmint. Apart from Huba Szeremley, we have regrettably no grower to report who would produce Kéknyelű wine to consistently reliable standards.

or eight early or late ripening varieties, chosen specifically for the site and climate, would go much further in rewarding the grower for the sweat of his brow." Interestingly though, some of the varietal names Schams so fervently objected to, like Juhfark ("Sheepstail") or Sárfehér ("Golden White"), have survived to this day, together with the grapes they designate.

Raising its head in Hungary in the 1880's, phylloxera dealt the first major blow to the country's viticulture, which had till then relied on a large selection of grape varieties and consistent good quality. When most of

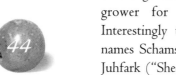

	Primary name used in Hungary	Other Hungarian name(s)	Branch	English name or translation	Other name(s)
Királyleányka				"Princess"	Feteasca regale
	A natural intraspecific hybrid of Kövér Szőlő and Leányka, native to the Carpathian Basin.				
Occurrence and Growing area in Hungary	Originating from Transylvania, today part of Romania, Királyleányka was introduced to Hungary in the 1970's. It first gained ground around Balatonboglár. About 1000 hectares, mostly concentrated in Balatonboglár, the Kunság, and the Mátraalja.				
Soil preference	Likes a looser soil, and will do quite well on loess or sand.				
Description	Shiny, densely textured leaves with slight articulation and wide open petiolar sinuses. Small compact bunches of round greenish-white berries flecked with black.				

■ THE WINE AND ITS BEST DOMESTIC GROWERS

Királyleányka makes a delightfully crisp but subtle wine often reminiscent of glucose drops. Its neutral flavors and firm acids make it ideal for blending with aromatic varieties, which it supports rather than overpowers. Clearly not a wine for longevity, Királyleányka is best drunk young and makes perfect sipping wine for a hot summer day. The best have come from Ottó Légli in Balatonboglár and Mátyás Szőke in the Mátraalja.

the indigenous grapes had been wiped out by the pest, reconstruction was carried out relatively fast but with little foresight. Despite the world-wide reputation achieved by Zsigmond Teleki, along with other Hungarian scientists and breeders, in selecting the best rootstocks and developing new ones, the varietal composition of entire wine regions evolved without an underlying concept or steadfast commitment to quality. The exigencies of mass production in the wake of World War II led to the establishment of mediocre clones which produced large yields but prevented sheer quality, let alone the true expression of the terroir. The research institutes worked away at breeding new varieties by the dozen, but most of these resulted from considerations of quantity and ease of industrial cultivation rather than quality.

In an effort to track changing global tastes in the eighties, Hungary performed a hasty overhaul of sorts on its varietal structure, committing large tracts to French grapes even in areas where these were clearly out of place. In this way, Cabernet Sauvignon and Franc, along with Merlot, often ended up in sites where they could not possibly get

45

	Primary name used in Hungary	Other Hungarian name(s)	Branch	English name or translation	Other name(s)
Leányka		Leányszőlő	Orientalis caspica	"Maiden"	Feteasca alba
	Probably native to Transylvania.				
Occurrence and growing area in Hungary	A total of 1000 hectares, mostly in Eger, the Bükkalja, and the Mátraalja. Smaller tracts are cultivated in the Kunság and Ászár-Neszmély. Not the most fashionable grape these days, Leányka has seen its production scaled back in recent years.				
Soil preference	Leányka is best in Eger, particularly in sites where it gets the lime it needs to ripen with adequate acidity. It makes a softer wine on pure volcanic soils, and will not yield better than blending wine when planted on sand.				
Description	Intensely articulated leaves with large open petioles, and a smooth shiny surface. Medium-sized, compact shouldered bunches of small round berries that ripen to a light brownish yellow color and have thin but chewy skin. A relatively early-ripening variety.				

■ THE WINE AND ITS BEST DOMESTIC GROWERS

The halcyon days of the legendary Egri Leányka are clearly over for now, although this grape can deliver high alcohol and even appreciable residual sugar in good years. Its wine is quintessentially floral, with hints of black locust blossom, wild flowers, and honeydew melon. Its soft acids make it imperative to time the harvest with care. Given appropriately low yields, Leányka is capable of fine quality and even longevity as a solo varietal, for instance from Tibor Gál in Eger. It is nevertheless more favored nowadays as a blending wine, supplying a key ingredient in Pók-Polónyi's fine cuvées (also from Eger). Quite a few growers predict a great future for this grape, and recommend it for barrique treatment along the lines of Chardonnay. If supported by new plantation and the discovery of an appropriate wine style, Leányka may yet become a wine of independent character in its own right.

enough sun and warmth. No wonder that the resulting wines were routinely criticized for their rawness and lack of concentration. This is also how Chardonnay and Sauvignon Blanc became the inevitable staple of almost every large winery, but rarely turned out better than mediocre or, at best, inferior in quality. Albeit Cabernet, Pinot Noir, and Chardonnay had been established

here and there in Hungary as early as the early 20th century, they have never run out of control anywhere in the country. All in all, Hungarian viticulture is clearly still dominated by traditional Carpathian varieties, both in terms of their number and the acreage devoted to them. This fact notwithstanding, prices and competitions at home and abroad demonstrate that international

	Primary name used in Hungary	Other Hungarian name(s)	Branch	English name or translation	Other name(s)
Olaszrizling	Nemes rizling	Occidentalis gallica	Italian Riesling	Welschriesling

Occurrence and Growing area in Hungary	The most wide-spread quality white grape in Hungary, grown in backyards and large wineries everywhere in the country—except in Tokaj. Currently grown on 6,500 hectares, of which 800 hectares belong to Badacsony, Balatonfüred-Csopak and Balaton-felvidék each. These regions are followed by Kunság and Mátraalja each with 800 hectares of Olaszrizling planted.
Soil preference	Particularly fond of volcanic soils; adept at processing minerals and trace elements.
Description	Small, distinctly compact bunches of round, yellowish green berries; speckled when ripe. Highly frost resistant but sensitive to rot. An even producer, but needs low yields to show what it is capable of.

■ THE WINE AND ITS BEST DOMESTIC GROWERS

Powerful yet refined when fully ripe, but harsh and sharp when made from unripe fruit, regardless of site. A fine sugar producer in better locations, with firm but elegant acids; capable of optimum balance. Prone to contract botrytis, the Olaszrizling supplies the rare Aszú of Mount Badacsony. When dry, the wine is tart in the way traditionally referred to as masculine, the nicer bottles often showing hints of burnt almond on the nose and on the palate. Olaszrizling is also suitable for blending and will reward a deferred harvest. The nicest examples come from the volcanic buttes of the Balaton-felvidék and the Somló, where Olaszrizling attains remarkable longevity; the very best will age for 15-20 years. In the Mátraalja and the Egerszólát district of the Bükkalja, the grape makes lighter, flowery wine marked by a distinct mignonette fragrance, as opposed to the burnt almond note typical of Olaszrizling grown further south. Equally amenable to maturation in steel or wood, Olaszrizling has often suffered scorn in the shadow of Rhine Riesling—a reputation routinely refuted by Hungarian examples. The finest Olaszrizlings today are produced by Huba Szeremley (Badacsony), the Scheller Estate (Balaton-felvidék), Mihály Figula (Balatonfüred-Csopak), Ottó Légli (Balatonboglár), as well as Lajos Gál and Vilmos Thummerer (Eger).

	Primary name used in Hungary	Other Hungarian name(s)	Branch	English name or translation	Other name(s)
Ottonel Muskotály			Orientalis caspica		Muscat Ottonel
	Assumed to be a cross between Chasselas and Muscat de Saumur, created in 1852.				
Occurrence and Growing area in Hungary	Found throughout Hungary, except in Somló, and Sopron. 1,380 hectares, with most of it divided among the Kunság, the Mátraalja, and Eger.				
Soil preference	Not especially demanding about growing conditions, but will make more enjoyable wine in cooler areas where it can retain higher acidity. Tends to be more deeply flavored on volcanic soils than elsewhere.				
Description	Regular-shaped leaves with five lobes and nearly or completely closed petiolar sinuses in between. Small cylindrical bunches, often shouldered, of yellowish berries shaded with brick red when fully ripe.				

■ THE WINE AND ITS BEST DOMESTIC GROWERS

Like all aromatic varieties, Ottonel Muskotály is especially susceptible to the timing of the harvest. If picked before the onslaught of full biological maturity, the grape's acidity can successfully offset its rather distinct sweet and perfumed aromas. In Ottonel Muskotály picked too late, these aromas can easily take a downward turn. The wine is rather soft in character, and will show to best advantage when vinified fully dry. As one of the most popular secondary grapes, Muscat Ottonel usually plays some role or another at most wineries in Hungary, not least in blending. Huba Szeremley (Szent Orbán winery, Badacsony) has been noted for his consistently fine Ottonel Muskotály. In the Mátraalja, Mátyás Szőke also makes it nice and dry.

varieties lead the market of Hungarian wines today—with the notable exception of noble sweet wines from Tokaj.

Of course, none of this is to question the merit of these international grapes. We merely regret the fact that often they were planted in sites without the climatic or geological potential that they deserve—sites where they yield wines without personality that could have been made anywhere else in the world. Then again, if a grape truly proves itself right for certain conditions, it will not make the slightest difference whether it has been in the area for 200 years or 20. Eventually, the market will always recognize genuine quality.

At present, then, the Hungarian palette of grape varieties is rather embryonic. Quite a few regions in the country are still bogged down by a legacy of large-scale industrial

	Primary name used in Hungary	Other Hungarian name(s)	Branch	English name or translation	Other name(s)
Pinot Blanc		Fehér Burgundi	Occidentalis gallica	"White Burgundy"	Weissburgunder, Weisser Klevner
Occurrence and Growing area in Hungary	Not one of the more common grapes in Hungary, Pinot Blanc nevertheless featured in the country's viticultural registers as early as the 1930's. While it crops up here and there, it has never come to claim a leading role in any of the regions. About 160 hectares, with the bulk located in Tolna, Balatonboglár and the Bükkalja.				
Soil preference	Pinot Blanc thrives especially well on deep, moist soils. Higher concentrations of lime have a beneficial influence on aroma formation.				
Description	Rather like Pinot Gris in its ampelographic characteristics, Pinot Blanc has slightly shouldered, compact bunches that are fairly heavy compared to the average bunch weight. The berries are small, thin-skinned, juicy, and greenish yellow when fully ripe.				

■ THE WINE AND ITS BEST DOMESTIC GROWERS

Pinot Blanc in Hungary is not much different from its peers grown elsewhere, most notably in Alsace. In problematic years its wine is often hard and sharp, while overloading may result in diluted, neutral flavors. By contrast, care in the vineyard and conscientious yields can deliver a crisp and elegant wine with distinctive hints of nuts (walnut, hazelnut) in its aroma and flavor. The nicest examples in the Carpathian Basin have emerged from areas around Lake Fertő (Neusiedlersee) belonging to Austria today, and from around Lake Balaton in Hungary proper. Ottó Légli on the southern shore (Balatonboglár), and Mihály Figula and István Jásdi on the northern shore (Balatonfüred-Csopak) have distinguished themselves with very sound Pinot Blanc wines over the years.

plantations geared for mass production. With a little improvement here and there, and certainly more care in cultivation, these sites could turn out large quantities of decent and drinkable table wines. Hungary's viticulture today is led by a handful of wineries that produce the country's top wines, but which still represent a tiny fraction of the total output. Having finished most of the work of investing in infra-structure and technology, these growers are now able to concentrate on shaping the varietal model of their estates and selecting the best clones for reconstruction and expansion. The excellent vintages of 1999 and 2000 also marked a turning point as the two years when some of the top new plantations around the country started bearing fruit, rewarding the vanguard with even better wines.

	Primary name used in Hungary	Other Hungarian name(s)	Branch	English name or translation	Other name(s)
Rajnai Rizling			Occidentalis gallica	"Rhine Riesling"	Weissriesling
Occurrence and Growing area in Hungary	Found in every wine region in Hungary, except in Somló, Sopron, and Tokaj. About 1,500 hectares, most centered in the flat Kunság region.				
Soil preference	While not particularly fussy in this regard, Rajnai Rizling will do best in harder *nyirok*-type soils or soils rich in weathered granite or basalt debris.				
Description	Compact cylindrical bunches with round, greenish yellow berries that are speckled when fully ripe. Highly tolerant of frost but vulnerable to rot, Rajnai Rizling is a good sugar producer and botrytis host in the better growing locations.				

■ THE WINE AND ITS BEST DOMESTIC GROWERS

Rajnai Rizling in Hungary was scandalously disgraced in the 1950's when the authorities decided to plant it en masse on the sandy soil of the Great Plain, mostly on account of its resistance to frost. Remarkably, the grape was able to produce appreciable acidity even in this sprawling flat region, although obviously not the depth, elegance and longevity expected from it in better circumstances. In a few regions in Hungary, given the appropriate soil and climate, Rajnai Rizling has been known to realize its true potential, but it never became the favorite of consumers prejudiced by unripe examples with coarse acidity. For years, Huba Szeremley (Szent Orbán winery, Badacsony) has led the Hungarian Riesling scene with expressive, memorable wines that are firm, full-flavored but subtle, especially in good years.

Hungary's wine regions have a storehouse of white varieties to rely on in their struggle to discover their identities. Red wine grapes present more of a problem. Eger and Szekszárd find they must revise the composition of their Bikavér blends, just as Villány is busy trying to rethink the role of Pinot Noir, the grape that was so popular here at the beginning of the last century. It was only in December 2001 that Michael Broadbent came out and said that Cabernet Franc had found a true home in Villány, but several professionals before him had felt this to be the case. Recent plantations of Pinot Noir in Eger have now yielded two or three vintages that seem to bode more than well for the future—a promise explained eloquently by the local soil and climate. These successes show that the world varieties, or these two at least, should certainly have a place in the Carpathian Basin, but only in the context of an appropriate varietal portfolio and rigorous clone selection. As for white grapes, the traditionally excellent per-

50

Primary name used in Hungary	Other Hungarian name(s)	Branch	English name or translation	Other name(s)
Rizlingszilváni		Intraspecific		Riesling Sylvaner, Müller-Thurgau
	A cross between Rajnai Rizling and Zöld Szilváni (Green Sylvaner); recently suspected of Rajnai Rizling and Chasselas parentage instead.			
Occurrence and Growing area in Hungary	Appeared in Hungary after World War I; mostly limited to industrialized plantations today. Most of the 3,200 hectares planted with this grape belong the Kunság, the Mátraalja, and Eger.			
Soil preference	Rizlingszilváni is very tolerant of deep, cool and damp soils, whether bearing clay or lime, but will not do well on thin topsoil or gravel.			
Description	Deeply articulated leaves with five lobes and a blistered surface. The medium-sized bunches are cylindrical, slightly shouldered and elongated in shape. Yellowish white berries, round and juicy.			

◼ THE WINE AND ITS BEST DOMESTIC GROWERS

Although cultivated widely by small-scale growers, Rizlingszilváni rarely produces outstanding quality—not least because it tends to force an early harvest due to its sensitivity to fungal disease and rot. Picked early, it often turns out harsh and coarse, although it is rather on the soft side when made from fully ripe fruit. The best are remarkably fragrant and light, but will invariably age and decline fast. In Hungary, Rizlingszilváni is typically sold in the table wine or country wine category.

formance of local varieties like Furmint, Hárslevelű, Kéknyelű or Juhfark makes life much easier for growers. And although the Olaszrizling, Szürkebarát and Tramini are not Hungarian in origin, they are capable of yielding wines of great quality and character almost anywhere in the country.

As usual, Tokaj deserves a special mention—this time for being the only official wine region in Hungary without any major concern about its well-established grape varieties. Supplying the backbone of pro-

duction and fleshed out by Hárslevelű, the Furmint seems to be able to deliver everything we have a right to expect from a grape used for sweet botrytis wines. Some of the top growers of Tokaj have argued that Muscat Lunel, which currently accounts for no more than 2-3% of the vineyard acreage in the region, should be given a greater role. Eventually it probably will, but don't expect big changes in this department for 5-10 years. The latter-day breed of Zéta (formerly known as Oremus) functions as no more

	Primary name used in Hungary	Other Hungarian name(s)	Branch	English name or translation	Other name(s)
Sárga Muskotály		.	Pontian georgica	Yellow Muscat	Muscat Lunel, Muscat Blanc, Muscat de Frontignan, Muscat Blanc á petits grains
Occurrence and growing area in Hungary	Perhaps the most ancient extant variety in the Carpathian Basin, Sárga Muskotály is claimed by certain sources to have been cultivated here in Roman times. At present limited to 260 hectares, mostly in Tokaj, Balatonboglár, and the Mátraalja, but increasingly planted in Tokaj where many say it is destined for a glorious future.				
Soil preference	Apparently feels at home on any type of soil, but prone to excessive yields on sand.				
Description	Moderately articulated leaves with closed upper lateral petioles and lute-shaped petiolar sinuses. Large, dense and shouldered bunches of small yellowish berries with a rusty shading when ripe, and a skin type that is thick but soft. A good sugar producer and botrytis substrate.				

■ THE WINE AND ITS BEST DOMESTIC GROWERS

Prized everywhere as one of the finest aromatic grapes, Sárga Muskotály could not attain its true expression in Hungary in former decades while it was mostly relegated to semi-sweet or downright syrupy versions. While it has a higher acid content than its cousin, the Muscat Ottonel, it still requires a relatively early harvest to retain freshness and varietal character. Solo varietal Sárga Muskotály tends to age fast, with the exception of sweet versions from Tokaj. Here, the variety accounts for no more than three to five percent of the total acreage under cultivation, although many local growers say it deserves a more prominent role. This argument makes good sense in light of the grape's elegant acids and propensity to invite botrytis. Some of the best dry and off-dry examples in Tokaj have been released by Degenfeld and Hétszőlő, while Vince Gergely's 2000 Muscat has been hailed as the finest expression of this grape's potential despite its massive alcohol. János Árvay has been the only one to date to make Aszú macerating exclusively Muskotály berries in pure Muskotály base wine. When more growers follow his example, the pure varietal Muskotály Aszú will surely become a hit genre, and we will learn something about its unknown aging potential.

	Primary name used in Hungary	Other Hungarian name(s)	Branch	English name or translation	Other name(s)
Sauvignon Blanc			Occidentalis gallica		Muscat Sylvaner
Occurrence and Growing area in Hungary	In Hungary, like Chardonnay, did not really began to conquer land here until the early 1980's. Today, it is grown everywhere in the country, with the exception of Bükkalja and Somló. Total growing area today 500 hectares, predominantly in Balatonboglár, the Mátra Foothills, the Mecsek Foothills, and Etyek-Buda.				
Soil preference	Prefers loose calcareous soils, but will thrive on sand and loess as well.				
Description	Medium-sized rounded leaves with five lobes and moderate articulation. Small compact bunches, shouldered or cylinder-shaped in appearance. Small and thick-skinned but juicy, the berries are a yellowish white color with black speckles. Sauvignon Blanc is characterized by extremely vigorous growth, requiring heavier than average pruning.				

■ THE WINE AND ITS BEST DOMESTIC GROWERS

Its distinctive aroma and taste have rendered Sauvignon Blanc one of the success grapes of the past decade—a spectacular career from which it has not necessarily benefited. The best Hungarian examples are grown in cooler regions with calcareous soils (Sopron, Ászár-Neszmély, Etyek-Buda). Producers like Hilltop Neszmély (Ászár-Neszmély), Etyeki Kúria, László Hernyák, or Nyakas (Etyek-Buda) have been making Sauvignon Blancs that satisfy high international expectations. Harvesting from slightly warmer sites, Ottó Légli (Balatonboglár) and Mihály Figula (Balatonfüred-Csopak) are skilled at rescuing sufficient acidity and delightful aromas in their Sauvignon wines. A leaner style has been honed by Eurobor on the cooler Völgység district of the Tolna region, while György Eberhardt in the Mecsekalja to the south has made a special botrytis version in suitable years.

than a hint of spice in Tokaj, as does the recently rediscovered Kövérszőlő (the "Fat Grape"), an ancient indigenous variety that is probably identical to the Fehérszőlő (the "White Grape") of pre-phylloxera times. While Hungary's viticulture seems to have no finalized notion of where it is going, it certainly has no shortage of remarkable and

valuable varieties to work with. Grapes such as Furmint, Hárslevelű, the aristocratic Kéknyelű, Juhfark, Ezerjó, or Kadarka surely deserve all the support they can get, if only because they are hardly ever encountered outside the Carpathian Basin. And yet, the country's annual wine competitions paint a picture ranging from the discordant

	Primary name used in Hungary	Other Hungarian name(s)	Branch	English name or translation	Other name(s)
Szürkebarát			Occidentalis gallica	"Gray Friar"	Pinot Gris, Ruländer, Tokay d'Alsace
Occurrence and Growing area in Hungary	Grown on a total of approximately 1100 hectares, most of it in the Mátraalja, followed by Badacsony, Balatonfüred-Csopak, and the Balaton-felvidék.				
Soil preference	Capable of great quality on a wide variety of soils, but particularly prefers warmer soils of volcanic origin.				
Description	Cylinder-shaped, compact bunches of a purple gray color when fully ripe. This often translates into a faint pink tinge to the finished wine, which is not regarded as a flaw. Szürkebarát is sensitive to rot due to its dense bunch structure, and will not ripen its acids sufficiently when overloaded. It yields the best quality when trained on the horned head, possibly on the low cordon.				

■ THE WINE AND ITS BEST DOMESTIC GROWERS

Possibly the most Hungarian of all grapes next to the Olaszrizling, not simply because of its prevalence throughout the country but also for its ability to meet the highest international standards. Szürkebarát has become practically synonymous with Badacsony, even though examples just as nice can be had from the Balaton-felvidék, Balatonfüred-Csopak, and Balaton-melléke (Zala). Planted on volcanic soils or clay-bearing sediments, in good years the grape can make full-bodied wine of oily structure that tends to have high alcohol and some residual sugar. Often marked by hints of liquorice and catnip, Szürkebarát is eminently suitable for cellaring and will invariably benefit from spending time in large barrels. For years running, some of the finest Hungarian Szürkebarát wines have come from Dr. Bussay (Balaton-melléke). Other reliable sources include SzakálVin (Badacsony, Balaton-felvidék), Szent Orbán Winery (Badacsony), and Mihály Figula (Balatonfüred-Csopak).

to the downright distorted in this regard. Defying the abundance of studies, treatises and various other publications extolling the virtues of old Hungarian grapes, and even despite the good prices attainable for them in domestic markets, these wines do not tend to perform well in contest. Why is this? Why is it that a faceless Chardonnay or a standardized Sauvignon Blanc is often rated much higher than a full-flavored, fiery Furmint, Hárslevelű, or Kéknyelű? Why should a smooth and spicy Kadarka or an intriguing Bikavér be overshadowed by a tannin-laden Cabernet or Merlot? Part of

	Primary name used in Hungary	Other Hungarian name(s)	Branch	English name or translation	Other name(s)
	Tramini	Piros Tramini, Fűszeres Tramini	Occidentalis gallica		Gewürtztraminer, Savagnin Rosé
Occurrence and Growing area in Hungary	Grown everywhere around the country except in Tokaj; less common in the Great Plain. 806 hectares, mainly in the Mátraalja, Kunság, and Mór regions.				
Soil preference	Does well on clayey or loess soils, but will benefit from stiffer acidity imparted by volcanic rock.				
Description	Small shapeless bunches, dense and sometimes shouldered. The short tendril length makes the cluster seem to sit directly on the cane. Small berries of light incarnadine color, often veiled in gray.				

■ THE WINE AND ITS BEST DOMESTIC GROWERS

Like Szürkebarát, Tramini is a perennial favorite of Hungarian growers. Although in recent years it has lost some ground to less fragrant and more fashionable international grapes, there will always be staunch fans who will seek out their Tramini year in and year out. Harvested from soils conducive to higher acidity, the grape will yield a wine that is more vivid and better balanced. The volcanic soils of Somló or the Balaton-felvidék grow a Tramini that is not so much perfumed as it is smooth, fleshy and fiery, although to a lesser extent the wine will always retain the grape's distinct China rose fragrance. Matured in wooden casks, Tramini can stay in good shape for years, but it is not adverse to stainless steel either.

It rarely keeps well from years defined by higher sugar but lower acidity. The best Traminis of the country are made by László Bussay (Balaton-melléke), Eurobor (Tolna), and Szőlőskert (Mátraalja). Another remarkable example is Evinor's Tramini from Sárospatak in Tokaj, where it can only be labeled as country wine.

the answer must have to do with the fact that these Hungarian grapes, often harvested from stiff volcanic soils, make full and large-scale wines with a high concentration of extract and minerals that need plenty of time and air to unfold in all their splendor. As these conditions rarely exist at competitions, panelists tend to grade them down compared to the international varieties that

are much more approachable and readily understood when young and fresh. And those few tasters who would have the depth of knowledge to judge these wines for what they are hardly ever come face to face with them.

Later in this book, we will list the principal grapes for each wine region described. Now we would like to simply introduce the

	Primary name used in Hungary	Other Hungarian name(s)	Branch	English name or translation	Other name(s)
	Zengő				
	An intraspecific Hungarian hybrid of Ezerjó and Bouvier, created in 1951.				
Occurrence and growing area in Hungary	Not a widespread grape, Zengő is cultivated on some 360 hectares, mostly located in Eger and the Mátraalja.				
Soil preference	Prefers volcanic subsoils and a high concentration of minerals.				
Description	Large round leaves with shallow petioles and low articulation; surface light green and blistered. Medium-sized, shouldered bunches have a dense structure. Berries small and round, thin-skinned and juicy, and greenish white in color.				

■ THE WINE AND ITS BEST DOMESTIC GROWERS

Rarely encountered solo, Zengő is typically used for blending. Its wine is vigorous, but it mellows out and can even attain elegance when aged in wooden casks, not least on account of its delicate locust blossom and wild flower fragrance. Zengő is a good sugar producer and therefore potentially high in alcohol. It has been known to contract botrytis on occasion. The best take on this grape in recent memory has been the Leányka-Zengő cuvée from Pók-Polónyi in Eger.

grape varieties, without any pretense to completeness, in terms of their scope and importance in Hungary's viticulture, and of the general style of the wines they make. Most of the international varieties grown in the country are no doubt well-known to vinophiles. Therefore, we are not going to describe these in great detail, we will focus instead on varieties more or less specific or unique to Hungary.

In addition to the red wine grapes listed above, larger quantities of **Blauburger** have recently been planted in Eger, as a substitute for Kadarka in Bikavér blends. Blauburger makes a spicy, full-flavored wine that seems more refined here than either

Kadarka or Kékoportó, the other grape that used to be popular for blending in Eger. A few local growers now also bottle Blauburger as a solo varietal.

Eger, together with Sopron, was also a first for **Syrah** in Hungary. Tibor Gál in Eger blended his virgin Syrah crop in his Bikavér, and has no intention of bottling the variety separately. Franz Weninger in Sopron created much more of a stir when his 2000 Syrah jumped directly to the top of the hit lists. Even those who had expected this tremendous level of concentration from Weninger's new attempt were caught off guard by the elemental force with which this wine exploded our notion of

	Primary name used in Hungary	Other Hungarian name(s)	Branch	English name or translation	Other name(s)
	Zenit		Intraspecific		
	An intraspecific Hungarian hybrid of Ezerjó and Bouvier.				
Occurrence and growing area in Hungary	This recent cultivar has been planted on about 550 hectares, predominantly in higher altitude sites in Eger, the Mátraalja, the Balaton-felvidék, and Balatonfüred-Csopak.				
Soil preference	Zenit thrives best on volcanic soils rich in minerals and trace elements.				
Description	Large dark green leaves with five lobes and closed petioles. Medium-size shouldered bunches of small greenish berries with black speckles and thick skin.				

▪ THE WINE AND ITS BEST DOMESTIC GROWERS

Assuming controlled yields and rich soil, Zenit makes a potentially long-lived wine with a stylish mineral-rich taste that needs to be matured for a few years before it reaches top shape. The best are subtly fruity but never in-your-face, with refined acids that are ample enough to help the wine keep well. For years, Sándor Tóth's Áldozói Zenit from the Balaton-felvidék has been considered the apotheosis of the variety.

what Sopron was, and could be, about. This Syrah unleashed a veritable purging fire and energies hitherto unknown in Hungarian reds, all wrapped in a huge body and accompanied by consummately orchestrated flavors. Some syrah has also been planted in Szekszárd and Villány, though without an appreciable harvest to date. A few more years will have to pass before we can form a responsible opinion about this grape that would be valid for a number of growing areas round the country.

Three additional white grape varieties, described briefly below, are grown in vast quantities in the Great Plain to make ordinary table wine.

Kövidinka, more likely than not of Hungarian origin, emerged around the middle of the 20th century around the village of Versec. Known in German-speaking areas as Steinschiller, and in older records as Ruzsica, the unfussy Kövidinka is largely limited to the Great Plain where it was planted—on 1,220 hectares—for its excellent tolerance of sandy soils. Kövidinka has a lower sugar content, and an acidity that is modest in quantity but appreciably fine in structure. It makes a soft, plain wine with some varietal character that is typically light and often thin. Although Kövidinka rarely yields better than table wine quality, its reli-

	Primary name used in Hungary	Other Hungarian name(s)	Branch	English name or translation	Other name(s)
Zéta (Oremus)					
	An intraspecific Hungarian hybrid of Bouvier and Furmint.				
Occurrence and growing area in Hungary	Effectively limited to 62 hectares in Tokaj.				
Soil preference	Only known from Tokaj, where it is planted in both loess and nyirok soils.				
Description	Medium-sized leaves that are barely articulated and often intact, normally with U-shaped open petioles. Small and compact cylindrical bunches of yellowish green, round berries, speckled with black.				

■ THE WINE AND ITS BEST DOMESTIC GROWERS

Zéta ripens earlier than either Furmint or Hárslevelű, but it is an equally good substrate for botrytis, and a competent sugar producer also noted for its fine acidity. Never bottled under the varietal label, Zéta usually ends up in the base wine blends used in making Tokaji Aszú.

ability and unassuming character make it an important source of decent mass-produced wines for the average consumer. The name of **Izsáki Sárfehér** (the "Yellow-White from Izsák") has been changed recently, if somewhat redundantly, to **Arany** ("Golden") **Sárfehér**, in the wake of international regulations banning place names in the official designation of grape varieties. Surrounded by uncertainty as to its origins, the grape has been known and cultivated in Hungary since the mid-19th century, initially as Német ("German") Dinka. Later it spread to the area of the village of Izsák in the Great Plain, which explains the

name it went by until recently. Arany Sárfehér is a late-ripening variety distinguished by the largest quantity of the stiffest acids among all the white grapes grown in Hungary. It is a very productive grape, particularly when trained to smaller stock forms, and is fairly resistant to frost. Its wine is thin, faintly aromatic, and low on flavor, with variable alcohol and pronounced acidity. While as still wine it deserves mention in the table wine category at best, the aforementioned traits make it a good staple for sparkling wines. Indeed, Arany Sárfehér is now used extensively as a key ingredient in the "cuvées" supplying the base for

	Primary name used in Hungary	Other Hungarian name(s)	Branch	English name or translation	Other name(s)
Cabernet Franc			Orientalis gallica		
Occurrence and growing area in Hungary	Like the Sauvignon, Cabernet Franc was known in Hungary at the outset of the 20th century, but its large-scale plantation occurred only in the 1960's. Today it is grown on some 910 hectares, predominantly in the Kunság, Szekszárd, and Eger. By far the finest examples emerge from Villány, despite that region's much smaller Cabernet Franc acreage.				
Soil preference	Cabernet Franc likes a cooler, better bound soil type, and it needs slightly less heat than the Sauvignon. It's an even performer on loess, adobe, and volcanic soils alike.				
Description	Slightly elongated but regular leaves with five lobes. Its shouldered bunches are small to medium in size, with small round berries that are dark blue and bloomy.				

■ THE WINE AND ITS BEST DOMESTIC GROWERS

Not long ago, Michael Broadbent wrote that he felt Cabernet Franc "comes into its element" in Villány. Indeed, no other grape in this region displays such individual personality. Here, Cabernet Franc makes a wine that needs time to get acquainted with, instead of bowling you over with clichés. Substantial and profound, it is not exactly love at the first sip for the apprentice vinophile. Ideally, it is mellow with ripe tannins and a taste marked by a distinctive tart note; always long-lived and an inevitable candidate for aging in wood. The best Cabernet Francs in Villány have been crafted by Ede Tiffán, who started working with the grape seriously at the beginning of the 1990's through his joint venture Domaine Mondivin. His 1993, 1995, and 1999 are luxurious. Public opinion is divided over Attila Gere's Cabernet Franc Selection, which the author of these lines holds in higher esteem than any other wine from this grower. Csaba Malatinszky has also released a superb Cabernet Franc from the universally excellent 2000 vintage. The variety has also found favor in Szekszárd, where it makes full, tannic wine that is excellent blended with Merlot—especially from Péter Vida and the Taklers. Cabernet Franc conquered a lot of ground in Eger as well, but most of it ends up as a component in Bikavér blends. Bucking the local trend, Béla Vincze has been producing a remarkable solo version for years.

59

	Primary name used in Hungary	Other Hungarian name(s)	Branch	English name or translation	Other name(s)
Cabernet Sauvignon			Orientalis gallica		
Occurrence and growing area in Hungary	Cabernet Sauvignon was already present in Hungary in the early 20th century, but it did not really became widespread until the mid-1980's. Since then, it has been firmly established everywhere, except in regions dedicated to white wine exclusively. Most prevalent in Villány, Eger, and Sopron with a total area of 2100 ha.				
Soil preference	Cabernet Sauvignon thrives on a variety of soils, but it will yield the best quality when planted in well-drained soils overlying marl, clay or limestone. In Hungary, Szekszárd's loess and Villány's limestone are perfect hosts for this grape.				
Description	Deeply articulated, round leaves with closed upper lateral petioles and sinuses. Small shouldered bunches, often bifurcating at the tip, and frequently containing underdeveloped green berries due to poor set. Berries are round, dark blue, and bloomy.				

■ THE WINE AND ITS BEST DOMESTIC GROWERS

It is for good reason that this grape makes the most highly esteemed reds in Hungary. Regrettably, the hasty plantations in the early eighties did not always use the best clones or the best methods. As a result, the majority of the country's Cabernet stock is not likely to ever produce great wine. These Cabs are often unripe and harsh, with a characteristic green pepper flavor—a far cry from wines harvested from scrupulously designed vineyards with strictly limited yields. This latter approach is now the name of the game in Villány, where dense Cabs offer the closest approximation of the grand Médoc style. These wines are big, tannic, full-flavored and slow to evolve, destined for longevity. While one could make an honorable mention of every leading winery in Villány, certainly including Ede and Zsolt Tiffán, Attila Gere, and Vylyan, the most remarkable solo Cabernet Sauvignon wines in recent memory have been associated with Csaba Malatinszky and Tamás Günzer. The grape makes a leaner, fruitier wine in Szekszárd, but one still suitable for long cellaring. Here, Ferenc Vesztergombi has led the pure varietal camp, although Cabernet in Szekszárd, too, has been preferred of late as a key ingredient in top house blends, supplemented by Cabernet Franc, Merlot, and perhaps Kékfrankos. In the cooler climate of Eger and Sopron, Cabernet will ripen well in good years and privileged sites, but this is hardly the norm.

	Primary name used in Hungary	Other Hungarian name(s)	Branch	English name or translation	Other name(s)
Kadarka			Pontian balcanica		Kadarska, Skadarska, Gamza
Occurrence and growing area in Hungary	Originally of Balkan extraction but now regarded as fully Hungarian, Kadarka conquered the most ground in the Great Plain and Szekszárd, but it is present in every major red wine region, including Eger and Villány. Before World War II, Kadarka was an indispensable ingredient in the Bikavér blends that made Eger famous. Today it is grown on a total of 1040 hectares nationwide.				
Soil preference	Kadarka favors loess soils, but a higher concentration of lime will not really keep it from yielding good quality. Grown on sand, it makes thin, dilute wine.				
Description	Medium to large leaves with three or five lobes; dark green, shiny, and coarse-textured. The medium-sized, cylindrical bunches are rather compact and have round, medium-sized berries that often retain their greenish blue tinge even when fully ripe. Sensitive to frost and difficult to grow in just about every other way, Kadarka needs traditional training, such as the horned head, to perform at its best. (Trained on the cordon, it makes inferior wine, although strictly low cordon training may result in acceptable quality.) This requires a tremendous amount of manual labor, but in good years the wine will reward it all.				

■ THE WINE AND ITS BEST DOMESTIC GROWERS

Over the past decade or so, Kadarka has become somewhat of a national obsession among wine consumers. Like Pinot Noir, its wine is relatively low in tannin, but all the more emphatic in its refined acidity. This, coupled with a rich spicy nose and a smooth structure, offers ample compensation for the lower color saturation and delicate body. A truly concentrated Kadarka is intriguing, charming, and elegant, but it rarely improves beyond its second or third year in the bottle. It is a popular ingredient in all kinds of blends owing to its ability to spice things up even when measured in tiny doses. Without a doubt, the most delightful Kadarka wines come [out Szekszárd] from growers such as Ferenc Vesztergombi, Ferenc Takler, Tamás Dúzsi, Péter Vida, or the Szt. Gaál Kastély. Anticipated to arouse massive interest over the coming decade, Kadarka is a grape that few red wine growers can afford to ignore in contemplating new plantation. Made in commercially more viable quantities to reliable standards, this wine could contribute an intriguing color to the palette of the world's wines. Its finest producers are already well worth seeking out in Hungary.

61

	Primary name used in Hungary	Other Hungarian name(s)	Branch	English name or translation	Other name(s)
Kékfrankos			Orientalis caspica	"Blue Franc"	Blaufränkisch, Lemberger, Frankovka
	Native to Central Europe.				
Occurrence and growing area in Hungary	For decades, Kékfrankos has been the leading red wine grape in Hungary, currently grown on 8260 hectares. Found everywhere in the country except Tokaj, Somló, and Badacsony, it claims the largest acreage in the Kunság, Sopron, Eger, Villány, and Szekszárd regions. Kékfrankos is a fairly recent variety that was still undiscovered in the early 19th century.				
Soil preference	A reliable grape in a diversity of conditions, Kékfrankos (with reduced yields) will tolerate slightly cooler microclimates (Sopron). It is at its best on mineral-rich soils and loess, but also widely grown on sand.				
Description	Large, unarticulated leaves with narrow petiolar sinuses. The bunches are shouldered and moderately dense, with dark blue, juicy berries covered by bloom.				

■ THE WINE AND ITS BEST DOMESTIC GROWERS

Kékfrankos makes a vigorous fruity wine with a tannin content that can be termed average. When made from ripe grapes and matured in stainless steel, it has a pleasant tart flavor that makes it suitable to accompany fine food. Although the best have the wherewithal to take on barriques, the traditional Hungarian standard remains a Kékfrankos that spends six to twelve months in large oak barrels. Both styles have their followers and fans. Franz Weninger uses this grape to make wines more distinguished than any red to have come out of Sopron and—let us risk the assumption—from Burgenland across the Austrian border. Relying on severely limited yields and well-chosen new oak, these Kékfrankos wines have fabulous concentration and a silky-creamy texture. By contrast, the examples from Szekszárd that are aged in large casks have distinguished themselves by their crisp, bouncy acids, subtle fruit flavors, and lighter concentration. Such very good traditionalist Kékfrankos can be had from Tamás Dúzsi, while the Taklers represent the trendy style marked by robust character and powerful tannin extraction. A synthesis of the two schools is offered by Vesztergombi, whose Kékfrankos is momentous, and elegant wine. Kékfrankos is also a good blending wine, notably for Bikavér in Eger and Szekszárd.

	Primary name used in Hungary	Other Hungarian name(s)	Branch	English name or translation	Other name(s)
Kékoportó			Orientalis caspica	"Blue Port"	Blauer Portugieser, Porthogeze
	Native to Central Europe.				
Occurrence and growing area in Hungary	An obscure grape whose origins—Austrian, Portuguese, or otherwise—have yet to be proven. Known in Hungary for ages; in Villány practically regarded as an indigenous Hungarian variety. It is cultivated on 1530 ha, mostly in Eger, Villány and Kunság.				
Soil preference	Grown on a diversity of soils, including loess, limestone, and sand, Kékoportó in Hungary is most common in Villány, the country's southernmost wine region. Also found in Germany.				
Description	Irregularly articulated round leaves of a shiny grass-green color. The large, shouldered bunches are moderately dense, with dark blue berries that are thin-skinned, juicy, and pleasantly sweet rather than acidic in flavor.				

■ THE WINE AND ITS BEST DOMESTIC GROWERS

The epitome of this variety is grown in Villány, where a few growers still make very low-acid Kékoportó that can be drunk practically without moderation—at least compared to other wines. Marked by characteristic hints of garlic and an animal nuance that generally owes more to the terroir than the grape itself, Kékoportó is a soft red that can be excellent for everyday drinking, but will not keep long unless made from strictly limited yields and matured in small new oak. The average Kékoportó has modest tannins and is best drunk within two or three years of the harvest. While it crops up in every Hungarian region where red wine is made, in most places it is used for blending. The earliest-ripening red

wine grape, Kékoportó can be processed quickly to make an offering en primeur for the feast of St. Martin's day on November 11th each year. As every grower in Villány will inevitably make his own special "Oportó," a stroll down the main street of Villány will reward you with many pleasant encounters if you yield to the temptation of open cellar doors.

sparkling wines produced in the Great Plain. 2,900 hectares.

Kunleány ("Cumanian Girl") was created as a cross between *Vitis amurensis*, *Vitis vinifera*, and the table grape Afuz Ali. It is a very productive grape that ripens with sugar levels of 16-17 degrees by the end of September. It is highly tolerant of frost and rot, and is not susceptible to either downy or powdery mildew. It makes a slightly acid-biased wine with a delicate aroma and flavor that is hard to tell apart from wines

63

	Primary name used in Hungary	Other Hungarian name(s)	Branch	English name or translation	Other name(s)
	Merlot		Orientalis gallica		
Occurrence and growing area in Hungary	Merlot in Hungary goes back to the middle of the 20th century, but it did not really gain currency until the 1960's. Since then, it has spread everywhere in the country, most notably in Szekszárd, Balatonboglár, the Kunság, and Eger. Particularly promising in Szekszárd, Villány, and Eger. Total cultivated area is 1950 ha.				
Soil preference	Merlot prefers cooler, moist soils like clay, nyirok, and loess.				
Description	Leaves with five lobes and open petiolar sinuses. Small to medium-sized shouldered bunches of deep blue, bloomy berries. Merlot is a sensitive and finicky grape to work with. No wonder Hungarians had to wait until the 1999 vintage to have some really nice domestic examples, which no longer seem to be the exception to the rule.				

■ THE WINE AND ITS BEST DOMESTIC GROWERS

In Hungary, this grape makes a distinctive wine not unlike Argentinean or Chilean Merlot, but always requiring maturation in wood for quality. In 1999 and 2000, the vastly different regions of Eger and Villány both yielded some truly fine Merlots. Aided by a great concentration owing to limited yields, these wines in their youth were fabulously fruity with bursting raspberry flavors. At two or three years of age, they began to assume fuller, deeper tones with emerging oak aromas. Now we seem to have a solid supply of fine Merlot to last for years—from Vilmos Thummerer and István Tóth in Eger, Ferenc Takler, Ferenc Vesztergombi, and Peter Vida in Szekszárd, as well as Attila Gere, Ede Tiffán, and Vylyan in Villány.

made from vinifera varieties. It is largely confined to the Great Plain, where it was planted widely as an even mass producer that could always be counted on to ripen on time. Kunleány really has no place in the quality wine category, but it can make a valuable contribution to sparkling wines.

Among Hungary's recently rediscovered old quality varieties, mention must be made of **Kövér Szőlő**, the "Fat Grape," which has now been re-approved for production in

Tokaj. Of unknown origins, the grape came to Hungary's present-day territory from Transylvania in the 19th century. It is also known by the aliases of Gohér and Bajor ["Bavarian"], although taxonomically it is not identical to either of these grapes. Kövér Szőlő is a low-yielding variety that is reasonably resistant to frost and drought, but vulnerable to downy and powdery mildew. While it is not picky about the soil, it definitely benefits from being planted in

	Primary name used in Hungary	Other Hungarian name(s)	Branch	English name or translation	Other name(s)
Pinot Noir		Kék Burgundi, Kisburgundi	Occidentalis gallica		Blauer Burgunder Blauer Klevner

Occurrence and growing area in Hungary	Early in the 20th century, Pinot Noir in Hungary was known by the name of Villányi Kisburgundi (the "Little Burgundian from Villány"), but the ensuing decades of mass production had no room for this grape. Even today, its largest regional plantation is limited to 100 hectares on the hills of Balatonboglár–in fact a large chunk in the total of 610 hectares under cultivation nationwide. Recent years have ushered in a Pinot Noir renaissance of sorts, although–happily enough–growers no longer like to try their hand at the grape unless they are clear about its assets and limitations.
Soil preference	Pinot Noir clearly prefers limestone soils, but will do very well on other deep soil types such as loess or calcareous marine sediments cropping out by volcanic rocks (as is the case in Eger).
Description	Regular pentagonal leaves, slightly articulated and with a blistered surface. Compact bunches; berries are small, dark blue, and round. Pinot Noir is susceptible to all kinds of fungal disease and rot.

■ THE WINE AND ITS BEST DOMESTIC GROWERS

As perhaps the most high-maintenance grape, Pinot Noir demands special care if it is to yield great wine. In terms of soil and climate factors, Eger seems to have all the potential that made Burgundy the champion of the variety. The elegant spectrum of acids, impeccable varietal character, and ample alcohol content of Pinot Noirs that have recently come out of Eger certainly bode well for a future of great success with this grape. Their tannins, creamy-smooth structure, and racy, almost lascivious flavors all fall into place by the time they reach two or three years of age. Now that Vilmos Thummerer and Tibor Gál have given us a taste of what this grape could achieve here, we have no choice but to ex-pect the finest Pinotsin all of Hungary to come from Eger. Pinot Noir seems to be headed for an entirely different style in the much hotter Villány region, where in fact it has more of a local tradition than in Eger. If Villány's growers are capable of rescuing enough acidity come harvest time, there is really nothing to advise them against growing the grape. No one who has tasted Vylyan's 1999 or the 2000 from Tiffán or Malatinszky will deny the merit and distinction of these wines. They may be robust and overly tannic when young, but will express the loveliest Pinot Noir character in their second or third year after the harvest–as we have just recently found out.

65

	Primary name used in Hungary	Other Hungarian name(s)	Branch	English name or translation	Other name(s)
	Zweigelt		Intraspecific		Rotburger
	An intraspecific hybrid of St. Laurent and Kékfrankos.				
Occurrence and growing area in Hungary	Zweigelt was introduced in Hungary in the 1960's, and it instantly became a staple for industrialized mass production. Currently cultivated on 2,460 hectares throughout the country, it claims the largest vineyard area in the Great Plain, followed by Eger, Szekszárd, and the Mátraalja.				
Soil preference	Not a demanding grape, Zweigelt thrives well on a wide variety of soils.				
Description	Barely articulated, round leaves with closing or entirely closed petiolar sinuses. Large, moderately compact bunches of bloomy, dark blue berries. Zweigelt is a rather heavy-bearing vintage variety whose yields must be severely cut to achieve quality.				

■ THE WINE AND ITS BEST DOMESTIC GROWERS

As a grape grown for decades solely for its extreme productivity, Zweigelt attains truly decent quality only on the offchance today. Except for large wineries, few growers take the trouble to deal with it, even though in conscionable yields it can make rather nice wine distinguished by buoyant acidity, spicy cherry and morello aromas, and a smooth structure. The potential of Zweigelt has recently been rediscovered by Luka in Sopron, and Vylyan in Villány, both wineries making superb interpretations of this much maligned grape. These rare attempts notwithstanding, Zweigelt remains mainly allotted for blending or bottled as a cheap commercial varietal.

well-sheltered sites where, fall weather permitting, it is predisposed to shriveling and botrytization. It generally ripens midseason with high sugar levels, ideally with botrytized berries ready for picking at the end of September. The significance of Kövér Szőlő is pretty much limited to Tokaj where it can do good service, strictly for purposes of blending, as a grape that ripens earlier than Furmint and produces a higher proportion of Aszú berries.

Gastronomy

Anyone could rightfully ask what makes Hungarian wines so special that they should presuppose a unique approach, or even some background knowledge, for proper tasting. And yet perceptive and knowledgeable experts allow that a wine like Tokaji Aszú may demand some local knowledge, even some advice, before one can fully appreciate the storehouse of pleasure that it offers.

It may seem an ambivalent task to write about food in a book dedicated to the wines of a country whose traditions exerted a decisive culinary influence for centuries, but which finds its role in the world's gastronomy thoroughly reshaped by the forces of history today. Undoubtedly, Hungary's farmlands have a unique potential not only for viticulture but also for growing fruits and vegetables. If coupled with the appropriate economic environment and a responsible, well-informed and quality-minded attitude on the part of the country's farmers, this potential could yield some of the finest produce anywhere. Many regions in Hungary used to have their special flavors, foods, and methods of preparing them, along with local wines to delight residents and visitors. In deference to a misunderstood concept of modernity, this wonderful diversity is being

Parma ham with
cream cheese

displaced by uniform foods pervading every nook and cranny of the country. Regional cuisines are disappearing fast as Hungarian cooking makes increasing use of alien ingredients, blurring periods, places, and palates. And yet we have the good news to report that the country has begun to exploit its geological and climatic potential. While there is plenty of room for improvement, some wines in certain Hungarian regions have crossed the threshold separating mediocrity from that which is unique and impossible to emulate.

Since this book is not a cookbook any more than its is a treatise on cultural history, my focus here will be Hungarian wine as we know it today. I will proceed under the assumption that the reader just getting acquainted with the country's wines will eventually want to try them with cuisines other than the Hungarian. Therefore, while my primary focus here is Hungarian food in its national and local versions, I will try to make my observations and tips general enough to be useful for considering culinary alternatives in a foreign context.

WINE FOR FOOD – OR FOOD FOR WINE?

This question is far from being a rhetorical one these days, when more and more Hungarian wines are of sufficient stature to inspire menus, rather than the other way round. Indeed, the very best deserve to inform our invention of dishes that will be the most effective to highlight their merit. Whichever the point of reference, the goal is always to attain greater culinary satisfaction than could be provided by a haphazard combination. A well-informed choice either way will help you get more out of both your wine and your food. In the ideal case, you may achieve utter harmony, understood as a synergy of sensory impressions that is greater than the sum of its parts. Of course, all this presupposes thorough acquaintance with the wine and the food, not only in terms of their respective flavors and components, but also of the ways in which they interact with each other.

This topic, so dear to some of us, has engendered a body of common lore—often more useful as a point of departure than a doctrine

to be blindly followed. One rule of thumb is that white wines must be served before reds and dessert wines, just as a plain wine should precede those that are more complex and elegant in character. By the same token, young wines must come before older vintages, and a gradation of alcohol content should also be observed. It goes without saying that there are always exceptions to prove these rules, if only because you can never make the same recipe taste exactly the same twice, even if using identical ingredients. Add to this the fact that wine is living matter that changes in the bottle, for better or for worse, and you will see no reason to be unyielding in your application of such conventions.

Everyone has heard of traditional marriages of wine and food made in heaven. They include foie gras with dessert wines; blue cheese with bigger sweet wines that are higher in alcohol; Muscadet with oysters; smoked salmon with barrique Chardonnay; or grilled lamb with a nice Médoc red. To mention just one Hungarian example, a fine dish of stuffed cabbage from Transdanubia can be superb with a mature but still vigorous Juhfark grown in Somló. All these combinations have stood the test of time.

If you venture beyond these tried and well-tested alliances in search of absolute harmony between food and wine, sooner or later you will hit some rather slippery ground. Just think about the likelihood that in the past, when the mentioned landmarks were established, it must have been much easier to determine sound and universally valid combinations. The bewildering diversity of ingredients available today can make it so hard to decide that it is often best to go back to the basics. In times of duress, try to consider what it is that makes a specific partnering of food and wine acceptable or positively delightful. It's not so much that the appearance of salmon goes well with the onion-skin color of a rosé, but that an oily fish will call for a crisp and bone-dry wine. Salty flavors partner well with a sweet accent. According to an equally reliable principle, acid foods will need an even higher-acid wine for the duo to succeed.

Thinking rigidly in terms of grape varieties will not take you very far. It is much better to consider the style and essential character of the wine in making a choice, and the current range of Hungarian wines certainly makes this consideration feasible. One simple rule you can easily verify for yourself is that the wine must always be slightly sweeter than the food it is to accompany. In a similar way, whether a red wine happens to have hints of violet or blackberry on the nose has less consequence for its basic character than the concentration, ratio and maturity of its acids and tannins. High-acid reds are much more versatile than heavily tannic ones, which in combination with some foods may result in a hang-to-dry sensation on the palate. A bottle of fully mature great red with a powerful concentration of tannin is often best when sipped on its own. If you must find something to complement it, a fine hard cheese could be a decent match, but choose another type of wine altogether to accompany a proper course of the meal.

Whatever the food and the wine, always remember to personally taste them beforehand. You can never rule out the possibility that a normally dry cheese turns out to be fatter than usual, or that a bottle from a winery you know well is somehow different in the given vintage year. In fact, wines with identical measured acidity will create a totally different acid sensation on the palate depending on the concentration of residual sugar or alcohol present. Therefore, the questions you want to answer first is whether your wine is soft and mild, downright flat, high-acid, or intensely marked by new oak; and whether it has any residual sugar and how much. If it's a red wine, you need to find out whether it is tannic rather than high-acid , or vice versa. Once you have determined these basics, you will need to "map" your food by similar coordinates of taste (salty, fatty, sweet, acid, tart/bitter) and texture (smooth or rough).

The color of meat and poultry (red or white meat) should weigh less in the balance than the technique of preparation and the seasonings used. Obviously, roasting will influence the fibers and the moisture/solids ratio differently than poaching the same piece of meat. And if you cannot forego a garnish of fruit to go with your saddle of venison, remember that not all wines will go equally well with the

same old sweet and sour cranberry sauce and the pungent taste of game. In Hungary, various meats and game are often served with a garnish of fruit or a sweetish fruit-based sauce. Now, you obviously cannot afford to disregard the presence of sugar in any form on the plate. For harmony, you must find a wine that will create a sense of sweetness on the palate without containing residual sugar, possibly derived from high alcohol, glycerin, extract, or even lengthy maturation in wood. More often than not this will take a fully mature red. If it is tart and still a little rough, you will be better off saving the bottle for a sauté of forest mushrooms or a fine cigar after dinner. Among other factors, such issues of compatibility more than adequately justify the gastronomic ban on "mixed garnish," a sort of culinary crime still often committed by restaurateurs in Hungary. If you disagree with this assessment, just try to pick a wine for a braided roast tenderloin of pork that is simultaneously accompanied by a spinach soufflé, quince stuffed with fennel and walnuts, and potato croquettes scented with nutmeg.

After all these caveats, I can all but hear dismayed voices clamoring for fool-proof solutions. Don't despair, for there is hope. In what follows, I will provide practical guidance for those wishing to discover the possibilities of Hungarian wine for themselves. Effective regulations divide this small country into 22 wine regions. As some of them are quite alike in their

Meat consommé as Lajos Kossuth liked it

Marinated salmon with olive

New potato
with red caviar

geology and climate, their wines tend to be comparable in character and style. In an effort to avoid repetitions, I will discuss these regions together from the point of view of gastronomy.

THE GREAT PLAIN: HAJÓS-BAJA, KUNSÁG, CSONGRÁD

Although the Great Plain of Southern Hungary comprises three official wine regions, most of the wines grown here are rather uniform in character despite local variations of terroir. Both reds and whites tend to be light, mild, and low in alcohol, with the possible exception of those harvested from the richer loess soils around the village of Hajós. These can approach Szekszárd reds in terms of tannin structure. The sore point that ails all three regions is simply the lack of really good wines. Very few growers in these parts seem to care for quality before quantity, even though lighter style, sand-grown wines could easily carve out a respectable niche in gastronomy—practically whenever firm acidity is not a requirement. In fact, modern culinary trends using a variety of greens, vegetables, and white meat would often call for such lighter wines typically with no more than 10% alcohol, particularly at lunchtime. If the grape variety is a better acid producer, its wine may do good service as a staple for a refreshing *fröccs* (Hungary's spritzer made with varying proportions of wine and soda) on a hot summer day.

So what exactly do these wines go well with? Perhaps it will be easier to answer if we turn the question around, asking what they should *not* be served with under any circumstances. High-acid foods, for one thing, are obviously unacceptable, as they threaten to cancel out any modest acidity your wine may have. Sweet flavors, whether of the main ingredient or the garnish, are also to be avoided—especially fruits which tend to be high-acid and sweet at the same time. These wines will not hold their own with complex dishes with intricate flavors or exotic seasoning, but will be just right for a plain course with a neutral taste. For dishes made with red paprika spice, a better Kékfrankos, Zweigelt or Kadarka from Csongrád or Hajós will demand a role. If the fare is *halászlé* (traditional Hungarian fisher-

man's soup flavored with paprika and often thickened with roe), the wine must be from Baja—a quaint small town on the Danube that goes against the grain of national nutritional statistics with its per capita consumption of over 6,000 grams of fish annually. No man worth his salt in Baja can exist without distinguishing himself in cooking *halászlé*, typically heavy on red paprika spice and enriched with "matchstick" noodles. This wonderful soup of freshwater fish calls for a light and spirited red, the best of which here, as in Szekszárd across the river, rely on the spicy Kadarka grape. As a rule, the other traditional foods of the Great Plain are associated with the lifestyle of shepherds, which assigned limits to the ingredients and methods of preparation available to them. A *gulyás* or *pörkölt* (stew) of lamb or mutton is often the ticket in these parts, along with a variety of homemade egg noodles. Onion and paprika are essential, if not very ancient, ingredients in these dishes. As rather fatty foods, they also demand a light red with a modest tannin content and reasonably firm acidity. The most intensely seasoned versions can be paired off successfully with a local Cabernet-based blend, but never one subjected to long maturation in wood. The key words for harmony here are freshness and fruity character.

ÁSZÁR-NESZMÉLY, PANNONHALMA-SOKORÓALJA

These two regions are quite similar in their geographical position and geology, with prevalent marl and clay overlain by brown earth soils. Both areas have a cooler climate than the national average, so the wines grown here are clearly of the northern type with a fine acid spine. The grape varieties under cultivation here are almost invariably white; reds have no appreciable significance, historically or otherwise. In better years and well-tended vineyards, the higher acidity can be coupled with high alcohol and good body, but almost all the wines will have the same basic elegance. The traditional varieties of Olaszrizling, Királyleányka, Leányka, and Rizlingszilváni have been increasingly supplemented by Chardonnay and Sauvignon Blanc. In short, the two regions yield wines that could serve as the foundation for composing a fashionable restaurant menu, including fresh greens with practically any dressing, vegetables (raw, grilled or in spicy marinade), as well as simply-prepared lean fish, whether freshwater or from the sea. Other seafood, even deep-fried, is also a good candidate for these crisp whites, while a nice Sauvignon Blanc from Neszmély will be very helpful with a dish of robust aromatic vegetables or greens such as asparagus, cauliflower, Brussels sprouts, or spinach. Something as potent as artichoke will call for a two or three-year-old barrique Chardonnay. The astringent flavors of this vegetable can be mated remarkably well with the tannins derived from small new oak barrels.

BADACSONY AND THE BALATON HIGHLANDS

The general decay that characterized the area around Lake Balaton during the decades of planned economy did not spare local gastronomic traditions. Bream, plain fisherman's soup and the occasional *fogas* (an otherwise fine freshwater fish, known in English as pike perch or walleye, that used to be more often deep-fried than grilled as advertised) did little justice to the sonorous wines that emerged here and there from a few family cellars in defiance of the times. The wines, almost invariably white, that are much more familiar to us today from Badacsony and other growing locations north of the lake, such as the Kál Basin or the hills of Szent-György and Csobánc, have always deserved better food than that. Rearing directly on the shore of the lake, Mount Badacsony itself is uniquely equipped to profit from the proximity of the large body of water below. Even in lesser years, the wines grown here incorporate the heat of the south-facing volcanic slopes so successfully that you can practically chew sunshine in a mouthful. The high sugar content of the grapes may be realized in high alcohol or some residual sugar, but will always impart roundness of body. The deprived vines send down very deep roots in search of nutrients to deliver plenty of acids and minerals to the fruit, essentially defining the role these wines can play in gastronomy.

Huba Szeremley's winery (Szent Orbán) on Mount Badacsony offers a virtually complete cross-section of the grapes grown in the region, while Ödön Nyári nurtures a noble wine tradition on the Szent-György a few kilometers away. A crisp Budai Zöld, Muscat Ottonel, or Irsai Olivér harvested in these parts, particularly from a year with sufficient moisture, have the type of zinging acidity that makes them ideally suited to accompany white fish or greens with a dressing made with lemon or balsamic vinegar. Olaszrizling is the region's most common variety. When made from fully ripe grapes, Olaszrizling wines convey minerals, an agreeable tart taste, and occasional hints of botrytis to complement the grape's otherwise stiff acidity. Examples without residual sugar go very well with rich fish, braised cabbage, and dishes with sour cream. The native pike perch mentioned above can attain perfect rapport with Olaszrizling, although as a light-flavored, fine fish it is equally delicious with a dry

Catfish with shiitake mushroom

Kéknyelű. In better years, this grape yields a suppler wine marked by a faint floral fragrance instead of the burnt almond aroma typical of Olaszrizling. If you have a rich course that positively calls for a wine with assertive acids, a local Rajnai Rizling can be the best choice. Beside these grapes, Szürkebarát

Fillet of Dover sole á la duchesse

71

Smoked swordfish
with cantaloupe

(Pinot Gris) has become practically synonymous with Badacsony. With its softer acids, higher alcohol and often noticeable residual sugar, Szürkebarát can have a natural affinity with dishes containing sweet flavors, such as fruit, baked or braised, or a sweet sauce served with the meat. Dark poultry or even wild fowl are further candidates, but avoid serving fish with a Szürkebarát that has any residual sugar or very high alcohol.

Not infrequently, the region will reward the conscientious grower with a massively sweet dessert wine typically relying on the Olaszrizling grape, which is a good substrate for botrytis in good years if the yield is held back. For years, Huba Szeremley has used this grape and the Zeusz variety to make sweet late harvest wines that offer a unique experience. With their citrussy apricot aromas and elegant tart flavors, these crisp sweet wines are a dream with duck's liver or foie gras, homemade smoked ham, and desserts made with *túró* (fresh, soft farmer's cheese from cow's milk; the sharp and salty *juhtúró*, made from ewe's milk, is never used for dessert). Comparable to a 4-5 puttonyos Tokaji Aszú in concentration, they have a rather high sugar content which complements salty flavors very well. The result can be celestial harmony, this time based on an equilibrium of contrasts rather than on a symmetry of similar flavors.

But what do you do in Badacsony if you feel like a nice steak of *szürkemarha*, the region's ancient and recently re-naturalized gray longhorn cattle? Although in the 19th century red wine grapes outweighed white ones on the northern shore of the lake, today you will have a hard time trying to find a local red to go with your beef. A handful of growers have dipped into Kékoportó and Kékfrankos on the Tihany Peninsula and Merlot in the Kál Basin, but these wines have yet to attain the well-established quality of the whites. Incidentally, the author of these lines is convinced that a full-bodied white with a sufficiently broad foundation of acid and extract can be just as appropriate with red meat as a mature tannic red. Acidity is the heart and soul of a wine. If your wine is short on acids, or has a sufficient quantity but in the wrong

structure or composition, the tannins, sugar or alcohol can be so overpowering as to completely mask the primary fruit flavors. And an excessively tannic, syrupy, or alcoholic wine will not get along easily with any food you may care to throw at it.

BALATONBOGLÁR

According to a malicious dictum, the only nice thing about the southern shore of Lake Balaton is the vista of Mount Badacsony on the other side that you can see from it... But with the eye of the grower-winemaker, it is impossible not to appreciate the gently rolling loess-bearing hills around the village of Balatonboglár. Geographically, they appear to be a continuation of the range at Szekszárd further south, but the white wines here have the advantage of a much higher acidity and, consequently, a crisper, more buoyant disposition. A light Királyleányka or a dry Muskotály or Sauvignon Blanc from this area will implore you to order a pike perch from the lake, but will do just as well with less grand fish such as *keszeg* (bream) or *garda* (razorfish), a personal favorite particularly when barbecued on a skewer. In contrast, the Balaton version of *halászlé* calls for a light acid-driven red such as Kékfrankos, possibly Pinot Noir, to offset the paprika flavors and the richer stock of this fish soup.

The region's white wines have traditionally been associated with the summer, for the simple reason that they are best drunk as thirst quenchers. In fact, I hope to be forgiven for proposing that, at this time of the year at least, a local Királyleányka or even a Chasselas should be enjoyed strictly in the form of a good *fröccs*. This indigenous wine spritzer has fallen out of favor with current trends in Hungarian cuisine, which tend to discount the fact that not all wines are created equal even for this modest purpose, and that nothing can beat a glass or two of *fröccs* with a nice helping of *lecsó* (a paprika-flavored stew of onions, sweet pepper and tomato, a sort of Hungarian ratatouille that is considered a summer staple).

The red wines around Balatonboglár have improved by strides in recent years. Some of the reds from János Konyári, St. Donatus, or

Öregbaglas can now give the best of Szekszárd a run for its money. Indeed, a grower in Villány has hailed one of Konyári's wines as "a red I wouldn't be ashamed to have in my own cellar." Although the region's reds are not as long-lived as their peers from Szekszárd or Villány further south, their silky warm tannins and complex flavors make for a distinct and very enjoyable style. Apart from the lighter examples already recommended for *halászlé*, a few truly big reds have emerged in the area. Ripe and fruity Merlot, Cabernet Sauvignon and Franc from a good vintage such as 1999 or 2000 will be ready to drink in their second or third year, owing to their quickly maturing tannins.

SWEET WINES

For now, Öregbaglas, the Swiss-owned family venture at the village of Kéthely, is the only winery in the region producing sweet wines, but it has made them consistently for years. Typically using late-harvested, nobly rotted grapes, these wines are bottled with a high concentration of sugar and extract that makes them comparable to a 4 or 5 puttonyos Tokaji Aszú. Redolent with primary grape aromas and a distinct botrytis character evident in hints of citrus, a nice Chardonnay or Tramini Beerenauslese or Ausbruch from the Öregbaglas winery can handle the same desserts as an Aszú would. The difference to keep in mind though is that these wines are much lower in acidity than a typical Tokaj, and as such will not yield the ultimate harmony with the sharper flavors of a dessert made with *túró*. Indeed, caution is in order when choosing a fruit for these wines, as a high-acid fruit could easily make them seem hollow on the palate. Stick with loosely textured, less intensely flavored sweets instead. Avoid whipped cream; a low-acid wine could come off as flat and lethargic when served with food rich in fat.

BALATONFÜRED-CSOPAK

This is a rather uniform wine region in terms of the character of its white wines. (Reds are few and far between, and limited to a handful of cellars with an enterprising spirit.) As elsewhere in the country, the leading grape

here is the Olaszrizling. Other traditional varieties include Szürkebarát, Tramini, and Muscat Ottonel, these days supplemented

by newcomers like Chardonnay and Sauvignon Blanc. What all these varietal wines have in common, irrespective of the vintage year, is their solid but not particularly stiff acid spine. This trait comes from the region's soil composition, which is quite different from the volcanic rocks of other growing areas on the northern shore of Lake Balaton. In Balatonfüred-Csopak, the predominant sandstone and, less frequently, adobe soils have a high content of lime and iron. Coupled with the beneficial climate, they impart a characteristic intensity to the region's wines, which tend to be elegant and full-flavored, but quite trim in structure. But why talk about soils on the excuse of gastronomy? Quite simply, because this is where it all begins. The specific features of a growing location—above all its *terroir*, understood to mean soil and climate collectively, plus prevailing varietal structure and cultivation methods—conspire to evolve the area's wine types, ultimately influencing your choice of the foods to go with them.

Throughout the region, cellars were never dug deep into the ground. More like facilities for wine storage than proper cellars, they were hardly fit as a place for aging wine for longer periods. As a consequence, the previous year's wine was usually consumed by the time the new vintage came along. It follows that the

A colorful composition of asparagus tips

Prawn with sugar snap pea pod

traditional white wine of the region is crisp and fruity, with acids untamed by lengthy maturation in wood. In a fortuitous coincidence for gastronomy, the wines of Balatonfüred-Csopak are naturally well-adapted to local cookery. The fish dishes here—typically supplied by the fresh catch of *fogas*, pike, catfish, bream, eel, and carp—rarely rely on mas-

Shanks of Guinea fowl with millet porridge

sive doses of paprika that would call for a high-acid red, allowing you to choose from among the region's own whites instead. As local fish, including the fried bream sold by street vendors, tends to be prepared plainly to emphasize the natural delicate flavor of the white flesh, you clearly don't want to overpower it with a wine that is bold, robust, or particularly brawny. Furthermore, the high sulfur content of fish can generate a disagreeable bitter taste on the palate when combined with a wine that has powerful alcohol or residual sugar, or is marked by the micro-oxidation that comes with aging in wooden casks. (These mature, full-bodied wines are better saved for roast poultry or a Bakony-style entrée prepared with mushrooms and sour cream.) To sum up, the rule to remember on fish is this: The simpler the mode of preparation, the younger and fresher your wine should be—and, of course, always fully dry (ideally, from Mihály Figula or István Jásdi). A richer fish recipe will take on a more mature white or a grape variety fit to receive

the barrique treatment, such as Chardonnay. But remember that excessively pungent spice in your food will always rob your wine of some of its character. The only exception is black pepper, which amplifies the sensation of acidity on the palate.

The considerable acidity of wines from Balatonfüred-Csopak makes them particularly desirable with foods that have a high acid content themselves, such as dressings, sauces and marinades using lemon or balsamic vinegar, as well as sour cream and sauerkraut (in Hungary, the latter two in fact often go together in the same dish). This is why an Olaszrizling from Csopak can be so delightful with a salad of fresh summer greens or a chilled vegetable soup—or indeed solo before the meal. A white wine doubling as an aperitif must be dry, not overly aromatic, and never strident. Serve it chilled (8-10 °C) and in small quantities (less than 100 ml), and always give it ample time to work its magic on the stomach.

BALATON-MELLÉKE (FORMERLY ZALA)

It's not very often that you will find commercially sold wines from this long-neglected region just beginning to emerge from oblivion, but when you do, you will not forget the encounter in a hurry. Wines from Dr. Bussay or the Németh Borház are two obvious arguments for the potential greatness of Zala County, one of two regions that for centuries supplied the royal Hungarian table with wine (the other being the Kál Basin in the Balatonfelvidék). These wines of old must have been full-flavored, substantial, and long-lived, and had a sophisticated local cuisine to build on. In turn, this rich culinary tradition was grounded firmly in the excellence of local ingredients, ranging from wild mushrooms to Zala River crawfish to big game. As for our own era, the few wines we have had the opportunity to sample are distinguished by their ripe flavors, huge body, high alcohol, and an aristocratic purity of taste, embodying a type very difficult to find on the world map of wine today. They have a particular personality that is overshadowed everywhere these days by the two styles dominating the international white wine scene: that of the crisp and

fruity white made in steel, and the barrique Chardonnay. While red wines have no tradition in Zala to speak of, there is quite a nice array of white grapes to choose from. Szürkebarát and Tramini, often vinified to retain some residual sugar, tend to be particularly full and fiery. The terroir encourages high acidity, even in varieties normally yielding softer wines, such as the Tramini. Besides the traditional Olaszrizling and a little Rajnai Rizling, Chardonnay performs well in Zala, although its basic character is sometimes altered by the powerful alcohol it produces here.

As regards the pleasures of the table, Zala wines are hardly a light summer affair. Instead, they reward the company of autumnal flavors, such as game, mushrooms, sweet cream, ripe walnuts, and almonds. These great wines have a smooth structure from the alcohol and a classy taste that enable them to hold their own with venison or wild boar, while their ample acids will fend off any hint of vulgar character that an aromatic grape is always in danger of communicating. Finally, these wines are also generous in the sense that they will forgive you for sipping them solo—without any food, and for your own solitary pleasure.

EGER AND THE BÜKKALJA

Eger still reminds many people of the Szépasszony-völgy, the wine tourist trap set up in the "Valley of the Lovely Lady." How many more wonderful wines will it take for this region to convince consumers of its true merit? How many more good vintages to make people realize that wine does not need to be sweet to be first-rate?

Eger is in a difficult position indeed. No wine region in Hungary, except perhaps around Lake Balaton, was discredited so thoroughly as Eger during the decades behind the iron curtain. What went by the name of Egri Bikavér and Egri Leányka in those days did not turn out as we wanted, and were certainly a far cry from the quality of the wines from Eger nowadays. What can we then say about wines from Eger and the Bükkalja with certainty? For one thing, we know that they possess elegant acids and the kind of fruity character that is much

appreciated around the world today. Obviously, this does not imply lightness of body or lack of substance, but simply that these wines are ideally suited to accompany fine food on account of their refined spectrum of acids. Whether white or red, a wine will always be a successful partner for food if its has a sufficient quantity of acids in a good structure. This rule will apply with particular force if the flavors themselves are masked by other components in your wine—typically by residual sugar in whites, and tannin in reds.

1999, and especially 2000 resulted in extraordinary alcohol levels throughout Hungary, making white wines uniformly flat or even clumsy with preponderant alcohol in regions where the acids just could not keep up. These wines are very difficult to match with food. Unlike this general tendency, the high-alcohol but proportionately vigorous whites of Eger can do perfect justice to rich dishes, whether the source of the fats is the meat, the sauce, or other ingredients. Regardless of the grape, a leaner example can be perfect along-

Polenta flavored with *juhtúró* (sharp ewe's milk cheese)

Mushrooms stuffed with mushrooms

side of a fine trout from the Szalajka Creek, indeed with any other finer fish. The long-established Hárslevelű wines of the Debrő district have undergone some very welcome changes for the past few years. Still often containing a hint of residual sugar, the modern-day Debrői Hárslevelű can provide an agreeable background for white meats pre-

Fried egg on a plinth
of celeriac, with caviar

Stuffed snails

pared with sweet spice or served with a sweet sauce. Do not be wary about these wines. When produced by a respectable grower—such as Lajos Gál, Lajos Varsányi, Ker-Coop, or Szőlészeti Borászati Kutató, the region's government-sponsored Research Institute of Viticulture and Enology—they will be entirely true to nature, and can be followed up by any course that demands a dry red.

The first red wines from Eger to really redeem the region's promise emerged from the fine 1999 vintage. Given adequate concentration, they are capable of a superb silky structure in which the sensible tannins do not overwhelm the generous fruit flavors. Almost without exception, the bigger wines are aged in small new oak, and are possessed of a distinct sweetness of extract that cannot be mistaken for residual sugar. These reds are of course dry, but they invariably benefit from that little roundness which can make a red wine really delightful.

The Bikavér, Eger's leading brand, also appears to have started out in a good direction. Although the constituent grapes or their ratio in the blend are not yet written in stone, efforts have been stepped up to tighten regulations for a Bikavér Superior of sorts. These endeavors will no doubt lead to improved wine quality across the board. More important than the varieties or their proportions in the cuvée, the rule to remember is that a mature

red will stand a much better chance on the dining table. Unripe tannins kill the taste of food as surely as they kill the other flavors of the wine itself. They develop an unpleasant astringent taste on the palate that overpowers everything, except perhaps the taste of fresh wild mushrooms. You can highlight any dark berry aromas or animal hints reminiscent of leather present in your red wine by using a little of the wine in cooking the food you are going to serve it with. Alternatively or in combination with this method, consider the fruit that the wine's bouquet reminds you of—blackberry, plum, morello cherry, etc.–as an ingredient. These words of advice apply to mature Bikavér and varietals with a higher tannin content, such as Cabernet Sauvignon, Cabernet Franc, Merlot, and their various blends. If you have a really nice bottle of ripe Eger red, it can be the perfect choice for a chocolate-based dessert that is not too sweet. In this case, the emphasis is on the bitter taste of chocolate, which can go surprisingly well with the tart tannins of the wine. Also common in Eger, wines made from high-acid grapes (Pinot Noir, Kékfrankos, Kadarka, Zweigelt) can stand up to paprika-seasoned dishes and even spicier foods, provided that they were not matured in heavily toasted new oak. Once again, it is the acidity which enables a positive interaction with the fatty flavors of the dish, while the bite of red paprika is echoed very well by the tartness of the wine's tannins.

ETYEK-BUDA

This old-new region recently succeeded in reclaiming its Buda district, albeit the one-time vineyards of Sashegy and Budafok have long since been devoured by the sprawling metropolis of Budapest. Both Etyek and Buda share the same calcareous soil that is ideal for cultivating grapes for sparkling wines. The exclusively white grapes grown here yield fresh, lean and fruity still wines, or go into the base wines for sparkling. Both these types are remarkably versatile in terms of gastronomic potential. In fact, no wine style is better prepared than a great dry sparkling to accompany an entire meal from hors d'oeuvre to dessert. As always, this special ability has to do with the acidity,

in this case enhanced by the carbon-dioxide generated in the wine in the course of secondary fermentation. But let us see the fare that these wines go so well with.

To begin at the beginning, or even before it, remember that a dry and light sparkling wine can be the perfect aperitif if given at least 10 minutes to exert its beneficial influence of "readying" the stomach. If you take further due care to serve it well-chilled, in the proper flutes and in small quantities to prevent it from warming up, you can be reasonably sure that everyone will reach for that second fill and sit down to dinner quickly. Provided that you keep quantities to a minimum, you can rely on a still white from Etyek to deliver the same effect, although the spectacle of a sparkling wine will certainly add—well, a sparkle.

At the outset of the meal proper the opportunities multiply, as a starter of greens, vegetables, fish or seafood is invariably a good foil for Etyek wine—still or sparkling. Whatever you serve as the hors d'oeuvre, keep in mind that a sour condiment in the form of lemon or vinegar will require a wine with at least an equal level of perceived acidity. I say perceived, because your subjective impression of how acid the wine is will not always tally with its analytical parameter. Higher alcohol or some residual sugar will make the wine seem less vigorous, for all the high measured acidity it may possess on paper. Foods are similarly prone to relativity when it comes to assessing their acid level. Typical Hungarian examples are *lecsó*, sour cream, and sauerkraut.

MÁTRAALJA

Thoughts of Hungary's mountainous north conjure up balmy winds, cool forests, the fragrance of flowery meadows, and the savor of animated fruity wines that can occasionally surprise with depth. Red wine grapes were common here in former centuries, but today the region is devoted almost exclusively to white varieties, including Irsai Olivér, Királyleányka, Ottonel Muskotály, Hárslevelű, and the requisite Olaszrizling. In addition to these native grapes, a number of growers have naturalized the popular Chardonnay to make fine buttery whites. As

none of these grapes suffer a shortage of acidity in the region, the wines tend to go well with high-acid foods. But watch out for wines from a good year and microclimate. These may contain some residual sugar, and thus perform best in the company of roast pork or poultry garnished with fruit. Have no qualms about serving the few really sweet examples with dessert. For years, the Szőlőskert Coop has supplied a consistently reliable sweet Tramini, and its Vitézvölgyi Hárslevelű also has considerable residual sugar. Other fine examples of the local sweet style include Mátyás Szőke's Muscat Ottonel and the particularly wonderful late harvest Muskotály from the Németh Winery. All these wines are lovely with lighter desserts composed around vanilla and citrus flavors.

The most prominent reds in recent years have been two Kékfrankos wines released en primeur. One is Szőke's tribute to *Márton nap* (St. Martin's day), the other is labeled in honor of Szt. Imre by the Nagyréde Winery. These lean, fruity reds have very subtle tannins that makes them perfect with paprika-flavored meat dishes, but they will do just as well—as they certainly should—with the traditional roast goose on St. Martin's day. The matured reds frequently rely on the Cabernet Sauvignon grape. Expect a light body and delicate acids in these wines rather than intense tannin. They can be just right with simply prepared game.

Snails stewed in red wine, with boletus

Fresh asparagus rolled in ham

Strudel with *orda*
(buttermilk curd cheese)

Fried chicken wing with
sun-dried apricot

MÓR

When we talk about Mór nowadays, the first thing that comes to mind is a high-acid, masculine white wine with a bite. And yet this tiny region should be capable of giving us much more than those few products from two or three better growers that are commercially available today. Móri Aszú is not a legend, either. The heritage is kept alive by the Bozóky family winery, which makes a rich sweet wine from nobly rotted grapes almost every year. Even the dry wines of the region tend to be very long-lived owing to their relatively high acidity and broad mineral foundation. The best may last decades and are comparable in style to a fine Riesling or Veltliner from the Rheingau (Germany) or Wachau (Austria). Spicy and unctuous but never heavy, they may be a little sharp when young, but if carefully grown and vinified, all they need is a few years of expert maturation to lose their edge and become well-balanced and stylish–though hardly charming or flattering. A case in point is a 1991 Királyleányka that Ákos Kamocsay made while under the wings of his former employer, the Mór State Farm. Tasted recently at 12 years of age, this wine was still pleasant to drink and had apparently retained much of its original substance.

The acids typical of all Mór wines, practically regardless of grape variety, can provide a good background for almost any basic flavor. The Ezerjó, a heavy-bearing local variety, is rarely capable of refinement even in the hands of the best winemaker. When harvested unripe, it is so aggressively harsh as to border on the undrinkable, and will never come round. Leányka, Rajnai Rizling, Tramini and, more recently, Chardonnay, deliver a much more even performance. You can trust these wines until their second year to enhance your fish, crisp salads, and dishes made with sour cream and/or sauerkraut. Particularly from very high-acid years along the lines of 2001, they can even handle positively sharp foods. The odd bottle of an exceptionally nice wine from this region, such as the 2001 Tatai "Karós" Ezerjó from the Németh Borház (the adjective in the middle means "stake-supported") can cope with sophisticated white meat entrées. As this wine offers an illusion of sweetness due to its high alcohol and glycerin, it will not shy away from dishes using fruits and even exotic spice. A sweet or semi-sweet late harvest wine or an Ezerjó Aszú from Bozóky or Hilltop Neszmély can rival Tokaj as the best accompaniment to *túró*, and possibly blue cheese.

In Mór, quintessentially a white wine area, you will be hard-pressed to find something to wash down meat that would properly call for red wine. But despair not, for you could do worse than a ripe and rich local white with at least 13% alcohol to suit your game–just make sure not to pick your herbs, spices or cooking technique with a big red in mind. Use white wine only for the sauce. Avoid rosemary, thyme, oregano, and basil, but be liberal with tarragon, marjoram, green or pink peppercorns, and sweet cream to thicken your sauce. Although I don't usually recommend grape varieties for specific flavors, I will make an exception here for Tramini, which can be uncommonly firm in this region, and whose distinct aroma has a great affinity with marjoram. As this herb is often used in Hungary to scent white fowl, sautéed liver and other giblets, a Tramini would seem to me a feasible accompaniment.

SOMLÓ

Somló wines tend to be even stiffer than those from Badacsony; they are positively hard and masculine, but nevertheless very full-flavored. The soil imparts distinct flavors to this tiny region's wines. A nice local white often conveys a mineral taste verging on the salty, but seldom displays identifiable herbaceous or fruity nuance. The reason why the finest of these wines can offer a unique experience has to do with their solid acidity as the best foundation for any composition of taste—the same kind of foundation on which the great wine monuments of Rheingau Riesling and Burgundy Chardonnay have been erected. The eroded volcanic butte of the Somló is home to the some of the most gifted Hungarian grapes, notably Furmint, Hárslevelű and Juhfark. While it is important to support these ancient varieties through our consumer habits, it is also vital to measure them against the highest of expectations. The term "indigenous" is not a magic word in itself, and will do precious little for these grapes if their pedigree is not simultaneously correlated with present-day quality.

Due to its massive acids, Somló wine is appropriate for a wide variety of high-acid foods that call for matching verve. Rich dishes with a high ratio of fat also demand a vigorous wine. A combination of these two food types, *töltött káposzta* (Hungarian cabbage stuffed with ground pork, flavored with bacon and paprika, and braised on a bed of sauerkraut) is something that I always serve with a bottle of Somló, preferably Juhfark or Furmint. The high acidity also renders these wines fit to accompany fine cream-based sauces. If the fare is fish, choose a younger wine for preference. Maturation flavors may impair the synergy between the fish and the wine.

The fact that Somló is a white wine-only region should be no cause for alarm if you fancy roast game on the menu of a local restaurant. Who says that a hunch of wild boar or a steak of venison will take offense if washed down with a white wine instead of a red? In fact, Somló is unique in Hungary's wide range of whites in that it has the body, alcohol, and elegance to safely cope with the most pungent game or forest mushroom, let alone duck or goose. All Somló wine needs to rest for two or three years to mellow out, and the best will inevitably spend time in wood. The micro-oxidation through the pores of

the cask and the high extract endow these wines with a secondary sweetness that helps them hold their ground against a sweet sauce. As always, keep in mind that the ingredients, seasonings, and the method of preparation should be more decisive in informing your choice of wine than any easy coincidence of color between it and the meat.

Strangely enough, Somló wine has a much poorer rapport with cheese than with vegetables or meat. The explanation is a simple one: An intensely flavored cheese needs a well-rounded velvety wine. Generally, Somló seems a little rugged for the purpose, although it has been known to indulge a ripe goat cheese or ewe cheese on occasion. Finally, a tip on serving: Always allow Somló wine to breathe, at least for 10-15 minutes before drinking. It is equally important to serve it slightly warmer (at 14-15 °C) than you would a typical dry white. At the end of the day, is there anything that could spoil the encounter between Somló wine and fine food? Just one thing: inferior wine quality. Everything I have written above is based on the assumption that you have a decent bottle to work with.

Celery with blue cheese

Goose with chestnuts

Fillet of fallow deer
with foie gras in pastry

Rabbit skewer

ment of acidity which makes them perfect with fine fish or crisp greens and vegetable bakes in the summer. Depending on the acid level of the food, a softer and more mature local white will do good service with dishes reflecting Austrian and Slovakian influence, such as *párolt káposzta* (braised cabbage often flavored with caraway), *vadas* ("hunter's style" beef or game marinated in spices and vinegar, roasted, and then briefly braised in a sweet and sour sauce based on puréed soup vegetables and sour cream), and *zsemlegombóc* (boiled bread dumplings finished in the oven, typically served as a garnish with *vadas*).

If you started the meal with a Kékfrankos, save some for the dessert if there is something with fine dark chocolate around, say *Gundel palacsinta* prepared according to the original recipe invented by the renowned restaurateur Károly Gundel about a century ago (crêpes stuffed with a filling of ground walnut and raisins scented with lemon peel and moistened with rum, finished in the oven and served with a dark chocolate sauce poured over; often flambéed for spectacle). Such a fine dessert deserves a mature Kékfrankos with completed malolactic fermentation—preferably three or four years old and/or from an outstanding vintage like 2000. The delicate bitterness of fine chocolate can be a heavenly match for ripe tannins, especially when the wine has some extract sweetness to boot. Finally, there is no reason for you to shirk a shot of ice-cold fruit brandy on a chilly, windy evening (which is not a rare occurrence in Sopron). Contrary to a popular misconception, clear fruit brandy is no foe of the seasoned vinophile, provided it is a completely natural product and of superb quality.

SOPRON

The town of Sopron and its environs occupy a subalpine zone that was known for centuries for its predominantly white wines. Today, two-thirds of the wine region is devoted to red wines, which tend to be high in acidity and tannin due to the frequently very calcareous soils, but lower in alcohol than the Hungarian average owing to the cool climate. This latter trait should not be a problem in light of current trends in consumer preferences; it is rather on account of the wines' tendency to a certain hardness of taste that Sopron will never be a universal favorite. The region's prevailing variety is Kékfrankos, a high-acid grape itself, whose character as a wine here seems to be undergoing a transformation in the hands of a few growers subjecting it to malolactic fermentation and longer maturation in wood. Whether high in malic acid or not, a glass or two of Kékfrankos from a better cellar can certainly go well with *babos pogácsa*, a sort of traditional scone with puréed beans in the dough. Equally important for Sopron's bourgeois culinary tradition, big game from the nearby forests also benefits from the company of a well-rounded but still vigorous red. Further popular choices to go with your Sopron red include baked pork hocks in any version. The pronounced acidity of the wine is useful in cutting the fat of such dishes.

Given scrupulous work in the cellar, the region's energetic whites can have a great refine-

SZEKSZÁRD AND TOLNA

People say good wine is easy to talk about. If this is true, a wine region with a deep tradition should be no more difficult for the writer to discuss. I must confess a positive bias for Szekszárd, perhaps because Szekszárd proper, the Völgység, and Bátaszék all yield wines for which no "black tie is required"—wines you can love without self-interest. Once you have understood them, they will always remain dear to you. The Szekszárd red is caressing rather than robust. Its tannins ripen to a velvety sheen quite quickly; even a heavy tannin producer like Cabernet Sauvignon will here turn a gentler face to us. The playful acids typical of Szekszárd engender a fabulous elegance that can make a concentrated red seem light. The fruitiness and spicy tang of Kadarka and Merlot, as solo varietals or in blends, need four to five years to fully develop, so don't skimp on the cellar time of these wines. However, don't expect appreciable acidity or longevity from the region's whites.

But what about food? Anything will go that is built around fatty, acid, or spicy hot flavors, or a combination of these. The affinity of Szekszárd red with freshly ground Hungarian paprika is a long-standing observation. The proximity of the deep alluvial forests at Gemenc and the Danube itself gave rise to a distinct local cuisine that finds an ideal synergy with most of the area's wines. Indeed, Szekszárd is one of the few regions in Hungary where you can feel confident choosing a local wine to go with local food. The classic example is Szekszárd's *halászlé*; a ripe local Kadarka would be hard to top as a complement for this soup of fresh river fish. For finer, less rustic flavors—such as lean game, small or big, with sweet sauce or spices—pick a more tannic red that is fully mature. Merlot in Szekszárd attains a velvety structure, adding to the reputation of the grape as the source of the most caressing wines.

Mention must be made of Szekszárd's traditional Bikavér blend, relying on Kékfrankos for bulk, Merlot for velvety texture, Cabernet for tannin, and Kadarka for acids and a hint of spice. Marginally more supple than its counterpart from Eger, the Szekszárdi Bikavér is nevertheless a powerful and firm personality by regional standards that you will find perfectly adapted to forest mushrooms and potently seasoned meats, grilled or pan-fried. (As usual, the cooking method and the seasoning should be more important considerations than the color of the meat.) Aside from Kadarka, Merlot, and Bikavér, Szekszárd has the potential to endow Cabernet Sauvignon and Franc with a distinct local character. The finest examples from exceptional years are properly

best sipped alone—as will befit any great red.

Finally, the region's fish, noodle and pastry dishes may convince you it would be a mistake to overlook Szekszárd white and rosé. Pike, carp and catfish all take well to a local white, especially from a year when the grapes produced more acidity than usual. Always remember that a rosé made to suit the Hungarian palate will behave more like a crisp, high-acid white wine in the culinary context, which explains why it goes infinitely better with fish than a flat or lethargic white. Other acid-friendly local foods to consider include *téfölös bütök* (salty leavened dough baked and rolled in fat and sour cream), *juhtúrós puliszka* (polenta baked with sharp ewe's milk cheese, sometimes sprinkled with diced fried bacon), and *csomboros töltött káposzta* (stuffed cabbage scented with savory). If the dish has something smoked in it, as indeed *töltött káposzta* often will, don't hesitate to use a local barrique Chardonnay.

TOKAJ

"*Tokaj ist evig* – Tokaj is for eternity," proposed a card of invitation to an extraordinary wine tasting to celebrate the opening of the new Hungarian Embassy in Berlin. The event was honored by such notable invitees as Michael Broadbent. But why do I bring this

A bit of foie gras

Cold foie gras with Tokaji Aszú jelly

up here? Because eternity may remind us of the infinite possibilities and permutations of taste that Tokaj affords. Indeed, sometimes it is hard to find a combination of flavor with which an inexplicably rich Tokaji Aszú would *not* be able to cope. The high extract, sugar, and firm acids of an Aszú conspire to make quick work of the most challenging dish, out-

Cheek of beef braised in Villányi Merlot, with géva mushrooms

muscling everything without creating a disagreeable interplay of flavors on the palate. And yet it would be foolish to suggest that a massively sweet Tokaj, particularly an Aszú, is *the* wine to drink with just about anything. It is in fact possible to isolate those flavors that will achieve consummate harmony with Tokaj—or supply a feasible counterpoint to it, as the case may be.

Let us begin with the dry whites. In the shadow of the great sweet botrytis wines, the region nurtures increasingly pure and impressive dry Furmint, Hárslevelű, and Szamorodni. Furmint yields a firm, high-acid wine with hints of quince and sweet pear compote on the nose that partners well with foods containing similar fruit flavors, for instance any meat, toast, grilled or pan-fried, and garnished with baked apple or pear, or a purée of quince. More charming, quicker to mature, and easier to approach than Furmint, Hárslevelű has distinct aromas of linden blossom and honey even in its fully dry version. Avoid sour foods with

Hárslevelű, as this grape is considerably lower in acidity, particularly when harvested from loess rather than clay or adobe soils. These two wines also get along well with fish, provided that the recipe does not call for paprika.

Dry Szamorodni can be the perfect aperitif when chilled to 8-10 °C, while its green walnut and yeasty aromas seem to destine this wine for rich turkey and other roast poultry. A garnish or stuffing of chestnuts, walnuts or figs would be very appropriate to highlight the matured flavors of your Szamorodni. Bear in mind that anything sweet on the plate will have to be matched with some sense of sweetness in the wine—whether derived from residual sugar, higher alcohol, or extract sweetness.

Dry Muskotály, still the exception to the rule in Tokaj, possesses the kind of acidity and alcohol that assigns it roughly to the same culinary limits I have outlined above. But beware: The forward but refined aroma of the Muskotály grape may make a fiery and concentrated wine seem light, and can be downright problematic with fish.

What all sweet Tokaj wines have in common is a nose reminiscent of ripe citrus fruits, a function of the high ratio of botrytis present. Younger examples that have never seen wood tend to convey more intense hints of apricot, lemon and orange peel, grapefruit, and sometimes fresh peach. Beyond remembering the sugar, for these wines you should choose light and delicate ingredients that can be prepared quickly and without fuss. Thanks to its high acidity, *túró* has a special rapport with any late harvest wine from the region, especially when scented with lemon or orange peel. The great classic match for sweet Tokaj is foie gras or duck liver, cast in the leading role or as a flavoring ingredient. The combination may be true and well-tried, but should never be applied without discrimination. For instance, if you have accidentally used more than a scrap of garlic or onion in preparing the liver, you will be better off digging up a bottle of young rustic red. Sweet botrytis wines in this context can only be justified, indeed preferred, as long as a gentle cooking technique (steaming, mousse, etc.) and a light hand with seasonings have helped retain the liver's inherent sweetness and rich fat. These dishes can handle plenty of fruit of any color—white, yellow, orange, or, best of all, brown.

Mature Aszú with a deeper tone (not only of color, but also aroma and flavor) calls for different foods to underline its hints of walnut, chestnut, fig, coffee, cedar, sandalwood, or tobacco. Goose and duck with the appropriate accoutrements come to mind, or the greatest of all blue cheeses, Roquefort. These magnificent wines deserve and reward sophisticated preparation, the resourceful application of intriguing herbs and spices, and a purposefully orchestrated, vibrant interplay between the food flavors and the accents of the wine. Finally, credit should be given to the hardened gourmet, in parlors small or large, who will sip nothing but 6 puttonyos Tokaji Aszú to moisten the smoke of his Havana cigar...

Two afterthoughts:

1. Any wine with residual sugar can be very nice with decidedly salty flavors, such as cured ham, salami if not seasoned with paprika, and certain types of cheese. The richer the food in acid or fat, the more vigorous your wine must be.

2. Desserts employing fine dark chocolate can be a way of saving your precious Aszú, insofar as they go just as well with a ripe red that has completed malolactic fermentation.

VILLÁNY AND THE MECSEKALJA

Villány and red wine are intertwined so intimately that we frequently forget about the other wines the region has to offer. Whites grown around the town of Siklós or in the Mecsekalja are full, soft and broad as a result of low acidity and typically high alcohol. They are a special case in that they make it easier to ask the question in the negative: What is it that you should never serve with a Siklós white, under any circumstance? Well, above all anything that has a sour flavor, due to a main ingredient, seasoning, or condiment—particularly salads, sauerkraut, or *lecsó*. Caution will be in order with lean white fish, although the smoked variety can be decidedly pleasant with these wines, particularly those matured in small new oak casks. The safest bet is poultry and other white meat, served with a rich cream sauce. The distinct rustic flavors of Villány

cooking provide few ideas that could be useful with the fabulously elegant reds that have emerged from the finest cellars of this region recently. The traditional local cuisine, considered too heavy today, relies on intensely seasoned pork and dry beans as its staples. Even the best growers of Villány tend to use Kékoportó to wash down such foods, whether consumed by the cellar or at home. Incidentally, these soft, caressing and jammy wines can be used to great effect as a ploy to wean a gullible friend off sweet red wines. Why should this be a goal? Because Hungary's climatic conditions practically rule out the possibility of red wines containing any residual sugar of *natural* origin. Kékoportó is best drunk young, in its first or second year. It is a good match for noodles, pasta and other rustic dishes lightly scented with garlic and/or rosemary.

The Kékfrankos grape in Villány is losing ground to the great Bordeaux varieties of Cabernet Sauvignon, Cabernet Franc and

Marinated breast of duck with prune

Terrine of Guinea fowl

Merlot. Many leading growers will no longer bottle it as a varietal wine, using it instead as a blending wine for their big cuvées. It's a pity, because Kékfrankos has a potentially lovely acidity and delicious fruitiness that can make it very enjoyable on its own. Two consecutive outstanding vintages, in 1999 and 2000, gave Villány a boost so big that it necessitates a gastronomic reassessment of the region. In

*Töltött káposzta -
Hungary's famous
stuffed cabbage*

as we have a right to expect. These reds are full, generous and complex, with sufficient but not firmly etched acids, and, at long last, velvety tannins. In short, they have everything in place to do justice to all kinds of dark meat, including beef, game, and wild fowl. A word of caution: Don't serve your Villány red with courses using a sweet sauce, garnish, or condiment, unless the wine has appreciable extract sweetness of its own. If the tannin content is ripe but predominant among the other flavors, your wine will stand up to the most pungent wild mushroom. A special case is supplied by truffles, which have recently made an appearance in several restaurants in Hungary. The finest real truffle, correctly used sparingly as a seasoning, calls for the kind of animal hints and barnyard character that a mature Pinot Noir will be most competent to supply.

Another way to exploit a ripe Villány red is with chocolate, provided that its tannins are flush with the taste, and the chocolate is of the finest quality. Like all big, tannic reds, Villány when fully mature can be mated successfully with cheeses, particularly those with a weight and concentration commensurate with those of the wine itself. This will invariably mean a hard cheese, most notably Parmesan and Pecorino, another Italian cheese from sheep's milk (in the matured Vecchio version for preference), their Spanish counterpart Manchego, the more loosely structured Cheddar from England, or Cantal or Gruyère Comté from France.

As the author of all the smart advice above, I must confess that my very favorite way to enjoy a treasured Villány red is with no food at all—just nursing a glass with a huge bowl, snug in a corner, in the company of good friends.

former times, if you wanted a nice red to go with a fine cut of red meat, you looked to other regions—unless you had years to wait for an otherwise impressive and precious Villány red to shake its rough tannin dominance and come round. Owing to a fortuitous combination of various factors, these two recent vintages really coaxed as much out of the grapes

TERRA BENEDICTA

SECOND CHAPTER – WINE REGIONS

Ászár-Neszmély

Badacsony

Balatonboglár

Balatonfelvidék

Balatonfüred-Csopak

Balatonmelléke

Bükkalja

Csongrád, Hajós-Baja, Kunság

Eger

Etyek-Buda

Mátraalja

Mecsekalja

Mór

Pannonhalma-Sokoróalja

Somló

Sopron

Szekszárd

Tokaj

Tolna

Villány-Siklós

Ászár-Neszmély

A sentinel watching over the Danube, this wine region is out of the limelight, but it fills a vital niche in Hungary's wine production. Ászár-Neszmély is a reliable source of wines for daily consumption, and a fine destination for a holiday trip.

Located on the right bank of the Danube in Komárom County, the wine region occupies the southwestern flanks of the Gerecse Range and its northern plateaus dipping toward the river (around the village of Almásneszmély), as well as the northern foothills of the Vértes and the Bakony Mountains, where the hills meet the Kisalföld (the "Little Plain"). The Ászár district of the region includes the communes of Bársonyos, Császár, Csép, Ete, Kerékteleki, Kisbér, Nagyigmánd, and Vérteshely; the Neszmély district comprises Baj, Dunaalmás, Dunaszentmiklós, Esztergom, Kesztölc, Kocs, Mocsa, Neszmély, Szomód, Tata, and Vértesszőlős. In respect of all these communes, only wines harvested from sites ranked Class I or Class II in the national cadastre can be labeled under the wine region's name. These sites in Ászár-Neszmély add up to 6,574 hectares, of which 4,223 hectares are recognized as Class I sites.

Ászár-Neszmély has a temperate continental climate with annual fluctuations of temperature far less wide than in the Great Plain. The region is characterized by relatively high humidity, moderate rainfall, and rather low heat quantity and insolation. Spring frosts are infrequent and not particularly severe when they occur. The cool and damp conditions are ideal for the production of delicate aromatic wines, almost exclusively white.

The region's geology is rather diverse. The Neszmély district has Triassic limestone and dolomite, Cretaceous and Eocene marls and shales, and Oligocene continental clay and gravel, all overlain by a mantle of Pleistocene loess. In the Vértesalja and the Bársonyos Hills, the prevalent rocks are Pannonian clay and sand sediments with thick Quaternary

loess. The soil is typically of the brown forest type, with *rendzina*—a dark soil that develops under grass on limestone and chalk—also occurring over sandstone, marl, loess, and sand. The soils are heavily eroded in the vicinity of Almásneszmély and in the larger area of the Western Gerecse. The terrain is characterized by gentle slopes and valleys. Around

Almásneszmély, the northern face of the loess-covered hills breaks off sharply toward the Danube, while the south-facing slopes are less steep and much easier to cultivate.

Neszmély and its environs boast a wine tradition going back to medieval times. Starting in

ÁKOS KAMOCSAY, VINTAGE 1946

In 1990-91, during the democratic transformation which swept away the monopoly of state-run wineries and cooperatives, a few enthusiastic outsiders glimpsed the opportunity to do a thing or two for the cause of Hungarian wine. Such people made up the team behind the Hungarian stand at VINITALY in 1992, which turned out to be a huge success owing in no small part to Ákos Kamocsay, since then best known as the head winemaker of Hilltop Neszmély. The amazement of visitors who stopped by the stand – "Are Hungarians really this good?" – was elicited by Kamocsay's 1991 Móri Rajnai Rizling, now widely recognized as a milestone for being the first reductive Hungarian wine *par excellence*. Not erring on the side of tropical exuberance, this crisp but weighty riesling hung on to its vigor for many years, and became a perennial star of wine shows. What Hilltop does nowadays is a direct continuation of this lineage. Although Kamocsay's wines sometimes seem overly eager to please international tastes, this is certainly a mark of an astute businessman who not only produces wine on the order of dozens of millions of bottles, but is also able to sell it all. Kamocsay is probably the only person in Hungary who can do both.

86

the 18th century, a few aristocratic estates took charge of caring for the good reputation of local wines. The second half of the 19th century saw the creation of a model vineyard and winery by the Esterházy Estate in Csákvár. The scrupulous professional work at this estate

paved the way for the official recognition of the Neszmély wine region in 1897. In 1959, the area was subsumed under what was then the Bársonyos-Császár wine region, in a move that reflected the preferences of a planned economy for state farms and forced collectivization. (The name Bársonyos, meaning "velvety," refers to a low plateau of loess-covered hills north-west of the Vértes Mountains.) In 1977, the wine region Ászár-Neszmély was restored to its former status as an independent wine region to encourage the reconstruction of neglected vineyards and promote quality wine production.

The leading grape varieties are Chardonnay (208 ha), Rizlingszilváni (205 ha), and Zöld Veltelini (120 ha), followed by smaller quantities of Cserszegi Fűszeres (50 ha), Olaszrizling (85 ha), Muscat Ottonel (67 ha), Ezerjó (186 ha), and Királyleányka (39 ha). The region's wines, invariably of the high-acid and lean "northern type," commanded great respect in former times. The most notable examples in the 19th and the early 20th centuries were the Neszmélyi Rajnai Rizling and the Neszmélyi Szemelt Rizling. This latter wine was made from "hand-selected" (*szemelt*) grapes as indicated by its name. Today, the wines are generally vinified in reductive conditions to retain intense primary aromas and the wide spectrum of fine acids that are so typical of this region.

Only three wineries in the area produce larger quantities of bottled wine. Prominent among them is the Hilltop Neszmély Winery, whose wines have won accolades in Hungary as well as abroad. Indeed, it would be no exaggeration to say that Hilltop has single-handedly breathed new life into this region. Aromatic, fruity, trim, and never more than medium-bodied, Hilltop wines have become the example to follow in Neszmély—as they themselves are faithful followers of a familiar international style. While this high-tech style is adapted deftly to suit local conditions, it tends to strangely mask regional character in a number of white wines that Hilltop sources from different wine regions around the country. The other two local producers worth mentioning are the Szöllősi Winery, also based in Neszmély, and Gimeskő-Vin in Kesztölc.

Badacsony

Badacsony has been a favorite hide-out of poets and their muses, and frequented by kings and fools. This hill on Lake Balaton has something for all; and wine never does taste as good as when there is water nearby.

The Badacsony wine region—magnificent country studded by buttes that used to be volcanoes—occupies the Tapolca Basin and some of the adjacent Kál Basin just north of the western part of Lake Balaton. It is flanked by the dolomite blocks of the Keszthely Mountains on the west, the Nivegy Valley trending from Balatoncsicsó to Zánka on the east, and a low range of the Southern Bakony Mountains on the north. Outlets to the towns of Sümeg on the northwest and Veszprém to the northeast are provided by two narrow valleys.

While the unmistakable silhouette of Mount Badacsony is visible from far away, the region is far from being limited to the slopes of this eponymous hill. More than one volcanic butte in the Tapolca Basin provides vistas and wines that can rival those of Mount Badacsony itself. Badacsony was designated as a wine region during the Reform Era of the 19th century, when the literate Hungarian gentry keenly followed a romance unfolding on the slopes of Badacsony between the beautiful Róza Szegedi and the noted poet Sándor Kisfaludy. The gradually consummated idyll, recorded by the poet in cycles like "Plaintive Love" and "Joyous Love," held the general public in thrall and admiration for years. Having been known only to wine drinkers till then, the name of the hill now suddenly sprang to national fame. What János Nagyváthy in 1819 called the "Badacsony Wine Region" was a vast wine-producing belt from Egregy to Felsőörs that probably comprised nearly 5,000 hectares.

The region's communes, which belong to Veszprém County administratively, include Ábrahámhegy, Badacsonytomaj, Badacsonytördemic, Balatonszepezd, Gyulakeszi, Hegymagas, Káptalantóti, Kisapáti, Kővágóörs, Nemesgulács, Raposka, Révfülöp, Salföld, Szigliget, and Tapola. The vineyards here have never been relegated to the bottom of the

87

basins; in addition to Mount Badacsony, they occupy the slopes of the following hills: Tóti, Szent György, Szigliget, Csobánc, Gulács, Haláp, Örsi, and Ábrahám. The sites making up the wine region total 4,772 hectares, including 3,462 ha classified as Class I. However, only 1,790 hectares of this potential area are actually planted with vines. This has to do with the dilemma besetting the entire resort belt around Lake Balaton, where land has proved much more profitable when sold as building sites for resort homes than used for wine production. As a result, some of the best potential terroirs on Mount Badacsony and Ábrahám Hill overlooking the Lake sport rows of villas and cottages instead of rows of vines today.

The region has a temperate continental climate with an average heat sum and insolation. What is special for the vines here is Badacsony's microclimate. This is shaped by the steep incline and favorable southern aspect of the slopes, which gives them shelter from cold northerly winds. Practically every account from the past hundred years or so also points to the benefit of extra light reflected by the surface of Lake Balaton. In reality, this factor is probably negligible, because the Lake, instead of illuminating the vineyards as a focused searchlight, disperses sunlight in every direction, and then generally not at a wavelength that the vines could utilize. Of much more consequence is the way this large body of water influences the temperature around it by moderating masses of cold air that often burst into the area, and by ensuring the movement of air in the vineyards. This latter contribution is particularly important physiologically as it helps to prevent a premature metabolism of acidity by enabling the vines to cool off on hot summer nights. The proximity of water is also instrumental in maintaining higher levels of humidity. All these factors combined result in a microclimate not unlike the sub-Mediterranean. Fig trees probably think so too, as they bear fruit in this area almost every year.

The Tapolca Basin and the contiguous Kál Basin were produced by a young, tertiary collapse, and are filled up by the Late Miocene deposits of the Pannonian Lake. On the dried-up bed of the Lake an intense volcanic eruption

deposited basaltic tuff and lava rocks in the Pliocene. While at certain places the basalt formed a continuous mantle (Hajagos and Fekete Hills), in the case of Mount Badacsony, Szent György Hill and Csobánc Hill it created small lava caps. The hard and resistant basalt covering these buttes preserved the underlying soft Pannonian-Pontian sediments from erosion. The basalt hills of Tapolca, known for their big wines, are surrounded by peat-moors not suitable for viticulture.

A smaller segment of the wine region between the villages of Badacsonyörs and Révfülöp consists of red Permian sandstone, a type of rock familiar from the nearby Balatonfüred-Csopak region. This geological discrepancy, the result of specious logic or lack of competence in demarcating wine regions, can be sometimes felt if one compares a wine grown on the sandstone of Badacsonyörs with one harvested from the volcanic slopes of Mount Badacsony itself.

The volcanic slopes are covered here and there by loess mixed with clayey and sandy Pannonian sediments in the lower parts, and increasingly with basalt and basaltic tuff debris at higher elevations. Accordingly, at the bottom of the hills we find clayey soils mixed with basalt debris, while the steep slopes, often cultivated on terraces to fight erosion, are covered with a basalt talus, lending rich acids, full body and flavor to local wines. In a few places, the pure basalt rock has evolved black *nyirok* soils. In addition to the famous weathered basaltic soil, pure adobe and, on rare occasions, calcareous soils can also be found (around Salföld and Tapolca).

The relief of the area is shaped by volcanic cones (the hills of Hegyesd, Kis-Hegyestű, Gulács, Tóti, and Királyné-Szoknyája) and truncated cones such as Mount Badacsony, Csobánc Hill, and Szent György Hill. (The truncated shape of the Halács Hill is the result of mining activity). Delimiting the Kál Basin from the south, the Örs, Ábrahám and Fülöp Hills are characterized by milder but better-articulated gradients.

Archeological finds in the area attest to a flourishing viticulture 2000 years ago courtesy of the Romans, who built one of their military

89

routes skirting Mount Badacsony. This road is known today as Római-út, and is still in use. The Hungarian Occupation of the Homeland at the end of the 9th century did not interfere with the legacy of viticulture that had continued unbroken since Antiquity. Charters from the 13th century show that some of the vineyards in the area were owned by the Church, while others belonged to the Altyusz family who built the fortified castle of Szigliget and the Almád monastery near Monostorapáti. Already at this time, some of the local wines ended up on the tables of the Royal court.

As a region that fell into the *végvár* belt, a zone marked by a string of fortified castles on the fringes of Hungarian-controlled territory, Badacsony became half depopulated and its viticulture declined during the wars against occupying Ottoman Turks in the 16th and 17th centuries. The area recuperated in the 18th century, when new plantation and more modern viticultural methods led to the production of wines that ultimately made Badacsony famous. A number of aristocratic families, some based well outside of the region, maintained estates and press houses on these hills. The members of the Tóti-Lengyel family, who owned the most gorgeous press house on Szent György Hill, commuted by boat from Somogy County across the Lake to supervise the work in the vineyard and to enjoy their wines in the original setting.

At the time, the wine region stretched all the way along the northern shore, and was known as *Balatonmelléke* ("Balaton District," a name officially applied today to the wine producing areas of Zala County west of the Lake). Mátyás Bél, the notable Lutheran pastor, educator, and encyclopedist of the first half of the 18th century, observed that *"the endless wine hills flanking the northern shore of Lake Balaton generally yield wines of quite a noble stature, but the very best come from the hills at Badacsony, Szent György, and Kővágóörs. The fruit of these hills tastes so delicious that the wines it makes are certainly among the best-known in the country, if not necessarily the ultimate among them..."* This excellence and reputation probably rested on the fact that these hillsides were excellent sites for hosting botrytis—as they are today. Another special product of the region was the *ürmös*, a bitter-

The built terraces are somehow 4-5 m high

sweet wine made from aromatic grapes, dark for preference, sweetened with honey or must concentrate, and flavored with herbs, in particular wormwood. First mentioned in 1788, *ürmös* was often sold in pharmacies due to its alleged curative powers.

By the 18th century, the Kéknyelű had emerged as the most expressive grape of the region. Although its distinct Badacsony

character was universally touted, Kéknyelű was really confined to the estates of the aristocracy who could afford to indulge this noble, but naturally low-yielding variety. The bulk of production continued to rely on other ancient Hungarian grape varieties, notably the Szigeti or Fehér Furmint, which was planted in mixed lots with Juhfark and Sárfehér in an attempt to emulate the day's famous white blends of the same composition from Somló and Neszmély. Along with Kéknyelű, these three grapes were widely regarded as yielding the finest wine of Badacsony. In the 19th century, Furmint was superseded by Olaszrizling and a fad for the red Kékoportó. Another grape unique to Badacsony was the Budai Zöld, planted in mixed lots with Kéknyelű to help fertilize this pistillate variety. The leading variety today is Olaszrizling (1,032 ha), followed by Rizling-szilváni (89 ha), Szürkebarát (86 ha), Chardonnay (145 ha), and Muscat Ottonel (45 ha). In addition to these prevalent grapes, small patches remain of Budai Zöld, Furmint, and Kéknyelű.

At the end of the 19th century, phylloxera destroyed almost all the vines in Badacsony and the Kál Basin. Retaining walls supporting the terraces were built to prevent erosion as part of the reconstruction effort. New wine legislation in 1893 recommended only white varieties for plantation, effectively transforming Badacsony into an exclusively white wine-producing area as we know it today. In 1936, the region was

buildings. Characteristically, the ensuing decades of "goulash communism" failed to come up with any new value to redeem the obliterated assets of nature, scenery, and economy that had evolved together to form an organic whole. To add insult to injury, the relative boom in the tourism industry enslaved the wines to a miserably substandard market. At their best, Badacsony wines are typically full-bodied and rich in extract, alcohol, and titrable acidity. As a result, they tend to cellar well, typically taking two or three years to reach their peak of development, and sustaining that quality for quite some time after that. The most famous wines, going back a hundred years, have been the Badacsonyi Olaszrizling, the Badacsonyi Szürkebarát, and the Badacsonyi

officially renamed Badacsony-Balatonfüred-Csopak, but it retained the villages of the Kál Basin—only to lose them shortly after with its subsequent division in 1941.

In those days, occasional ridge tillage, narrow spacing, stake support, regular horned head training, and short spur pruning still characterized local cultivation methods. With the stepped-up conversion of the Lake Balaton area into a resort zone after the Great War, many of the best growing sites fell victim to an explosion of weekend cottages. In the wake of forced collectivization under the single-party state, the combined lack of spiritual attachment and market demand for quality wines led to the destruction of vineyards and unique winery

Kéknyelű, distinguished by its spicy bouquet. This latter variety had drifted to the brink of extinction by the end of the 20th century, for obvious reasons of economies. Kéknyelű is a very problematic grape that has female (pistillate) flowers only, leading to a difficult berry set. Even if it gets the special care it needs, it remains a low producer, and will only reward the effort if the market is willing to pay a higher price for the wine. Thanks to new plantation, Kéknyelű has sprung back to some 10 hectares in Badacsony, from the dangerously low hectare and a half only a few years ago.

The vintage permitting, Badacsony has a significant production of more or less sweet wines. Szürkebarát, Muscat Ottonel and, to a

The southern slope of Mount Badacsony before World War II

emerging, once again, from the Szent Orbán Winery. We keep talking about Badacsony wines, although not all of them are harvested from the slopes of Mount Badacsony proper. In fact, some wines from neighboring hills, such as the Csobánc, the Gulács, or the Szent György, have been known to challenge the preeminence of the hill that gave its name to the region. The philosopher Béla Hamvas had this to say about the taster's quandary: "*The difference between Badacsony and Szent György wines will be the subject of my lectures for an entire semester if I ever gain an appointment to the faculty of the Department of Vinology. What we have here is the text-book example of how two great wines can differ. The Badacsony is like a world-famous artist, while the Szent György is like the artist who has hardly ventured beyond the confines of his room all his life, but has created a greater opus than his celebrated colleague. Both are possessed of greatness, but the one I would call Olympian, the other Chinese, a greatness of the Tao type. It is strange how I seem to be unable to choose between them… A while ago I all but made up my mind in favor of the Szent György, but when I drank a glass of Badacsony*

smaller extent, Tramini are commonly vinified in the off-dry or semi-sweet style, although the Szent Orbán Winery has come up with excellent dry versions in recent years. Before the Great War, the better wineries often made Aszú, and even Eiswein. The tradition is apparently being resurrected by wonderful late harvest Zeusz and Olaszrizling

HUBA SZEREMLEY, VINTAGE 1940

Best termed an "estate owner," Huba Szeremley is not a qualified enologist; for that matter, neither is his "first mate," Béla Fölföldi, who actually makes the wines. What is then the secret of the excellent wines–from over 100 hectares in Badacsony and nearby hills, more recently from about 500 ha on the Great Plain under the Helvécia label, and soon from the 150-hectare Nagygombos property northeast of Budapest? Not that this is the only mystery surrounding the man, whose life has been a pet topic in the tabloid press. To mention just one thing, you must admit that someone exploring Persian viticulture as the guest of the Shah is not an everyday occurrence.

Mr. Szeremley, known to Hungarian wine cognoscenti simply as Huba, has set himself three goals (or rather, this is how many we can mention here within the bounds of confidentiality): to provide Hungarian consumers with an impeccable but affordable table wine; to firmly reestablish *szürkemarha*, Hungary's ancient gray longhorn cattle, and *Mangalica*, an indigenous pig breed that yields fine ham for curing, as solid culinary support for Szeremley's wines; and finally, to make red wine in Badacsony. Coming from anybody else, these ambitious plans would seem hopelessly utopian. With Szeremley, we may expect them to be turned into reality.

His Kéknyelű has been the example to follow in Badacsony. The small quantity of Riesling he makes is easily the best in the country (mind you, this is the noble Rajnai Rizling, not the Olaszrizling variety). His sweet botrytis wines have found a special niche in the shadow of Tokaj's giants. He gave a new lease of life to old grape varieties like Budai Zöld and Bakator, and reinforced the position of Zeusz, a fairly recent hybrid–and the list could go on. Who could make an inventory of all the achievements of this one man?

Riesling, I had to side with Badacsony. Then I swore by Badacsony until I had a chance to taste the juice of Szent György over again. In any case, what is to prevent me from being Greek and Chinese at the same time?"

Far from such lofty dilemmas, the quality of the region's wines hit rock bottom in the late 1980's. At that time, it seemed all but impossible that the wines would ever again live up to their old fame. Indeed, this battle for quality has not yet been won in Badacsony, where a number of factors still work to the detriment of a high culture of wine rather than to its advantage. Sándor Tóth describes the region's predicament in these words: *"The touristy shore of Lake Balaton caters to the masses with an emphasis on the quantity of wine that can be gulped down in one sitting, not to mention its mind-altering properties. Clearly, this amounts to the shameless devaluation of a magnificent local culture of wine that is rooted in historic times. The other district uphill and further inland has been largely spared by the hordes of tourists. Consequently, the press houses and cellars here have survived in their original form, so well-suited to the surrounding landscape."*

This dismal situation, created for the casual tourist on the shore, is being braved by a number of growers who have done a lot since the Wall came down to restore Badacsony wines to the quality that earned the reverence of former generations. The smaller ones include István Tombor in Köveskál, György Varga in Révfülöp, József Csanádi in Badacsony, Kálmán Pupos in Szigliget, and Ödön Nyári with the landmark press house on Szent György Hill. Also based on Szent György Hill and adding a dash of color is the Biovitis Winery, makers of organic wines known as *biobor*. (The word alone makes you wonder when the category "chemobor" will be invented to label the fake wines sold in the tourist traps on the shore).

Huba Szeremley's Szent Orbán Winery plays a seminal role in the region as the largest producer of top quality wines. Indeed, if Szeremley had not set up his wine venture here, we could hardly talk about Badacsony as we know it today. Already the first wines to have come out of this innovative cellar make the name Badacsony ring true once again.

The local traditions of architecture engendered a great diversity of press houses—buildings erected over the cellars where the wine was

made. Most of them are protected monuments today. At the end of the 18th century, the wine region was studded with rudimentary press houses, better peasant dwellings with ancillary buildings for domestic animals, two-story press houses built by middle-class owners, and refined manors belonging to the landed aristocracy. The press houses built by the lesser nobility often alloyed motifs of the so-called "rustic baroque" with similarly folk-inflected neoclassicist elements. The finest examples of this curious genteel-rural style are Róza Szegedy's house on the slope of Badacsony and the Tóti-Lengyel Borház on the southern face of Szent György Hill. Further gems of architecture include the small hillside chapels dedicated to the patron saints Orbán (Urban) and Donát (Donatus) to enlist their help in protecting the vines. Larger cellars—such as the Esterházy Cellars in Szigliget or the huge wine cellar of the Episcopal Palace in Sümeg—were evidently the privilege of the great estates. A fine cellar was built in 1815 in Tapolca by the Lessners, a wealthy Jewish family of wine merchants.

The Tarányi
Press House
(Szent György Hill)

93

The Badacsony region is also an inexhaustible storehouse of folklore and customs associated with wine. To mention just one example: *mustméz*, or "wine honey," a syrupy substance made by reducing must in copper cauldrons placed on a three-legged iron stand over fire, played an important role less as a beverage than as a sweetening agent in rural households and a treatment in folk medicine.

WHERE TO EAT ?

Around Lake Balaton, true gourmet experiences don't grow on trees. There are many agreeable restaurants with decent flavors and that requisite "Balaton feeling," and then there are establishments—unfortunately, the vast majority—catering to the palates of the masses with pedestrian dishes and at best mediocre wine lists. Needless to say, it's all about fish of all descriptions—small and large, pike-perch, eel, bream and carp, both the common and the crucian variety—but the quality is erratic. And yet there is a certain place here that

we have absolutely no bone to pick with in the fish department. It's a genuine epicurean destination, where the good folks realize there are more ways of mingling fish than the perennial *halászlé* or fisherman's soup (just think of fish pâté or terrine), and that the sheer quality of the finned ingredient matters as much as the quality of the wine used in cooking. And to top it all, it's a place with an authentic Balaton flavor, although it is not located directly on the shore. The Szent Orbán restaurant, perched on the side of Mount Badacsony, first won our admiration with a tangy fish cream soup made from pike-perch, catfish and bream—but no carp—and scented with lemon balm.

Served with a glass of Huba Szeremley's Mennyegzős Cuvée, which proved to be the perfect match, this soup was the exception that proved the old Hungarian rule that soup and wine don't mix. Completing this royal composition of flavors was a patty of fresh minced fish submerged in the soup, with a decoration of fish roe and milt in the center. Of course, such finesse takes a highly inventive chef, such as Lajos Takács, who maintains a herb garden at the back of the restaurant and has been known to decorate plates with delicious grape buds lightly sautéed in oil… And then there is that *bodzaszörp*, a grandma-style Hungarian cooler made with a syrup infused with fragrant elder blossoms and stirred with soda, which the kids will inevitably get instead of the ubiquitous Coke or orange juice from a box. For the adults, it's of course wines from the proprietor Huba Szeremley, to wash down an excellent fillet of gray longhorn or a cured ham of *mangalica*—both raised by the house. The only thing you shouldn't expect here is a quick meal, not to mention *fast* food. This place takes its time, and the patrons should do the same. Lajos Takács's flawless taste and unwavering touch guarantee that you will get the best you can get around Lake Balaton, literally elevated above the hubbub and clutter on the shore.

SZENT ORBÁN BORHÁZ
8261 Badacsony, Szegedi Róza út 22. Tel.: (36) 87 431 382.

Balatonboglár

Mountains always seem the tallest when viewed from another summit. It is from the southern shore of Lake Balaton that the extinct volcanoes across the water seem the most magical, and it is from here that the greatness or modesty of other wine regions is best perceived. The hill at Balatonboglár is tall enough to afford both perspectives.

U pon hearing the name of this region, any Hungarian will recall summer vacations, day trips, sailboats on the luminous waters of Lake Balaton, the green velvet of the vine-covered hills, and a table with the inevitable chequered tablecloth in the backyard of a cottage or on the patio of a restaurant, where some decent wine can be enjoyed on a hot afternoon. Being Hungary's largest tourist destination that also happens to be a wine region, the southern shore of Lake Balaton seems destined to make recreation complete by offering well-organized wine tasting opportunities. The wine region stretches along the northern slopes of Somogy county (the Külső and Belső-Somogy Hills), ranging on the shoreline from Zamárdi through Földvár and Lelle to Balatonberény, and extending to the south to an imaginary line connecting the villages of Andocs and Tab. It includes the communes of Andocs, Balatonberény, Balatonboglár, Balatonendréd, Balatonkeresztúr, Balatonlelle, Balatonszemes, Karád, Kéthely, Kőröshegy, Kötcse, Látrány, Lengyeltóti, Marcali, Ordacsahi, Somogysámson, Somogytúr, Szólád, Szőlősgyörök, Visznek, and Zamárdi. The total area of the wine region is 9,984 ha, of which 8,156 hectares are occupied by Class I sites. However, less than one third (2,899 ha) of this acreage is planted with vines.

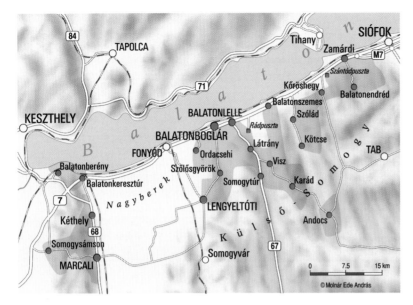

The local climate is quite beneficial for the cultivation of vines, with 1950-2000 hours of sunshine a year, a reasonably good heat sum (for instance, the mean temperature in July is 20-21 °C), and an annual rainfall of between 600 and 800 mm. The lack of extremes of climate makes vintage quantities fairly consistent.

Despite its extensiveness, the wine region shows a rather monotonous geological picture. The main mass of the hills consists of sandy-clayey lacustrine sediments deposited by the Pannonian inland sea in the Late Miocene. Remarkably, shells of long-extinct Congeria clams, called in Hungarian *kecskeköröm* or "goat's hoof," can still be found here and there in the soil of the vineyards. Two hills near the shore, the Kápolnadomb at Balatonboglár and the Várhegy at Fonyód, were created by tiny basalt volcanoes during the Pontian-Pliocene. In the Quaternary, the lacustrine deposits were covered by aeolian loess, today the primary parent material forming the soils of the vineyards—sand-bearing slope loess, loam, brown earth, brown earths and, sporadically, sand. The most common soil type is moderately cohesive loam.

The surface is mildly accentuated, with the hills dissected by gravel-filled valleys and delimited on the north by sand bars and peat moors near the shore. The southern slopes are characterized by gentle gradients, while the north faces often break off sharply (e.g. the loess wall of the Fonyód Hill).

Tracking down the history of local viticulture, we find that for a long time no distinctions were made between wines from the northern shore and those from the south. For instance, the Bishopric of Veszprém in the 14th century maintained well-tended vineyards south of the Lake, whose crop was vinified to make what was simply called "Balaton wine." Red wine grapes gained ground in the

OTTÓ LÉGLI, VINTAGE 1959

Légli's estate took shape between 1988 and 1992. Today his wife and daughter—both named Anna—assume a central role in running the family winery. Balatonboglár is a promising region, but not one known for spectacular breakthroughs and hardly ever eulogized for its wines. Talented as he has been from the start, how did Légli succeed in hoisting himself to the top flight of the country's growers? He has made it by scrupulous, reliable work, an early decision to think in terms of individual vineyards, and by never filling 25% Olaszrizling in the bottle if the label said Pinot Blanc... Let us add that his principal "partner," if this is the word for a distributor, is the same Attila Tálos of the Budapest Wine Society who has "discovered" and pushed into the limelight quite a few fine growers, including Imre Györgykovács and Krisztián Ungvári. Remarkably, Légli is an open-minded winemaker of enterprising spirit, but he never acts on reckless impulse—often a fault with people of similarly innovative disposition. His stylish wines are distinguished by a subtle vitality and a graceful note of citrus, with the exception of his exquisitely labeled barrique Chardonnay.

area during the era of Ottoman Occupation, and remained decisive until the onslaught of phylloxera. In the late 19th century, the southern shore was divided into smaller wine districts. The Kéthely district between the Nagyberek, a wooded marshland on the southwest shore, and Kisbalaton, a small lake connected with Lake Balaton by the Zala River, produced mainly red wines. The sandy vineyards between Balatonkeresztúr an Balatonszárszó typically made *siller*, a type of very light red bordering on rosé, while the district between Siófok and Balatonfőkajár was known for both white and red wines.

The phylloxera which wiped out two thirds of the country's vines did not spare the Balaton region, where only Mount Badacsony emerged relatively unscathed, thanks to the measure of applying carbon disulphide in the vineyards. The Hungarian State spared no effort in trying to mitigate the damage. It disbursed loans for vineyard reconstruction, promoted awareness among growers, and encouraged plantation in locations with a loose sandy soil, known to be immune to the root louse. One of these new vineyards was the Máriatelep property, established in 1891 on an extensive grazing range donated to the government by Count Tasziló Festetics. The main grapes chosen for plantation here were Olaszrizling, Zöldszilváni, Ezerjó, and Nagyburgundi ("Great Burgundy," today known as Kékfrankos) as the single red-wine variety. This project exemplified the rising tendency toward a preference for white wine grapes in the area. Although the Festetics property and the estate owned by the Benedictine abbey in Tihany evolved an advanced local culture of grapes and wines, the region as a whole did not begin to flourish until large-scale plantations were carried out toward the middle of the 20th century. Red wines also started to make a comeback at this time.

During the decades of communist rule, the production of the region was supervised and integrated by the huge Balatonboglár Winery. By the late 1980's, this state-owned giant developed a wide range of products that included the Chapel Hill series—smaller lots of better quality wines made for export—as well as substandard

wines and even cheap bulk sparkling for the masses. Today, the winery is called Balatonboglári Borászat, or BB as it is popularly known, and is owned by Henkell and Söhnlein.

In the late 1800's and the first half of the 20th century, the wine region went by the name of Balaton-melléke, and between the two World Wars was also referred to as the Somogy-Zala region. In 1949, it lost its wine region status, to be reinstated in this right in 1982 as the Dél-Balaton ("South Balaton") region. Two villages were added to it in 1997. In 2001, regulators yielded to pressure from BB and renamed the region as Balatonboglár, effectively giving precedence to a lobby over public interest. It would be nice to know what compelling arguments the agents of the winery proposed to convince the decision-makers that the name of a village with mostly mediocre wines, and a natural potential no better than in other communes in the area, should be chosen to lend its name to the region.

Today, Királyleányka is the area's leading grape variety (326 ha), followed by Chardonnay (293 ha), Zöld Veltelini (259 ha), Olaszrizling (211 ha), and Rizlingszilváni (156 ha). There are smaller quantities of Rajnai Rizling, Sárga and Ottonel Muskotály, Tramini and Sauvignon Blanc. Red wine grapes are represented by Merlot (170 ha), Kékfrankos (112 ha), the two Cabernets (together 90 ha), Pinot Noir (97 ha), Zweigelt (64 ha), and Kékoportó (58 ha).

One of the country's largest sources of mass-produced wines, the region has recently made a whole-hearted commitment to controlled vinification methods, at least as far as white wines are concerned. Fruity, aromatic and light, these wines tend toward softness on the vast lower end of the scale, but the better Pinot Blanc, Királyleányka and Chardonnay bottles can be fabulously elegant and vibrant in their acidity. In the quality light wine category, there is some very agreeable dry Irsai Olivér and Szürkebarát to be had. As a curiosity, the Öregbaglas Winery makes a varietal Semillon and increasingly fine naturally sweet wines.

The region's run-of-the-mill reds are mild and only moderately tannic, which makes them feasible red wine choices for consumers with hyperacidity. At the other end of the spectrum, for some time there has been a steady if small supply of full-bodied, more tannic yet elegant reds, more often than not Cabernet Sauvignon, which faithfully express the hidden merits of the region—and of course the people who make them.

BB produces many ordinary wines with poor acidity, very unlike its own Chapel Hill series. These full and firm wines are grown on the Kápolnadomb ("Chapel Hill") at Balatonboglár and on the slopes of the Várhegy at Fonyód. The soil of these volcanic hills is very different from the prevalent geological patterns of the region. Combined with more scrupulous selection and better technology, these soils go a long way to explaining the excellence of the Chapel Hill line. In addition to these products, the region's best wines have come out of the cellars of Ottó Légli in Szőlőskislak, János Konyári and the St. Donatus Winery in Balatonlelle, as well as the aforementioned Öregbaglas at Kéthely. Wines of formerly high repute from these parts included Boglári Muskotály, Boglári Chardonnay, Boglári Cabernet Sauvignon, and Kőröshegyi Olaszrizling.

The cellar rows at the János-hegy, Boróca-hegy and Hosszúdűlő vineyards between the villages of Buzsák and Táska are well worth a visit—not for their wines so much as for their quaint historic appeal.

Balatonfelvidék

Having witnessed glory days and rocked the cradle of cup-bearers to the king, the Balatonfelvidék is a magic treasure chest waiting to be opened.

I n all fairness, there are three wine regions that might equally deserve to be called *Balaton-felvidék* ("Balaton Highlands"): in addition to the wine region actually bearing the name, Balatonfüred-Csopak and Badacsony are also located on the uplands north of Lake Balaton. Actually, the natural potential and the wines of the region officially called Balatonfelvidék are so similar to those of Badacsony that there is practically nothing to justify their designation as two distinct wine regions. After this caveat, let us see how the Balatonfelvidék itself is divided. Geographically, it is split into two parts: an eastern wing between Badacsony and Balatonfüred-Csopak, which includes the northern section of the Kál Basin and areas north of that, and a western wing that basically

corresponds to the area of the Keszthely Mountains. The two segments do not communicate as Badacsony is wedged between them.

Administratively, the wine region is split between Veszprém County and Zala County, and includes the following communities: a) Balatonhenye, Hegyesd, Köveskál, Minszentkálla, Monostorapáti, Szentbékkálla in the Kál District; b) Balatonederics, Csabrendek, Lesencefalu, Lesenceistvánd, Lesencetomaj, Nemesvita, Sáska, Sümeg, Sümegprága, Zalahaláp in the Balatonederics-Lesence District; c) Balatongyörök, Cserszegtomaj, Gyenesdiás, Hévíz-Egregy, Rezi, Várvölgy, and Vonyarcvashegy in the Cserszeg District. The Balatonfelvidék has a total of 5,164 hectares authorized for regional status, but

99

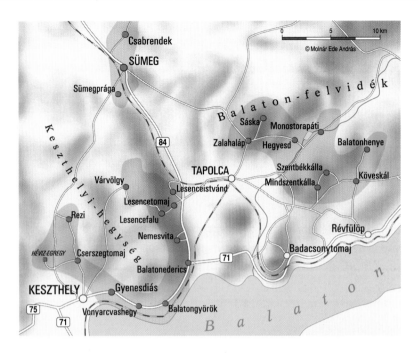

Red sandstone on the northern shore of Lake Balaton

this includes only 57 hectares of Class I sites. Only 1,497 hectares are under cultivation,

The climate, generally akin to that of Badacsony, is sunny, temperate, and conducive to predictable yields. Some areas further inland from the Lake may have less favorable conditions, but the region as a whole can be regarded as warm compared to the national average.

Each of the region's two wings has its own distinct geology. The bedrock of the eastern wing consists of Triassic dolomite and limestone overlain by Pliocene sands, but of much more consequence are the Pliocene basalt and tuff that make up the hills delimiting the Tapolca Basin and the Kál Basin from the west and the north. Whether in the form of bedrock or weathered debris mixed with the soil, these volcanic rocks have a decisive influence on the taste and character of the wines. The near-identical geology and soil structure, as well as the analysis of the wines, organoleptic and chemical, make it seem unreasonable to divorce this area from the Badacsony wine region.

The western wing of the Balatonfelvidék, notably the environs of the Keszthely Mountains, is characterized by a bedrock of Triassic dolomite and marls (Rezi, Balatonederics, Balatongyörök), less significant occurrences of Pannonian sand, and a total absence of basalts. The wines from these parts may be less full than in the Kál Basin to

VIRÁG TÓTH, VINTAGE 1979

One of the prominent producers of the region is the Scheller Estate (Hét Kál Vidéki Scheller Szőlőbirtok) in Monostorapáti, where Sándor Tóth (vintage 1937) rekindled a family winery first established in 1772. The extraordinary concentration of volcanic matter in the soil of the Táltoshegy and Áldozó vineyards, coupled with a consistently late harvest, help the family craft momentous, firm and long-lived Chardonnay (labeled as Kereklevelű or "Round Leaf," the old Hungarian name for this grape) and Zöld Veltelini, a potentially great variety unduly neglected in Hungary. Both of these wines need to be laid down for a few years to come into their own. Tóth's daughter, Virág, brings further refinement of taste, and now also a degree in enology, to steering this remarkable family venture.

the east, but they have a very appealing delicacy and elegance.

Seen as a whole, the region has a great variety of soil types, including rendzina over dolomite, limestone and marl, and moderately cohesive lessivage brown earths, brown earth, chernoziom, and lithic-loamy talus over Pannonian clay, weathered sandstone and Pleistocene loess. The basalt lava and tuff evolved lithic and earthy erosional soils and black *nyirok* (e.g. on the Fekete Hill at Szentbékkálla). Combined with these soils, the gentle articulation of the terrain—with valleys, escarpments, and moderately steep pediments—provides ideal conditions for growing fine wine.

There is a 2000-year tradition of viticulture in the Balatonfelvidék, supported by an unbroken string of archeological evidence since Roman times. Hungarians themselves began cultivating vines here more than 1000 years ago. The region rose to prominence in the early Middle Ages, not least as a source of wines for the royal pleasure of the Árpád Dynasty. The monasteries of Almád and Salföld on the periphery of the Kál Basin also produced wine for their own use, or else had the locals grow the wine for them.

In the first half of the 19th century, what was then called the Balatonmelléke (Balaton District) officially included all the growing areas that are today divided between three wine regions, namely Badacsony, Balatonfüred-Csopak, and Balatonfelvidék. Regulations enacted in 1897 renamed this wine area collectively as Badacsony, which engendered several further designations and titles and ultimately led to the separation of the region, in the early 1990's, into Badacsony proper and the rump western section of the Balatonfelvidék. The actual regional name *Balatonfelvidék* did not appear in the language of wine legislation until 1999, but now it seems to have finally taken root.

The Balatonfelvidék is essentially a white wine region, with Olaszrizling still leading the list of grape varieties with 784 hectares, followed by the fashionable Chardonnay (231 ha) and much less Rizlingszilváni (88 ha) and Szürkebarát (79 ha). Zöld Veltelini (68 ha) and Zenit (39 ha) both seem very promising.

The wines do not display consistent regional character. Those from the eastern wing can be easily taken for a wine grown in Badacsony, while the wines from the western wing resemble those of the Balatonfüred-Csopak region. This state of affairs is a faithful reflection of the picture suggested by the area's geological make-up, demonstrating the power of particular soils to take precedence over grape varieties. In addition to intense, firm Olaszrizling, some

A vineyard overlooking Lake Balaton

101

In the area of Monostorapáti, the genre of the *főbor* ("prime wine" or "principal wine") is enjoying somewhat of a renaissance. This is the ancient Hungarian name for Szamorodni-style wines, best known from Tokaj, for which the nobly rotted berries are picked along with grapes unaffected by botrytis (unlike for the Aszú, which is made by macerating hand-selected botrytized fruit in base wine or must). The result of this simplified late-harvest technique is typically a concentrated, high-alcohol wine that often contains residual sugar.

During the past decade, local growers have begun to realize the importance of quality over quantity. Still, few will volunteer to limit the yield in their vineyards, despite the centuries-old common knowledge that overloaded vines never produce great wine. As the villagers of Monostorapáti say, "The woman making love to many has not one true love of her own."

Other wineries of repute in this eastern part of the region include Kál-Vin, Szakálvin, and Ódon. Further to the west in the Balatonederics-Lesence District, the young Lesence Estate is equipped with top-drawer technology, but needs more time to prove itself. Based in the Cserszeg District but also growing grapes further west and around the town of Tata to the northeast, the Németh Winery has attained remarkable success, owing to its reliance on excellent enologists and the underestimated but fine terroirs of Zala County.

The wine culture of the Balatonfelvidék is symbolized by the cellars and press houses that continue to define its landscape today. Beside the unsophisticated cellars of local villagers, the members of the lesser nobility and the middle classes erected quite a few distinguished buildings in the rustic baroque and neoclassicist style. The Festetics Présház in Cserszegtomaj and the Taverna in Gyenesdiás are two wonderful examples.

The end of winter dormancy

full-bodied Chardonnay and zesty Zöld Veltelini wines have come out of this region. In better years, Muscat Ottonel, Zenit and Szürkebarát are often vinified in the semi-dry or semi-sweet style. Historically, the Olaszrizling harvested from the Bece Hill was the most highly regarded wine of this region.

Balatonfüred-Csopak

From Anna Balls to spa resorts, and from buoyant wines to intellectual ones, this region has something in store for everyone. If you like a charming white, you can nose around in Almádi or Aszófő, while the famed Berekhát vineyard at Csopak will give you a taste of noble pride.

The wine region spans a 12 km-long strip between Zánka and Balatonalmádi on the northern shore of Lake Balaton. Geographically, the region forms the eastern part of the Balaton-felvidék, understood as a geographical unit instead of the wine region of the same name. Administratively, it includes the Veszprém County communes of Alsóörs, Aszófő, Balatonakali, Balatonalmádi, Balatoncsicsó, Balatonfüred, Balatonszőlős, Balatonudvari, Csopak, Dörgicse, Felsőörs, Lovas, Mencshely, Monoszló, Óbudavár, Örvényes, Paloznak, Pécsely, Szentantalfa, Szentjakabfa, Tagyon, Tihany, Vászoly, and Zánka. The wine region's total area of 6,341 hectares includes 5,792 hectares of Class I sites, but only 2,143 hectares are actually planted. One reason for this low level of utilization is the fact that many excellent vineyards were divided up by non-local owners for building weekend cottages. These sites are lost to wine production for a long time to come, perhaps forever.

The temperate continental climate of the Balatonfüred-Csopak region is similar to that of Badacsony. The angle of the slopes and the articulation of the terrain have produced some excellent microclimates in the area. The region extends to the north as far as the ground surface keeps rising; quality wine production ends where the terrain melts into the flat Veszprém plateau. The explanation for this is

Balatonfüred is a cultural center as well as the heart of a wine region

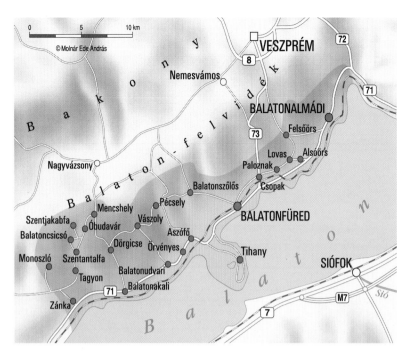

a simple one: whereas the southern slopes are sheltered, the level ground above is ruthlessly exposed to the cold northerly winds sweeping down from the Magas-Bakony Mountains.

The region's geology is rather complex. The most ancient formation is Silurian metamorphic phyllite, a type of schist, with volcanic intercalations that grow excellent wine near the villages of Alsóörs and Lovas, albeit on a very small area. The schist is overlain by Upper Permian sandstones, which have produced distinct red soils enriched in silica. Overlying these sandstones in turn are the diverse carbonate rocks of the Triassic period—marl, calcareous marl, dolomite—whose weathered calcareous matter imparts a white color to the soil. The combination of red and white soils invests the land with a unique appeal.

The stratification described above is characteristic of the region east of the Tihany Peninsula. The bedrock to the west consists of similar Triassic calcareous formations, but here they are mixed with the green weathered debris of an early tuff diffusion, and both schists and red sandstones are missing. In smaller basins, sandy-clayey Pannonian sediments are evident in patches. Young Pliocene basalt makes an appearance where the region borders on the Kál Basin to the west. The most visible example of this basalt outcrop is the Hegyestű, a crag dubbed the "Pointed Needle" near the village of Monoszló. The slopes here are covered by a thin blanket of loess, often no more than a couple of feet thick. With its prevalent basalt rock, this Monoszló district and its wines resemble the Badacsony region closely, whereas the wines grown near Balatonfüred and Csopak proper are more akin to those from the western wing of the Balaton-felvidék region, where dolomite and limestone also reign supreme. The flagrant disregard for natural geological boundaries in delineating this wine region lends an odd sense of ambivalence to the region's wines.

Soil conditions are equally varied, with forest soils over schist, red Permian sandstone and Quaternary loess, as well as rendzina that formed over Triassic limestone, dolomite and marl. The influence of these calcareous soils can be felt readily in the distinct, firmly etched acidity of wines grown around Csopak and Balatonfüred.

The hills making up the Balaton-felvidék rise gently from the sand bars and peat moors just north of Lake Balaton. The terrain is diversi-

A vineyard near Csopak with the charactersitic red soil of the region

105

fied and intensely articulated without steep gradients. The range parallel to the shoreline is dissected by valleys running inland from the Lake (e.g. the Nivegy Valley, famous for its wines) and smaller intermountain basins, such as the Pécsely Basin.

Viticulture in this part of Pannonia possibly started before the Roman Conquest, and was certainly highly advanced during the tenure of the Romans here. This is corroborated by the ruins of Villa Urbana, a roman residence from the 2nd or the 3rd century that was unearthed at Baláca-puszta. Clusters of grapes and vineyard scenes are recurring motifs of the ornamental relief and the frescoes found in this villa.

A wealth of written evidence shows that viticulture in the area that is the Balatonfüred-Csopak wine region today was well-established in the earliest centuries of the Hungarian nation. The country's first king, Saint Stephen, presented the nuns of a cloister established in 1018 in the Veszprém Valley with a fine lot of vines near the village of Paloznak, complete with a *szőlős* or "viner," meaning a serf charged with tending the vineyard. According to a charter from 1082, the Bishop of Veszprém had a holding of vines in Csopak. In 1211, the town of Balatonfüred became the property of the Church when it was acquired by the Tihany Abbey. In later times, the aristocracy owned substantial vineyard acreage in the region, not to mention the kings and queens who also became proprietors.

During the Ottoman Occupation, this strip along the shore formed part of the last line of Hungarian defense against the conquering Turkish troops. The area around the fortified castles were exposed to ceaseless skirmishes, contributing significantly to the eventual reduction of vineyard acreage in the region.

In the first half of the 19th century, Balatonfüred, often called Füred for short, emerged as the "capital" of Lake Balaton, where members of the nobility and an increasingly well-heeled bourgeoisie came from all parts of the country to spend their holidays, take hydrotherapy, and fill up on cultural events. In the summer season, the town ran a fully fledged theatrical program, and often hosted dignitaries of Hungarian politics and literature for a few weeks of relaxation. Each year, an especially large number of visitors convened to attend the so-called Anna Ball, still a popular annual event today. The girl who created a stir with her beauty at this gala had a good chance of returning home engaged. All this hustle and bustle of course provided excellent publicity for the area's wines, whose fame was carried to every corner of the country by those who spent their holidays in the town.

MIHÁLY FIGULA, VINTAGE 1952

Having graduated from the Budapest University of Horticulture, Figula paved the way for his private career by working for large wineries in Balatonfüred, Sopron (8,000 tons of grapes per year!), Győr, and Csopak. However, as the family counted among their ancestors such notables as István Tolnai, the prominent estate owner of Balatonfüred, Figula clearly could not wait too long before establishing a venture of his own. In 1993 he came out with a few thousand bottles, and has kept increasing his production ever since. Relying mostly on vineyards around the village of Balatonszőlős, Figula makes excellent delicate wines, always distinguished by their emphatic acidity, regardless of the vintage year. In our assessment, his Pinot Gris and Olaszrizling routinely outclass his trendy Chardonnays.

The phylloxera devastation only caused a temporary setback in the successful production of local wines. For a long time, the area of Balatonfüred and Csopak was lumped together with the Balaton-melléke and then with Badacsony, and only gained independent wine region status in 1959. In 1997, the communities of Mencshely and Tihany were added to its territory.

Balatonfüred-Csopak is dominated almost exclusively by white wines today, but this has not always been the case. Red wine production here was quite significant in the 19th century, but was largely abandoned in the early 1900's. Red wines resurfaced after the Great War, but remained confined to a very small area within the region. Nowadays the leading variety is Olaszrizling (886 ha), followed by Rizlingszilváni at a distant second (201 ha). Over the past decade and a half, Chardonnay has gained a lot of ground (145 ha).

Olaszrizling wines, generally regarded as the most successful in the region, show an interesting variation of character from east to west. Those grown in Csopak tend to be elegant, delicate and light even at higher concentrations of alcohol and acidity. Those around Balatonfüred, Balatonszőlős and Arács have more body and extract but can be softer in certain years. Around the villages of Akali and Zánka, near the western boundary of the region, Olaszrizling can yield a positively heady wine. This overview seems to be valid for the moment, but the varying philosophy, yields and technical sophistication of the emerging private estates may soon cause a few surprises and alter the ways in which we think of the region's wine styles.

In the shadow of the all-important Olaszrizling, the formerly well-regarded Akali Muskotály seems to be disappearing from the shelves. It's a pity, because this wine attained somewhat of a cult following domestically in the troubled second half of the 20th century, on account of the fact that it was available in a semi-dry and a fully dry version—very unlike the semi-sweet or downright syrupy Muscat wines that were the name of the game in the era of planned economy. Mention must be made of Mihály Figula's innovative Semillon, a non-

native variety that seems to be very promising in this region. The two red-wine enclaves are the Tihany Peninsula and the vicinity of Dörgicse, producing red and rosé from Kékfrankos (69 ha in Tihany), Merlot, and Zweigelt (46 ha in Tihany).

Along with Figula' excellent family winery based in Balatonfüred, the cutting edge is represented by the Jásdi Winery in Csopak. These two outstanding producers are followed by a number of promising wineries of a lower rank, including but not limited to Fodorvin, Zoltán Hudák, the Pántlika Winery, the Salánki Family Winery, and Vinarius. Although Balatonfőkajár falls out-

The Jásdi Winery

107

A renovated press house near the village of Aszófő

Permian red sandstone near Paloznak (Balatonfüred-Csopak region)

Calcareous soil over Triassic marl, limestone, and dolomite (Balatonfüred-Csopak)

side the official wine region, the natural potential of the village and the style of the very promising wines made here by Lajos Feindl links this winery intimately to Balatonfüred-Csopak.

The wine-hill architecture in this region is typified by cellars built by the lesser nobility, such as the Kusztodiátus cellar in Dörgicse. Foremost among the larger cellars is that of the Tihany Abbey, built around 1822 and boasting naves 69 and 43 meters long. The Ranolder-Jásdi cellar in Csopak is also quite impressive in its aristocratic grandeur. The row of peasant cellars in the village of Aszófő is a protected national monument, but is falling rapidly into disrepair.

Balatonmelléke

This is one wine region bursting with quiescent force. Bussay and his fellow-magicians have now begun to coax the genie—the spirit of the place—out of its bottle, and lure it into their own.

The "Balaton District" wine region consists of three groups of villages scattered around Zala County. The Csáford District on the slopes of the Keszthely Mountains includes Csáford, Pakod, Vindornyalak, Vindornyaszőlős, Zalabér, Zalaszántó, and Zalaszentgrót. The Szentgyörgyvár District directly west of Lake Balaton comprises Dióskál, Egeracsa, Garabonc, Homokkomárom, Nagyrada, Orosztony, Sármellék, Szentgyörgyvár, Zalakaros, and Zalaszabar. The Mura District along the Mura River on Hungary's western border is made up of the communities of Csörnyeföld, Letenye, Murarátka, Muraszemenye, Szécsisziget, Tormafölde, and Zajk. The wine region occupies a total of 6,079 hectares, of which 4,107 hectares are ranked as Class I growing sites. Only 1,524 hectares are actually planted with vines at present.

Zala county has a well-tempered climate that is cooler and wetter than the Hungarian average. The Mura District in fact has the highest annual rainfall in the country at 900 mm, but because almost all of this moisture arrives in four large doses, the vines here do not get any fewer hours of sun than elsewhere on the same latitude.

Most of the region consists of gentle hills with a core made up of the sandy-clayey sediments of the former Pannonian Lake, and covered by a thin stratum of Quaternary loess. Somewhat distinct from this general geological pattern is the area around Vindornyalak, Vindornyaszőlős and Zalaszántó, where the vineyards climb on the northern basalt slopes of the Keszthely Hills, overshadowed by the volcanic dome of Tátika. Throughout the region, loess-bearing loam alternates with brown earth.

Charters and other written records attest to a flourishing local viticulture since mediaeval times. By the late 19th century, this region west of Lake Balaton had become one of the largest sources of generally fine wine in the country. Subsequent to the phylloxera epidemic, this highly evolved culture of wine faded away fast, and the traditional wine grapes were supplanted by direct-producing varieties like Noah, Delaware, and Othello. Also known for its production of

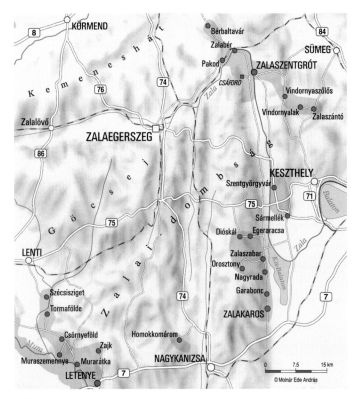

table grapes, notably Chasselas, Zala before the Great War formed part of the South Transdanubia-Balatonmelléke region. The region as we know it today was designated in 1997 as Zala, but was renamed in 2000 as the Balatonmelléke region.

The most widely planted grape in this fundamentally white-wine region is Olaszrizling (138 ha), followed by Rizlingszilváni (64 ha), Zöld Veltelini (65 ha), and Chardonnay (56 ha). Királyleánka, Rajnai Rizling and Zala Gyöngye together amount to less than 100 hectares, while 96 hectares are planted with red-wine varieties. More responsible plantation policies over the past couple of decades have scaled back direct producers to under 7 hectares in sites of regional status.

In its current incarnation, the Balatonmelléke wine region is still largely unfamiliar to professionals and wine consumers in terms of its quality and quantity potential, since very few wines have been commercially released to date. Among the handful of outstanding producers special credit is due to the Vinum Veres Winery, known for characterful, rich aromatic whites harvested in Csáford, and the very first bottling, in the late 1990's, of the rare Pintes variety. The Németh Winery, already mentioned in connection with the Balatonfelvidék region, is now also sourcing most of its wines from Zala County. Based in Muraszemenye-Csörnyeföld in the southernmost tip of the region, Dr. László Bussay makes small batches of white wines that are superb even when measured against the highest national standards. These include big and round dry examples as well as wonderful, resounding wines with some residual sugar and a faint echo of the wine style of Alsólendva just a stone's throw beyond the Slovenian border.

A relic of local folk architecture is the *boronapince*. These characteristic "log cellars" survive today in dwindling numbers along the southern border in Rédics, Muratátka, the Vörcsök Hill, and around Alsólendva. National monument status has been awarded to the last *boronapince* in the village of Nagykávás, but it seems nothing can save another row of crumbling log cellars from eventual demise. With their neat thatched roofs, these cellars used to be quite a spectacle to behold on the wine-hill at Nagykutas.

LÁSZLÓ BUSSAY, VINTAGE 1958

Here is a man who has come to embody an entire wine region as the only grower bottling wine in the Balatonmelléke near the Slovenian and Croatian borders (5 hectares producing and 5 hectares as yet unplanted). Based in the village of Muraszemenye, Bussay had been an expert huntsman before he turned to making wine as a pastime, so the visitor may get lucky and test the synergy between the man's wine and his gifted ways of handling game in the kitchen. A district practitioner by profession, Dr. Bussay has had easy access to information about where the best wines used to be grown in the area. Whenever he chose a site—on the slopes of the Pál, Kövecs, and Vörcsök Hills—the main consideration was never economy but sheer quality. He observes the same commitment in the work of plantation and cultivation. Bussay himself had always been aware of the great potential of Zala County. When he released his first bottles with their distinctive, wonderful labels, the wines were immediately recognized for their grand style, resting on a solid foundation of acidity and extract. One is tempted to call these wines downright inspiring—not just in the sense that they encourage spirited conviviality, but also that they might move us to help rescue this dormant wine region from eternal sleep.

Bükkalja

This is a truly special Hungarian phenomenon: a designated wine region without a single bottle to its name that would be available in the wine stores of Budapest... And yet the region's heritage and potential warrant the advance confidence that the wines, when they appear in commercially feasible quantities, will be good enough indeed.

Since the phylloxera devastation, the Bükkalja ("Bükk Foothills") has been overshadowed by the neighboring Eger region. This was not always the case. In the 19th century, when the slopes of the Bükk Mountains belonged to the Miskolc wine area, wines grown around the town of Miskolc often fetched a higher price than those of Eger. In 1970, the Bükkalja became an autonomous wine region, but most of its wine today is bottled by various Eger-based producers under their own label.

Situated at the southern reaches of the Bükk Mountains between the towns of Eger and Miskolc, the region is part of Borsod-Abaúj-Zemplén County, and includes the communes of Bogács, Borsodgeszt, Bükkaranyos, Bükkzsérc, Cserépfalu, Cserépváralja, Emőd, Harsány, Kács, Kisgyőr, Kistokaj, Mályi, Mezőkövesd, Miskolc, Nyékládháza, Sály, Tard, Tibolddaróc, and Vatta. The region spans an enormous growing area of 17,636 hectares, of which 15,323 hectares have been ranked as potential Class I sites. Under the circumstances, it is difficult to see why actual cultivation is limited to 1,183 hectares. The situation becomes even more incomprehensible if we consider the favorable climate. The Bükk range rising behind the south-south-southwest-facing

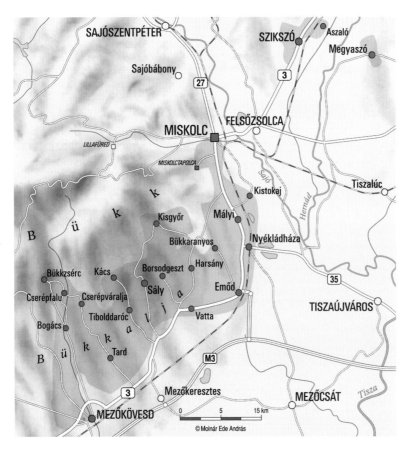

Vines in the region are first mentioned by a charter from 1313. In the 15th and 16th centuries, a number of villages were actively engaged in viticulture, with Diósgyőr and Miskolc as the centers. In the 18th century, the local wine trade began to flourish as increasing quantities of must from grapes harvested in Tokaj were vinified and matured in Miskolc, where the local rhyolite tuff rock lent itself to carving fine, extensive cellars for this purpose. The region's own production was plentiful, and the wines, especially from Miskolc, were known and well-liked throughout the country. In the 19th and 20th centuries, the village of Tibolddaróc was a renowned source of base wines, mostly using Olaszrizling and Furmint, for sparkling wine production. At one time, the Tibolddaróci Olaszrizling even attained a measure of repute as the region's best varietal wine.

Today, the wines produced in Bükkalja are almost exclusively white. It has no traditional grape varieties to speak of, unless the direct producers, which have survived in massive quantities here and there in the region, can be regarded as "traditional." The grapes recommended for the region are Chardonnay, Cserszegi Fűszeres (79 ha), Leányka (741 ha), Olaszrizling (120 ha), and the red wine varieties of Cabernet Sauvignon, Cabernet Franc, Kékfrankos (61 ha), Merlot, and Zweigelt (68 ha).

Little is known about the region's true potential, mainly because the often zesty, vigorous and aromatic wines that can be tasted in the local cellars rarely make it into the bottle. Also, many small growers have got stuck with direct producer grapes and find it hard to make a change. Two promising growers based in Bogács, László Prókai and Ottó Szerencsi, started out a few years ago, and are still searching for a style that will best suit their wines.

The Bükkalja region harbors an astonishing number of peasant cellars carved in the rhyolite tuff rock. They often form entire street-like rows in the villages, most notably in Tibolddaróc (1000 cellars), Bogács (600 cellars), and Cserépfalu (450 cellars).

slopes protects the vineyards from cold northerly winds, but also captures much of the moisture coming in. This can lead to arid conditions, often with no more than 130 mm of rainfall in the summer season.

The geology of the region is relatively complex. The bedrock underneath the northern slopes consists of Triassic and Jurassic black shales and limestone, eocene and Oligocene deposits although grape production is negligible here. Similarly to Eger, further west, the most valuable sites are located on the southern slopes with a streak of Miocene rhyolite tuff underneath, overlain by Pannonian clay, sand, and lignite. The youngest formation in the area is Quaternary loess. The rhyolite tuff has produced black *nyirok* soils, but elsewhere brown earth and brown forest soils dominate. Further south from the foothills, chernoziom and prairie soils over Quaternary deposits gradually take over. The mild gradients and escarpments that characterize the terrain would make the region ideally suited even for industrialized cultivation.

Csongrád, Hajós-Baja, Kunság

*Three wine regions, with much in common in the style of wines, and even more in
the people who make them... The Great Plain is not a bad terroir, as long as you
know what to expect from it: sound, unpretentious wines for everyday drinking.*

CSONGRÁD

The Csongrád wine region is located in
the Great Plain on the right bank of
the lower Tisza River at Hungary's
southern border. Administratively part of
Csongrád County, the region's communities
are grouped in four districts as follows: a)
Csongrád District: the town of Csongrád itself; b) Kisteleki District: Balástya, Csengele,
Kistelek, Pusztaszer; c) Pusztamérges
District: Forráskút, Öttömös, Pusztamérges,
Ruzsa, Üllés; d) Mórahalom District: Ásotthalom, Bordány, Domaszék, Kiskundorozsma, Mórahalom, and Zákányszék. The total
area is 14,311 ha, including 2,595 and 8,474

hectares in Class I and II sites, respectively.
The remainder consists of potential sites
ranked as Class III which, unlike elsewhere in
the country, are recognized as part of the wine
region as well.

Like the Kunság region, Csongrád is characterized by an extreme continental climate,
with low rainfall and the highest average temperatures of the country. The abundance of
sunshine (2050-2100 hours annually) and
heat helps the grapes ripen with a high degree
of sugar. In the hot and arid summer season,
the sandy soils not only warm through quickly but they also reflect the rays of the sun back
to the vines, sometimes resulting in temperatures of 60 °C near the surface. The fall is

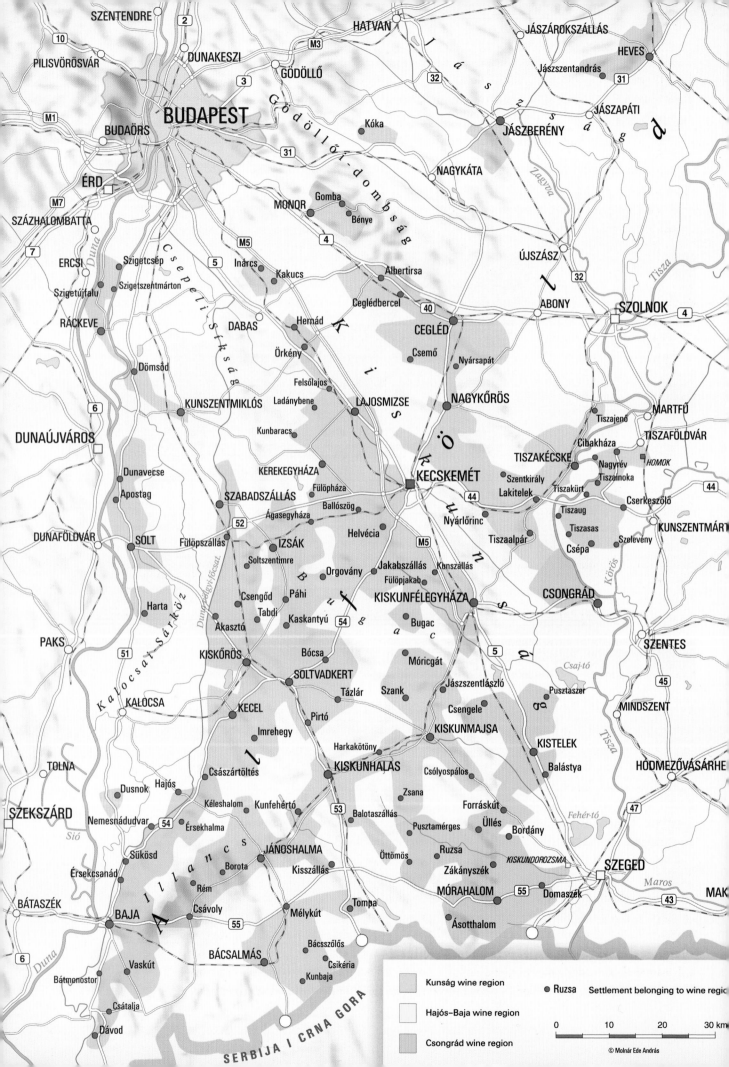

SZENTENDRE 2

10 PILISVÖRÖSVÁR

DUNAKESZI

M3 HATVAN

JÁSZÁROKSZÁLLÁS

HEVES 31

GÖDÖLLŐ

Jászszentandrás

BUDAPEST

3

Kóka

JÁSZAPÁTI

BUDAÖRS

JÁSZBERÉNY

M1

ÉRD

31

NAGYKÁTA

Zagyva

M7

Gomba

SZÁZHALOMBATTA

MONOR

Bénye

Gödöllői-dombság

ÚJSZÁSZ

32

7

Szigetcsép

Inárcs

Kakucs

Albertirsa

ABONY

Tisza

SZOLNOK

ERCSI

Duna

5

M5

Szigetszentmárton

Ceglédbercel

40

Szigetújfalu

Hernád

CEGLÉD

4

RÁCKEVE

DABAS

Csepeli síkság

Örkény

Csemő

Nyársapát

MARTFŰ

6

Dömsöd

Felsőlajos

TISZAFÖLDVÁR

DUNAÚJVÁROS

Kis

LAJOSMIZSE

NAGYKŐRÖS

Tiszajenő

KUNSZENTMIKLÓS

Ladánybene

Cibakháza

HOMOK

Dunavecse

Kunbaracs

TISZAKÉCSKE

Nagyrév

44

Apostag

KEREKEGYHÁZA

Szentkirály

Tiszainoka

ö

Fülöpháza

Tiszakürt

SZABADSZÁLLÁS

Lakitelek

Cserkeszőlő

DUNAFÖLDVÁR

Ballószög

KECSKEMÉT

44

KUNSZENTMÁRT

52

Ágasegyháza

k

Tiszaug

SOLT

Fülöpszállás

Helvécia

Tiszasas

Szelevény

u

Nyárlőrinc

IZSÁK

M5

Tiszaalpár

Csépa

Soltszentimre

Körös

n

Orgovány

Jakabszállás

Kunszállás

Harta

Csengőd

Páhi

Fülöpjakab

CSONGRÁD

s

PAKS

Tabdi

KISKUNFÉLEGYHÁZA

51

Akasztó

Kaskantyú

54

á

SZENTES

Bugac

c

KISKŐRÖS

Bócsa

g

Móricgát

5

45

KALOCSA

SOLTVADKERT

Jászszentlászló

Pusztaszer

Tázlár

Szank

MINDSZENT

KECEL

Pirtó

Csengele

g

Imrehegy

KISKUNMAJSA

KISTELEK

TOLNA

Harkakötöny

l

Balástya

Császártöltés

KISKUNHALAS

HÓDMEZŐVÁSÁRHE

Dusnok

Hajós

Csólyospálos

SZEKSZÁRD

Kéleshalom

Kunfehértó

Zsana

Forráskút

47

Sió

Nemesnádudvar

54

Balotaszállás

Üllés

Érsekhalma

53

Pusztamérges

Bordány

Fehér-tó

Sükösd

JÁNOSHALMA

Ruzsa

Öttömös

Érsekcsanád

Borota

Kisszállás

Zákányszék

KISKUNDOROZSMA

SZEGED

BÁTASZÉK

Rém

MÓRAHALOM

BAJA

Csávoly

Tompa

55

Domaszék

Maros

6

55

Ásotthalom

43

MAK

Duna

Vaskút

BÁCSALMÁS

Bácsszőlős

Bátmonostor

Csikéria

Csátalja

Kunbaja

Dávod

SERBIJA I CRNA GORA

Kunság wine region

Ruzsa Settlement belonging to wine regio

Hajós–Baja wine region

0   10   20   30 km

Csongrád wine region

© Molnár Ede András

typically warm, long, and sunny, followed by an extremely harsh winter. Frost damage is not uncommon in the fall and the spring.

The prevailing bedrock is Holocene alluvial calcareous sand, with more cohesive alluvial mud around Csongrád and, less frequently, Pleistocene loess or aeolic drift sand. Soil types include alluvial soils without calcareous content, acid sand and black earth from the Tisza River; as well as calcareous aeolic sand mixed here and there with loess, in part originating from the Danube. Sandy soils tend to have a low humus and nutrient content, but the relatively high ground water levels (3-6 m below the surface) are easy for the vine's roots to reach. The terrain is typically flat throughout the region, with gentle dunes no more than 2-3 m tall.

The first record of viticulture in the area is in the 1075 charter of the Garamszentbenedek Abbey, which refers to vineyards around the village of Alpár along the Tisza River. The town of Szeged and the other *oppodiums*—commercially important settlements with privileged trade and tax rights—had their own estates of vines in the 14th century, not only locally but also in the famous Syrmia further south (today in Serbia). The 15th century saw new vineyards planted in the immediate vicinity of Szeged. During the Ottoman Occupation, wine was an important source of income for the Ottoman officials and landowners. The first red wine grapes arrived in Hungary from the Balkans around this time, led by the Kadarka variety. The prevailing training method of the day did not employ any form of support for the vines.

The departure of the conquerors ushered in the civilization of the Great Plain where conditions had grown quite savage during the Ottoman Occupation. In 1779, Queen Maria Theresa issued an edict urging the plantation of vines in the Great Plain as a measure to bind the quicksand. Plantation on a large scale continued in the 19th century, and came to play a crucial role in replenishing the country's wine production when it was decimated by the phylloxera invasion. This root louse cannot survive in loose sandy soils with a quartz content over 75-80%, and thus it did not wreak havoc in the

Great Plain as it did elsewhere in the country. The extensive plantation projects were also instrumental in converting the uninhabited reaches of *puszta*, the wasteland steppe, into a farmland with scattered *tanya*, Hungary's equivalent of the ranch.

For most of the 20th century, wine growing remained an important business in the area, but began to decline in the 1970's as the government gradually withdrew subsidies covering production costs. The process ended with the collapse of Hungary's Eastern-Bloc wine markets, which in turn set off a radical reduction of the acreage under cultivation—all this despite the fact that in 1990 Csongrád attained independent status as a wine region. Now that the Eastern markets are no longer around to encourage the production of inferior wines, professionals and consumers are curious to see whether Csongrád will be able to readjust to the higher quality standards dictated by the West.

A little over half of the region's production consists of white wines today, with Olaszrizling (120 ha), Kunleány (82 ha), Rajnai Rizling (96 ha), and Zalagyöngye (94 ha) being the main varieties. Red wine grapes are represented by Kékfrankos (352 ha) and Zweigelt (127 ha). Formerly, the most popular varieties included Kadarka, Kövidinka, and Izsáki Sárfehér.

The wines generally resemble those of the Kunság region, although quality wines in Csongrád claim a higher share of the total production. They tend to have a medium to high alcohol content but fairly low acidity if the grapes are harvested ripe. Although fine wine production in commercial quantities is unheard of in these parts, the area has certainly had its own popular wines over the last century, such as Pusztamérgesi Olaszrizling, Csongrádi Kadarka, Csongrádi Cabernet, and Csongrádi Kékfrankos. Two local growers of distinction are Miklós Csikai in Csongrád and Sándor Somodi in Ásotthalom, who makes decent, clean wines occasionally capable of gusto. These wines hold out the promise of progress and improvement inherent in this much-abused region.

Vines planted in sand

HAJÓS-BAJA

The wine region is located on the western reaches of the low loess plateau between the Danube and Tisza Rivers, making a transition into the sandy terrain of the Kunság region to the north. Administratively part of Bács-Kiskun County, it comprises the communities of Baja, Bátmonostor, Császártöltés, Csátalja, Csávoly, Érsekcsanád, Érsekhalma, Hajós, Nemesnádudvar, Rém, Sükösd, and Vaskút. None of the region's 14,874 hectares have been designated as Class I growing sites, though 6,631 hectares earned Class II rank. Only 1,681 hectares of this acreage are under cultivation at present. The wine region as we know it split off from the Alföld region in 1990, although its area was somewhat reduced in 1997.

The climate is similar to that of the neighboring Kunság region, with a harsh winter and an extremely hot summer characterized by some of the largest heat sums and insolation in the country. While the annual rainfall is modest, the vines are well-adapted to the arid conditions. A greater risk is presented by frost,

particularly in the winter and the early spring.

Hajós-Vaskút is a typical example of a flat wine region—none of the loess banks exceed 200 m in height—although its geological features are somewhat distinct from those of other wine producing areas in the Great Plain. While those are underlain by a sandy bedrock, here the very low mounds consist mainly of Pleistocene loess, with aeolian sand intruding only in smaller patches. Soil conditions are more favorable as well, with prevailing loess-bearing loam and calcareous chernoziom soils instead of sand.

The history of the region has been inseparable from that of the Great Plain. An important turn came about in the 18th century, when the ethnic Slav minority was displaced by a new wave of German settlers who brought know-how and an ethos of hard work to cultivating the vineyards. Following the phylloxera epidemic, the acreage under vines here increased significantly, and the varietal composition slowly settled to the present-day pattern. This is characterized by a two-to-one dominance of white varieties over reds, headed by Kunleány (191 ha) and Cserszegi Fűszeres (191 ha). These are followed by Chardonnay (92 ha), Királyleányka (62 ha), and Rajnai Rizling (74 ha). Red-wine grapes are represented by Kékfrankos (209 ha), Zweigelt (99 ha), Cabernet Franc (49 ha), and Cabernet Sauvignon (41 ha).

Owing to the properties of the soil, the white wines are mild with low acidity. This softness is better-balanced in the region's reds (e.g. Hajósi Cabernet Sauvignon), some of which attain a quality comparable to that of hill-grown wines. Foremost among them are the red wines produced by Brilliant Holding at Nemesnádudvar under the Villa Stephen label, and the Sümegi Winery based in Érsekcsanád. The region's best-known sight is the *pincefalu* or "cellar village" near Hajós. This is a complex of several hundred cellars carved in loess and adorned with baroque frontispieces. A quaint village in its own right, this network of cellars and alleys was created by ethnic Swabian growers in the area. The village of Nemesnádudvar also boasts a number of cellar rows.

KUNSÁG

The vast Kunság—named after the Cumans, a Turkic-speaking ethnic group that settled in Eastern Hungary in the 13th century—is the largest wine region not only in the Great Plain but in the entire country. Situated between the Danube and Tisza Rivers, with a small section around Tiszaföldvár east of the Tisza, the wine region is shared by the five counties of Bács-Kiskun, Csongrád, Heves, Jász-Nagykun-Szolnok, and Pest. It consists of 95 communities grouped in eight districts, covering a total growing area of 103,863 hectares, including 1,436 ha in Class I, 26,196 ha in Class II, and the rest in Class III sites. Only 29,544 ha of this available area is planted with vines.

The climate in the middle of the Great Plain is rather varied during the growing season, but generally it is characterized by extreme continental features, such as a hot summer and a very cold, dry winter. The high heat sum and insolation, especially along the Lower Tisza River, is typically accompanied by low precipitation—on the long-term average, 100 mm less than would be safe for viticulture. Summer drought, severe winter, and frost damage in the fall and in the spring are all fairly common, and the vines often suffer scorching and heat stroke. All these factors combined render the risk of production higher in the Kunság than in any other region in the country. While the high heat sums would seem to justify an early harvest, local traditions prohibited picking "sand-grown" grapes before St. Michael's day on September 29th.

The region's geological patterns are colorful but hardly complex, with the bedrock typically comprising Pleistocene and Holocene shifting sands, less frequently loess and fluviatile aleurit silt from the Danube. The predominant soil type is calcareous sand, which here and there forms a thin mantle covering cohesive loam and clay subsoils. The low specific heat capacity of sand allows these soils to heat through quickly in the summer, contributing to the low acid content of the wines. There are areas with light-colored, shifting sand with a low humus content; elsewhere darker sands mixed with loess can have a higher concentration of nutrients. A third type is the acid sand soil evolved from the Tisza River. Even though Hungarians refer to the wines of the Great Plain collectively as *homoki* or "sand-grown," not all of these wines are actually grown on sand. When mixed with loess, sandy soils here are often covered by a layer of black earth, and alluvial deposits

in sites rising above the flood plain of the rivers can also develop chernoziom soils.

In the flat areas, the ground water level is relatively high at 2-5 m below ground. The water table is located deeper underneath the sand dunes. Consisting mainly of Quaternary sands, the dunes often "migrate." Binding the sand and preventing aeolian erosion have been important technical challenges in the area.

A charter provides documentary evidence of wines having been made here as early as the 11th century. Wine production continued through the Middle Ages and even during the Ottoman Occupation, typically as a secondary pursuit serving local needs, but also producing a small surplus for export. Of course, these wines were neither of outstanding quality nor particularly famous. Plantation of both vines and other fruit on a larger scale began in the late 18th century, for the main purpose of binding the shifting sands, but these plantations had not really attained national significance until the phylloxera attacked and destroyed 90% of the vines in the hillside—

117

—vineyards country. The vines of the Great Plain survived because loose sandy soils are impervious to the root louse. This immunity gave a temporary boost to the value of vineyards in the Kunság, and the area planted with vines multiplied by the end of the 19th century. Profits from wine sales also increased due to the elimination of much of the competition around the country. In 1892, a government decree established the Viticultural Research Institute in Kecskemét, relying on highly qualified professionals such as János Mathiász, the world-famous root-stock breeder. A second wave of new plantation in the 1960's still favored the old varieties yielding plain, dilute wine. It was only in the 1970's that a preference emerged for quality varieties and grapes suitable for sparkling wine production.

Initially termed "Kiskunság," the region was isolated in 1990 from the Alföld or Great Plain region, then augmented by significant additional acreage in 1997. Although it has never been considered as one of the traditional wine producing areas, it was already mentioned among the wine regions designated in 1897—admittedly merely as a source of what the regulators termed "orchard wines." The little local tradition there is to talk about is mostly limited to the spur-pruned or cane-pruned low head training and the winter covering of the trunk. These cultivation methods are still widely used in the smaller vineyards of the region.

Today, white varieties outnumber red wine grapes about three to one in the Kunság. The largest area is devoted to Izsáki Fehér (2,879 ha), followed by Zala Gyöngye (2,715 ha) and Ezerjó (2,617 ha). Cserszegi Fűszeres, Kunleány and Olaszrizling are each cultivated on 1,000-2,000 hectares each, while Bianca, Chardonnay, Ezerfürtű, Királyleányka, Lakhegyi Mézes, Muscat Ottonel, Rajnai Rizling, Rizlingszilváni, and Zöld Veltelini each can claim a few hundred hectares. Black grapes are headed by Kékfrankos on 2,787 hectares, followed by Kadarka, the region's traditional dark grape (861 ha) and Zweigelt (604 ha). Cabernet Franc, Cabernet Sauvignon, Kékoportó and Merlot

are each planted on over 100 hectares. Planted on 116 hectares, direct producers occupy the largest vineyard acreage anywhere in the country.

The Kunság produces the bulk of Hungary's commercially sold wines, relying on a wide range of grape varieties far in excess of those listed above. These "sand-grown" table wines tend to be light and soft, with little body and a flat taste. The whites are typically flabby, often with high sugar degrees and alcohol. The reds are plain with no trace of complexity, although the better grapes have the potential to produce better quality, particularly with conscientiously limited yields. Top quality wines are practically nonexistent in these parts. Around the turn of the 19th and 20th centuries, vineyards planted in sand exceeded the national average crop of 5-6 hectoliters per *hold* (about 9-10 hectoliters per hectare) three or four times. Although some authors cited these figures with a measure of pride, growers today should think twice about such yields being conducive to competitive wines for an increasingly finicky global market.

Under the circumstances, we will be forgiven for not listing various wineries making at best run-of-the-mill wines. A completely different mindset—and reduced yields—characterize the Helvécia Winery, owned by Huba Szeremley, and the Ruttner Farm based in Ceglédbercel. The runner-up producers, including Eszesvin, the Fritmman brothers, Szigetvin, and Szikrai, still accord a role to sweetened wines, which sometimes account for 50-70% of their product range.

The Kecskeméti Pecsenye Fehér and the Kecskeméti Leányka, both sweet whites, were two better-known wines from the Kunság between the two world wars. At one time, the Csengődi Olaszrizling was a name to reckon with among dry whites. In the second half of the 20th century, the Alföldi Nemes Kadarka, a late-harvest semi-dry red bottled in smaller lots, rose to popularity with a certain clientele who liked their red low in acid and tannin, but high in alcohol. Kadarka was also the staple grape for making *siller* or *kástélyos* type wines.

Eger

Eger faces a peculiar predicament. Elsewhere in Hungary, fame may lag behind the greatness of the wines; here, it is the wines themselves that should live up to their reputation at last. That this will eventually happen seems guaranteed by the quality of vineyards such as the Eged, and now by the commitment of the growers.

The region evolved on the southwestern foothills of the Bükk Mountains, where the gradually tilting terrain of the Great Plain abruptly rises toward the peaks. The Bükk Range shelters the vineyards on the slopes from northerly winds, and has created a favorable local climate. The official region comprises the Heves County communities of Andornaktálya, Demjén, Eger, Egerbakta, Egerszalók, Egerszólát, Felsőtárkány, Kerecsend, Maklár, Nagytálya, Nosz-vaj, Novaj, Ostoros, and Szomolya in the Eger District, as well as Aldebrő, Feldebrő, and Verpelét in the Debrő District. The total designated growing area is 22,162 hectares, including 18,302 ranked as Class I in the cadastre, but vines are cultivated only on 4,395 hectares of this vast acreage.

Like the Mátraalja region, Eger is characterized by a late spring, a rather short growing season, and an annual median temperature of 10.1 °C, well below the average of other

New plantations reclaiming the higher slopes of the Nagy-Eged

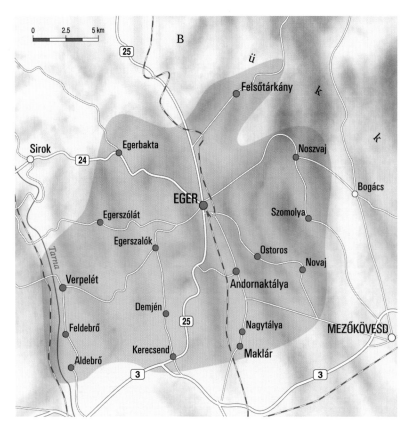

cally on the *verő*, the local name to describe cosseted south-southwestern slopes that emerge from the cool midst of the valleys below) to enjoy an extra treat of sun. In these fine vineyards, the annual insolation can exceed 2200 hours, and the heat sum during the season averages 3400-3600 °C. The region as a whole is subject to a temperate continental climate, with an uneven pattern of rainfall. Most of the moisture arrives in May and June, leaving the second half of summer dry and sunny. Even so, the *verő*, particularly on Mount Nagy-Eged, occasionally suffer from brutal rainstorms which have the power to destroy grapes and soils alike. Although the annual rainfall, averaging 595 mm over the last 40 years, is more or less sufficient, its peculiar distribution and forms of appearance, including hailstorms, regularly damage the region's vineyards.

Eger's geological make-up is rather diverse. The bedrock of the northern section—most notably of Mount Nagy-Eged—consists of Mesozoic marine rocks, such as Triassic and Jurassic limestone, dolomite, and shale. These partially folded hard rocks are overlain by Eocene and Oligocene limestone, clay marl and sandstone. These formations are decisive underneath the triangle formed by Eger, Felsőtárkány and Noszvaj, which encloses

wine regions in the country. This has to do with the northern location, a higher elevation above sea level—for instance, Mount Nagy-Eged rises over 500 m—and the intense articulation of the terrain. It is, however, the same dissected morphology that has enabled growing sites with excellent microclimates (typi-

Typical carved cellars around Andornaktálya

Elected members of
the wine community
of Eger in 1871

some of the finest vineyards of the region: the Tekenőhát at Noszvaj, the Kis-Eged, and the Áfrika at Eger proper, so named for its unusually hot microclimate. The Kis-Eged is also known for the 30-million-year-old fossilized leaf of *Vitis hungarica*, an ancestor of the grape-vine as we know it today, that was found on the slope of this hill.

The southern zone of the region is characterized by younger Miocene formations above Oligocene rocks, in particular rhyolite tuff and the far less common rhyodacite. Vineyards with these volcanic rocks underneath make the biggest, most fiery wines of the region around Maklár, Szomolya, Ostoros, Demjén, Egerszalók, Andornaktálya, Novaj, and the southern sector of the town of Eger. Rhyolite tuff has also played a central role as a rock eminently suitable for carving cellars in. This rock hides 99% of the cellars in Eger, including underground networks of passageways dozens of kilometers long, as well as the famous catacombs underneath the fortified castle of Eger.

VILMOS THUMMERER, VINTAGE 1953

The village of Noszvaj has some fine vineyards, but what really makes it worth the trip from Eger is the astonishing spectacle of a realm carved in tuff rock–dwellings, cellars, even an aristocratic pantheon. Here, at the periphery of the residential area, Vilmos Thummerer and his wife Katalin, a qualified horticulturist herelf, work away at their flourishing business–a genuine family winery. Thummerer only uses stainless steel to make his white wines, which nevertheless do not lack convincing force. His reds boast a balance and aromatic finesse which make them very approachable despite their considerable weight. In addition to his Bikavér, his Tekenőháti Pinot Noir–the first bottling of this variety in Eger–created quite a stir among vinophiles. This was followed by a Bordeaux-style prestige blend dubbed Vili Papa Cuvée (evidently a tribute from grandchildren to "Granddaddy Bill's" best wine). This is a judiciously wooded but fabulously concentrated red with a fruitiness that has enthralled everyone able to afford the seduction.

The outcrops in the west-northwestern section of the region, including at Egerbakta and Egerszólát, are conglomerates of gravel and terrestrial clay deposited during the Middle Miocene, with intercalations of a younger rhyolite tuff which boost the soil's concentration of trace elements. As the terrain dips and flattens toward the Great Plain in the south, the Miocene formations are increasingly overlain by Pannonian clayey-sandy sediments,

Pliocene paludal beds, and Pleistocene loess.

The soil pattern of the region is equally colorful, indeed quilt-like in places. In the mountainous north, the lithosoils make for smaller yields but particularly characterful wines. East of Eger, rendzina soils over limestone dominate, while west of the town black *nyirok* over weathered volcanic rock is excellent for viticulture. At lower altitudes south of Eger, loess talus and loam have evolved over rhyolite tuff. Brown soil reigns supreme in the valley of the Eger Creek, where most of the region's vineyards are located, although the alluvial soils in the flood plain of the Creek are far less suitable for quality wine production. The low-humus prairie soils on the southern periphery and to the west in the Debrő district yield zesty, often high-alcohol wines, while the sandy soils around Verpelét came to play an important role in the late 19th century, due to their immunity to phylloxera.

From the point of view of grape-growing, the terrain can be divided roughly into two zones. One consists of a low, 200-300 m high sequence of gentle rhyolite tuff hills running north to south. The major traditional vineyards of the region are located on these hills, including the Rác, Hajdú, Agárdi, Pap, Kis and Nagy Galagonyás Hills west of the Eger Creek, as well as the Bajusz, Cigléd, Királyszék, Almagyar, Kőporos, Sasdomb and Tihamér east of the same creek. The other zone consists of terraces built from gravelly alluvium on either side of the valley, on which excellent *nyirok* soils and a few patches of loess have developed.

Viticulture in the area was already an economic factor around 1010 A.D., when King Stephen founded the Eger Bishopric, renouncing the whole county's tithes to the Church to provide further incentive for wine production. Walloon settlers arriving later in the 11th century gave further impetus to local viticulture and brought with them French traditions. The area's most celebrated hill, the Eged, was in fact named after St. Giles (Saint-Gilles in French and Aegidus in Latin), the patron saint of a Benedictine abbey in France. Under the influence of the invited Italian and French settlers, the region soon embraced the use of wooden barrels and cellars for maturing the wines, instead of simply keeping them in wine skins.

Until the end of the 16th century, local viticulture continued to flourish. During the tenure of István Dobó as captain of Eger's fortified castle, sales of wine made a significant contribution to financing the defense against Ottoman invaders. As wine quality came to matter more, and accumulating stocks of wine needed more space, real cellars carved in tuff by well-heeled merchants and peasants began to supersede vaulted cellars and the plainly modified natural cavities in *darázskő* ("honeycomb rock", an old Hungarian name for volcanic tuff) that had also served as wine stores till then. By the second half of the century, a labyrinthine cellar network had grown under the town.

After skirmishes and a siege that lasted decades, the Ottomans finally took Eger in 1596 and held it for 91 years. Despite their religious abstinence, the Ottomans allowed viticulture to survive because the taxes imposed on wine provided a source of income they could not afford to give up. In fact, the period also saw the appearance in the region of Kadarka, a red-wine grape whose first cuttings were probably brought along by Serbian growers fleeing north from the Ottoman invasion. In the space of a few generations, black grapes began to displace the ancient white varieties in Eger. However, they could hardly have been regarded as a complete novelty; the account books of Bishop Hippolit Estei had sung the praise of Eger's red wines as early as in 1507. At this time, the town's best vineyards were located at Almagyar, Tihamér, and Cigléd.

Once the Ottomans had been driven out, wine production increased steadily to exceed 80,000 *akó* (over four million liters) a year by the end of the 18th century. The share of white wines continued to dwindle in the Episcopal cellars, and reached a low of 18% of the total inventory in 1767. Red wines were entered in the books under two categories: as *vinum subrubrum* (a very light red almost like a rosé, called *siller* today), and the much scarcer *vinum rubrum*, or true red wine. The majority of growers were accustomed to blending the little white they had with their reds; only a few larger and finer estates continued to make

DR. TAMÁS PÓK,, VINTAGE 1957

Pók became known to vinophiles at large as the winemaker of the Antinori-Zwack winery that was established in 1993 on the former Apponyi Property in Bátaapáti, Tolna County. At the time this must have seemed an ultramodern enterprise, but after a few good years Pók left for Eger, where he set up his own winery in partnership with István Polónyi. Not a man of high-flying ambition, Pók can seem a little scholarly at times—if only because he has much higher professional qualifications than the average winemaker in Hungary. He is still searching for the way at his own winery, although his Egri Bikavér and flagship blend, called Rhapsody in Red, earned him recognition in a short period of time. A less self-effacing winemaker with Pók's talent would have garnered all the laurels a long time ago.

white wine and strictly pure red wines. These circumstances turned out to be all-important in bringing about Bikavér, Eger's famous blended red wine.

From the end of the 17th century to the division of Poland by Russia, Austria and Prussia in 1772, the Polish aristocracy was the principal buyer of Eger wines. However, the political collapse in Poland and the concomitant loss of this important market did not prove fatal for Eger, which continued to flourish and rose to prominence among Hungarian wine regions by the 1800's. Cellars continued to multiply, and

TIBOR GÁL, VINTAGE 1958

A flying winemaker from Hungary? You bet! Tibor Gál started out in Eger but really made it at Lodovico Antinori's estate in Bolgheri, where in six years he crafted such monumental wines—and leaders of Wine Spectator's top list—as the 1998 Masseto and Ornellaia. These days, Gál shares some of his precious time between Italy and South Africa, leaving his unmistakable signature on the wines he assists with. In Hungary, he keeps an eye on the production of at least ten wineries as their official consultant, while back at home in Eger he is at work to prove that the local terroir is capable of turning a winemaker's most ambitious dreams into reality. He has undertaken to bring about an Egri Bikavér revival, and has made a statement with stylish Cabs and Chardonnays free from international cliché. He is also championing the cause of Pinot Noir, a grape he believes more likely than the Bordeaux varieties to achieve world-class performance in Hungary. To top it all, he has planted some Syrah and Viognier, two varieties hitherto unknown in Hungary that seem to be doing very well in his vineyards already. Belying his young age, Gál is one of the most widely respected wine authorities, with organizing skills unequaled in Hungary. His ventures may have seemed unduly bold to some at first, and have in fact been known to elicit skepticism among colleagues, but time has always proven him right so far. A father of four, Gál is steering a 50-hectare estate of his own. Multiply that acreage by a large factor to figure in the exceptional terroir, and you will begin to get a better idea of the worth of this man.

ond half of the 19th century, when severe soil erosion forced growers to abandon a number of vineyards, including some of the region's best sites on Mount Eged. The area under cultivation began to shrink not only around the town of Eger but throughout the region as well. The coup de grâce was delivered by the phylloxera, which found ideal conditions in the cohesive clay soils and the monoculture of the region. In Eger, the root louse destroyed vines on a scale (93.51%) unequaled anywhere else in the country.

It was after the reconstruction of vineyards at the turn of the 19th and 20th centuries that the Bikavér emerged as Eger's most famous wine and attained a world-wide reputation. The excellence of this branded blend owed its success to a combination of factors, including the Kadarka ingredient, the unique terroir, the broadening knowledge in the field of enology, and improved cellar equipment. The appearance of Bikavér triggered a new period of boom for Eger, then known as the Eger-Visonta region, which lasted several decades.

The heyday of the area ended after the Great War, at which time the name of the region was simplified to Eger. Starting in the 1960's, the mass-producing industrialized wineries dumped Eger wines of at best variable quality on domestic and international markets. The abuse of Eger's repute ended with the social-political transformation of 1990, which enabled small and mid-size wineries to assert themselves with a representative range of products. The state-owned large wineries responded to the winds of change by reforming themselves as joint stock companies, while the communist-era "cooperatives," set up under the forced collectivization scheme, "cleaned up their profile" and became limited liability companies or genuine (voluntary) alliances of growers. Wine legislation adopted in 1997 added the villages of Szomolya, Aldebrő, Feldebrő, and Verpelét to the official region.

In the 19th century, and especially during vineyard reconstruction in the wake of the phylloxera epidemic, white grape varieties regained most of their former predominance. For a while, even some of the Kadarka crop

in suitable years even some naturally sweet red wines were made from botrytized grapes. The first symptoms of decline surfaced in the sec-

was vinified as white wine–a *blanc de noirs* of sorts–despite this red-wine grape's formerly decisive role as an ingredient in Bikavér. In the 1940's, this hallmark blend still normally contained 70% Kadarka, supplemented by 15-20% Nagyburgundi (Kékfrankos) and 10-15% Medoc Noir. Some Kadarka ended up as *siller*, and sometimes a small part of the crop that contracted noble rot in the upper section of the Eged, widely considered as Eger's finest vineyard, would be made into a sweet red dessert wine.

Today, most of the region's black grape vineyards are located in the narrower Eger district, although even here they amount to less than 60% of the total area under cultivation–despite recent trends favoring red wine varieties exclusively for new planting. The Debrő district yields mostly white wines, and accounts for the bulk of the region's production of Hárslevelű. The leading white grape though is the Leányka (354 ha), followed by Rizlingszilváni (330 ha), Muscat Ottonel (204 ha), Olaszrizling (177 ha), and the latter-day hybrids Zenit (140 ha), and Zengő (119 ha). Királyleányka, Hárslevelű, Cserszegi Fűszeres, and Chardonnay each occupy less than 100 hectares.

Among red wine grapes, Kékfrankos reigns supreme with 849 hectares, followed by Zweigelt (317 ha), Kékoportó (293 ha), Cabernet Sauvignon (210 ha), Blauburger (181 ha), Merlot (144 ha), Cabernet Franc (143 ha), and Turán (85 ha). Although Kadarka dominated the region's red wine production for centuries, only traces of it remain today.

The average vineyard property size of about half a hectare represents a multitude of handkerchief-size parcels (90% of all Wine Community members), plus a handful of larger producers with a few dozen hectares each. Most of the vines were planted 10-15 years ago, although quite a few vineyards 30-35 years of age survive from the first wave of large-scale plantations, designed for high cordon training.

The most popular dry whites are the Egerszóláti Olaszrizling and the Verpeléti Olaszrizling, while Leányka, Tramini and Muscat Ottonel are often vinified in the off-dry or semi-sweet style so characteristic of

BÉLA VINCZE, VINTAGE 1961

If merchants stand in line to lay their hands on someone's wine, that wine must be pretty good indeed. The case of Béla Vincze is even more extreme: several proud retailers claim they sell more of his wines than the competition…Vincze's reds can indeed command respect, but they are very appealing at the same time. Although massive, full-bodied, and enduring, they do not need long to evolve a hallmark animal nuance, often combined with an equally distinct hint of extract sweetness.

this region. In better years, these wines can have good body and a refined taste. The Egri Leányka is an aromatic, short-lived white that often contains some residual sugar, although the dry Leányka of the G.I.A. winery, since the 1990's, has expressed the true and very special flavors of this variety which the sweeter versions cannot begin to convey. For decades, the semi-sweet Debrői Hárslevelű and Verpeléti Muskotály have been highly popular, if equally variable, white wine choices from the Debrő district.

Kékfrankos, Cabernet Franc and Merlot have long since replaced Kadarka and Kékoportó as the decisive black grapes in Eger. One local red wine style in addition to dry Bikavér that attained a certain popularity was the notoriously semi-dry Medoc Noir, originally made from a strain of a French grape known as Mornen Noir or Cot Rouge. These days, this dubious red has been su-

A statue of Szent Orbán in the Síkhegy vineyard

them a respectable position among Hungary's red wines. Traditionally, Eger's best red was of course the aforementioned Bikavér ("Bull's Blood"), originally a fiery blend of Nagyburgundi (Kékfrankos), Kékoportó, and Kadarka. The brand was properly established by a man named Jenő Grőber, who borrowed the memorable name from Szekszárd and also perfected the recipe of the blend by adding Medoc Noir for body. Bolstered by efficient marketing and scrupulous quality control, Egri Bikavér became one of Hungary's best-known wines and enjoyed universally high esteem until World War II.

The heavily industrialized mass-production during the communist era degraded this brand to the point where it became at best barely acceptable and often simply undrinkable, creating an aversion in the better foreign markets that is still making itself felt today. Just how much of its appeal the blend has lost is illustrated by the fact that the small and medium-size privately owned wineries in Eger, which started out in the early 1990's, did not take on the Bikavér as their declared flagship product, but typically relegated it to a second label. Indeed, some small local growers in the appropriate locations still sometimes hawk wine called "Bikavér" to unsuspecting tourists that is really just a blend of inferior lots and grape varieties that they could not possibly sell in any other form. On the positive side, the local Wine Community in 1997 adopted a Bikavér Code. The most significant provision of this regulation defines Bikavér as a blend of at least three grape varieties chosen strictly from a specified list. If this system of quality assurance is genuinely adhered to by the majority of growers, and accompanied by appropriate strategies of enforcement, the region will have made a big step toward restoring the honor of what is potentially its best brand.

The composition of Bikavér at the turn of the millennium differs from the original version in that Kadarka is no longer one of the three or four grapes in the blend. Run-of-the-mill Egri Bikavér typically relies on heavy producer grapes such as Kékfrankos, Zweigelt, and Kékoportó. Only the so-called

TÓTH ISTVÁN, VINTAGE 1961

A many times champion in triathlon, Tóth has a personality that never fails to leave an imprint on the wines he makes. These wines are obviously destined for glory. The question for him seems to be what kind of race tracks are available for the contestants for the hard work of preparation and training. There are big names aplenty in Eger. Tóth's wines are big as well, but it is not so much by dint of raw power as through geniality and distinctive aromatic finesse that they finally win the day. If you have tasted Tóth's Bikavér selection, you probably can't help but start believing that Egri Bikavér has a future after all. The man is judicious with new oak, but all the more open-handed when it comes to time in the barrel, aging his wines quite a bit longer than the norm in the region. If you are after a truly unique experience, you must try to find a way to get into Tóth's cellar. (A confidential tip: start looking around the viaduct...)

perseded by the similarly semi-dry Egri Medina (an interspecific cross of Medoc Noir itself).

Eger reds are typically medium-bodied but reasonably tannic and dark, although in cooler vintage years they tend to lose both color and tannin, and can be on the harsh side. In terms of body, tannin and alcohol, the regional average rarely achieves the standards of Hungary's southern red wine regions, but the most prominent examples will not be dwarfed by the tallest giants from Villány. Their elegance and complex harmony of taste give

"artisanal wineries," which account for a fraction of the production, accord a significant role to Cabernet and/or Merlot in the cuvée. The top wines tend to come out of small and medium-size family wineries, led by the Vilmos Thummerer, whose pioneering effort was recognized in 1995 with the Winemaker of the Year award. He was soon followed, in the order of appearance, by G.I.A. (Tibor Gál, Winemaker of the Year in 1998), Endre Bakondi, Béla Vincze, the Pók-Polónyi Pince, Ferenc Tóth, István Tóth, the Kőporos Winery, and others. One of the latest promises is József Simon, whose new plantations give us reason to assume that his 2000 Dom Simon, a red cuvée, has turned out to be an excellent blend not by chance but by design.

Among the larger wineries, Ostoros-Bor has distinguished itself with sound, well-received wines. Benefiting from the consultancy of Lajos Gál and the scientific work of György Lőrincz, the Research Institute of Viticulture and Enology run by FVM, the Ministry of Agriculture and Regional Development, has assumed a vital role in promoting new equipment, methods, and know-how. In 2000, a narrow circle of local growers founded the Eger Wine Guild with the aim of raising standards even higher and forging a collective market presence.

The vast network of cellars underneath the town of Eger has taken nearly a thousand years to construct. Today, only a small portion of this labyrinth serves its original purpose of wine storage. The older tunnels often cave in, causing serious disruption to the city's traffic and utility services. The cellars at Verőszala and Árnyékszala within the city limits are still used by wineries today. There are well-known cellar rows at the Nagykőporos, Kiskőporos and Tetemvár vineyards, as well as in the Tihamér Valley and the Szépasszony Valley. The latter spot is on the must-see list of every tourist agency, although the inferior wines on offer there do more harm than good to Eger's reputation. The heritage of cellar construction is so rich

throughout the region that we cannot possibly enumerate every sight of interest. Without any pretense to completeness, let us single out the villages of Ostoros and Andornaktálya for their impressive rows of cellars that are certainly worth a visit.

Major wine-related events include the "Eger Wine Tournament" on Vincent Day, the feast of Egri Bikavér on St. Donatus Day, the Feast of Eger Vineyardists on the first Sunday of Advent, and the consecration of wines on St. John Day.

The Egri Borok Gyertyás Háza ("Candle-lit House of Eger Wines") stands as the stronghold of local wine and gastronomy.

This cellar provided shelter and the comfort of faith during the Ottoman Occupation

Etyek-Buda

*Today, Etyek makes the most sense as a source of grapes for nearby sparkling wine pro-
duction—the place where the magic of bubbles begins and ends. And yet it would be nice
to know more about this former supplier of great still wines to the great capital city...*

An amphitheater
of cellars

The Etyek-Buda wine region stretches
from the southern tip of the Gerecse
Range to the Buda Hills to the east
and the Velence Hills to the south, and is
shared by the three counties of Komárom,
Pest, and Fejér. It can be divided into three
districts: that of Etyek proper (Bicske,
Csabdi, Etyek, Vál), the southern slopes of
the Velence Hills (Kajászó, Nadap, Pákozd,
Pázmánd, Sukoró), and the Buda Mountains
(Budajenő, Budakeszi, Pilisborosjenő, Telki,
Tök, Üröm). The "Buda" element of the
compound name is quite misleading, because
this region has nothing to do with the former
Buda wine region along the Danube, from
Szentendre in the north to Tétény in the
south, which for 600 years produced what

were known throughout Europe as "Buda
wines." The total area of the wine region is
5,632 hectares, including 3,927 hectares in
Class I sites. Only 1,480 ha, or 30% of this
potential area, are planted with vines today.
The annual temperature here (9.5-10.5 °C) is
somewhat lower than the national average,
but the rainfall comes quite close at 400-800
mm. Air moves around freely in the area, reducing the risk of fungal disease and frost
damage in the vineyards. The Vál Valley is
one of the windiest parts of the country.

The geology of the Buda district is dominated by Triassic dolomite and limestone. In
the vicinity of Etyek, these rocks crop out
from under younger sediments at a distance
from the village, near Bicske. In the Buda

Mountains, the old bedrock is overlain by Oligocene sandstone and younger limestone. The oldest and most important formation in the narrower Etyek area is loose and porous limestone (less commonly also marl and gravel) of Sarmatian origin, evident in small outcrops east, west, and south of the village. The famous cellars of Etyek were dug in this easy-to-work rock. The bulk of the hills here consist of sandy clay and marl sediments of the Pannonian stage, overlain by Pleistocene loess and, in places, Holocene shifting sand. In contrast, the whole range of the Velence Hills is made up by Carboniferous granite of intrusive origin.

In the hills around Etyek, the parent rocks responsible for soil formation are typically loess, sand, limestone and, less frequently, dolomite. These rocks evolved loam soils with a high concentration of active lime, which yield the region's characteristic "calcareous wines." In the Velence Hills, the prevalent soil is weathered granite mixed with loess. In the Buda district, chernoziom and basic brown earth are the most common, here and there with a significant concentration of lime. Throughout the region, the terrain is moderately articulated without steep gradients. The vineyards occupy gentle hillsides of various aspect, dissected by erosional valleys and ravines.

In its present form, Etyek-Buda is one of the country's newer wine regions, although the fame of wines grown on the slopes of the Buda Mountains goes back to medieval times. During the reign of the late Árpád Dynasty in the 13th century, wine provided the citizens of Buda with their main source of income. In the wake of the Ottoman Occupation, Serbian immigrants settled down in the city and its environs; their legacy is still felt today in local place names in the Tabán and Gellért Hill districts of Budapest. Owing to the influence of the Balkans that these settlers communicated, red wines gained the upper hand in the local vineyards. The Buda-Sashegyi Kadarka attained a Europe-wide reputation in its day. Following the expulsion of the Ottoman conquerors, the ethnic scene was diversified further with the arrival of German vineyard hands who set up house in

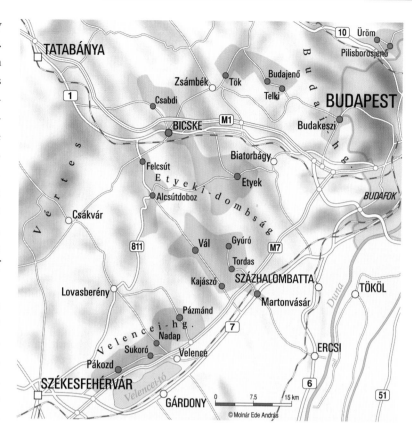

Promontor just outside the city to the south (today Budafok).

In 1890, the phylloxera ruined most of the vineyards that had been spared by industrialization and the sprawling city. By the first decade of the 20th century, viticulture in the area of medieval Buda was consigned to the annals of history. Etyek itself rose to prominence in the middle of the 19th century as one of the centers of Hungarian wine production, owing to the diligence of German settlers and the proximity of the Törley House, which sourced the grapes for its famous sparkling wines from this region. After the Great War, the communist system had no plans for Etyek other than to provide base wines for cheap sparkling. For decades, the region sold practically no products under its own name, although the small growers continued to make wine for their own needs.

The region was resurrected in 1990, at first as Etyek, on the reconstructed vineyards around Velence, a formerly prosperous region ruined by the phylloxera a century before, and on the vineyard holdings of the giant Hungarovin that had superseded the Törley Estate in Etyek. In 1997, the Wine Act added

Granite outcrop in the southern section of the Etyek region

129

a few wine producing communities at the foot of the Buda Mountains, changing the region's name to Etyek-Buda. The Etyek-based grower Tibor Bátori became one of the first new-era private growers in the country to release a bottled product, setting a national benchmark in the *small winery/top wine* genre with his Öreghegyi Chardonnay and Sauvignon Blanc.

The old grape of Etyek was Schlamper, a German variety unsuitable for making quality wine, while black Kadarka probably dominated in the Buda district. The modern Etyek-Buda is a quintessential white wine region, with 784 hectares of Olaszrizling and 261 hectares of Chardonnay. Zöld Veltelini, Szürkebarát, Sauvignon Blanc, and Rizling-szilváni can each claim an area of 50 to 100 hectares. Like other white wine producing regions in Hungary, Etyek-Buda seems to suffer under the stifling dominion of the Olasz-rizling variety, which keeps in check the finer grapes—such as Chardonnay and Sauvignon Blanc—that have done the most in recent times to enhance the region's good name. Although red wines are still the exception in the region,

Hungarovin's estate in Pázmánd has come out with a few Pinot Noir and Cabernet wines of note. These wines, together with those about to be released by the Pázmánd Kúria, look set to revive a local tradition, whereby the red wine of the village of Nadap next door commanded respect far and wide in the 16th century.

The soils of Etyek-Buda are not cut out for firm wines of great character, but are certainly capable of imparting vibrant acidity. This is one reason why Etyek is the best source of grapes for sparkling wine production in Hungary. Apart from base wines for sparkling, Etyek's wine style follows western trends for elegant, cold-fermented dry wines without too much body. Outstanding producers in the narrower Etyek area include the Etyeki Kúria, Tibor Nagy Gombai, László Hernyák, Pervinum, the Sánci Winery, Zoltán Kendl, Hungarovin, Gyula Orosz, and Imre Pekk. The Buda district still has very few producers bottling wine. Most remarkable among them are the Nyakas Winery in Tök and the Kovács Winery.

Although not strictly part of the region, Budafok deserves another mention for its wine-related monuments of architecture. The extensive cellars here were carved in porous limestone between the 18th and 20th centuries; they are yet to be surveyed in their entirety. Especially impressive is the export cellar of Hungarovin, with its 25 passages totaling 3.5 kilometers in length, and the Törley Cellar, built in 1886 for sparkling wine manufacture. The György-villa—a baroque mansion in Budafok owned by Hungarovin today—is a fine example of the grand style that used to characterize country wine houses.

Cellars carved in the same limestone are still a landmark in Etyek, although their number has diminished from 560 before World War II to 150 today. The finest cellars here were built in the *Kecskegödör* ("Goat's Pit"), on the Újhegy and Öreghegy Hills, as well as near the village center in an amphitheater layout. The cellar row of the nearby village of Páty, although of lesser architectural distinction, is well worth a visit.

Mátraalja

If the Sár Hill ever gets replanted, the reputation of Mátraalja wines will at last outgrow the village limits of Abasár. The residents of Gyöngyöstarján surely would not mind...

One of the larger wine regions in Hungary, the Mátraalja ("Mátra Foothills") is located south of the Mátra Mountains between Hatvan and Domoszló, extending roughly to the line of the M3 freeway to the south. It includes the Heves County communities of Abasár, Apc, Atkár, Detk, Domoszló, Ecséd, Gyöngyös, Gyöngyöshalász, Gyöngyösoroszi, Gyöngyöspata, Gyöngyössolymos, Gyöngyöstarján, Halmajugra, Hatvan, Karácsond, Kisnána, Markaz, Nagyréde, Rózsaszentmárton, Szücsi, Vécs, and Visonta. The total growing area is 32,497 hectares, including 24,261 hectares in Class I sites. Only 5,446 hectares of this extensive area is planted with vines today.

The region's climate is a tempered continental one. The range of the Mátra Mountains protects the vineyards on the slopes from northerly winds, helping to shape a diversity of favorable microclimates. Spring typically arrives late in the year. Because the peaks also arrest much of the precipitation, conditions tend to the dry, with most of the rainfall occurring in May and June. The number of sunshine hours during the growing season varies between 1250 and 1500. The mean temperature is 9-11 °C annually, and 14-18 °C during the growing season. The effective heat sum is 3100-3400 °C, while the annual precipitation fluctuates between 550-700 mm.

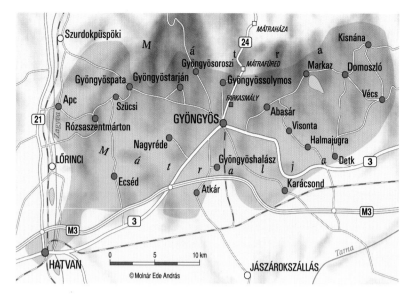

The region's decisive geological formations are all volcanic rocks, both acid and neutral, such as pyroxenic andesite, and tuffs of andesite and rhyolite. The volcanic paroxysm in the area occurred some 14-16 million years ago, during the Badenian stage of the Middle Miocene. After the volcanic range lifted up of the Miocene sea, over time a variety of rocks, including Sarmatian clay marl and sandstone, were deposited at the base of the mountains, followed by the sandy-clayey sediments of the Pannonian Lake, and paludal woody lignite. During the Pleistocene, these older formations were overlain by alluvial gravel and diverse clay.

Occasionally subject to erosion, the diverse soils include chernoziom, brown earth, brown forest soil, as well as sands enriched in humus. Most of these soils are not particularly calcareous, but in places their active lime content can be as high as 60%. The finest of them all for viticulture is the black *nyirok* soil, which evolved on the foothills and the piedmont slopes from easily weathered volcanic glass rich in trace elements, mixed with lacustrine clays and sandy loess. This soil typically yields crisp and aromatic wines with a high alcohol content that can be quite full-bodied in the best years.

We have no knowledge of which people first started cultivating vines in the region. In the 13th century, charters begin mentioning vineyards around the town of Gyöngyös, whose wine had attained such a reputation by the 15th century that the city council banned the sale of local wine unless its quality was first ascertained by an inspector. Later, during the Ottoman wars, the Ottoman invaders vied with the Hungarian lords themselves in imposing various taxes on the growers of Gyöngyös, ultimately contributing to the recession of viticulture in the area.

The region gained independence from the Eger-Visonta region in the 20th century. In the 1940's, it was still referred to as Gyön-

MÁTYÁS SZŐKE, VINTAGE 1942

A machinist by trade, Szőke is a self-taught winemaker whose name became synonymous with the true Mátraalja tradition in the era of planned economy. These days, he has some followers but no one has yet challenged his preeminence in the region. While Szőke makes mainly white wines as dictated by the region's varietal emphasis and terroirs, he also has a celebrated rosé and some sumptuous fruity reds capable of outclassing the majority of Eger wines in exceptional years. Szőke is not averse to innovation, but he is not given to reckless experimentation. His venture is a large one by family winery standards, but the quality of the wines is unimpeachable and always reliably consistent with the given category. Little wonder that some of his flagship products, for instance his barrique Chardonnay, have recently caught up with the leading edge of Hungarian wine. Szőke has no need to worry about posterity, either. One of his two sons, Zoltán, is a qualified enologist who will take the best possible care of the family winery.

132

gyös-Visonta; the present name Mátraalja dates from 1959. The villages of Aldebrő, Feldebrő and Verpelét were annexed to the Eger wine region in 1997.

In former centuries, the region's staple consisted of Kadarka-based red wines such as the Visontai Vörös, praised as recently as in 1947 as potentially smoother and spicier than the reds of the neighboring Eger. The Kadarka grape was also vinified to make the noted Gyöngyösi Siller. These days, white grapes have gained the upper hand, with Rizlingszilváni topping the list (869 ha), followed by Chardonnay (400 ha), Olaszrizling (368 ha), Muscat Ottonel (383 ha), and Szürkebarát (326 ha)—and a dozen or two of less common varieties. The most widespread red wine grapes are Kékfrankos (317 ha) and Zweigelt (217 ha). Direct producers have been cut back in recent years, but in the smaller farms they still represent a regrettably large portion of the crop. The villages of Abasár, Nagyréde and Markaz supply a significant part of the country's grafts from their nurseries.

In addition to Olaszrizling, Rizlingszilváni, Leányka, Hárslevelű, Tramini, and Chardonnay, the Mátraalja also produces the largest quantity of, and potentially the best, Muscat Ottonel wines in Hungary. The region's better-known dry whites include Olaszrizlings from Gyöngyös-Visonta, Abasár, Gyöngyös, and Atkár. High sugar degrees in exceptional years and from the best vineyards may result in wines with some residual sugar, such as the Domoszlói Muskotály or the Kompolti Muskotály.

The top producers of the region are Mátyás Szőke, József Ludányi and the Német Winery (all based in Gyöngyöstarján), Sándor Kiss and Son in Pálosvörösmart, and the Szőlőskert Coop in Nagyréde. This latter operation is one of the very few large wineries in Hungary producing easy-drinking wines in massive quantities, but always to reliably high standards. Near the town of Hatvan, Tibor Gál and Huba Szeremley are setting up a very promising estate called Nagygombos (70 hectares planted + 23 hectares fallow).

While the peasant folk carved their cellars in loess, lesser noblemen and aristocrats had the resources to cope with andesite and rhyolite, rocks much harder than loess to work with. Some fine examples of the local cellar architecture can be found on the Castle Hill of Gyöngyöspata, where the press houses were built in a tiered arrangement. The region's largest cellar is the Haller Cellar in Gyöngyöstarján. Having been under construction since 1740, this cellar has grown from 271 to 750 meters in length, and 6 meters wide in places. The village of Abasár hides another huge cellar carved in rhyolite. Legend has it that the early Hungarian King Aba Sámuel is buried somewhere in its pas-

sageways. The most frequented and possibly the most spectacular sight in the area is the Farkasmály Promontorium near Gyöngyös, consisting of 26 cellars arranged in three tiers one above the other. The construction of this cellar complex started in 1785, and continued well into the 19th century.

Beside Tokaj, the Mátraalja is the only region in Hungary where the noble mold called *Cladosporium cellare* thrives in the cellars. For an explanation, one could do worse than point to rhyolite tuff as the common substratum for this remarkable fungus.

Mecsekalja

A Sleeping Beauty of bygone days waiting for the awakening kiss, the Mecsekalja is lovely even in its dormancy.

The Mecsekalja ("Mecsek Foothills") region occupies the southern slopes of the Mecsek Range and the Baranya Hills. It can be divided into two parallel zones running from east to west: a northern one between Szigetvár and Mecseknádasd, and a southern one stretching from the village of Keszü all the way to the town of Mohács on the Danube. Located in Baranya County in its entirety, the region extends to the following communities: Babarc, Bár, Bóly, Cserkút, Dunaszekcső, Hásságy, Helesfa, Hosszúhetény, Keszü, Kispeterd, Kővágószőlős, Kővágótöttös, Lánycsók, Mohács, Monyoród, Mozsgó, Nagypeterd, Nyugotszenterzsébet, Olasz, Pécs, Pécsvárad, Szajk, Szederkény, Személy, Szigetvár, and Versend.

The total potential growing area of 6,998 hectares includes 6,416 hectares ranked Class I. Astoundingly, only 673 hectares of this very highly valued area is planted with vines. One reason for this is that some of the famous old vineyards have been engulfed by the urban zone of the city of Pécs, and now have residential buildings and industrial installations erected on them. The high rate of industrialization in the area makes it unlikely for the plantations to expand beyond their present size.

134

Together with Villány, the Mecsekalja is Hungary's warmest wine region, endowed with the longest growing season and a sub-Mediterranean climate. A hot and sunny summer is usually followed by a mild winter with rare frosts. On the most sheltered southern slopes, fig trees not only weather through the winter but will actually bear fruit. Precipitation levels are low throughout the area.

The variations of bedrock material and geological features trace the region's geographical articulation. In Mecsek Range proper to the north, the most common formations are Permian red sandstone and Triassic calcareous rocks—much like the bedrock of the Balatonfüred-Csopak wine region. These hard rocks are overlain by looser Miocene sands, shale and, occasionally, limestone. The brown earth that have evolved over the red sandstone are acid, leached, and ferriferous. These soils yield medium to full-bodied wines that are high in alcohol but low in acidity. Remarkably, the wines here exhibit the same overtone of burnt almond that characterizes Olaszrizling wines grown in Csopak north of Lake Balaton, on very similar red sandstone bedrock. Weathered sandstone and loess have also served as parent rocks for podzolized and lassivage brown earth, while rendzina soils appeared over limestone and marl. Covered by a thin mantle of loess, the southern slopes evolved loess and adobe soils. Further south, the Baranya Hills have a core of Pannonian clay marl alternating with calcareous sandstone, still within reach of the grape-vine's roots. This formation is overlain by a 2-3 meter thick layer of loess, which has evolved brown earth and calcareous chernoziom soils. This pattern is particularly characteristic of the zone between Bóly and Mohács.

Viticulture was brought to the area by the Roman legions, and it survived the vicissitudes of the great migrations. This is borne out by an extant Carolingian charter from 890 A.D., in which Arnulf, King of Franconia, confirmed Wittmar, the Archbishop of Salzburg, in his property of vines at the town of Pécs. In 1015, King Stephen, founder of the Hungarian state, presented the Abbey of Pécsvárad with 110 vine-dressers and six

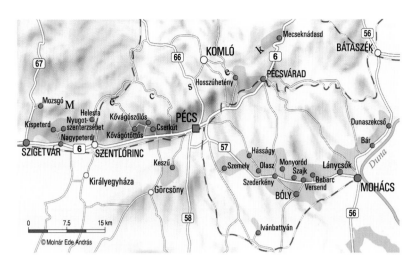

coopers. During medieval times, the region's most treasured vineyards at Pécs were Mons Aureus (the Roman name of the hill known as Aranyhegy today), Tettye, Donatus, Deindol, and Makár.

In 1694, Baranya County was granted its own crest, whose grape motif probably illustrated the *heveng*, a local delicacy made by hanging ripe clusters on branches of sloe to shrivel and desiccate the berries in the warm autumn sun for longer storage. At about this time, the Provost of Pécs took it into his head to make an Aszú in the Mecsekalja to emulate Tokaj. Not realizing that botrytis would not develop in the local climate, the good clergyman ordered cuttings and even earth to be brought from Tokaj to indulge his sweet dreams—all in vain. This is probably how the Furmint grape first showed up in this southern region. In the 18th century, the variety was mainly planted in Szentmiklós. (The region stopped making Furmint in the second half of the 20th century; the last known examples were intensely sweet and had 13.5% alcohol.)

The 1830's saw quite a revolution take place. Stakes appeared in the vineyards where the vines had been trained without any form of support, and the Provost tried to meet increasing domestic demand for better quality wines by importing the Cirfandli grape from Austria. This variety—of no relation to California Zinfandel despite the similarity of the name—has since become the near exclusive and endangered specialty of Pécs. The phylloxera at the end of the 19th century destroyed 80% of the vineyards. Despite some

Mecsekalja region. Although Kadarka used to hold sway in the area, it has been completely displaced by white varieties, particularly Olaszrizling (111 ha), Chardonnay (70 ha), Rajnai Rizling (55 ha), and Zöld Veltelini (47 ha). There is hardly a trace of the formerly celebrated Furmint, and Cirfandli could barely claim five hectares in 2000.

Owing to the warm climate and the scarce precipitation, the region's wines are generally full-bodied and often contain residual sugar and/or high alcohol. In fact, the Mecsekalja is a favorite hunting ground for devotees of off-dry or semi-sweet wines with a hint of spice. These wines can have charming acidity to offset some of the sugar, but they lack the spine needed for keeping, and will age fast. Almost impossible to find today, the Pécsi Cirfandli has a distinct floral nose evoking a meadow in full bloom, and a spicy, complex taste usually rounded off by a gram or two of residual sugar. Until the 1960's, a certain cult following sustained the Pécsi Olaszrizling, a very high alcohol (13,5-14%) but low-acid (4.5-5%) white.

Spearheading the region's minuscule production of bottled wine is György Eberhardt in Mohács, followed by a few promising producers such as the Pécsi Bor Winery, István Radó, Tibor Somogyi, and the Vaskapu Kastély Winery. The classic style of the Mecsekalja is perhaps best represented today by the wines made by the Research Institute of Viticulture and Enology based in the city of Pécs. The most impressive cellar in the region is the vast Pannonia-Cézár cellar in Pécs, which boasts 20 passageways and a combined length of 2.5 km.

new plantations, the region has never recovered from this blow, and has barely a trickle of bottled wines today.

Before the second half of the 20th century, the Mecsekalja constituted part of the official Villány appellation. In 1997, several villages were added to the now independent

Mór

Yet another hugely underrated region, Mór is distinguished by wines that never flatter but remain serious and dignified even in the sweet botrytis version. Some also say they show to best advantage when married off to other grapes in a blend. Then again, can any wine need higher praise than being compared to a good spouse?

The wine region consists of the Fejér County communities of Csákberény, Csókakő, Mór, Pusztavám, Söréd, and Zámoly. The 1,994 hectares designated for regional status include 1,459 hectares in Class I sites, but the plantations are actually confined to 799 hectares today.

The moderately cool and rainy climate follows the general pattern in northern Transdanubia, although some much more favorable microclimates have developed on the south-southwestern slopes. The annual number of sunshine hours ranges from 1900 to 2000, including 1450-1500 hours during the growing season, when the median temperature is 16,61 °C. The last spring frost usually occurs between April 20th and 25th. The distribution of rainfall shows prominent peaks in May and August, averaging 433 mm during the growing season. The outlet of the Mór Trough to the northwest exposes the terrain to gusty winds, reducing the risk of fungal infection in the vineyards.

The Vértes Range consists of Triassic flinty dolomite, with large-grained, brittle Main Dolomite providing the bulk of the hills. *Dachsteinkalk* is limited to the immediate vicinity of the village of Mór, while Cretaceous rocks are represented by smaller patches of marine limestone, marl, and shale. The Mesozoic structures are overlain by Eocene bauxite, marl, as well as limestone especially rich in the marine nummulitic protozoa that Hungarian geologists call *Szent László pénze*, or "St. Ladislaus' coins." The more recent formations include Oligocene fluvial gravel and variegated clay. Here and there, this intricately composed bedrock is covered by Pleistocene loess.

The loose Quaternary soil of the vineyards, which is formed mainly over Oligocene sands, consists of sandy loess, piedmont clay debris, gravel, and talus. The loess evolved brown forest soil, while the dolomite and limestone at higher elevations are overlain by rendzina soils alternating with red earth. The calcareous bedrock imparts a relatively high lime content to the soil. Also significantly for the vines, the Oligocene rocks have a high concentration of potassium derived from biotite mica.

The tectonic Mór Trough formed in the Quaternary when the two ranges on either

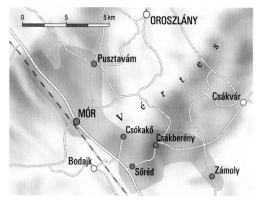

side uplifted to occupy their present-day position. The foothills of the Vértes Range flanking the Trough on the northeast consist of gentle hillsides dissected by erosional and derasional valleys, yielding to steeper piedmont slopes at higher altitudes. Needless to say, the vineyards–most famously the Árpádhegy, the Öreghegy, the Látóhegy, the Cserhát, the Kecskehegy, the Örömhegy, and the Táborhegy–are all situated on the south-southwestern slopes of the Vértes Range. The north-northeastern flank across the Trough is unfit for viticulture due to its exposure to cold air masses from the Bakony Mountains.

Mór and its vicinity turn up in 12th century charters as parts of the Csókakő castle manor. Documents dating from 1138 and 1231 mention the vineyards and serfs of Bodajk, a village adjacent to Mór, and, respectively, the vineyards of Csákberény and Vajal (today a neighborhood in Mór). The name of Mór itself first surfaces in the 15th century. The steady development of the region's viticulture was arrested by the Ottoman invasion in the 16th century. 28 of the 32 villages under the protectorate of the fortified castle of Csókakő ("Jackdaw's Rock") perished in the ensuing Ottoman wars, and the abandoned vineyards soon ran wild. For the work of reconstruction we have to give credit to the German settlers who moved here in the course of the 18th century. Mór also benefited tremendously from the arrival of the Capuchin monks, who became the best vine-dressers in the area. The 18th century thus brought a fresh start to Mór instead of directly carrying on the ancient tradition. It was probably around this time that the Ezerjó grape first materialized in the region's vineyards.

Mór reached the pinnacle of its fame in the 19th century. At least in part, its renown no doubt rested on its export of late-harvest sweet wines, which often fetched a price second only to Tokaji Aszú. The region emerged from the phylloxera epidemic with less damage than wine producing areas with cohesive soils, as the sandy loess here provided relative immunity against the pest. The district of Mór belonged to the Neszmély wine region until 1901, when the village applied for and received independent wine region status.

Many growers in Mór continue to rely on elements of traditional cultivation, including narrow spacing, bald-head training, and disbudding (which the locals call *gyomlálás*, or "weeding"). Uniquely, the Ezerjó is by far the most widely planted grape at 311 hectares, followed by Chardonnay (66 ha), Rajnai Rizling (96 ha), Rizlingszilváni (74 ha), Sauvignon Blanc (66 ha), Szürkebarát (83 ha), and Tramini (112 ha). This kind of varietal structure is actually rather typical of North Transdanubia, where viticulture has strong ethnic German roots.

Mór wines tend to be hard, fiery, and long-lived. The reputation of the region's best-known wine, Móri Ezerjó, has been severely tarnished in recent times. This has to do with the fact that Ezerjó is a very fastidious grape that is rather sensitive to rot starting early in the fall. For this reason, many growers often harvest their Ezerjó at an early date to avoid damage. However, this invariably means less than ideally ripe grapes and, consequently, wines with an unpleasant bite. Those few willing to risk a late harvest are sometimes rewarded by a firm but elegant wine of great fire and personality. In the best years, Ezerjó is often vinified in the off-dry or semi-sweet style. The rare Ezerjó Aszú is a medium to full-bodied sweet dessert wine made from shriveled grapes attacked by botrytis. It typically contains 13-14% alcohol, 10-12‰ residual sugar, and 11-12‰ acidity.

A wide-spread notion holds that Mór wines are *meszes*, or "limy." As the popular verse puts it, *A móri bor meszes, / Aki issza, eszes.* – "*The wine of Mór has lime in part, / this is what will make you smart.*" The clever rhyme notwithstanding,

laboratory analysis has not confirmed an actual lime content in Mór wines, let alone verified any intelligence-enhancing effect on those who drink it...

In addition to its hallmark Ezerjó, Mór can boast some fine old vintages of Leányka that are still impressively vigorous. Királyleányka and Muscat Ottonel, two varieties recently recommended for the region, have produced wonderfully aromatic and trim wines. In the wines harvested from the best sites, the powerful acidity derived from the soil is balanced by a body to match, but it will always stay in the foreground. Many of the region's wines may seem absolutely dry when they contain one to four grams of residual sugar. In some years, the early-ripening quality varieties may even yield wines on the semi-sweet side. The prominent producers of this small region include Endre Bognár in Csókakő, the Bozóky Winery in Mór, Hilltop Neszmély, and István Lincz, also based in Mór. The Széchenyi press house and the Dömötör Cellar, now used by the Bozóky Winery, are two of some 15 larger press houses and cellars that are still standing in Mór. A charming tradition that has been handed down by the ethnic Swabian dwellers is that of the wine soup, consumed as part of the revelry after the hard work of harvest. According to German custom, a variety of sweet pastry and biscuits are served with this soup, including *kvircedli* (Kwiezetl), *Katzenpratzl* ("cat's paw") and *Nusstangli*, a type of walnut bar.

Pannonhalma-Sokoróalja

While Pannonhalma has never really been a wine area of national significance, enthusiasts have speculated for centuries that the wine made around Szent Márton Hill cannot have been all that bad if the priests of the abbey would drink nothing else. They must be doing something right on that hill!

The imposing Benedictine Abbey of Pannonhalma

Pannonhalma-Sokoróalja is located in northwestern Transdanubia, on the fringes of Kisalföld, Hungary's "Little Plain," south of the city of Győr. The core area extends to the three hills of Pannonhalma, Csanak, and Szemere, none of which are higher than 317 m. Part of Győr-Moson-Sopron County, the wine region includes the communities of Écs, Felpéc, Győr-Ménfő-csanak, Győrság, Győrszemere, Győrújbarát, Kajárpéc, Nyalka, Nyúl, Pannonhalma, Pázmándfalu, Ravazd, and Tényő. The total designated area adds up to 3,944 hectares, including 3,236 hectares in Class I sites. Regrettably, no more than 618 hectares of this potential acreage is under vines today.

The region has a temperate continental climate, with moderately cool temperatures, sound precipitation levels, and heat sums and sunshine hours corresponding roughly to the Hungarian average. The bulk of the Sokoró Hills consists of Late Miocene (Pannonian-Pontian) lacustrine sand and clay, along with Quaternary gravel and sand. These formations evolved brown soil and thin loamy loess soils, interspersed with patches of sand in a mosaic-like pattern. The terrain is accentuated, with the best vineyards situated on the gentle southern slopes of the Sokoró and Bakony Foothills.

Pannonhalma-Sokoróalja is one of the oldest wine-producing areas in Hungary. Documentary evidence attests to a flourishing viticulture in the villages and holdings of the Benedictine Abbey on Szent Márton Hill, at the early date of 997 A.D., just one year after the foundation of the Hungarian state. More than a millennium ago, the founding charter of the Abbey itself enshrined the privilege of making wine. The Benedictine priests provided the dwellers with guidance on tending the vines, not only from the pulpit but in the vineyards as well. In the 19th century, a number of smaller growers with commercial production established themselves in the shadow of the Abbey's great estate, but the process of

diversification was cut short by the scourge of phylloxera. In 1990, after a long period of dormancy, the area received wine region status in recognition of its awakening viticulture. Having been supplemented by another two villages in 1997, Pannonhalma nowadays has a number of cooperatives and smaller growers to burnish the region's name.

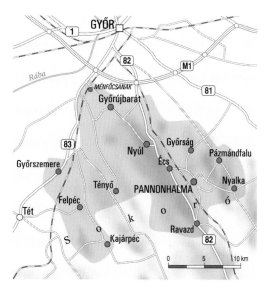

Like most white wine areas in Hungary, Pannonhalma is dominated by the Olaszrizling grape (190 ha) and, at a distant second, Rizlingszilváni (81 ha). Historically, Rajnai Rizling was quite influential here, but has lost much of its importance today. Other varieties planted in appreciable quantities include Chardonnay (32 ha), Ezerfürtű (39 ha), and Tramini (37 ha). The wines, typically cold-fermented, are lively and refreshing, with good regional character. In the 1980's and 1990's, the local cooperative still produced a Pannonhalmi Rajnai Rizling in the heavier, oxidative style. This wine—the region's best-known product in former centuries—is now relegated to collections maintained by "wine museums." More recent wines of note include

great news for the region, which somehow managed to avoid the headlines, is that the Pannonhalma Abbey in 2002 signed a deal with Magyar Külkereskedelmi Bank, whereby this major financial institution bought into Mártonhegy Kft., the company set up to oversee wine production on the church property. The purpose of the transaction is to revive the ancient tradition of monastic viticulture on the hill that lends its name to the venture.

the Báródombi Olaszrizling, the Pannonhalmi Olaszrizling, the Pannonhalmi Tramini, and the Pannonhalmi Chardonnay.

As Pannonhalma only received wine region status in 1990, the production of quality wines under the region's own name is quite recent. There have been releases from Miklós Horváth, the Szemennyei Winery, and the Pannonhalma Cooperative, but the top wines so far have emerged from the cellars of Hilltop Neszmély and the Szöllősi Winery. A piece of

Throughout the region, the visitor will encounter cellars of the *lik* ("hollow") type. These are actually cavities dug into the loess walls flanking the gulleys—locally known as *horgas*, a variant of *horhos* in standard Hungarian—that used to serve as storage for tools and wines, and even as makeshift dwellings for the growers. The most representative examples can be seen near the villages of Győrújbarát, Nyúl, and Écs.

Construction of the Abbey's cellar is under way (on the left)

141

Somló

"We had better discover Somló for ourselves before the world gets there!" This piece of good advice was offered a few years ago at a gathering of friends we call the College of Wine. At about the same time, Christoph Wagner had this to say on the pages of the Gault Millau magazine (1998/6): "Wines around the world are increasingly made in the same style, and many great wine personalities fall by the wayside. The growers of Somló, too, will likely make increasingly good wines maybe ten years from now, but these will have less distinct character to be identified by. It is precisely this genre of 'good' wines where the role of provenance and terroir is relegated to the background. Now Somló Hill is possessed of a terroir, in the true sense of the term, which no other wine region in the world could possibly emulate."

What are the distinguishing features that make Somló so special? The list is a long one. To cite just two examples from recent memory, it was here that growers prevailed over the Hungarian wine bureaucracy when they managed to legalize Juhfark, the region's ancient indigenous grape variety. It was here that the industrialized vineyards planted in the lowlands to meet the quotas of a planned economy first ran wild when the political winds changed. The people of Somló did not need the plain wine of the plain; they wanted the high-flying wines they could only make higher up on the hill. Somló also benefited from being avoided by the waves of cheap tourism that continue to plague popular Hungarian wine regions such as Sopron and Eger, not to mention the shores of Lake Balaton. Somló has preserved this relative tranquility at the expense of the unprecedented fragmentation of its vineyards. Although we have no precise data available, if we divide the total growing area of 700 hectares by 3400, the estimated number of growers today, we get an average property size of a mere 0.2 hectares, or about half an acre! Before 1999, no one in the area had a modern bottling line of a reasonably capacity, and the production of the best growers—invariably owners of handkerchief-size plots—was limited to a few thousand bottles a year until recently. But before comparing the region's past and present, let us hear the personal testimony of two famous authors about what the wine of Somló meant to them.

Sándor Márai, the eminent novelist: *"When I grow old, I will want to have a cellar… I will not pick up a book less than a thousand years old, and will sip a five-year-old Somlói to smooth the way of reading… The wine of Somló is the repository of the noblest qualities inherent in the Hungarian people: Eastern wisdom and Western civilization. It has a little of Asia's serenity and a little of Europe's inquisitiveness—the most fortuitous blend in both wines and people."*

Béla Hamvas, the noted philosopher: *"Very few wines are universal in the sense that all of humanity can be imagined to drink it together at a great feast—say, the feast of world peace. Of all Hungarian wines, I would only recommend Somlói for this purpose. Curiously, this is also the wine of the lonesome."* [And yet Hamvas relates how a Hungarian count recommended an Indian Raja to drink Somló wine to regain his virility—allegedly with remarkable success.] *"Somlai is a wine of fire, grown on a volcano with no water anywhere near. The hill rises above a great plain and is shaped like a crown. Among all our wines, for me Somlai is the non plus ultra… and while any serious hill-grown wine has more affinity with life after forty than with youth, Somló is a wine for true old age. It is the wine of the sage, who has learnt the greatest knowledge to be learnt: that of quietude."* Elsewhere Hamvas relates his penchant for consuming a variety of wines with a single meal, and concludes that *"the sine qua non immediately preceding coffee will have to be Ruszti Aszú or a glass of Somlai, preferably twenty years old."* *

THE FACTS

ORIENTATION

Somló is situated on the eastern periphery of the Kisalföld ("Little Plain"), not far from the towns of Ajka and Pápa. The Somló Hill itself is a solitary volcanic butte rising 432 m above sea level, with plantations reaching an altitude of 350 m. However, the official wine region named Somló also includes the Kis-Somlyó and the Ság, two smaller hills some 20 kilometers to the east and northeast of the eponymous butte. In this introduction, we will focus on Somló proper, often referred to as *Nagysomló* ("Great Somló") to differentiate it from its lesser brother.

NUMBERS

Somló encompasses 700 hectares today, and was shrinking steadily since World War II until recently. In 1998, growers posted a total crop of 4700 tons (white grapes only). Varieties include, in alphabetical order, Chardonnay (45 ha), Ezerjó (15 ha), Furmint (35 ha), Hárslevelű (40 ha), Juhfark (25 ha), Olaszrizling (350 ha), Rajnai Rizling (15 ha), Rizlingszilváni (30 ha), Tramini (15 ha), and other miscellaneous grapes (30 ha).

CLIMATE

Insolation: 1950-2000 hours; median temperature: 9.8 °C; precipitation: 600-700 mm (annual figures). Remarkably, the Somló is the only volcanic butte north of Lake Balaton where vines can be found even on the northern face of the hill.

GEOLOGY

The core of Somló consists of Pontian (Miocene) lacustrine deposits overlain by clay-marl and sandstone, on which a huge volcanic eruption spilled a spread of basalt and tuff. These two rocks make a vital contribution to the topsoils and thus to the character of Somló wines. At the foot of the hill, sandy-clayey soils and loess adobe dominate, while higher up on the hillsides the basalt and weathered tuff debris have evolved excellent soils uniquely rich in trace elements and minerals. Some of these substances have been leached out of the soil of the steeper slopes to enrich the adobe soils at the lower elevations below.

143

* Note Hamvas's spelling *Somlai*, an older variation of the adjectival form *Somlói*; we retained both versions in the above quotes for purposes of illustration. Speaking about tradition and orthography, we might as well recall the noun form *Somlyó* [pronounced *shom-yo*], an old alternative to *Somló* [*shom-lo*], the accepted spelling and pronunciation of the proper name today.

Castle ruins on top
of the hill

TURNING POINTS OF HISTORY

The fortified castle perched on top of Somló is first mentioned in a charter drawn up in 1093; wine production on the hill can be documented since 1135. The three chapels on different sections of the hill, dedicated to Szent Márton, Szent Margit, and Szent Ilona, were built during the 14th century; the first cartographic representation of the castle survives from 1528.

The next documented stage in the hill's sketchy history is 1570, when 121 growers on the hill paid a form of tax known as the "hill toll" to the conquering Ottoman forces. More than a century later, Napoleon's troops passed through the region, claiming an equally severe sacrifice from the villagers in pillage and loot. But the most lethal threat to the vineyards arrived in the form of the phylloxera in the late 19th century. The application of carbon disulphide seemed to deliver results at first, but it did not prove to be a permanent protection against the root louse. As elsewhere in the country, the reassuring solution was to graft noble scions onto American rootstock, even though this measure transformed the region's set of grape varieties to a significant degree.

Throughout history, the hill has been divided between the Church and the lay aristocracy. A lack of ownership by the "free estates," including the bourgeoisie and the lesser nobility, hampered development for centuries. In 1933, a rather successful cooperative was founded, only to be swept aside by the drive for nationalization in the wake of World War II, though it is true to say that large industrialized plantations never made deep inroads in Somló as they did elsewhere in the country. Even in the "halcyon days" of planned economy, the Badacsony State Farm

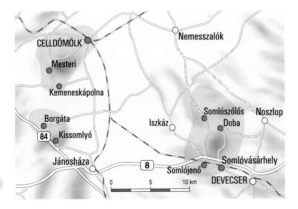

IMRE GYÖRGYKOVÁCS, VINTAGE 1950

A man who calls every bunch of grapes he grows by name, Györgykovács is a qualified horticulturist with an unlikely remote background in telecommunication engineering. Local food specialties are hard to come by in the press houses of Somló, simply because the region has hardly any to offer, but Görgykovács and his wife Gyöngyi, his steadfast support, always treat their guests to some well-chosen delicacies to suit the excellent wines. The Györgykovács winery is a genuine manufactory in the classic sense of the term, based on a single hectare of vines. The legend started in 1994, when a lawyer named Gyula Dávid took the recently discovered Györgykovács under his wings, and relieved this gifted winemaker–and a man totally incapable of managing his own affairs–of the daily chores that come with business. As for the wines themselves, they are invariably fermented and aged in wood, but they are so pure they can inspire doubt in those who cannot believe they have never seen stainless steel. As far as we are concerned, we simply marvel at the man's ability to keep his barrels so impeccably clean. Such rigorous hygiene in the cellar certainly pays dividends. We have yet to encounter a Györgykovács bottle with any type of flaw (except of course for the very occasional corked bottle, which is not the winemaker's fault). Györgykovács's wines do not distinguish themselves by overwhelming concentration, but by an accomplished balance of taste that is often transmuted to ethereal harmony with age. They are exceptionally long-lived; some barrel samples from 1989 and 1990 that the man "bunged up on the run" still hold their ground firmly. Beyond his sheer good taste and penchant for purity, Györgykovács is characterized by a punctilious attitude bordering on anxiety–a spirit possibly instilled by a grandfather, who was the cellar master of the Abbey of Zirc.

controlled no more than 37 hectares in the area, and by 1987, 79% of the area suitable for growing high-quality wines was in the hands of individual growers.

Another important date in the chronology of the wine hill is February 27, 1629, when Somló's first wine law was enacted (the original of this milestone document is kept in the museum of Pápa). This statute regulated life on the hill, mainly by listing the fines to be levied against various offenders. Decrees from 1743, 1803, and 1864 provided for communal norms, including the rules of purchasing and selling plots of vine, and the hierarchy of officialdom on the wine hill. The lowest rank in the wine community was that of the simple *szőlőpásztor* ("vine shepherd" or vine-dresser), followed by the *hegymester* ("master") and the *hegybíró* ("magistrate") above him. The loftiest position was that of the *hegyelnök* ("president"), a largely ceremonial echelon reserved for members of the nobility.

Important detailed accounts of Somló were published in 1736 and 1836 by Mátyás Bél and Elek Fényes, but the work that remains most useful to us today is *A Nagy Somló hegyről* ("On the Great Somló Hill"), a treatise printed in 1848 by Sándor Cseresnyés, the Chief Medical Officer of Veszprém County. Already at this time, Somló was clearly distinct from the other wine-producing areas west of the Danube, not only geographically, but also in terms of its ownership structure, the mindset of its growers, and the taste of its wines.

The chapels already mentioned played a major part in the life of the community. From the road hemmed by poplars that most people will take off of highway 8 to approach the hill, the most conspicuous one is the Szent Margit Chapel to the right, but certain stretches of the road also afford a view of the Szent Ilona Chapel on the left. These landmarks have been vital for the locals not only for their beauty as places of worship, but also as points of orientation. Except during the dreary years of Soviet occupation, the hillside chapels always served as holy destinations for collective pilgrimage, a peculiar form of folk ceremony practiced around the Carpathian Basin. The procession would wind its way up on the hill chanting supplications for a blessed harvest. Although a priest was invariably present, the apocryphal chants and prayers were rife with transmuted pagan motifs. They remain some of the most important vestiges of ancient Hungarian folk poetry.

TONGUES OF LAVA

Even from the best lookout points on the hill, it is impossible to trace the lava as it must have poured down the side of the volcano eons ago, but getting closer to the ground it is easy to make out the signs of former volcanic activity. The messengers are nuggets of basalt, worn by time and erosion to a size seldom larger than a cherry. In some places on the slopes, there is no soil as such in evidence, because every inch of the ground is covered by the *kukoricabazalt*, or "corn basalt." The blanket made of these grains of weathered volcanic rock is intermittently present as you work your way up towards the imaginary caldera, but if you trace it skirting the hill along a contour line, it will break off abruptly in a perpendicular direction. These spits or "tongues" of lava impart extraordinary concentration and opulence of flavor to the wines grown on them, provided that the yield is not allowed to cross a certain threshold. These are the great wines of Somló, marked with a classic mineral note in their taste. Yes indeed, the lava tongues could speak volumes about why a plot of vines in Somló can sell for several times as much as another plot of the same size next door.

THE GROWERS

FAZEKAS WINERY, Somlóvásárhely — A well-known grower based near the Margit Chapel, with traditional, even classic Somló wines displaying all the virtues and flaws that come with the style. Happily, the former far outweigh the latter in the balance.

KÁROLY FEHÉRVÁRI — Traditional Somló wines in the oxidative style, but never erring on the side of excessive oxidation. Wines of character for those who like well-matured flavors in their glass.

BÉLA FEKETE, VINTAGE 1926
Having spent a lifetime career in forestry, Béla Fekete has always made wine for a hobby, but did not begin to plant on any scale of consequence until a few years before his retirement. Together with his wife Borbála and son Zsolt, Fekete runs a scant five hectares, but the ideal aspect and the magnificent soil of his plantation make this small estate virtually priceless. The wines have a very powerful

mineral character owing to the "corn basalt" in the soil. Remarkably, the boundary of the lava tongue can be pinpointed with an accuracy of two meters in Fekete's vineyard.

In some years, such as 1993, Fekete's Hárslevelű, his main grape, collected nearly the maximum score from tasting panels in Hungary, although his Furmint and Juhfark can be a little more forceful than the optimum. Aside from this, they are always true expressions of Somló character, and matured just to the right point. Remarkably, Chardonnay delivers an excellent performance in Fekete's estate; the 1998 attained five-

A terrace just below the basalt "organ pipes"

147

ENDRE TORNAI, Somlóvásárhely — A family winery whose 1988 Olaszrizling can be regarded as the wine that marked the fall of the Iron Curtain in Hungary. When Thummerer in Eger and Polgár in Villány came out with a bottled product, Tornai's wines had already been available in the better grocery stores in Budapest for some time. Upgraded in 1999 with 4000 hectoliters of storage capacity and a modern bottling line, the winery represents the pinnacle of technology in Somló today.

THE WINE

It is difficult to add anything wise to the assessments quoted from Márai and Hamvas earlier, except that Somló may well serve as a touchstone of all Hungarian wine. But how does the world at large form an opinion? The wines of Somló, like those of Tokaj or Badacsony, demand to be appreciated and judged differently than through the customary set of evaluation criteria. These are wines of mystery that will divulge their secrets only to those who can understand the language they speak. To put it in more practical terms, these wines will never get the credit they deserve if tasted and assessed the same way as a cold-fermented wine made from a western grape variety with specific yeasts. Lumped together with such wines, a Somló may easily come off as nondescript and uncouth—very unlike the wonderful experience it will afford when given sufficient bottle age, sufficient time to breathe when that bottle is opened, and tasted at a temperature of 13-15 °C, slightly warmer than usual for a dry white.

Anyhow, Somló is not a spectacular wine that bowls you over; it will never make a cheap show of its talent. It is decidedly aloof when young, but at two years of age it will open up beautifully in the glass after some unhurried exposure to air. It must be laid down, and will keep for a very long time. In this respect, it can compete with the best of dry Tokaj. It ages gracefully, but will assume unusual animal nuances reminiscent of fine Russia leather. (Many growers in Somló will consider this association an insult, but the

star status in its peak form. The winery is essentially a reliable one, although it has suffered from improvised, stop-and-go development on occasion. Nobody familiar with the history of the estate will hold this against the family.

ISTVÁN INHAUSER — Based on the Somlószőlős side of the hill, Inhauser supplied the stores of Budapest with the finest wines, young and old, that came out of Somló in the mid-1990's. Also known as a producer of viable quantities of classic but very approachable Juhfark, Inhauser has won undying recognition for vindicating this grape in defiance of the authorities.

note is often clearly present in mature items, and is far from being objectionable in our opinion.) On average, Somló has the distinction among Hungarian dry whites of possessing the highest concentration of extract. Partly for this reason, it is an enduring wine that tolerates transportation well. It also has medicinal powers attributed to it far beyond the confines of this tiny wine region.

Is cold-fermented, reductive Somló wine a feasibility, on the analogy of Tokaj, as it were? It certainly is, but only at the expense of sacrificing some distinct regional character. But what do we regard as good Somló wine; or an unadulterated one, for that matter? Is there a yardstick at all? These are rhetorical questions. Only one thing seems certain: no wine in Somló could or should be made without maturation in wooden casks.

The career of Somlói Aszú offers some interesting lessons. Starting in the 16th century, peasant serfs and aristocratic estates both made smaller or larger quantities of late-harvested sweet wines called Aszú, as in Tokaj. The serfs did not pay a tithe contribution out of these sweet wines. This caused friction with the landowners on such a scale that the National Diet put the case on its agenda in 1655. At long last, Queen Maria Theresa in 1779 abolished the tithe levied on Aszú wines. Curiously, a book published nearly 200 years ago describes Somló's desiccated grapes as making a "wine or *ürmös* that is strong, sweet and enduring, but hardly a match for a Badacsony in sweetness."

GRAPES OLD AND NEW

Prior to the phylloxera epidemic, at least 30 different grapes were cultivated in Somló; most sources list 36-37 varieties. Nowadays we know that the grapes that perform best on the hill are the same *Furmint* and *Hárslevelű* that made Tokaj famous. Hárslevelű yielded the finest wine in Somló until 1997, when its ascendancy was challenged by the increasingly planted Furmint. The success of this variety was sealed by Imre Györgykovács's 1997 vintage. In the early 1990's, a few small growers made some very nice wines from the Királyfurmint clone of the grape. But who walled up any of these wines to see if they are any good today?

Olaszrizling – Rich and vigorous, with good mouthfeel; concentrated and elegant. Accounts for half the output of Somló today.

Juhfark – Relentlessly harsh if unripe; can be wonderful if made from fully ripe grapes. Mildly tannic. Csomorika is a grape that few can tell from Juhfark. Many Juhfark bottles actually contain a portion of Csomorika, and are not always the worse for it.

Tramini – Makes a very appealing, pure and ageworthy wine in Somló. Unusually for the grape, Somlói Tramini is but faintly aromatic, and has a broad acid foundation.

But what about the trendy international varieties? Does the powerful terroir of Somló outmuscle the varietal character of *Chardonnay*, or is it a synergistic combination capable of engendering fabulous wines? There is indeed a chance for such a miracle, because the soil here possesses the same minerals that shape the greatest white Burgundy, along the lines of Mersault or Montrachet. This is another area where Somló departs from Tokaj, which is yet to give us an enjoyable and enduring Chardonnay. It is also one more reason to discover this wonderful solitary hill before the rest of the world gets there.

Sopron

No other wine region in Hungary has been abused more than Sopron. In fact, we do not even know if its true face is red or white; and we will not even mind if it takes the advice of a neighbor from Austria to show it to us.

The westernmost wine-producing area in Hungary, Sopron has had a firm reputation for its wines and well-organized wine trade since medieval times. The sub-alpine region occupies slopes of the Sopron Mountains skirting the southern and western shores of Lake Fertő, and is a direct continuation of the vineyards across the border in Burgenland, Austria (under the Leitha Mountains and around Rust). The

northern section of the Sopron region, the one marginally better suited for viticulture, forms a triangle between Fertőrákos, Balf, and Lake Fertő, and dips toward the Lake. The other main section is located east of the town of Sopron to the village of Fertőszentmiklós; vineyards also line the road to Harka to the south.

The region traditionally extends to the Győr-Moson-Sopron County communities of Fertőboz, Fertőendréd, Fertőrákos, Fertő-szentmiklós, Fertőszéplak, Harka, Hidegség, Kópháza, and Sopron. A few years ago, the vineyards around Kőszeg, Csepreg and Vaskeresztes were added on, boosting the region's potential acreage to 4,287 hectares. This total area includes 3,236 hectares in Class I sites, although only 1,705 hectares are actually under vines.

The temperate continental climate is free from extremes, although the sub-alpine influence results in lower median temperatures and higher rainfall than the national average. The summer is cooler and wetter than anywhere else in the country, but the winters are beneficially mild. Gusty winds are fairly common throughout. As the old local adage goes, "In Sopron, it's either raining or windy, or else the bells are ringing."

The metamorphic crystalline gneiss and mica schist that make up the Sopron Mountains were formed during the Paleozoic period. These old formations are overlain by Miocene gravel, shale, limestone, sandstone, and coal seams, all covered by a stratum of Quaternary loess. The weathered Sarmatian and Pannonian debris, limestone and loess evolved clayey loess and brown earth soils, as well as loose Pleistocene sands. The *ranker* is a soil variety that typically develops over crystalline schist bedrock. Despite the less than ideal climate, the articulation of the terrain has facilitated the emergence of fine microclimates on the hills around Lake Fertő and the sheltered southern and eastern slopes of the Sopron Mountains. While the growers themselves are keenly aware of the differences between the individual terroirs, these distinctions have not yet become common knowledge. An exception is the Spern Steiner, which has recently attained a wider reputation through Franz Weninger's excellent single-vineyard wines.

Sopron was probably founded by the Celts. The Romans called it Scarabantia, and there is archaeological evidence to suggest that they tended vines on the slopes around the town. After the establishment of the Hungarian state, vineyards in Sopron County are first mentioned in an endowment contract dated 1230. A charter signed by King Stephen V in 1270 reveals that the bowmen of Sopron owned extensive vineyards and made large quantities of wine. In 1277, the founding charter of the town of Sopron described vines within the city limits and provided for the levy of tithes on wine.

Settlers from Lower Austria arrived in the area in the 13th and 14th centuries. The sizable German-speaking minority diversified Sopron's population and naturalized advanced technologies of grape processing and winemaking. In the 14th and 15th centuries, the wine of Sopron became one of Hungary's most sought-after export commodities in Europe. By the beginning of the 17th century, the city had adopted protective laws not only banning the local sale of wines from other regions, but even imposing a tax on any wine shipment passing through. The regulations effectively made tavern rights a privilege of local growers, subject to certain stipulations. In the early 1700's, Sopron exported thousands of hectoliters of wine to various European locations, including Silesia (a region divided between the Czech Republic, Germany and Poland today). Until the end of the 18th century, wine remained the chief source of income of the Hungarian and German citizens of Sopron.

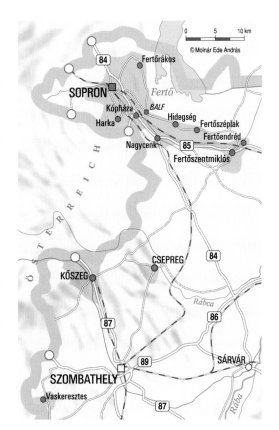

The viticulture of Sopron is recorded in the very first Hungarian treatises discussing wine in a professional manner. In 1723, Mátyás Bél correlated rising water levels of Lake Fertő with a better quality and more abundant crop. Correspondingly, he associated ebbing waters with an inferior harvest. The explanation probably has to do with the fact that wetter years were more conducive to berry growth and noble rot.

As elsewhere in the country, the 19th century saw a shift toward quantity-oriented wine production. The process was cut short in the 1890's when phylloxera reared its head in Sopron, and promptly obliterated nearly all the vines. In the aftermath of the epidemic, wine production took a new turn that makes itself felt to this day in the altered varietal structure of the vineyards, and the diminution of the sector's significance in the economy and life of the city. To make things worse, the triumphant Allies in 1946 ordered the large-scale deportation of the ethnic German population who had tended most of the city's vines. The final blow came with the setting up of state farms and centrally managed cooperatives.

151

Robert Wenzel makes sweet botrytis wines in Rust in Austria, just across the border from Sopron

tant second on 109 hectares, followed by a near equal proportion of Cabernet Sauvignon (106 ha). The most common white grapes are the traditional Zöld Veltelini (85 ha), which dominated the entire region at the outset of the 20th century, and the more recently planted Chardonnay (33 ha). This inevitably raises the issue of why and how black grapes rose to prominence in the wake of the phylloxera epidemic in a region that had been devoted to white wine production exclusively. The answer is that the new social class that had emerged with industrialization wanted cheaper, mediocre wines. Always quick to respond to changing demand, the astute growers of Sopron abandoned the low-yielding quality white varieties in favor of Kékfrankos, a heavy-producing grape, especially when trained on the cane-pruned cordon. The turnaround will seem all the more remarkable if one considers that, in 1861, red wines accounted for a mere 10% of Sopron's total output of 21,970 hectoliters, and even that 10% consisted of Kékoportó. Nowadays, Kékfrankos is widely considered native to Sopron, even though it is more likely of Austrian origin.

Back in the 18th century, the Furmint grape used to make the best wine in Sopron. In suitable years, late-harvested Furmint was vinified as sweet Aszú, whose popularity abroad and chemical properties that allowed safe transportation over long distances made it an important export commodity. Decimated by the phylloxera, Sopron's production of Aszú wines dropped from 1000 hectoliters in 1893 to 500 in 1894, and 200 in 1895. Once the pest had made a clean slate of the vineyards, the Soproni Aszú never came back, although the sweet tradition was upheld in Rust west of Lake Fertő. After a hiatus that started in 1919, sweet botrytis wines are made in better years once again around Rust (today part of Austria), more often than not using the Furmint grape.

Sopron's cool climate and calcareous soils yield red wines that are high-acid but not particularly tannic. They also tend to be

Lacking any motivation by pride of private ownership, these outfits were hardly well-equipped to care for the abandoned vineyards. Another consequence of the industrialization was an all-out displacement of traditional head training and cane-pruned high training methods. The privatization drive that followed the demise of the communist regime resulted in improving quality and a sensible reduction of vineyard acreage.

The wines of Sopron—and, to a lesser degree, those of Kőszeg—were held in such high regard that growers had reason to guard against theft and burglary by moving their wine into the city for storage. As a result of this security measure, the cellars were not built out in the vineyards, but within the city walls—in particular, under the houses where the growers lived. This custom also made sense in light of the stringent ordinance banning non-local wines within the city walls. With cellars located outside the city limits, the council would have been unable to precisely monitor inventories and sales.

Sopron today is a predominantly red-wine producing region, with Kékfrankos holding sway on 1,113 hectares. Zweigelt is the dis-

somewhat lower in alcohol, which is not necessarily a drawback given the recent shifts of taste in red wines. These potential merits notwithstanding, the often hard red wines of Sopron do not have universal appeal, although their peculiar "butch" style has a certain following. (Preferences of taste aside, the more important question to ask is why red wines just a stone's throw away across the Austrian border far outstrip the average quality of their Hungarian counterparts.)

Sopron also has some production of slightly jagged rosé from Kékfrankos, but the dry whites are of more interest. Although these can be on the hard side as well, they are generally fresh, aromatic, and, if vinified with care, capable of finesse of acidity. A case in point is Sauvignon Blanc, which has yielded some very convincing local examples in recent years.

The last half decade or so has brought explosive change, owing to a dozen growers who set their sights higher, and also to the favorable location near the Austrian border. This allows Sopron residents to directly profit from visitors–mostly Austrian–who jump across the border any time of the year, and whose presence encourages higher standards in all aspects of catering–including the quality of the local wine. Among the winemakers, special mention must be made of Austria's Franz Weninger, whose 1997 Kékfrankos harvested in Sopron moved the goal posts, and has been a sort of driving force in the region. Other producers of note include the Gangls, Hauer, Jandl, Zoltán Iváncsics, Lővér, Luka, Dr. Szita and Son, Taschnervin, and Vincellérház, as well as three large wineries, namely Vinex, Hungarovin, and Hilltop Neszmély (formerly Interconsult).

Uniquely in Hungary, Sopron is home to the tavern-type establishment known as the *Buschenschank*. The institution goes back to the 17th century, when the city emulated Lower Austrian regulations by allowing residents who took the civic oath to pour wine–strictly their own product–at their narrower place of residence. The licensed neighborhood taverns were marked by a sign

using a branch of fir suspended from a long pole over the entrance. The sign was decorated with a white or red canvas ribbon or a straw cross, depending on whether the house poured white wine, red, or a mature old vintage. The wines were actually served and consumed in the courtyard of the house or, in winter or bad weather, in the main room indoors. The proprietor of the *Buschenschank* made it a point of honor to pour his finest wines. No wonder it was often difficult to get a place in the best houses during the peak hours of service.

The growers who grew, made and poured the wines belonged to the old Sopron class of the *ponzichters*, whose German ancestors had settled down in Sopron in medieval times and attained citizenship. This typically urban ethnic group pursued a very different lifestyle than the simple villagers. The name *ponzichter*, originally also used as a slur, is a distorted form of German *Bohnenzüchter*–a reference to these ethnic German growers' custom of planting beans between the rows of vines. Starting in 1919, the *ponzichters* found themselves in a curious stand-off with the students of the Academy

Franz Weninger of Burgenland, making the best Hungarian Kékfrankos in Balf, Sopron

of Mines, Metallurgy, and Forestry that had just relocated from Selmec to Sopron. The students never tired of inventing ways to vex the venerable citizens, and enshrined them in vitriolic verses with the obvious purpose of *épater la bourgeoisie*. The *ponzichters* did not much mind being made fun of, as the packs of students inevitably wound up in their *Buschenschanks* to spend their allowance they got from back home.

Wine tourism is a booming business in Sopron these days, helped along by designated wine trails and a host of wonderful sights we have no room in this book to discuss. Let us simply recommend a few cellars that are also relics of a rich heritage of rural architecture. The vicinity of Kőszegszerdahely and Cák is famous for the *kalabuk* type log cellar, characterized by a forward-leaning truss and a thatched reed roof. A quite similar row of cellars can be found in Szentkút (Heiligenbrunn) in Burgenland, just two kilometers from the Hungarian border. The Vasi-Hegyhát Plateau, which is no longer part of the official wine region, provides a wonderful hunting ground for quaint log

József Horváth, the passionate owner and chef of Ráspi with truffles

cellars dispersed in villages such as Oszkó, Döbörhegy, Szarvaskend, Hegyháthodász, and Petőmihályfa. For the most part, the cellars in Vaskeresztes and Felsőcsatár were built in the rural neoclassicist style, and reflect a more sophisticated culture of wine.

WHERE TO EAT

No gourmet of a professional bent would likely accept on face value the assertion that the best restaurants in Hungary are invariably those that decline to serve the underage with a dreary soda pop, offering instead a non-alcoholic spritzer flavored with a sweet and tart home-made syrup of fresh elder blossom or strawberry—or, for that matter, of any of fifteen other fruits, as is the case at József Horváth's RÁSPI RESTAURANT in Fertőrákos. And yet this passion for the symbolic elder cooler and other miracles of hand-picked natural goodness is a common denominator that Horváth shares with Lajos Takács of the Szent Orbán Borház in Badacsony, and Pascal Lemann of the Ős Kaján in Tolcsva. Needless to say, all three chefs cherish fine wine, swear by hand-crafted, unrepeatable dishes, recoil from any ingredient shy of utter perfection, and refuse to debase their sanctuaries of culinary rapture by churning out grub on the run. True enough, there are other places with a discriminating wine list, where one feels flawlessly taken care of in all aspects of well-being, and where dining can be a truly uplifting experience. So what is it that really elevates this unlikely gastronomic triumvirate above the rest? It must be that elder thing after all, and what it stands for: the rejection of everything artificial, ready-made, trendy, or unconscionably profitable. A few kilometers from Sopron, József Horváth has turned the little village of Fertőrákos into a Mecca of culinary enlightenment for Hungarian and Austrian patrons. As for his cooking, we would be hard put to nail it down to a style. It is neither avant-garde nor nouvelle cuisine, any more than it is traditional or modernist. The man simply lives his creative dream in the enchantment

of smell and taste. He will reveal himself to fellow sensitive souls, and he is receptive in his turn to well-taken commentary—not flattery, but constructive criticism. He is an institution in the most dignified sense of the term. It would be difficult to single out any sensory impression at Ráspi. Should it be the heavenly flavor of boletus, the tart fragrance of invigorating garden herbs, or the succulence of the home-made chocolate-wrapped cherry brandy? Let everyone decide to his or her preference. One thing is indisputable: Horváth's ingredients include everything Hungary has to offer, from truffles to forest cornelian and from brook trout to Balaton pike-perch; but strictly nothing foreign to the country. Salmon, shellfish and lobster may be delicious, but are out of the question at Ráspi. Instead, look out for home-made noodles and bread, just the way grandma used to make them. There are no fancy steamers or shiny chrome in the

Spring a'la Ráspi

kitchen. But there is a large, well-stocked cellar, a wooden statue, and a carved marble sink—all the handiwork of a man blessed with a creative imagination. This is not a place for just dropping by. It's an encounter for which you must be prepared, in spirit and with time to abide.

155

Szekszárd

Whoever first said Szekszárdi was the wine of love was certainly not far off the truth. Szekszárdi is not monumental but still somehow festive. It does not bowl you over but fills you with experience. Not awe-inspiring but certainly unforgettable, it is a wine to return to, any time of the year—or any time of one's life.

Szekszárd's finest vineyards flank the old part of the town

Szekszárd is located between the Tolna-Baranya Hills and the Danube, just west of the river's flood plain called the Sárköz. Although the region is regarded as consisting of "hills" according to official geographical taxonomy, the hill rising in its heart is known to locals and vinophiles as *Szekszárdi-hegy*, or Szekszárd Mountain. The vineyards that made this land famous lie on the eastern slopes of the range running north to south from the town of Szekszárd to Báta. They include the renowned Őcsény, Decs, and Sárpilis,

although the villages themselves after which these vineyards are named are located 3-5 kilometers away, on the alluvial flats.

The wine region extends to the Tolna County communes of Alsónána, Alsónyék, Báta, Bátaszék, Decs, Harc, Őcsény, Sióagárd, Szálka, Szekszárd, Várdomb, and Zomba. The total designated acreage is 6,001 hectares, including 3,789 hectares in Class I sites, but only 2,225 hectares are actually under cultivation today.

The temperate continental climate is characterized by a hot summer and a mild winter. The annual mean temperature is 11.7 °C. In the summer, temperatures sometimes rise to 34 °C, contributing to the large heat sum of 1950-2050 hours of sunshine, including 1480 hours during the growing season. On the downside, low precipitation levels (of about 600 mm on the 19-year average, and less than 400 mm during the growing season) can cause drought in some years. Importantly for sensitive varieties like Kadarka and Merlot, spring and autumn frosts are infrequent. Red wine grapes also benefit from a fall season that is both warmer and dryer than the Hungarian average, and therefore very helpful in reducing the risk of rot in the vineyards. Winter is shorter and much less severe than in the Great Plain to the east. As a result, Szekszárd has one of the longest growing seasons of all the wine regions in Hungary.

Occupying altitudes of 100 to 120 m, The Szekszárd Hill and the entire range were formed during the most recent period of Earth's geological history. The core of the hills consists of the Late Miocene deposits of the Pannonian Lake, cropping out here an there in the flanks of transverse valleys. Landslides on the vine-covered slopes often reveal the lacustrine shale, clay-marl, sand, and, occasionally, sandstone, all of which formed 6-8 million years ago. After the Pannonian Lake filled up, the gradually uplifting surface evolved red clay and talus in the Quaternary, subsequently overlain by Late Pliocene eolian loess. This mantle of loess, generally a few meters thick but reaching a depth of 30 m to the north of Szekszárd, is the decisive formation underneath the region's vineyards, and is a fine parent rock that develops excellent soils for red wines. These clayey loess soils typically contain 5-7% active lime, with some of them exhibiting a carbonate saturation as high as 10-30%. They yield richer, more complex wines than less intensely calcareous soils, for instance sand. Brown forest soil also occur in the Geresd Hills to the southwest.

In the northern fringes of the range, the all-important rock that comes near the sur-

face underneath the loess blanket is nutrient-rich red clay. It is this formation that evolved Szekszárd's celebrated *vörös föld*, or "red earth" subsoil, tinted a rusty red by oxidized iron. Shallow enough for the vine's roots to reach after breaking through the layer of loess, this soil typically has a neutral pH, occasionally a little on the acidic side. East of the foothills, the alluvial soils in the flood plain of the Danube are hardly suitable for viticulture.

Szekszárd's terrain has a variegated morphology. The 285-m tall Óriás-hegy ("Giant Hill") rises like a colossus among the surrounding dwarf hills. The low elevation (150-250 m) of the slopes and plateaus helps minimize the risk of frost. The intensely accentuated range is dissected by steep, erosional-derasional valleys and ravines, both transverse and longitudinal, providing a great variety of distinct microclimates. The best wines are grown on the slopes facing south and southeast; vineyards of a western and northern aspect yield a slightly lower quality. The finest vineyards are Csatár, Remete, Parászta, Csótányi, Iván, Fatai, Bence, Nagymihály, Előhegy, and Porkoláb; as well as the eastern Bakta,

Loess overlying the famous red earth of Szekszárd

5

Palánki-puszta

PALÁNKPU

Sió

Hidas-sziget

Hidas-sziget

Palánki-sziget

Leányvár

Rózsamáj

Füstöstő

Sz. Mihály-dűlő

PALÁNK

Völgységi-patak

Hidas-sziget

Borkút

Palánki-hegy
231

Palánki-völgy

Faddi-völgy

Fuksz-völgy

Jobbparászta

56

Malomta

5

Malom-oldal

Balparászta

Bikó

Parásztai-séd

Malom-dűlő

Hidas-völgy

Petre-völgy

Saul-völgy

Szalai-völgy

Cser-hát-hegy
274

Bottyán-hegy
210

ÉSZAKI-
KERTVÁROS

Epreske

Gyertyános-dűlő

Hosszú-völgy

Bagó-völgy

Kopasz-hegy

Előhegy

Benedek-völgy

Öreg-Petre-hegy

Jobbremete

MÉREY-LTP.

ÚJVÁROS

Kerék-hegy

Balremete

FELSŐVÁROS

Szekszárdi-séd

Kor

Éles-hegyhát

Nagy-bödő-hegy
256

BARTINA

Kálvária-h.
205

YBL-LTP.

TÁRTSAY-LTP.

Baranya-völgy

Kiskert

Kis-bödő-hegy
256

Kisbödő-völgy

Csötönyi-völgy

Porkoláb-völgy

Bartina-hegy
235

ALSÓVÁROS

Szekszárdi-séd

Csatári-árok

Faluhely

BAKTA

Bükkös-erdő

Bodzás-dűlő

Gyűszü-völgy

Bakta-hegy
195

SZEKSZÁRD

Szilfa-dűlő

Cseresznyés

Csatári-völgy

CSATÁR

Felső-erdő

Gurovica

Almási-erdő

Szőlőhegy

56

Szállás-völgy

Tót-völgy

CINKA

Szállás-völgy

Újhegy

Szőlőhegy

Ebes

Residental area; Garten

Forest; Wineyard, Orch

Pared roads

Other road, Unpared ro

Railway

1 : 32 000

0

© Molnár Ede András

Bartina, and Palánk, and the western Bödő, Tökös, Cinka, and Gesztenyés. As part of the vineyard reconstruction after the phylloxera, growers formed terraces and implemented other measures to fight the constant threat of erosion. The paved roads in the hillsides double as conduits for rainwater.

The first relics of a local viticulture date back to Roman times. One of them is an 11-ton marble sarcophagus, with a decoration on a side panel illustrating a bearing grape-vine growing out of a double chalice. In another sepulcher, the inscription on a sacrificial chalice placed next to the body proclaims a curious wisdom: "Make an offering to the shepherd, drink, and you shall live." During the six centuries that elapsed between the winding up of the Roman colony and the arrival of Magyar tribes, the migrating people that passed through and sometimes stayed on in the area apparently carried on the legacy of tending vines. This is suggested by the round earthenware flasks found in the graveyards of the Avar, a now extinct nomadic people originating from central Asia. These canteen-shaped vessels probably contained wine to smooth the way of the Avar warriors to the nether world.

Subsequent to Roman times, the first unambiguous evidence for viticulture here is the founding charter of the Benedictine Abbey from 1061, in which King Béla I lists the royal grants to the Church—including three vineyards named Csin, Bika, and Fövestelek. The monks established up-to-date cultivation methods and built a fine, enormous cellar using the local sandstone saved from the construction of the monastery. This was the predecessor of the cellar underneath Garay tér today. The ecclesiastic estate continued to cultivate the vineyards to exacting standards, as attested by the 1267 charter of the Szekszárd Abbey.

The southern Slav culture of red wines, along with the Kadarka grape, was introduced to the region by Serbian refugees fleeing from the Ottoman invaders. Wine production continued relatively undisturbed in 1541, when the Ottoman Turks turned

Szekszárd into an administrative center known as the *sanjak*. In fact, some of the vineyards were acquired by Muslims, who thought that ownership was even more profitable than levying taxes on someone else's wines. These times probably gave rise to the tradition of the collective vineyard watch, which uniquely survives in the villages of the Sárköz, the area just east of the Szekszárd Hills. The service was performed by the maidens stowed away in the hillside vineyards, where they could feel safe from Ottoman warriors. Banded together, the girls managed to keep away thieves of all description, winged or human.

It was also during the Ottoman Occupation that the admirable technique of "sealed fer-

On special days, wine actually flows from this well

ZOLTÁN HEIMANN, VINTAGE 1959

Heimann's story illustrates the power of wine to interfere even with the life of a top-ranking corporate executive. His is one of the oldest families of growers in Szekszárd, so Heimann could not help but submit to the compelling family tradition, even as the former CEO of Béres and Bábolna, two of the most successful model companies in recent Hungarian memory. Having finished construction of a fabulous cellar on the wine hill, Heimann set about expanding his estate and modernizing existing vineyards. The planted grape varieties illustrate the estate philosophy well, with a stress on domestic grapes such Kékfrankos and Kadarka, augmented by Merlot and Cabernet Franc. The top house blend called Cervus is a consistently full-flavored and intriguingly spicy wine, owing to the Kadarka ingredient and extensive maturation in wood. Heimann never tires of improving his Bikavér, the style he believes is destined for leadership among all Szekszárd wines. Recently, he has been planting grape varieties hitherto unknown in Hungary, such a Viognier and Sagrantino. Working away in the spirit of ceaseless experiment, this winery is still just starting out, but Heimann has a very clear vision of where he is headed.

mentation" evolved in Szekszárd. The crushed grapes were poured into vats tapering toward the top for fermentation. The cap was periodically punched down using a type of wooden plunger called the *csömösz* or *csömöge*. Once

fermentation was complet, the nearly dry surface of the cap was daubed with mud. The extraction of tannin and color continued underneath the air-tight seal, resulting in dense, stable wines with a remarkable ability to withstand long-distance transportation. These positive developments aside, the plundering Ottomans eventually managed to depopulate Szekszárd and its surroundings. When the conquerors left, the seven Hungarian and two ethnic Serbian families who ventured back in 1695 to undertake reconstruction cultivated 55 "plots"—probably no more than 20 acres in total. In the early 18th century, the Benedictine abbots gave tax breaks to local growers, stimulating plantation and attracting ethnic German settlers to the area.

In 1812, the wine community adopted *Articles of Viticulture* to regulate the procedure of plantation, vineyard work, and wine-making, codifying a common law that had been tacitly understood and practiced in the region for ages. The Articles also enacted stringent provisions conceived to protect property and wine quality in the best mutual interests of the growers.

It was in the 19th century that Kadarka emerged as Szekszárd's leading wine, inspiring such immortal works of art as

TAMÁS DÚZSI, VINTAGE 1949

A father of seven, Dúzsi is a college graduate from Gyöngyös who set up his privately-owned winery in 1994. He is a believer in working away in humble circumstances without subordinating quality. For him, keeping the business (but not the stature of the wines) to modest dimensions means no credit payments and no need to look for investing partners. Ten hectares seems just about the upper limit of an estate he is willing to handle. Above all, Dúzsi is a wizard with the Kékfrankos variety. There may be takes on the grape that have more fruitiness or concentration, but Dúzsi's Kékfrankos somehow always shows up among the best. It is a remarkably pure red—no, make that exceedingly pure. Even more importantly, it has personality. Several vintages of his Kékfrankos Rosé have won the title of the best Hungarian rosé, hands down. Interestingly, Dúzsi nurtures an intimate relationship with Szekszárd's literary tradition as part of building the image of his own wines. His trademarked archaic spelling "Szegzárdi" on the labels is a case in point.

Schubert's Trout Quintet. Another musical genius, the Hungarian Ferenc (Franz) Liszt was for decades a regular guest at the house of Antal Augusz in Szekszárd, where he often availed himself of some of the noblest old vintages of the local red. Perhaps the best-known eulogy of the Kadarka grape was penned by the poet János Garay, himself a native of Szekszárd:

The Heimann cellar

Just like a maiden's bluest eye,
The grape of Szekszárd from afar
Doth twinkle through the leaves ajar
Under the clearest autumn sky.

Garay made another important contribution to promoting the region's wine when he composed the *Szegszárdi bordal*, the "Szegszárd Libation Song" (note the archaic spelling of the town's name) for the harvest at the Kristofek family estate, to which he was invited. Using an original metaphor, Garay calls the aged local red *bikavér* ("bull's blood") in the poem, giving birth to what

was to become Szekszárd's famous brand name. This first grand chapter of viticulture in Szekszárd ended in 1875 with the onslaught of the phylloxera. The pest eradicated the mass-producing white grapes—Szlankamenka, Dinka, Bakator, Mézesfehér, Lisztesfehér, Rakszőlő, Járdovány, Csókaszőlő—clearing the way for more Kadarka, which became the predominant grape of Szekszárd after the Great War. Some Kékoportó, Kékfrankos, Medoc Noir, and Cabernet (both Sauvignon and Franc) were also planted as part of the

161

FERENC TAKLER, VINTAGE 1950

Yet another self-taught winemaker, Takler started out as a machinist. If he had stuck with this original occupation, he would hardly have attained the stardom he enjoys today. The involvement of his two sons, András and Ferenc, gave a huge impetus to the family winery. Takler's wines cannot help but remain true to their Szekszárd roots, even though their extreme concentration and extraordinary reliance on new oak may seem out of character. Traditionally, Szekszárd wines have been known for their distinctive light touch and a sort of talkative mood, both in the sense of being smooth and approachable, and of inspiring relaxed chat. As these qualities clearly have to do with the region's terroir, they cannot be stamped out or repressed even in wines as radically new-fangled as Takler's. His wines also happen to fit in perfectly with recent trends in consumer expectations, and are sought-after accordingly. The current flagship is a blend called Regnum, followed by a number of similar wines in the Takler "fleet."

reconstruction effort, but these grapes were far outweighed by Kadarka throughout the region.

Viticulture in Szekszárd remained relatively successful after World War II, albeit not immune to the dead-ends and false starts that characterized the planned economy. Due to large-scale planting projects, black grapes now account for 63% of the region's total acreage, although in the larg-

er wineries Kékfrankos trained on the high cordon has almost completely displaced Kadarka, which fell out of favor as a problematic late-ripening grape that is sensitive to both rot and frost. Things have changed radically since 1947, when Fornády hailed Kadarka as "yielding such a sweet must in better years that it will take a long time to ferment, making a wine that is thoroughly enjoyable even in the off-dry version."

PÉTER VIDA, VINTAGE 1953

Prophets have never had it easy, in their own country or elsewhere, but a miraculous helper usually comes to their rescue. For Péter Vida, this is the Kadarka variety, of which he uniquely owns quite an impressive contiguous plot in the famed Bakta. A rare grape in a vineyard where the old Szekszárd saying holds that vines could not be bought but only inherited–this is Vida's main asset. We can only hope that the day comes when the encroaching housing project will depart from this grand cru quality site, loaded on trucks as concrete rubble… It's an experience to taste Vida's wines while listening to the man talk about the beauty of the hills and the wines themselves. His strong suits are of course his Kadarka, and a superbly crafted blend based on Cabernet Franc, which was awarded the highest score in a large sample of Hungarian reds tested by Alles über Wein.

FERENC VESZTERGOMBI, VINTAGE 1948

Vesztergombi is an emblematic figure in Szekszárd, also in the literal sense of being possessed of an ancient family crest with an unambiguous reference to wine: the Aesopian fox holding a bunch of grapes in its paws. Although we know that good wine needs no bush, a nice heraldic sign in the naïve folkloristic style from the late 1700's will surely not hurt the marketing. Of course, the father and his son Csaba make sure that truly good wines are not lacking in the Vesztergombi cellar, the first winery to have ventured to bottling in the region. Their 1992 Bikavér was a milestone, not just in Szekszárd but in the history of Hungarian wine at large. Less than a decade later, they erected another landmark in the Csaba Cuvée, an absolutely gorgeous, large-scale red. Hailing it, as some commentators have, as proof that Szekszárd has finally caught up with Villány is a huge mistake. We are talking about two totally different regions with their own special style. Ferenc Vesztergombi himself sees to it that no such "catching up" happens, because he knows this could cost Szekszárd its cherished identity. His most potent weapon to protect Szekszárd's distinct character is his Kadarka (probably the closest approximation of the region's legendary Kadarka style), but his Merlot, Bikavér and Rosé are also benchmark wines in their own right. As for the new cellar, it will provide a worthy residence for the family's finest wines.

Today, Kékfrankos remains the most widely planted grape in Szekszárd (626 ha), followed by Zweigelt (294 ha), Merlot (207 ha), Cabernet Sauvignon (170 ha), Cabernet Franc (143 ha), and Kékoportó (138 ha). The acreage devoted to the formerly decisive Kadarka has shrunk to 57 hectares. Clearly of secondary importance and popularity, white wines can show decent form in better years, but they will remain invariably low in acid and soft in character, yet fairly high in alcohol–possibly because of the warm climate. The leading white grape is Chardonnay (124 ha), followed by Olaszrizling (111 ha) and Rizlingszilváni (70 ha).

Although Szekszárd's soil is not conducive to high acid levels, the excellent, full-bodied red wines of Szekszárd tend to be rather vigorous owing to the high tannin extraction during extended maceration. In recent years, crisp but quite fiery rosés have appeared, diversifying the selection of almost black, tannic red wines. Practically limited to a few smaller family wineries, Kadarka makes an unusually aromatic, spicy red wine with a wonderful ruby color and mild acidity. This grape was traditionally also vinified as *siller* or *fuxli*, occasionally even as a *blanc de noirs*

white. The name *fuxli*–also known among ethnic German growers as *fixli* or *fuchsli*–referred to the color of this low-alcohol, refreshing wine, comparable to a rosé. (*Fuchs* means "fox" in German, but these wines had nothing to do with the "foxy" taste often associated with *labrusca* varieties.) *Fuxli* was made from black grapes by quick processing, sometimes with some white blended in. A shade darker than *fuxli*, *siller* is a fresh, fruity wine that resembles a very light red in color and on the palate. It is made by macerating the must on the skins for 24 to 48 hours, depending on the ripeness of the fruit, then transferring it to wooden casks to complete the fermentation.

The full-bodied and intense Szekszárdi Bikavér is a blend of two or three grapes (Kadarka used to be a frequent ingredient). The recipes are secret and vary from grower to grower, although the wine community is gearing up for the adoption of a

163

"Szekszárdi Bikavér Code" in the foresee-able future. Under current regulations, Szekszárd is the only region apart from Eger entitled to use the Bikavér name. This privilege makes all the more sense considering that Szekszárd had actually trademarked the name before it gained currency in Eger.

Beside the prominent family wineries, a number of larger producers have firmly established themselves in the area, notably Aliscavin, the Aranyfürt Cooperative, and the Liszt Winery. Despite their presence, Szekszárd remains by and large a region of small growers running family businesses.

The distinctive cellars of the area are carved in loess, although vaulted cellars were constructed as well. The finest example of this latter type of cellar is the Várpince in downtown Szekszárd, which goes back to the foundation of the Benedictine Abbey in 1061. Architecturally speaking, the old cellar row at the Leányvár vineyard in Sióagárd survives relatively intact. The "Pink Wine House" near the northern city limit of Szekszárd was built in the historicist style, and is a protected monument today. In recent years, some of the smaller and midsize growers, including Heimann and Takler, have embarked on building impressive cellars with an artistic flair.

Tokaj

Is Tokaji the wine of kings or the wine of liberty? Does it hold sway over you or does it set you free? Whatever the answer to these complex questions, Tokaji certainly has the potential to become the wine of wines, the finest of its kind on earth—to the delight of the next generation after us. In the consensus of the authors of this book, it should also serve as the ideal national emblem of Hungary: a tangible product and a sensual-spiritual experience—more exalted than paprika, less politicized than the Sacred Hungarian Crown—that could help shape the country's image abroad, as well as buttress a sense of national identity at home.

Tokaj, Tokaji, Tokay, Tockay, Tocai—the enumeration and clarification of the permutations of the **name** alone can be a daunting task. Here, as in Bordeaux, the name of a key town came to refer to an entire wine region around it, according to the classical rule of *pars pro toto*. However, the wine region is officially designated as Tokaj-Hegyalja. The word *Hegyalja*—in old documents often translated into Latin literally as *regio submontanea* or *districtus submontaneus*, but also appearing in the form of *"Hegalya...unter das Gebürge"*—means "Foothills" in Hungarian. *Hegyalja* is a common geographical term, used to denote six or seven completely different areas around the country. The word *alja* itself ("bottom, lower part") in designations such as *Bükkalja, Mátraalja, Mecsekalja* indicates that the region lies at the "foot" of the corresponding mountain range (the Bükk, the Mátra, and the

View of city of Tokaj and Mount Tokaj with the Tisza River from the south

165

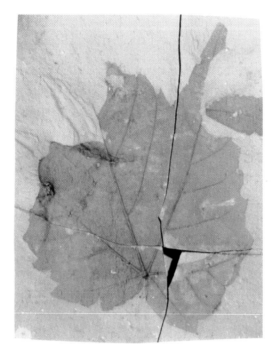

A 11 million-year-old fossilized leaf of *Vitis teutonica*, the predecessor of *Vitis sylvestris*, and thus of *Vitis vinifera* (Kővágó vineyard near Mád)

Mecsek Mountains, respectively). In this way, these regional titles follow a different principle than the compound name *Tokaj-Hegyalja*, in which the *Hegyalja* part does not refer to the slopes of Mount Tokaj, the prominent volcanic cone at the southernmost tip of the region, but to the foothills of the entire Zemplén mountain range (which in turn forms the southern range of the Tokaj-Eperjes Mountains). Hungarians in general often use the name *Tokaj* to mean the whole region, but the people actually living in the area refer to themselves as being from the *Hegyalja*, to distinguish themselves from the residents of the town of Tokaj itself. However, even they prefer to call their wine *Tokaji* (the *–i* ending in Hungarian turns a place name into an adjective) regardless of the narrower location within the region from which the wine actually originated. In colloquial usage, then, it is not considered an error to call the larger growing area Tokaj, as long as we remember that, strictly speaking, this is not the accurate name of the wine region at present. In order to eliminate some of the confusion, complication, and ambiguity, legislative efforts are now being made to change the official designation to the simple form *Tokaj*.

The first known occurrence of the name, in the form "Tokay," is in the 13th-century genealogy and history entitled *Gesta Hungaro-*

rum, penned by the famous chronicler Anonymus. The *Gesta*, and many sources after it, refer to the emblematic hill of the region not as Tokaj but as Tarcal, today the name of a village at the western foot of the hill. Remarkably, Tarcal was also the name of the hill in Syrmia far to the south, today known as Fruska Gora in Serbia, which yielded the most famous wine of medieval Hungary.

Having settled—or, rather, left open—the issue of names, let us see which **communities** belong to the region. Records enumerating the administrative units have existed since 1641, but these early sources are riddled with gaps and contradictions. For instance, one of the documents does not mention a single village north of Tolcsva. A landmark in the history of Tokaj is a document approved by the National Assembly in 1737, which lists the following villages as entitled to sell wine under the Tokaj name (the list is in alphabetical order, and the names in parentheses are the modern/full names of the settlements): Bénye (Legyesbénye), Erdőhorváti, Golop, Keresztúr (Bodrogkeresztúr), Kisfalud (Bodrogkisfalud), Kistoronya, Liszka (Olaszliszka), Mád, Olaszi (Bodrogolaszi), Ond, Patak (Sárospatak), Rátka, Szántó (Abaújszántó), Szegi, Tarcal, Tállya, Tokaj, Tolcsva, Ujhely (Sátoraljaújhely), Vámos-újfalu, Zombor, and Zsadány (Sárazsadány). In addition to these villages, other accounts refer to Bodroghalász, Bekecs, Hercegkút, Károly-falva, Makkoshotyka, Monok, Szerencs, Szőlőske, and Végardó. All in all, the various records mention at least 32 settlements. Today, Kistoronya and Szőlőske belong—as Malá Tŕňa and Viničke—to Slovakia, which has had no scruples about using the Tokaj name. In fact, Slovakia is making ceaseless attempts to expand the Tokaj appellation in its territory far beyond these two villages near the Hungarian border, to areas where a wine quality comparable with even the less prestigious wines of the authentic Tokaj region cannot be guaranteed. Current Hungarian wine legislation lists 27 communities with a right to label their wines as Tokaj. In alphabetical order, they are Abaújszántó, Bekecs, Bodrogkeresztúr, Bodrogkisfalud, Bodrogolaszi,

Erdőbénye, Erdőhorváti, Golop, Hercegkút, Legyesbénye, Makkoshotyka, Mád, Mező-zombor, Monok, Olaszliszka, Rátka, Sárazsa-dány, Sárospatak, Sátoraljaújhely, Szegi, Szegilong, Szerencs, Tarcal, Tállya, Tokaj, Tolcsva, Vámosújfalu. The vineyards around most of these communities were first classified in the 18th century, in a manner that was rather rigorous on its own terms at the time, but is not particularly useful today.

As the birthplace of world-famous wines, Tokaj has a better-documented **history** than most wine regions in Hungary. It is beyond the scope and purpose of this book to provide a chronological account of the events whose influence is still tangible in the region—such as the Walloon immigration (not yet conclusively proven), the arrival of Italian settlers in the 12th century, the Rákóczis' accumulation of wealth and prop-erty (c. 1600-1660), the influx of Ruthenes and especially Germans, the activity of Greek, Serbian, and Jewish merchants, etc. Readers interested in historical details are directed to the literature listed in the references.

The wine region could potentially encompass 11,149 hectares. Over the centuries, the area actually planted in Tokaj has been both larger and smaller than the 5,446 hectares under vines today. At this point, it seems unlikely that all of the 9,829 hectares rated Class I in the cadas-tre will ever be fully planted.

Located in northeastern Hungary, the Zemplén Mountains have a cool **climate**, as does the entire Eperjes-Tokaj Range within the Carpathian volcanic chain. The mean temperature in the foothills is 9-10 °C annually, 21 °C in July, and −3 °C in January. The favorable south-southeastern aspect of the foothills has con-tributed to the evolution of excellent micro-climates on the slopes. The average temper-ature fluctuation is 13 °C annually, normal-ly coupled with long, sunny summers and dry autumns also with a lot of sun. Precipitation measures between 500 and 700 millimeters a year, with an early-sum-mer peak. A high level of humidity, due to the region being situated leeward of the confluence of the Bodrog and Tisza rivers,

supports a unique fungal flora, which includes the all-important botrytis.

The best vineyard sites occupy the south-ern slopes where they are sheltered from northern and northwesterly winds by rela-tively tall, forested peaks. For optimum viti-cultural potential, these sites must have an outlet to the east or the west, as shut-in val-leys have a limited circulation of air, and are more prone to stubborn frosts. Superb vine-yards meeting these criteria include the Szarvas and Nagyszőlő on the southern flank of Mount Tokaj (also known as Kopasz-hegy or "Bald Hill"), the Disznókő south of Mád, the Zsákosak at Erdőbénye, and the Meszes at Olaszliszka.

The **geology** of Tokaj is quite sim-ilar to that of the Mátraalja region, illustrat-ing the ability of any two areas with compa-rable natural conditions to produce vastly different wines as a consequence of differing traditions, cultivation methods, grape vari-eties, and techniques of vinification.

The volcanic activity which began 15 mil-lion years ago and defined the geology here

The famous castle of Sárospatak on the bank of the Bodrog River

THE INFLUENCE OF GEOLOGY

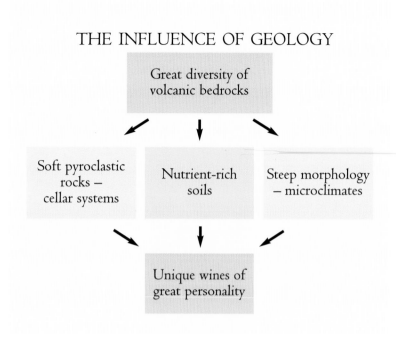

Great diversity of volcanic bedrocks

Soft pyroclastic rocks – cellar systems

Nutrient-rich soils

Steep morphology – microclimates

Unique wines of great personality

terms of silica content. In addition to these lava formations, pyroclastic rocks, most significantly tuffs, also occur in large quantities. During and after the principal eruptions, a variety of postvolcanic activity left its stamp on the rocks of Tokaj. Volcanic rocks tend to weather faster than other igneous types. The process is aided by postvolcanic currents and hot springs, which deliver to the surface large quantities of alkali, potassium and other trace elements that enrich the volcanic detritus. The major centers of postvolcanic alterations are located in the area of Mád, Erdőbénye, Tolcsva, and Sárospatak. The southern fringes of the range were overlain by aeolian loess in a wide arch at a much later stage, during the Quaternary.

The region's basic **soil** mantle developed during the Quaternary. On the steeper slopes, the thin soils are typically mixed with weathered andesite, and are quite hard to till. In the low valleys, loess soils of the slope, adobe, and glacial variety evolved. Volcanic glass, which weathers readily, continues to mingle with the soils today, enriching them with trace elements and minerals.

for 6 million years, created a great diversity of formations and morphologies in the Tokaj-Eperjes Range. The wide variety of volcanic rocks that can be found in the area includes rhyolite, rhyodacite, dacite, andesite, and even basalt, which is much more typical of the volcanic hills of Western Hungary. These differ mainly in

Autumn mist on the Bodrog River is essential for botrytis to develop

In 1867, József Szabó differentiated between three basic soil types, both in writing and on maps, from which all the other sub-types can be derived. Most widespread is the clayey *nyirok* (a red erubase soil created by the weathering of volcanic rocks, particularly andesite), which commonly contains rock and rock debris. When too wet, *nyirok* gets so gluey that it sticks to the spade; if it dries out, it will yield to nothing short of a pick-ax. It does not absorb water very well, and has low permeability. Its red color, from the ferrous hydroxide, turns darker as its humus content increases. Yielding the most powerful and substantial wines in Tokaj, *nyirok* is the soil of the Király vineyard at Mád and Mezőzombor, the Meszes at Olaszliszka, and the Várhegy at Sátoraljaújhely.

Of slightly lesser value is the soil type known as *yellow earth*, which is formed from loess. Its varieties in Tokaj are loess talus and adobe (both mixed with talus, debris, and fossils), along with sandy loess on the Kopasz-hegy at Tokaj and the hills north of Olaszliszka. Loess has good water management, good drainage, and a low lime content. This soil type is typical mainly on the southern rim of the range, but it also spreads west toward the Hernád River, and south toward the Great Plain. The loess blanket of the Foothills can be traced from Abaújszántó to Tokaj, and from there to Bodrogkeresztúr. The Szarvas at Tarcal is a famous example of vineyards with loess soil. Loess does not feature in the interior of the Tokaj-Eperjes chain or in the valleys, but on the southeastern slope of Mount Tokaj it can be found at altitudes as high as 405 meters.

The last basic soil type is the *rock flour* that forms from intensely silicified rocks and pumice. In essence a lithosoil produced through mechanical weathering, rock flour is a fine-grained debris of white rhyolite, pumice, and perlite. It is less coherent, not very malleable, and it does not retain water. Its heat capacity is inferior, so vines planted in it may easily dry up during a drought or freeze in extreme cold. Rock flour is the soil

Nyirok, a weathered volcanic soil (Tokaj, Pajzos vineyard)

169

Grapes heavily infected by noble rot necessitate maceration before pressing

type of the Pereshegy at Erdőbénye, the Tolcsvai-hegy, and the Oremus vineyard at Sátoraljaújhely.

As a consequence of the steep **morphology,** the area is highly vulnerable to soil erosion. The volcanic cones of the Tokaj-Eperjes Mountains rise abruptly behind the escarpments, overlooking the mildly accentuated pediment surface and the flood plain of the Bodrog River. These days, the vineyards are confined to the southern and eastern slopes in the foreland of the peaks, but there was a time when vines cultivated on terraces conquered the steepest faces, and almost reached the top of Mount Tokaj. The terrain in the viticultural zone is intensely articulated with valleys and streams.

For a description of Tokaj's varieties, we refer the reader to **the grape varieties** chapter of this book. Suffice it to add here that the two leading grape varieties, Furmint and Hárslevelű, are often harvested, pressed, and fermented together throughout the region. To some extent this makes sense, as their ripening schedules are not sufficiently different for growers to eschew the convenience of joint processing, not to mention the fact that many older plots still in cultivation are mixed plantations, containing the two varieties side by side.

Before providing an overview of Tokaj's modern **wine types**, a few words about the nomenclature of the past are in order. For centuries, the two main categories were *szűrt bor* ("filtered wine") and *csinált bor* ("made wine"). The former referred to wines made much the same way as most wine is made today, by simply pressing the grapes and fermenting the must. The latter denoted wines produced by the more complicated Aszú process. Clearly distinct from this noble sweet category was the typically dry *ordinarium*. Even in the old days, a distinction was made between free-run juice and press juice, although they were not necessarily handled separately. *Főbor* ("principal wine") was the old name of Szamorodni-style wine, at least insofar as it was made by pressing the harvested fruit as it came, with-

out separating botrytized berries from grapes unaffected by the noble rot. From 1707 onward, Essencia, the highest grade of Tokaji, was also increasingly referred to as *legfőbb bor,* meaning "supreme wine" (*legfőbb* is the superlative of the adjective *fő*).

Nowadays, the wines of Tokaj are grouped and categorized in nearly as many ways as there are authors. For our part, we follow the simple classic taxonomy, which happens to agree with many years of experience in the Austrian courses of the Wine and Spirit Education Trust.

A. DRY AND SEMI-DRY

1. Fresh or briefly matured wines. Typically fermented dry but potentially containing some residual sugar (below semi-sweet category levels). With a few exceptions, they are fermented in stainless steel and will last three to five years, depending on the vintage. For the most part, these wines are made from grapes, most of which are overripe, left in the bunches after the aszú berries have been picked out.

2. Matured dry wines. Invariably matured in wood, with a small proportion also fermented in wooden casks. Very long cellaring potential. As botrytis is undesirable in these wines, the grapes must come from high-altitude vineyards (about 250 m above sea level) set up specifically for this purpose. Expensive wines (e.g. from Szepsy and Árvay).

3. Szamorodni. Quality comparable to Beerenauslese, but fermented dry and subjected to subtle maturation (under a film of yeast). Contains botrytized grapes. A dead ringer for the Vin Jaune of the Jura.

4. Főbor. A category known and used for centuries, but dropped due to a shrinking assortment of wine types as a result of a tendency toward equalization over the last fifty years. Closest to Szamorodni in style without being matured in oxidative conditions, Főbor can be either dry or sweet, depending on the natural proportion of spätlese-type overripe fruit and shriveled, possibly botrytized berries.

B. SWEET

1. Szamorodni. Typically made in the sweet style, when the sugar content of the grapes is so high that the must will not ferment fully dry. The residual sugar of Sweet Szamorodni is comparable to a 2 or 3 puttonyos Aszú, sometimes more. It needs to be matured for two or three years, and is lightly oxidized in character.

2. Reductive sweet wines. Ready for release in a year or sixteen months after harvest, this new "satellite" genre emerged over the past decade as a necessary fallout of the lack of time and capital investment required to mature Aszú wines for a longer period in compliance with regulations. Often marked by mineral character, they may contain 50 to 180 g/1 residual sugar and a ratio of botrytized berries comparable to Aszú wines. Some wineries make them in stainless steel exclusively, while others–Árvay, Szepsy, Oremus–use new oak barrels for both fermenting and maturing these wines. This new category includes wines with the potential to exceed the organoleptic characteristics of an Aszú. The example that most readily comes to mind is the 1999 Szepsy Cuvée, which many regard as the finest Tokaji of all time. (We are of the same opinion.)

3. Aszú (3 to 6 puttonyos) and Aszúeszencia The chart shows minimum residual sugar and extract required per grade.

wine type	Sugar (g/l)	Extract (g/l)
3 puttonyos Aszú	60	25
4 puttonyos Aszú	90	30
5 puttonyos Aszú	120	35
6 puttonyos Aszú	150	40
Aszúeszencia	180	45

4. Essencia. The free-run juice of hand-picked pure botrytis berries, with over 450 g/1 sugar (but levels of 800 g/1 or more are not unheard of). Essencia takes years to achieve a modest alcohol level of 4-5%. It is rarely sold commercially, and smaller wineries will not handle it separately. It is generally used for blending to improve the concentration of Aszú wines.

5. Fordítás. Made by refermenting wine or must poured on Tokaji Aszú "paste" (marc) left after pressing. Sweet wines, typically with more than 60 g/1 sugar.

6. Máslás. Made by refermenting new wine or must poured on Tokaji Aszú lees. Sweet wines, typically with 50-90 g/1 sugar.

Vessels for collecting aszú berries, then and now

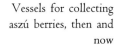

171

THE ASZÚ PROCESS

Tokaji Aszú can be defined as a sweet wine with a high concentration of residual sugar that is made from hand-selected shriveled grapes affected by *Botrytis cinerea*, macerated in wine or must before pressing, and matured in oxidative conditions without the addition of spirits of a higher alcohol content. To our knowledge, no other wine available commercially in the world meets all these criteria.

Botrytis *cinerea*, a species of fungus that causes both gray rot and noble rot, needs high humidity and sufficiently ripe berries with a high concentration of sugar as the two fundamental conditions for it to exert its benign influence by "attacking" the grapes. When it does, it affects the fruit in two ways: It increases the evaporation of the water content from the berries, and produces special aromatic substances inside them. If the shriveled berries have a "smooth-shaven" wrinkle surface and exhibit a color between yellow and brown, it is considered a good quality aszú crop. If the berry surface looks gray and "bristly" with mould, the grapes are less valuable.

According to former statistics, aszú **vintages** used to occur in three years per decade on average. In some years, such as 1962, only a trickle of Aszú was pro-

duced. This is no longer the case. The production of Aszú wines is now feasible even in an unfavorable year, such as 1997. In such years, the quantities will, naturally, be much smaller. Proper vine loading and grape maturity are both prerequisites for an adequate concentration of sugar and other substances, which the berries need to achieve in order to contract botrytis. Consequently, we have reason to "rewrite" the aszú vintage charts of former times, which used to be based primarily on considerations of quantity .

In the past, **harvest** in Tokaj meant removing entire bunches of grapes and transferring them to boards or tables where the aszú berries were picked out of the bunches one by one, by hand. Working in this manner, a harvester was able to produce two kilograms of aszú berries an hour. These days, the better wineries—as a rule, members of the Pannon Wine Guild and/or the Mád Circle—pick out the botrytized berries without removing the bunches from the vines. This method often takes three to five "passes" through a vineyard during a harvest season, but it has obvious advantages. First, it prevents potentially harmful further alterations in the berries after they have been shriveled and botrytized to an ideal degree. This means that the berries will be—weather permitting—as good as possible. Second, the berries left on the vines will become infected by botrytis more easily.

Before pressing, the harvested botrytized grapes are **soaked** for a period of 16 to 36 hours in fresh must, *murci* (fermenting wine), or new wine that has completed fermentation. This "leaching" is crucial to the extraction of as much substance as possible from the shriveled berries, and to achieving a concentration very few wine regions in the world can rival. (In those few that do, though, some other factor, for instance botrytis, will invariably be missing from the equation).

Let us back track and speak of what was traditionally the first phase after harvest: the crushing of the grapes gently to avoid seed damage. The berry pulp known as the "dough" or "paste" was for a long time cre-

ated by treading the grapes by foot, but more recently by crushing them with rubber rollers. The experiences of the past decade have shown us that it is perfectly possible to make excellent Aszú wine without mechanically splitting the grapes first.

To this day, the soaking of botrytized berries is a distinctive feature of making sweet Aszú-type wines throughout the Carpathian Basin, including around Lake Balaton and at Rust in Burgenland, Austria. Following this unique maceration process and pressing, the Aszú will take shorter or longer (sometimes months) to ferment, depending on a number of factors including temperature and sugar levels. The best growers shun the use of selected yeasts, preferring instead to rely on wild yeasts naturally present in the vineyards to trigger fermentation. Another characteristic trait of Tokaji Aszú is that it is made using relatively little sulphur, resulting in low levels of free sulphuric acid in the finished wine.

Barrels are obviously an issue, in more ways than one. The 136-liter **gönci** cask served until quite recently as a framework for measuring concentration. The grade of the Aszú depended on how many *puttony** (a 27-liter harvester's hod) of botrytized berries were blended with a gönci caskful of dry wine or must. These days, Aszú is made in barrels of optional capacity, not to mention the stainless steel tanks used by several wineries. Not surprisingly, the concentration of a finished wine is no longer determined with reference to a puttony number (though it is still described in these terms), but by official analysis prior to the authorization of its release.

Let us briefly touch upon the troublesome issue of **refermentation**, before addressing the functional contribution of barrels. This phenomenon, known all too well by producers of sweet wines across the world, can occur if the spontaneous fermentation of the wine stops for some reason—for instance, because the yeasts cannot tolerate the given alcohol level. Over time, some of the alcohol evaporates, reactivating the yeasts, which causes major

Making a barrel in Tokaj

Staves drying in the courtyard of a cooperage

173

* The form *puttonyos* on Tokaji Aszú labels is not the plural of the noun as some non-Hungarian commentators have erroneously suggested, but an adjective formed by a suffix comparable to English —ed, as in "seven-headed monster." In this way, *3 puttonyos Aszú* = "3-hodded Aszú." (Incidentally, the plural of *puttony* would be *puttonyok*, although note that Hungarian uses nouns in the singular after numerals. For that matter, neither is *gönci* a plural form, but an adjective denoting provenance, as in *Tokaji*. Gönc is a village in the northern Zemplén Mountains that used to be famous for its cooperage.

damage by using up the sugar reserves of the wine if it is left unattended. Growers in Tokaj say that their wine has "straightened out" when it has lost all its residual sugar to refermentation. Much like a dry Szamorodni, these "straight wines" can actually be very fine, but they invariably spell losses for the grower who had set out to make a precious sweet Aszú. There are a number of ways to combat refermentation. One of them, the removal of "awakened" wine to another location for heat sterilization, is only feasible at large wineries, and will rob the wine of much of its aroma. The other measure, theoretically available to all, is to

The famous cellar near Szegi, owned by the Kereskedőház

** Atkin, *Tradition and Innovation in the Tokaj Region*, p. 16.

fortify the wine by adding distilled spirit to stop the fermentation. However, fortification is now prohibited by law in Tokaj, as it was back in 1908, although even Atkin rightly emphasizes that "Refermentation [...] was deliberately prevented during the Communist period**." This leaves sterile filtering as the only legal solution today.

Returning to the **barrels**, it is instructive to remember that in Tokaj the staves used to be split, rather than sawn, from unblemished logs until the early 20th century. As elsewhere, oak was invariably the best wood for this purpose, owing to its even growth and its regular, dense grain structure that the splitting method did not damage. By contrast, sawn staves often have their fibers cut through, which can easily result in leaking barrels. This explains the importance of using split staves for barrels in Tokaj, also as a measure for guarding against the evaporation of alcohol. When matured in such a barrel, an Aszú of sufficiently high initial alcohol level (of at least 13%) will not lose perilous quantities of alcohol. In other words, a sound Aszú can easily pull through the two

years of barrel time required by the regulations nowadays, provided of course that adequate hygiene and sulfur levels are observed. Before bottling, the Aszú will be cold-stabilized and sterile-filtered.

Many sources, including Iván Balassa, insist that Tokaji was always shipped in its barrel. This seems to be borne out by tax records from the 17th to 19th centuries, which indicate large barrel inventories in Tokaj year in and year out. Such large barrel parks only make sense if we accept that most of the wine was sold in the barrel it had been stored in. The invariable use of new wood improved stability and, inevitably, imparted a distinct flavor to the wines. As sawn staves gradually displaced split ones, they left a mark on the quality of the wines. The process of decline–if not the leaking barrels–was sealed by the production and trade policies of the Communist era. The eastern markets clamored for their "Aszú" in such quantities that it was impossible to satisfy the demand other than through substandard mass-production methods and forced oxidation. The few better wines had to be blended off with the many worse, and the resulting equalized products quickly corrupted the consumer's notion of what Tokaji Aszú was truly all about.

But what *is* **true Aszú** like? If an Aszú has been made in accordance with current regulations–which stipulate, among other things, three years of maturation, including two in wooden casks and one in the bottle–but was bottled as early as is permitted, without longer aging in wood, then it will exhibit fresh fruit flavors in the lead while still young. A vertical tasting of wines held in honor of the 10th birthday of the Disznókő Winery demonstrated that, over the course of ten years, an Aszú, initially variously decried or hailed as a copycat Sauternes, can take on all the traits of color, taste, and aroma that we used to prize in the Aszús made in the 1960's and '70's–but without the flaws inherent in those wines.

Embracing and implementing **micro-oxidation** is a key factor in making good Aszú. Micro-oxidation, which essen-

The tasting room of
the Oremus winery

tially occurs through the pores in the barrel's wood, is certainly not amenable to making wines that will seem 10-20 years old at three to four years of age–this can be achieved, if it must, by not topping off barrels and by frequent racking. What microoxidation does do is establish a subtle process of maturation that the wine will complete in the bottle. Over time, Tokaji handled in this way will develop rich tertiary aromas and flavors, without losing its acidity and mineral taste, unmatched by any other sweet wine in the world. Identifying such wines simply–and censoriously–as "reductive Aszú" is just that: a reductive argument, and a huge mistake. All it takes to expose this fallacy is a quick taste of the genuinely reductive sweet wines we described in category B/2 above. Despite their mineral notes, high sugar, and botrytis flavors, these wines will never be mistaken for an Aszú, which owes its distinct character to intensely shriveled berries, the ensuing maceration, and the circumstances of oxidation. Primary fruit aromas define an Aszú until it has reached three to five years of age. Thereafter, the wine will slowly develop hints of sun-dried fruits, various nuts, and caramel or toffee. This process results from the natural alteration of sugars in an acid medium over time.

Among the natural factors, high **acidity** makes a fundamental contribution to the unique character of Tokaji, particularly Aszú. As is well-known, the high concentration of titrable acidity does not necessarily equal a forcefully acidic taste. Because Tokaji Aszú is invariably made from overripe grapes, harsh malic acid is never a problem, but the wine will have high levels of other, more benign acids that keep the often extraordinary sweetness from being cloying. (The same principle underlies the wonder of Trockenbeerenauslese from the Mosel and the Rhine.) The decisive influence of the acidity notwithstanding, one must keep in mind that ripe tannins and minerals are responsible for some of the most subtle and delicious forms of astringency on the palate. Working in a synergistic combination with the acids, these substances can attain a perfect balance with the intense sweetness of Tokaji Aszú.

This cottage now only serves to collect rainwater for spraying

The **minerals** and trace elements, present in the soils of Tokaj in a form that is readily accessible for the vine's roots, contribute their own flavors to the wines. This is why the first single-vineyard Aszús after the "great leveler" era of the command economy have been such a revelation. Due to the diversity of terroirs in the region, the wines show ever new facets of Tokaji Aszú to us. Especially fascinating are the Aszús made from Hárslevelű grapes grown on loess soils, for instance from the celebrated Szerelmi vineyard. These wines can be likened to an amorous man courting the lady of his heart: they are tender without losing virility.

Last but not least, **cellars** are indispensable in shaping the character of Tokaji Aszú. About 98% of the region's sweet wines are aged in 4-5 meter wide single-vaulted cellars dug in volcanic tuff. These cellars have a constant temperature of 9-11 °C, depending on their depth below the ground and other circumstances, and are never subject to fluctuations over the year. Even more important are the adequately high and constant levels of humidity, owing to the presence of the black mould called *Cladosporium cellare* that clings to the cellar walls. Pleasantly warm and dry to the touch, this fungus performs a vital function in the cellar by acting as a humidity buffer, while also making a spectacular black backdrop for the tasting of golden wines.

No account of the region would be complete without mention of the **Tokaj Renaissance** Association, an assembly of winemakers committed to superlative quality. The members of the group, also called Classified Vineyards of Tokaj, have built on the legally defined minimum parameters by implementing their own self-imposed criteria for wine production, and even making the release of their wines the subject of joint evaluation. No wine can display the logo of the Association if it has not been approved by this community.

GROWERS AND WINERIES

JÁNOS ÁRVAY

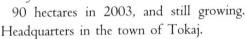

Contact: see Tokaj Renaissance
List of Members

90 hectares in 2003, and still growing. Headquarters in the town of Tokaj.

Two personalities of great caliber can peacefully inhibit the same sphere of life, even if they started out differently and choose to walk separate ways in the present. And yet János Árvay shares with István Szepsy, the grand master of Tokaj, two things that really matter: the same interpretation of what tradition means in the region, and an uncompromising drive for quality.

Árvay (vintage 1955) is a true-born native of Tokaj, carrying on a family estate that goes back many generations (and which shrank to a few hectares during the communist era). In the Hungary of the 1980's, a winemaker who wanted a career had no choice but to take a job at the Borkombinát, as the integrated state-run winery was called, or possibly at one of the cooperatives. When the French insurance company AXA arrived in Tokaj as one of the first foreign investors, the ever restless Árvay wasted no time and joined the nascent Disznókő estate. Starting with the first hack of the hoe, it was very hard work, which often had to be done in very harsh circumstances. But Árvay persevered, and soon became the head winemaker of the region's new trend-setting winery, where the golden age came with the great 1993 vintage.

Disznókő's superb fruity Aszús that were ready to drink in two years provoked fierce attacks, but Árvay, reassured that he was doing the right thing, remained cool as a cucumber. To give the reader a sense of the "vibes" in Tokaj at that time, let us imagine the following exchange. Fictitious grower of "traditionalist" Aszú: *"You are not saying a Frenchman will tell me how to make Tokaji Aszú, are you?"* The cool answer: *"No, that he won't. But he may know a thing or two about how to make a sweet wine without aldehydes and volatile acidity…"*

As any Hungarian was wont to do, Árvay kept working on his family estate on the side, putting a few splendid Aszús of his own on the table. The chance for a big break presented itself in 1999, when he received an offer for a joint venture by an investor who trusted him with making the decisions and running the business. Árvay went shopping for vineyards at a time when the well-maintained lots in good places had been sold out, but he managed to procure a few excellently sited smaller parcels, as well as about 15 hectares of 50 to 70 year old vines, with gaps in the rows but planted with all the highly prized old clones characterized by small berry and bunch size. Most of these sites occupy very steep hillsides, so mechanized cultivation was and is out of the question. Árvay bought some exquisitely exposed fallow land as well, bringing the estate up to its current size in 2003 of 90 hectares. Finally, he acquired the former Casino building in downtown Tokaj, now being refurbished and converted into an elegant chateau-type estate center and winery.

The 1999 and 2000 wines have more than met the very high expectations. The pure varietal Hárslevelű Aszú offers an unequaled intensity of taste and level of concentration to the lucky few who have had a chance to taste it. The dry Furmints, from the Lajosok and Teleki vineyards, did not encounter the resistance they had been expected to provoke on account of having been both fermented and matured in small new oak, as indeed all of

Árvay's wines are nowadays. This is of course a cost-no-object approach typical of Árvay and his partner, motivated as they are by the singular aim of discovering and showing the world just how much Tokaj is capable of. Maceration in old wine, forced aging in half-full barrels, and stabilization by any artificial means except sterile filtering are all a big no-no in this winery. Each lot is kept simultaneously in Hungarian, French and American barriques, and comparing them often produces astonishing results. The best wines are released under the *Hétfürtös* label, in tribute to the exceptionally low average yields for the cordon trellis system, literally at "Seven Bunches" per vine.

The performance of a winery fundamentally depends on both financial means and taste. The latter factor has a lot to do with experience, with how many wines, and what kind, the winemaker has had an opportunity to taste. Árvay no doubt counts as a "frequent flyer" among Hungarian winemakers, and shows up at every major international wine event, though he prefers exclusive presentations, especially in America, to noisy fairs.

AUREUM VINUM

Contact: see Tokaj Renaissance
List of Members

Established in 1988 and operated by a company called C.O.S. (Color, Odor, Sapor), the winery is in joint Hungarian and foreign ownership. The majority shareholder is Wilhelm Kirzner. It's not easy to obtain information about the size of the estate (figures are not even posted on the Net) but the processing facility, designed by Dezső Ekler, seems to suggest that the wines are made from purchased grapes. They are clean and full-flavored, showing many features in common with the so-called traditional style in Tokaj.

BODVIN

Contact: see Tokaj Renaissance
List of Members

A winery in Mád, owned by Géza Bodnár (Canada) and his brother Endre back home, with most of the 10 hectares of vines located in the Király and Veres vineyards. Barely known in Hungary, Bodvin sells most of its product on the American and Canadian markets.

CHATEAU DERESZLA

Contact: see Tokaj Renaissance
List of Members

Formerly known as Bodrog-Várhegy, this 50-hectare estate (30 producing) is owned by the D'Aulan family of Champagne. Most of the vines, aged between 20 and 60 years, are planted in excellent loess and *nyirok* soils in first-rate vineyards such as the Henye (13 ha), the Zsadány (6.6 ha), the Lapis (3 ha), the Dereszla (2.3 ha) and the Décsi (2 ha). Dereszla works with strictly limited yields and a significant proportion of small new oak barrels, kept in four different cellars. Contact: László Kalocsai. Winemakers: György Brezovcsik, Alain Rousse.

CHATEAUX MEGYER AND PAJZOS

Contact: see Tokaj Renaissance
List of Members

Two wineries under shared management, founded in 1992 on what was the largest fruit-bearing acreage owned by a new venture in the region at the time. Formerly owned by the CFVGT consortium, now in the majority ownership of Jean-Louis Laborde. Management: Hajnalka Szabó; winemaker: Sándor Zsurki; director of trade: András Győrfi.

Pajzos makes distinctively rich-flavored wines from 65 hectares west of Bodrogolaszi. The manor cellar in the Pajzos vineyard is the ideal place for maturing the wines. The winery's choice is stainless steel for vinifying dry wines and even many of the sweet late harvest wines, made instead of Aszú but often comparable to a 5 puttonyos in sugar concentration. Outstanding among them are the 1997 and 1999 Muscat Lunel. There is also a memorable 1999 Hárslevelű, an ice wine, and even a rare Essencia, in the 0.5-liter bottle. Somewhat overshadowed by the bigger brother, *Megyer* makes often steely Furmint and high-acid Aszú from 80 hectares of vines in cooler sites than the Pajzos estate. The wines display all the virtues and vices of cold fermentation, but are highly sought after by fans of the bracingly fresh style. The Várpince ("Castle Cellar") in Sárospatak is a must-see.

DISZNÓKŐ

Contact: see Tokaj Renaissance
List of Members

Stephanie Berecz

The white pavilion and the boulder shaped like a wild boar, after which the vineyard and the winery were named

For many pilgrims to Tokaj, the Disznókő winery with the Sárga Borház, the "Yellow Wine House," has meant the gateway to the region, figuratively as well as in the literal sense of the word. It is also the winery that has garnered the epithet *Paradeweingut* from a German wine magazine. We were there to marvel when this model facility was being constructed. Recently, at the celebration marking the tenth anniversary of the winery, we had the opportunity to taste a decade's worth of Disznókő wines, particularly Aszús, made by János Árvay. It was a resounding success indeed. In the early days, Jean-Michel Cazes was a frequent guest in Tokaj. It was under his management and that of Daniel Llos that the winery began to make those "clean" Aszú wines. At that time, Stephanie Berecz was an apprentice from France; today she is *chef de la cave* at Disznókő, and a "Hungarian" mother.

The winery processes the crop of 100 hectares, making splendid Aszús and reductive sweet wines, both to the highest quality standards. Importantly, the estate boasts a sizable plantation of the Zéta grape, formerly known as Oremus, the fourth permitted variety in Tokaj in addition to Furmint,

Hárslevelű, and Muscat Lunel. The 1993 Disznókő 6 puttonyos Aszú, now on the verge of maturity, has been widely regarded as a benchmark wine and a watershed in the history of Tokaj.

DOBOGÓ

Contact: see Tokaj Renaissance
List of Members

Owned by the Gelsey and Zwack families, Dobogó sources top-drawer 6 puttonyos Aszú from more than 30 hectares of vines near Mád and Tállya, centered on the Szt. Tamás and Betsek vineyards. Winemaker: Miklós Csontos; exclusive distribution: Zwack Unicum.

TAMÁS DUSÓCZKY

Contact: see Tokaj Renaissance
List of Members

The descendant of an aristocratic family, formerly estate owners in Tokaj, Tamás Dusóczky has labored and followed his vision tirelessly to create his small empire. He currently owns 5.7 hectares in the Kővágó (not yet producing), one of the lesser known vineyards in Tokaj that is nevertheless capable of legendary quality. Most of

179

the Kővágó vineyard, which has a well-documented history dating back to the early 14th century, was bought back in 1998 by Waldbott and Dusóczky, whose ancestors were the former owners. In the new plantings they have favored the „Madárkás" variety of the Furmint grape, which used to be the best clone in Tokaj.

EVINOR

Contact: see Tokaj Renaissance
List of Members

A flourishing family enterprise run by Sándor Simkó on 18 hectares, including some highly prized lots in the Kincsem and Zsadány near Tolcsva. Remarkably, Evinor's varietal composition diverges from the norm in Tokaj, with Hárslevelű accounting for more than half of the estate, and appreciable quantities of Chardonnay and Sauvignon Blanc surviving from the former state-run plantations. Evinor is also known as a reliable source of Essencia, which is the highest grade of Tokaji and is seldom available commercially.

FÜLEKY

Contact: see Tokaj Renaissance
List of Members

Owned by Baron Sigmund Kripp, Graf Franz von Pfeil, Grafin Isabelle von Walderdorff and Grafin Stephanie von Pfeil, the estate consists of 19 hectares of vines, including in the Király (Mád), the Palandor (Olaszliszka), the Szentkereszt (Mount Tokaj), the Somos (Szegi) and the Veresek and Sajgó (Bodrogkeresztúr) vineyards. The winery itself is located in Bodrogkeresztúr; visitors are received at the Füleky Manor in the same village. The wines—pure and crisp, fruity Aszú, and sweet but fresh late harvest—have an understated acidity without creating a sense that anything is missing. They are as captivating and charming as their maker, Judit Bott.

GRÓF DEGENFELD

Contact: see Tokaj Renaissance
List of Members

Coming along in strides, this winery relies on fine sites on loess and *nyirok* soils west of

Harvest season at Chateau Degenfeld

Tarcal, enabling a great variety of wine styles. Having completed a winery of the highest standards, Degenfeld has set up a Regional Trade Center, opened an elegant restaurant and inn with a wine store next door in downtown Tokaj, and is putting the finishing touches to what will certainly be the most sophisticated hotel in the region.

Known for straightforward but luscious wines with a firm sense of style, the winery is tradition incarnate. Count Sándor Degenfeld is old enough to have witnessed Tokaj before it lost its identity during the dreary years of communist rule, and has fond memories of a childhood spent in the Castle of Sárospatak with the crème de la crème of the aristocracy. His daughter, Countess Maria contributes her talent and a low-profile presence to the great comeback, staged by her husband, the talented businessman Thomas Lindner, who runs a tight ship with a steady hand. The winemaker is Miklós Prácser.

GUNDEL

Contact: see Tokaj Renaissance
List of Members

Formerly named Lauder-Láng after the families that continue to own it, this winery had to do lengthy soul-searching before it found its true identity some two years ago. Now Gundel is a worthy contender in the top flight of Tokaj, owing in no small part to Zsolt Kálmán, the dynamic manager and excellent PR communicator.

HÉTSZŐLŐ

Contact: see Tokaj Renaissance
List of Members

Tibor Kovács (vintage 1956) graduated from the Budapest University of Horticulture, and went on to obtain his doctorate from the same institution. In the meantime, he studied viticulture and enology in Montpellier. Now he is the proud manager of Hétszőlő, Tokaj's most spectacular estate, centered on the famous 48-hectare vineyard on the southern slope of Mount Tokaj or, as the locals call it, the Kopasz-hegy ("Bald Hill"). Whether viewed from afar or scrutinized between the rows, everything is perfectly neat and tidy in this vineyard, from the retaining walls through the trellis system to the micro-terraces and roads. All this would

The fabulous Hétszőlő vineyard

not be here without the man who had the grazing range plowed and in a matter of five years conjured up a veritable garden of Eden, which whould certainly deserve a place in "The World Heritage of Vines," should such a tome ever be published.

The wines are typical of the loess soils and the warmest possible southern exposure. Although the Hárslevelű grape accounts for only 20% of the estate's vines, it has a great significance for enabling styles of Tokaji that have not been copied to date, not to mention the pure Hárslevelű Aszú. This is a wine of captivating complexity that is gentle and charming without the faintest trace of frailty, and one that has become irreplaceable in the selection available from Tokaj today. So how did Kovács end up as the target of a crossfire in the media that lasted for months? Simply because he insisted that his Aszú was ready to drink in two years from the harvest. Needless to say, those wines were kicked out by the Wine Authorization Board for "lack of Tokaji character." If the decision split the audience, it was rather into the camp that had tasted the wine and the one that hadn't than anything else. Today, most of his detractors have come round, and are ready to admit that Kovács has been right all along.

Tibor Kovács

181

Tokaj Oremus
Tolcsva

KIRÁLYUDVAR

Contact: see Tokaj Renaissance
List of Members

An 80-hectare estate on the cutting edge, relying on the name and authority of István Szepsy as the manager, and the investment of Anthony Hwang, an American business-man, without whom the "Royal Manor," the center of the decisive former crown property, would still likely be the dilapidat-ed set of buildings that it was a few years ago. Today, this Hungarian answer to Chateau d'Yquem releases exquisite wines, most notably the 1999 6 puttonyos (a mere 2,779 bottles) from the superlative Lapis vineyard–possibly the most gorgeous wine that has been made in Tokaj to date. The winemaker is Zoltán Demeter, a prominent member of the younger generation in Tokaj, who also uses the facility to assemble tiny lots of his own magnificent "boutique wines."

MONYÓK

Contact: see Tokaj Renaissance
List of Members

József Monyók and his son Norbert run one of the oldest successful family wineries in Tokaj. Their Aszúeszencia wines have been in the limelight for decades, and they never cease to collect their share of gold medals at national competitions. The secret of the winery is the frame of mind of the growers whose generosity adds to the warmth of the wines.

OREMUS

Contact: see Tokaj Renaissance
List of Members

Owned by Vega Sicilia, this 128-hectare domaine controls 82 hectares of fruit-bearing vines in the Oremus (Sátoraljaújhely), the Mandolás, Gyopáros, and Szentvér (Tolcsva), the Teleki (Tokaj), the Deák (Tarcal), as well as in seven lesser vineyards. Strictly enforced principles include harvest in crates, maceration prior to pressing even for the dry wines, transfer of fruit and must exclusively by gravitation, and fermentation in wood (limited to 80% in the case of dry Furmint). Each year, the winery uses 800 barrels, made from wood sourced and dried in-house. The aging cellar has room for 2500 barrels. 60% of this capacity consists of 136-liter Gönci casks, 30% of larger, 210 liter Szerednyei barrels, and the rest in Burgundy barriques, all medium toast (m+). The cellar masters are Gyula Borsos and Sándor Sipos.

András Bacsó, the head winemaker and technical director (vintage 1953), is a man of striking modesty, like most great personalities of Hungarian wine today. While he is a gifted winemaker, he is more likely to go down in the annals of Tokaj history as the brilliant organizer who hammered Oremus together. He had been a key figure before in the region, but he does not pride himself on his tenure at the helm of the former Borkombinát. He is all the more enthusiastic about the new face of the Oremus estate, where the completion of a superlative winery refocused the attention on the vineyards themselves. Bacsó enjoys the unqualified trust of the owners of Vega Sicilia, and has been given the green light to make all the decisions himself, whether it is about new plantation or the reconstruction of a splendid Chateau as a guest house.

The library of selected older vintages, starting with the 1972, that Oremus acquired from the Borkombinát as part of the privatization deal, exhibit a similar style as the winery's own recent products: relatively low alcohol (hardly ever exceeding 12%) and no trace of Essencia added for a "face-lift" effect. The very popular Aszús are well-rounded and often mild, with just a faint hint of firm character, but all the more elegant for that.

Márta Wille-Baumkauff

PENDITS (FORMERLY MWB)

Owner and manager: Márta Wille-Baumkauff
Contact: see Tokaj Renaissance
List of Members

This is a remarkable family enterprise, with its headquarters in the former cellar of Flórián Biliczki, a noted liqueur manufacturer before the Second World War. The prime property of the 11-hectare estate is the eponymous Pendits vineyard near the village of Abaújszántó, whose unique microclimate and southern exposure in 1867 earned it a place among the region's first growths according to the *Tokaj-Hegyalja Album*, the definitive survey of "The Foothills" in those days. In addition to this famous site, the winery has lots in the Király and Holdvölgy near Mád, and in the Deák in Tarcal. In the Pendits itself, the heroic work of vineyard reconstruction is under way. If you have not walked up that hill and watched the family members fell trees, toiling side by side with heavy machinery, then you probably have no proper idea of what the workings of faith and dedication can accomplish in the wilderness. Seeing the forest taking over the crumbled walls, no one in his right mind would have thought that these terraces would ever be restored. Now the best part of the site is planted with vines, strictly as a feat of self-reliance, without any government support...

András Bacsó

183

The entrance to the Pendits vineyard

ISTVÁN SZEPSY

Contact: see Tokaj Renaissance List of Members

Tokaj has several great winemaking personalities, if only because the place is not fit to humor fickle, half-hearted dilettantes or small-time speculators. In any case, tending vines has never been the favorite occupation of those out to make a quick buck or an easy killing. Moreover, Tokaj is currently searching searching for the path that will lead back or forwards to the true Aszú identity, through the rediscovery of old traditions and, to some degree, through inventing the very basics of winemaking. This work of exploration must of necessity build on indirect evidence. You may taste all you can of a gorgeous, 150-year-old Tokaji with the original label that you bought at Sotheby's, these wines will never give you the key to the secret (although they will certainly support the assertion that Tokaji Aszú is as great as any great wine in the world). This effort will require the unearthing of long-forgotten purchase and sale contracts and musty tax inventories, then reading between the lines to find answers to a question that few have bothered to ask: What was Tokaji certainly *not* like? The next step is to explore and tame the old vineyards abandoned half a century ago that have been spared the deformities of socialist-era clone selection, but are bitterly difficult to access and exceedingly labor-intensive to properly care for. With their small berries and bunches, these vines could yield a wine that would put us in more intimate touch with the reality of the past. We all know that this is not the complete picture, but taking another road could easily lead to the pitfall of creating a pseudo-tradition.

The reason this train of thought is not the introduction to the Tokaj chapter of this book, but to the portrait of a winemaker, is because István Szepsy (vintage 1951) has single-handedly propagated this way of seeing Tokaj, and has come closest to realizing this ideal through his actions. Indeed, he could be seen as the sovereign prophetic leader of the region, were it not for his well-known humility. What he says today to the cameras and

The wines clearly have that rare, true Aszú breeding and class. Year in and year out, the reductively vinified Botrytis Selection is a splendid epitome of eternal sweet youth. And all this wonder is buttressed by a fragile lady whom everyone knows and adores simply as Márta.

ROYAL TOKAJI WINE COMPANY

Contact: see Tokaj Renaissance List of Members

1,200 hectoliters of Aszú wines, 100 tons of aszú grapes purchased a year: these figures give an idea of the volumes handled by this largely foreign-invested winery, which plays a major role in determining the reception of Tokaji abroad. The somewhat heterogeneous raw material, including estate-grown grapes from 110 hectares scattered in several vineyards as well as fruit bought on contract, yields many decent wines and a few excellent ones. While quality itself leaves little to be desired, the character of the wines seems to hover between the allegedly traditional, oxidative school and the fresh modern style that emphasizes fruitiness. Eliminating the ambivalence would certainly benefit owners and consumers alike. Contact: Zoltán Áts.

the microphones is precisely what he said years ago when he was struggling with bread-line worries and trying to maintain a few-hectare family estate to his own standards. This is the secret of a man confirmed in the truth of a faith which no force of adversity has ever been able to wrench from him.

Szepsy does not much like to talk about his 17th century ancestor, Máté Lackó Szepsy, the protestant minister who was for a long time credited with the serendipitous creation of the first Tokaji Aszú. Does he suffer from an "anxiety of influence" of sorts, finding the legacy more of a burden than a source of inspiration? Does he feel he had no free choice but to follow in the footsteps of the preacher who made his sweet wine in the mid-1600's, and whose spirit may be guiding his hand as he writes the Szepsy name for the second time in the annals of Tokaj's history? No one can know for sure. What is certain is that the tradition of wine was handed down in the form of fragmented parcels of vineyard that have always remained in the hands of the family. This is all-important, even if these lots would have seemed run-down at the time the forced collectivization engulfed most vineyards in Tokaj. There was the Szepsy vineyard near Bodrogkeresztúr that had borne the

family name for centuries, and which István Szepsy was able to reacquire only a few years ago. And there was the father, who had to endure dispossession in the name of communist egalitarianism, a much more severe blow than any of the purely economic hardship that the ancestors had to face from time to time. Living close to this man, Szepsy was given to understand what it was like to look ever forwards, armed with the tenacious faith of hard-nosed Calvinists.

Having said farewell to a series of large wineries, in 1992 Szepsy found himself on the edge with three children, Gabriella, István and Kinga, who had to be sent to school, and with the chores of running the few hectares he had to his name. Then came the release of his 1989 six puttonyos Aszú, his first successful wine, which convinced some growers and consumers that great Tokaji was not just about sheer concentration. As the accolades proliferated through the grapevine and in print, the detractors who perceived the wine as a threat kept saying there was too little of it for anyone to bother. Well, this assessment has not really stood the test of time, has it?

Let us now say a few words about how the need for truly reductive sweet wines arose in Tokaj. Beyond the obvious rationale of

István Szepsy

Szepsy in the cellar of the Királyudvar winery

185

A mound of rocks removed from the extremely stony Úrágya vineyard

demonstrating the region's multifaceted potential by diversifying the available range of wine types, the new style had to come about because few modern growers and consumers have the means or the patience to wait 8-10 years for a fully mature Aszú. The natural alternative has been reductive sweet wines with comparably impressive parameters that can be just as precious as an Aszú, but are ready for drinking at as little as one or two years of age. This wine type also functions as a point of reference for those who berate young, fruity Aszú for being "reductive," not realizing the absurdity of applying this buzz-word to wines that are by definition more or less oxidized to some degree as a result of aging in wood. Whether the oxidation is forced and carried to the point of almost being fraudulent, or gentle micro-oxidation only through pores in the barrel, is another question. What experimentation has taught us is that Tokaji Aszú can continue maturing perfectly in the bottle, without first spending long years in casks. Indeed, this now seems to be the path towards Aszú enlightenment.

Szepsy is a charismatic winemaker who spent his childhood in the company of his father, in the magic stage set of Tokaj's wine hills to where all roads led between the playground and the soccer field. He was 17 when they harvested the grapes for the 1968

Aszúeszencia, the wine that has been a reference point for him ever since. Today, his work is supported by a devoted wife, Anna, and the reassuring knowledge that two of his children now attend the same university in Budapest where he obtained his degree himself. When Szepsy's life turned into a career, he was almost automatically elected president of the Tokaj Renaissance Association, but before long it became apparent that a personality of his stature would pry open the mould of the organization. Although these days many winemakers in Tokaj follow his call, he resigned the honor as soon as it turned out that his ideals did not completely match those of the Association. In the meantime he received a prestigious government award, but he refuses to think of this as the decisive milestone of a constantly evolving career.

Anthony Hwang was not the first foreigner to come up with the idea, on the first sip of his wine, of working with Szepsy, but he was the one to recognize the greatness in him and to have the confidence to invest in his ambitious plans that a man of such caliber deserved. This investment began to pay off very quickly indeed. It is hard to believe, but Királyudvar, given a second lease on life over the ruins of the former royal property, has delivered the same unflinching commitment to quality on 80 hectares that characterized Szepsy's own 20-hectare estate (since then grown to 30 hectares).

Szepsy has been vindicated any number of times, including at the 2001 Best of Sweet showdown in Austria, and the Symposium of Masters of Wine in 2002. More importantly perhaps, Szepsy himself claims that, for all their success, the excellent vintages of 1993, 1999, and 2000 did not allow him to create the truly great reference wine for Tokaj. Let us remember that, while everyone now venerates or simply admires Szepsy's seminal wines, the creations do not yet reflect the full potential of the creator. Not until he has realized his wildest dreams and won final recognition for them as the ultimate form of self-expression, will the world accord the wines the same lofty niche that it has already reserved for their maker.

SZEPSY'S SWEET YEARS

In the Aszú style, Szepsy makes only 6 puttonyos wines, plus some Aszúeszencia or Esszencia in certain years. Single-vineyard Aszú releases have been limited to a few outstanding vintages such as 1993 and 1996.

1989 (600 bottles)

Szepsy's debut turned out to be a fine Aszú indeed, even by his own elevated standards. Due to the experimental nature of the technology employed, the wine has matured relatively quickly, but the few extant samples suggest that it will stay in top shape for at least 35-40 years.

1990

Szepsy sold all his wine on contract to the Royal Tokaji Wine Company, founded that same year.

1991
(600 bottles; Aszúeszencia 240 bottles)

Made from the crop of the Danczka vineyard under lease, these wines had high acidity but were slighter in body.

1992

Szepsy worked with crop from the Danczka under lease, and from his own lot in the Nyulas vineyard. Financial constraints forced him to sell three barrels of Aszú in bulk.

1993 (2,900 bottles; Aszúeszencia –
Király vineyard: 380,
Danczka vineyard: 900 bottles)

Szepsy's own plantation in the Danczka started bearing fruit, and the Király also yielded a crop for the first time—albeit just a single barrel. The wines were relatively soft in character due to the tender age of the vines.

1994

All the four barrels of wine Szepsy made in this lesser year were sold abroad. Delicate but vigorous wine.

1995 (2,200 bottles)

The evolving estate (5 hectares by 1995) produced a high-acid, high-potential Aszú.

For the last time in Szepsy's practice, the aszú berries were macerated in finished new wine, instead of fermenting wine or must.

1996 (6,000 bottles, plus Esszencia)

With further proprietary plantations turning productive, Szepsy began to use must or fermenting wine exclusively for macerating the aszú berries. Characterized by higher acidity and alcohol levels, the wine was matured in casks that had served to ferment a single vintage of dry white. This Aszú is positively charming to the point of being flattering, with plenty of botrytis character.

1997 (3,400 bottles)

The excessively dry fall produced scant levels of noble rot. The wine is clean and vigorous, with an overall vegetal character and good structure, owing largely to the top performance of the Király vineyard.

1998 (7,000 bottles)

The rainy fall did not permit a first-class aszú harvest; the berries were diluted and hardly attractive in their flavors. The inauspicious start notwithstanding, the wine emerged from the three years it spent in

187

wood with a sound structure and powerful botrytis aromas. It is impressively long already, but the tannins will need some more time to polish.

1999 *(8,000 bottles, plus Esszencia)*

The long-awaited excellent year, with additional benefits as vines in further fine vineyards, the Szepsy and the Úrágya, began to bear fruit. The Aszú from the Lapis vineyard (Királyudvar winery) is the great surprise: zinging, minerally, and dense, yet eminently elegant. The acidity is rather massive at 12.4 g/l but perfectly mature and flush with the wonderful spectrum of flavors.

2000

Szepsy's own new plantations in the Betsek and Szent Tamás turned productive, as did lots controlled by the Királyudvar Winery in the Lapis, Betsek, Nyulászó, Dertze, and Henye vineyards. The wines are increasingly mineral, tight-knit in their structure, and refined in their acidity. The 2000's are softer than the 1999's, but show more body.

2001

A year of large quantities, with an explosive botrytis set. At present, as elsewhere in Tokaj, Szepsy's wines display excessive botrytis and tannin. Both will gradually come round with age, but the wine is expected to remain firm and never to ease into charm.

2002

Everything seemed ideal until late September, and then the rains inflicted heavy damage. Even so, Szepsy's wine has a powerful structure, intense fruit, and an exceptional aging potential.

Aszú vs. Cuvée from Szepsy and Királyudvar

The *Aszú* process relies on hand-picked and separately kept aszú berries on which the bloom of botrytis continues to work its magic even in storage. Starting with the 1996 vintage, the berries are macerated in fermenting new wine to maximize the extrac-

tion of tannins, minerals, and acids. The method also results in bigger body and twofold fermentation. Since the extended maturation is not conducive to maintaining high levels of free sulphuric acid, the wine takes a subtle turn toward oxidation as it matures in wood for 28 months (Királyudvar) to three years (Szepsy). The 200-250 liter oak casks (roughly the Szerednyei size) are first, second or third fill, assorted depending on the vintage year.

To make the *Cuvées* (Auslese-type sweet wines), Szepsy crushes whole bunches as picked, without separating botrytized berries from unaffected ones, and leaves the must on the skins for about 16 hours. Although the Cuvées actually have a higher proportion of botrytized grapes than the Aszú wines, their botrytis character tends to be milder. These wines ferment only once, and the circumstances of maturation (one year in new oak) are closer to the reductive.

TOKAJ KERESKEDŐHÁZ

The successor of the communist-era Borkombinát, the "Trading House" remains fully owned by the Hungarian state. Its holdings have dwindled to about 80 hectares but still include the legendary Szarvas vineyard, a former crown property. Regarding however its capacity for processing and its aging/storage facilities, it is still the largest winery in all of Tokaj, and still committed to buying grapes from nearly 3000 small growers. Revamped as the Crown Estates, the operation makes 3 to 6 puttonyos Aszú, Aszúeszencia, as well as a line of fresh dry wines under the Castle Island label. The cream of the crop on offer is an inventory of great old vintages of Tokaji, including wines from the late 19th century.

TÖRÖK

Contact: see Tokaj Renaissance
List of Members

A family winery with 5.7 hectares in the Bomboly, Őzhegy and Középhegy vineyards near Mád. The traditional cellar has a 1500 hectoliter capacity, and facilities to receive visitors for a tasting.

ÚRI BOROK

Contact: see Tokaj Renaissance
List of Members

The owner and maker of "Genteel Wines," Vince Gergely (vintage 1962) is a prominent representative of his generation, who keeps working away quietly in Mád in a cellar that used to belong to the Baron Orczy family, deliberately limiting his selection to high-octane 6 puttonyos wines. Gergely is a man of few words, who believes that the grape material is much more important than how up-to-date the technology in the winery. The truth of this aphorism was driven home to him a few years ago, when the price of a better wine press bought three hectares in the famed Szt. Tamás vineyard. Today, no plots are available in the Szt. Tamás, but those presses are still for sale. At present, he owns nine hectares in the Szt. Tamás, three in the Danczka, and three in the Bojta, including two hectares planted with Hárslevelű, a grape he sets great store by, and a single hectare of Muscat for blending with the base wine. His holdings include some venerable old vines, some aged 70 years, the principal asset being of course the well-maintained Szt. Tamás, which has never been collectivized.

Gergely uses exclusively new wine or fermenting wine instead of must for macerating his aszú berries, because he believes that the presence of alcohol is indispensable for optimum extraction. At the same time, he does not split or crush the aszú berries for fear of bruising the skin and the seeds; he says that the berries, swollen by soaking, will release all their aromatic compounds anyway, without mechanical intervention. He is painfully aware that this method is potentially wasteful of other substances in the fruit, but he holds that such a sacrifice is intrinsic to maximizing Aszú quality. Lately, Gergely has been making some 1,500 bottles of dry wines each year to form a better idea of what his vines can do. These wines are not available commercially, they merely serve to introduce the in-house tasting of the great sweet wines. He is just as unyielding when it comes to the wines of substandard years, refusing to sell them even in bulk. As for the Aszús, they have an uncommon purity of taste and concentration, with a faint echo of the "traditionalist" school, and a distinctive, consistently recurring hint of citrus peel oil. Gergely's pinnacle of achievement so far has been the 1993 Aszúeszencia, with repeat performances in the works from the excellent 1999 and 2000 vintages.

LŐCSE ESTATE AND WINERY

The estate controls 80 hectares, including 15 hectares currently producing, near the village of Erdőbénye. Having enlisted the help of highly-regarded professionals, the new owners wasted no time in establishing a winemaking concept and a business strategy.

The goal is to create a mid-size winery dedicated to making top-quality Tokaji that pays tribute to modernity while building on tradition. For Lőcse, 2003 will be a year of launching development and planting vineyards. The grape varieties to be planted have been selected with a balanced composition in mind. In addition to Furmint and Hárslevelű, Sárga Muskotály (Muscat Lunel) will be given a significant role, and there are plans for some Kövérszőlő as well. Production volume is expected to peak at 100,000-200,000 bottles a year.

LŐCSE ESTATE
AND WINERY

Vince Gergely

The construction of the processing facility and the designing of Chateau Lőcse are now under way. The value of the investment over the coming years is estimated to exceed one billion forints, making the Béres Group the largest Hungarian-owned investor in Tokaj. The wines will be released under the Lőcse label. To help ensure professional prestige, the owners hired Sarolta Bárdos, a young and talented winemaker who has already earned the respect of the trade, to fashion the style and image of the wines.

TOKAJ VINTAGES

Vintages in Tokaj have been recorded continuously since 1801. The much-publicized old chart that many people are familiar with rates vintages by up to five stars. Although we do not know exactly what criteria were used, it seems reasonable to assume that the main consideration was the quantity of the botrytis harvest rather than the sheer quality of the aszú berries (although the two may to some extent overlap). In general, the rating of the vintage has always reflected the performance of the noble sweet wines; dry wines are not normally taken into consideration in Tokaj.

As far as we know, no extensive inventory of Tokaji survived the havoc of World War II, although individual bottles with the original label still surface here and there from private collections. The allegedly pre-war wines in commercial circulation today invariably come in bottles manufactured over the past few decades. This circumstance, along with other considerations, have convinced many commentators, including the authors of this book, that these wines cannot be authen-

Bottles of authentic Tokaji from the 19th century

tically dated to the vintage years claimed for them. Precise tracking of Tokaj vintages only becomes a realistic possibility starting in 1956, while the earliest vintage of Tokaji the authors of this book have bought commercially is 1972. Having said this, we are afraid that the shadow of a doubt, no matter how small, will always hover above the identity of any vintage preceding 1990. In addition to the former state monopoly, some family wineries have now also released Aszúeszencia-grade wines from the 1970's. These wines are invariably suspect due to the otherwise good-faith and even legal practice of rejuvenating older wines by the addition of Essencia of a younger vintage. With these caveats, let us see a brief overview of selected vintages.

1947: a great year beyond dispute. 1957 outclassed 1956, although both are rated five stars. Less comprehensible is the four stars some charts attribute to 1962, a year we think was no better than two stars. 1963 and 1964 were fine years, as was 1969. The greatness of 1972 is now firmly established and uncontested, both in terms of quantity and quality. The wines are highly variable in their taste though, probably owing to differences in permitted Essencia treatment. Further good vintages of Tokaji were 1975, 1983, and 1988, bringing us to the period of verifiable identity. Since the Wall came down, authenticity has been guaranteed not only by speedier bottling and general commercial availability, but by the demise of the faceless Aszú phenomenon that characterized the communist years.

1991 changed the way we look at vintages in Tokaj in more ways than one. Formerly, the consensus was that only three years out of any given decade would yield an "aszú vintage," practically understood as a massive quantity of botrytized grapes at harvest. However, the high concentration of sugar, a critical precondition for noble rot to attack, can be achieved in any year if the yield is held back and the harvest not rushed. The other key factor is adequate moisture in the form of rainfall or dew, which is again available most of the time. In this way, some aszú grapes can always be harvested in the

best looked-after vineyards, although their quantity may be just a fraction of the crop in a really good year. A case in point was 1997, a notoriously problematic year that petered out in a very dry fall season. Some growers managed to pick aszú grapes and make their Aszú wines even in this year, although in much smaller quantities than they normally do.

These days, the qualification of a vintage year depends more on the quality than the quantity of the botrytized grapes available. For instance, 2001 yielded an overabundance of aszú fruit, sometimes in places where botrytis had been unknown in living memory. Unfortunately, the affected berries were "fuzzy" and a grayish purple color, effectively hauling back the rating of the aszú vintage to where it can be regarded as a middling year at best.

1991 ***

A cool and wet year that yielded an average overall quality and good quantity.

1992 ***

A very promising start settled down to strong average. The year Disznókő made its first yardstick wine.

1993 *****

An exceptional year, in terms of both quality and quantity. The Aszús have come along very nicely and are in wonderful shape. The best investment at present.

1994 **

A sad year with no quantity or quality to report. Good Aszú was harvested only in places where the grapes survived the persistent rains, such as the Szarvas vineyard of the Trading House.

1995 ****

This one would have needed just a little push to cross the line separating a good year from a great one. In 2003, the Aszú wines are well ahead in development and still have plenty in reserve.

1996 ***

An ambivalent year, marred by late summer rains. Some very nice Aszú was made, but only from the fruit of sheltered, meticulously maintained vines.

1997 **

A dry fall throughout the Carpathian Basin permitted only very modest levels of botrytization. Where there were any aszú

A bottle of 1811 Tokaji Essencia, bottled around 1840, and imported by a London merchant in 1905

berries to collect, they were eminently sound and thus made some fine wines in diminutive quantities.

1998 **

Ceaseless rains washed away bright hopes. Quantity was understandably large, but the grapes were lacking in properly concentrated aromas.

1999 *****

An excellent year that delivered both quality and quantity, with a hallmark stress on fine acid composition (other regions also posted crops with good acidity). Two years after the harvest, some wineries began to struggle with baffling problems of stability.

2000 *****

The classic great year. Vegetative growth ended early, leaving the grapes to ripen with extremely high sugar content, particularly on the best southern slopes. Dry wines often had staggering alcohol levels, as high as 17%. Rain in the last days of September proved crucial for botrytis propagation. With the fascinating acidity of the 1999's, this could have been the benchmark year for Tokaj for a long time to come.

2001 ***

An auspicious start drowned in September rains. Botrytis infection happened like an explosion (hardly conducive to great quality) but growers risking the wait eventually harvested fine aszú grapes in adequate quantities.

2002 *** - ****

Once again, great expectations held up until late September, when stubborn rains arrived. In the second half of November, the aszú berries that had remained on the vines were very nice pickings.

These brief descriptions reflect regional norms. A few top wineries with a relentless limitation of yield and the fortitude to wait for full ripeness came out with five-star wines even from years rated two stars on the average.

ŐS KAJÁN

A French-Hungarian restaurant in Tolcsva may seem almost as implausible as a Hungarian-French one somewhere in Burgundy would. And yet, it was in this muddy village, noted for its church with a red painted gallery and a spire clad in wooden shingles, and, more recently, as the home of Oremus's splendid new winery building, that Anne Roy and Pascal Leeman of France settled down and opened what has become a gourmet destination.

Undoubtedly the most worthwhile restaurant in the Tokaj region, the **Ős Kaján** ("The Arch Taunter") was named, according to the blurb on the menu, after *"one of the most important gods of Hungarian heathen mythology [. . .] the god of gold and the god of the underworld's sun."* This sounds nice and archetypal enough in a new-agey sort of way, especially in the heart of the land of the world's finest golden wine, sunken for so long, where many things have recently statrted rising again having reached their nadir. In reality, though, the ambivalent, mythic character called Ős Kaján–an alternative translation could be "The Ancient Sneerer"– was invented by the symbolist poet Endre Ady, in a poem that he wrote in 1907 in, of all places, Paris. Ős Kaján appears in the title role as the poet's powerful, nightmarish alter ego and challenges him to a drinking bout. The drunken vision of this "debauched Apollo," who "hails from the East," is blurred with that of a Dionysian figure, possibly combining the solar clarity and life force of poetry with the inscrutable darkness of the impulses that drive the creative imagination behind it.

Unlike Ady's pal and foe, however, Pascal came from the West, bringing a ray of hope and a Bohemian flair to this easternmost of Hungary's wine regions, where vinophiles had all but despaired of seeing the culinary light beyond the occasional rapture of scrambled eggs with wild mushrooms that one could savor for breakfast if put up in one of the peasant houses deeper in the mountains. The Ős Kaján is also headquartered in an old peasant house, but one renovated with eclectic good taste (plenty of *objets trouvés*), mingling refreshingly disparate décor elements such as cowshoes (always mysterious for today's urban kids) and contemporary art (sometimes worth scrutinizing).

From the bright front room, dominated by a burst of sunny orange and yellow colors, wrought iron, and glass, a hallway leads to the inner *polgári szoba*, the "bourgeois room," which provides a pleasant contrast owing to its air of privacy and the darker hues of antique wood. There is also a smoking room with a weathered couch where you can enjoy a pipe or cigar over a book on Tokaj from the owners' impressive library—with or without a glass of Tokaji from the equally impressive assortment of local wines—or just take a nap. Finally, there is an exquisite sun lounge with small-panel French windows to the ceiling, which opens into an unpretentious banquet room on one side, and onto the vegetable and herb garden on the other.

Egy varázslatos hely — Tokaj Hegyalján.

Yes, Anne and Pascal grow their own; and whatever they cannot grow they make a point of sourcing locally: goat cheese from the nearby village of Károlyfalva, trout from the streams, and game from the forests of the Zemplén. The menu, regularly revamped to

MÓRICZ PREYSZ (1829-1877)

The inventor and the first user in practice of pasteurisation. According to the notes of Bertalan Szemere (minister at the end of the XIX.c.) it was more than a problem to make constant the tokaji wines in that time. Our export decreased – and the reason was mostly originating in this field. Preysz, using the method of after-fermentation found out that the microorganism could be killed with heat sterilisation. According to our present knowledge it is not the optimal way of preserving aromas in wine, but in those days the method itself was epoch-making in bio-chemistry. The first lecture for the publicum was held in 1861, while Pasteur let his results of the same researches be published in 1863.

accommodate the ingredients in season, is organized into four styles: the rustic, the gourmet, the Tokaj-purist, and the French-inflected. I have very fond memories of a hunter's salad with crisp greens and cured sheep's ham; *palacsinta* (crêpe) with creamy spinach and *juhtúró* (sharp and soft farmer's cheese made from ewe's milk); pheasant garnished with faintly exotic savoy cabbage and *lepcsánka* (hash browns); and oven-dried apple crisps scented with a honey-bake spice blend I am bound by confidentiality not to divulge. From the menu that is current when this goes to print, be certain to try the delicious rabbit liver sautéed with *vargánya* (boletus) from the "Flavors of Tokaj" list. And if the evening before it so happened that you succumbed to your debauched side and tasted a little too much Tokaji wine, do the Burgundian thing for a change and go for the egg poached in red wine. Pascal swears by its curative powers. But if you haven't had your fill of the sweet life, your best bet for dessert is of course more Tokaji—preferably with more goat cheese and Fourmé d'Ambert, the excellent French blue.

Eating here is always a charming experience. As the proprietors themselves declare, *"The intention to open new doors opens up ways leading to enchantment as well. It is especially true if we regard our limits as diving boards and not as obstacles."*

In a world of global trash passed off as human food, and of the ubiquitous phony smile proffered as a sign of genuine hospitality, it is so nice to have Anne and Pascal around. They greet you as true friends, cook like playful demigods—and even speak almost like native Hungarians when they come to your table for a chat.   (p.l.)

Tolna

Tolna as an independent wine region, and not just as the county by the same name, still sounds unfamiliar to most people. It was only designated in 1998, on the Völgység district west of Szekszárd, augmented by two more areas north of this core territory. In a sense then, Tolna is one of the oldest wine producing areas in Hungary, boasting a 2000-year history as part of the Szekszárd region.

I n its newly conceived form, the Tolna region extends to the following communities: Bölcske, Dunaföldvár, Dunaszentgyörgy, Györköny, Kölesd, Madocsa, Paks, Tengelic, and Tolna in the Tolna District; Aparhant, Bonyhád, Bonyhádvarasd, Dúzs, Györe, Izmény, Lengyel, Mórágy, Mőcsény, Mucsfa, and Mucsi in the Völgység District; as well as Felsőnyék, Hőgyész, Iregszemcse, Magyarkeszi, Nagyszokoly, Ozora, Pincehely, Simontornya, and Tamási in the Tamási District. With only 2,636 of the designated 11,324 hectares actually under vines, the region's growing potential is far from being exhausted, especially considering that 7,362 hectares of this area qualify as Class I sites in the cadastre.

Compared to Szekszárd, the temperate continental climate is slightly cooler in the Völgység and Northern Tolna, with a medi-an temperature of 16 °C during the growing season, and also somewhat wetter (700 mm precipitation). The southern reaches have a warmer continental climate more akin to that of the Great Plain, although the rainfall here is higher than in the arid Szekszárd region.

While the geological make-up is almost identical to that of Szekszárd, a few features more closely resemble those of Balatonboglár to the northwest. The main formation consists of the clay and sand sediments of the Miocene Pannonian Inland Sea, overlain by Quaternary aeolian loess. This loess mantle is thinner in the Tamási and Völgység Districts, but around the town of Paks it reaches depths of up to 30 meters. The soil patterns are rather uniform throughout the region, with loess adobe and brown earth dominating over loess bedrock, as well as sandy detritus in the vicinity of Tengelic and Tolna. For the most

195

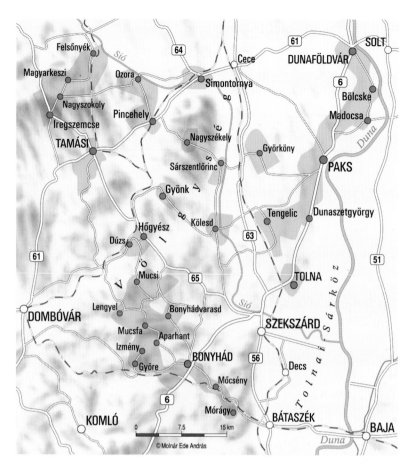

where the surface is more heavily dissected by smaller valleys and ravines.

Tolna is a predominantly white wine region today, with Chardonnay as the most widely planted grape (357 ha), followed by Zöld Veltelini (189 ha), Olaszrizling (166 ha), Rizlingszilváni (98 ha), Rajnai Rizling (86 ha), and Pinot Blanc (77 ha).

Many people are of the opinion that the wines of the Völgység Hills are inferior to those of Szekszárd proper. We believe that such an assertion cannot be responsibly made until the wines have been monitored regularly for a number of years. One must keep in mind that Tolna for decades functioned as a sort of hinterland, with wines typically blended under Szekszárd labels. In its present form, it is a fledgling wine region possessed of quite a few terroirs comparable to those of Szekszárd, but it has hardly had the time to put forth or substantiate a claim to distinct individual quality.

Because the terrain is amenable to industrialized cultivation, the leading producers are large wineries. The Danubiana Winery, based in Bonyhád, has been known for sound whites and reds, including the particularly commendable Gróf Károlyi label. These are wines for everyday drinking, made in massive quantities but to very decent standards—a rare combination in the Hungarian market. The Eurobor Winery in Bátaapáti has established itself for years as a producer of high quality wines, including some medium-bodied but full-flavored reds often on a par with Szekszárd, and, more importantly, elegant cold-fermented whites capable of realizing the region's true potential. Another producer worthy of note is Gálaker in Simontornya.

part, the terrain is gently accentuated. Steeper morphologies are limited to the Tamási-Hegyhát Plateau and the Völgység District,

The Apponyi cellar (Bátaapáti)

In and around the Tolna wine region many cellar rows and entire "cellar villages" survive to proclaim the former advanced wine culture of diligent ethnic German growers, so unjustly deported from the area in the aftermath of World War II. Especially remarkable among them are the cellar rows at Györköny and Nagyszékely. Built around 1780, the Apponyi Cellar in Bátaapáti stands as a fine example of the grand style that characterized the estates of the landed aristocracy.

196

Villány-Siklós

If Ferenc Kölcsey, the 19th-century poet, were alive today, he would probably want to mention a red wine in addition to the divine "nectar" of Tokaj in Himnusz, the Hungarian national anthem. If he did, there is little doubt that the tribute would go to Villány.

The second question to settle is what explains Villány's unrivaled popularity among domestic red wine buffs. What is behind this region's irresistible appeal? First, it has to do with the anthropomorphic dimensions: everything in Villány is of a human scale, approachable in a down-to-earth kind of way. Second, it is the prestige of sites that yield the most expensive red wines in the country. Third, Villány was the first Hungarian region to produce wines of a quality that stood comparison with eminent, similarly styled European reds. This parity has proved to be of enormous marketing value,

and is undoubtedly a great accomplishment for a small, little-known European country.

Villány preceded other areas in Hungary not only in the sense of being the first region where small growers began to bottle their wines, but also in attracting foreign investment, in the prices achieved by its wines and, last but not least, in its promotion of a massively tannic red wine style. Although this style has had its detractors, it is certainly a valid proposition. It is for good reason that red wines around Hungary have come to be seen and judged in terms of whether they live up to the standards of Villány in concentration, aging potential, and price.

Aerial view of the Szársomlyó Hill and Villány

197

White wines are a different matter altogether. On a southern latitude like this, it is difficult to make a fine white with a sound acid/alcohol balance without tricks and tweaking in the cellar. At the very least, it takes a very well-timed harvest, and often a lot more. Growers in the Siklós District have been pulling this off for centuries, but the fact remains that, down south, it is much easier to excel in the red wine genre. As always, the final assessment will lie with the consumer.

ORIENTATION

The southernmost wine region in Hungary, Villány is situated near the Croatian border below the 46th parallel–roughly at the same latitude as the northern part of Bordeaux. The region extends to the following communities, divided into two districts:

a) Villány District: Kisharsány, Nagyharsány, Palkonya, Villány, Villánykövesd;

b) Siklós District: Bisse, Csarnóta, Diósviszló, Harkány, Hegyszentmárton, Kistótfalu, Márfa, Máriagyüd, Nagytótfalu, Siklós, Szava, and Turony.

NUMBERS

The nominal designated area of the region is 4,522 hectares, all Class I and Class II sites. According to wine community statistics, the effective growing area under vines is 1,450 hectares (the Ministry of Agriculture has it significantly larger at 1,870 ha), including 655 hectares planted with white grapes and 730 hectares devoted to red wine production (plus table grapes and miscellaneous). As is the rule in Hungary, the most wide-spread white grape is Olaszrizling (425 ha), followed by Rajnai Rizling (93 ha), Chardonnay (63 ha),

Hárslevelű (48 ha), Zöld Veltelini (42 ha), and Tramini (28 ha). Among black grapes, Kékoportó still holds sway with 318 hectares, followed by Cabernet Sauvignon (204 ha), Kékfrankos (86 ha), Zweigelt (76 ha), Cabernet Franc (49 ha), Merlot (47 ha), Pinot Noir (13 ha), and a few other varieties of negligible significance. This data, the latest available, from May 31st, 2000, reflects inconsistencies dependant on the source. As such, it is for information only, and is not suitable for precise reference beyond illustrating major statistical trends and proportions.

CLIMATE

Like that of the Mecsekalja region, the climate of Villány mingles continental features with sub-Mediterranean elements. It is the warmest region west of the Danube, with an annual median temperature of 11 °C, a hot summer (mean 21 °C in July) and a relatively mild winter. The vineyards begin to warm through early in the spring, particularly on the sheltered southern slopes. This extends the growing season by a significant measure. Even with an annual precipitation of 600-650 mm, Villány is an essentially dry region, where the Mediterranean influence makes itself felt in a sharp peak of rainfall in the autumn. While the intense insolation (2070-2100 hours per year) and the great active heat sum are ideal for vines, the high risk of hailstorms lowers the reliability factor of production. Despite its modest elevation, the range rising above the vineyards does good service in blocking the masses of cold air from the north, thereby contributing to the emergence of very special microclimates.

GEOLOGY

Although the range is called *Villányi-hegység* or Villány "Mountains" in Hungarian, and it certainly merits that term on account of its geological structure, most of it really consists of fair-sized hills. At 444 meters, even the Szársomlyó, which stands as the tallest peak, barely rises to the height needed to qualify for the title "mount" according to Hungarian geological convention. The Tenkes to the west is only 409 meters high.

The imbricate range was basically created by five vast plates thrust one on top of the other. Its core is made up by calcareous rocks deposited in the marine basins of the Mesozoic, including dense and hard Triassic dolomite and limestone. The Tenkes Hill, which is somewhat detached from the main mass of the range, and the hills of Csarnóta and Szava also consist of thin and thick-bedded Triassic limestone and dolomite. After a very long interval, these old rocks were overlain by younger Jurassic limestone, including the Szársomlyó Limestone that built up the hill of the same name some 150 million years ago. The calcareous sequence is topped by the 120-million-year-old Nagyharsány Limestone from the Early Cretaceous period. One of the few outcrops of this rock is a familiar sight in the Szársomlyó, clearly visible as one drives by Nagyharsány. As Tertiary formations are entirely missing in this area, the limestone slopes are covered directly by Pleistocene sandy loess, which is the main parent rock responsible for soil generation.

No vines have been planted on naked limestone and dolomite; the vineyards are located in areas where these old rocks have a few meter-thick top layer of loam, adobe loess, or brown earth. In places where the loess topsoil thins out, the vine's roots go down deeper to reach the calcium-rich calcareous strata in the subsoil. Directly above the limestone outcrops, the very thin loess mantle is mixed with dolomite and limestone debris. This is where the high-acid wines are grown, while the pure loess soils yield somewhat softer wines. In addition to these soils, red clay can be found at the bottom of the slopes; the higher plateaus and northern slopes have formed rendzina and chernoziom as well. For the most part, the region's soils are fairly heavy, water-retentive, and hard to till, and only moderately vulnerable to erosion.

The present-day surface of the Villány Mountains took shape quite recently in geological terms, during the Quaternary. Running roughly east-west, the range is dissected by gentle valleys, longitudinal as well as transverse. The mild gradients and the natural escarpments delineated by the geological structure provide optimal terrain for high-quality viticulture.

TURNING POINTS OF HISTORY

Even though Villány remains largely unexplored archaeologically, excavations in the early 1980's delivered unambiguous proof that the Romans cultivated vines in the area. The best-known find is the remnant of an altar unearthed as part of a Roman villa near Nagyharsány, which records the plantation of 400 *arpensis* (about 45 hectares) of vines by the master of the house named Venatus and his son. The deep plowing in preparation for large-scale plantation in the 1960's had actually turned up evidence for a sporadic viticulture predating the Romans, from the Neolithic Age to the period of Celtic settlement in the Iron Age. Unfortunately, the ploughs often damaged the artefacts, reducing the amount of useful information they could provide.

Grape-growing in the early years of the Hungarian Kingdom is evidenced by the 1065 founding charter of the Pécsvárad Abbey, which provided the Church with a contingent of vine-dressers. Following the Mongol

The Kopár ("Barren") vineyard certainly deserves its name

Invasion, the vineyards of the Villány area were gradually restored, albeit at a variable pace depending on the location. This we know from a ranger's document dating from 1352.

Later, the occupying Ottoman forces curbed wine production without completely abolishing it. In fact, the constant skirmishes proved much more detrimental to the vineyards than the Islamic religious ban on alcohol itself. As the population was decimated along with the vines, there was a shortage of hands left to attend to the remaining vineyards. In this way, things in Villány took a long time to get back to normal after Ottoman rule in the area had ended with the Battle of Szársomlyó in 1687. As elsewhere in the country, the majority of the abandoned estates devolved on the court in Vienna, where the monarchs used them to make gifts to worthy subjects. One of the beneficiaries was Eugene of Savoy, the commander who had distinguished himself in the campaign against the Ottomans. When he died without an heir, his huge estate reverted to the daughter of Maria Theresa, and then to her husband, the Archduke Carl Albrecht. Encompassing 26 villages with a center in Bellye, today Bilje in Croatia, the estate was leased from the Treasury by two Armenians, who found that "the sloth and ignorance of the Serbs" hindered the efficient cultivation of the property. Nevertheless, the Bellye Estate continued to exert a decisive influence on Villány's economy for three centuries. The other great property in the area, comprising 24 villages and managed from Bóly, was owned by the Batthyánys, but the Duke of Montenuovo collected some of the income by entitlement through marriage.

The first wave of immigration had brought southern Slavs to Villány even before the Ottomans were driven out, and by 1715 some 40 Serbian families were firmly established in the village. Starting from 1740, German settlers arrived, introducing advanced agricultural know-how, hard-working habits, and a grape, known today as Kékoportó, which was destined to become a key factor in the region's wine and life. Surveys show that by 1767 ethnic Germans outnumbered Serbian settlers in Villány. In 1864, the village had 1745 residents. 35 years later, the population

of 2200 comprised 74% Germans, 18% Hungarians, and about 8% Serbians.

Villány experienced its first golden age during the 1850's and 60's, followed by a second period of boom after the phylloxera epidemic. At this time, the village and its vicinity attained nationwide significance owing to its overhauled varietal structure, and its Europe-wide export of cuttings of fruiting varieties grafted onto resistant American rootstock.

The appalling deportation of ethnic Germans in the wake of World War II rivaled

Zsigmond (Taussig) Teleki was born in the southern Hungarian town of Pécs in 1854. For a while he worked as an apprentice in his father's grocery store in Villány, but soon left for Budapest, where he financed his secondary education himself. Working in Vienna and then for a wine merchant based in Würzburg, Germany, Teleki traveled in Europe extensively, and honed a perfect command of German, English, and French. He returned to Hungary six years after the outbreak of phylloxera, and established an experimental stockyard in Villány. The famous rootstock variety Berlandieri x Riparia, bred by Teleki, proved perfectly suited to producing high quality grapes even when planted in the desolate, intensely calcareous hillsides of Villány. When Teleki died in 1910, his sons Andor and Sándor carried on the stockyard with great success until World War II, maintaining subsidiaries in six countries, and even running an export business overseas. Ironically, Franz Kober in Oppenheim eventually collected most of the recognition by subjecting Teleki's clones to further selection.

the atrocities committed by the Ottoman invaders hundreds of years before. Fortunately, a few families, such as the Tiffáns, were able to escape deportation by leaving their homes and hiding out in the area for years, until it became safe to return.

SIKLÓS AT A GLANCE

The area around Siklós is known today as the white wine district of the region. Just before the phylloxera, white wines here outnumbered reds two to one in most years, although in former times red wine production had been more important in this district as well. In 1895, the vineyards around Siklós occupied 691 *hold* (394 ha) or about one tenth of the farmland under cultivation. Established in 1855, the local wine community numbered 445 members by the end of the 19th century.

In 1935, the 820 *hold* (about 467 ha) of vineyards had more than 600 owners, and amounted to 11% of tilled land. Although Olaszrizling was the most common grape, Kadarka clearly outshone it in popularity. These varieties were followed by Oportó (today called Kékoportó), Chasselas, Rizlingszilváni, and Bánáti Rizling. Among the growers, mention must be made of Sándor Jantsits, whose production topped 1,200 hectoliters in some years. His son, Dr. Sándor Jantsits, a man of extraordinary erudition, remained a decisive force in the region until 1960, and made a lasting contribution to Villány with his model estate.

THE FINEST VINEYARDS OF VILLÁNY

JAMMERTAL

Probably so named in commemoration of the Battle of Szársomlyó in 1687, the 50-hectare "Vale of Sorrows" is considered second in quality only to the Kopár. The wines of this fine vineyard exhibit a distinctive animal note when ripe.

CSILLAGVÖLGY (Sterntal)

The first vineyard you will see on your right as you head west out of the village; about 250 ha. Approachable wines, and quickly maturing by Villány standards.

REMETE

The "Hermit" occupies some 70 hectares on the eastern flank of the Szársomlyó. Wines of firm character.

ÖRDÖGÁROK (Teufelsgraben)

So far, vines have been confined to the southernmost part of this vineyard. Now the Tiffáns, Bock, the Günzers and others are busy clear-cutting in the northern section to reclaim what are supposed to have been the best sites in the "Devil's Gulch." If they succeed, this will mean new plantation on a total of 50 hectares.

The cellar row in Villánykövesd

KOPÁR

The name of this legendary vineyard, meaning "Barren," refers to the bleak limestone debris directly above the vines. Occupying the southern face of the Szársomlyó, the Kopár has a wonderfully sheltered microclimate, where bud-break regularly occurs two weeks sooner than in the finest vineyards anywhere else in the country.

VÁRERDŐ

The "Castle Wood" is a well-protected vineyard facing west that has an excellent microclimate. The majority of the industrialized plantations have now been converted to suit modern demands.

KONKOLY

Large-scale landscaping works since 2002 have cleared the way for Attila Gere to plant a model vineyard geared for stellar quality. A site of symbolic significance, embodying the rebirth of Villány.

GÖNTÉR AND ZUHÁNYA

Two vineyards near the town of Siklós, better known for white wines. Owners include Malatinszky and Vylyan.

GRAPES

HISTORIC SNAPSHOTS

1494: An inventory of wines shipped to King Ulászló (Wladislas) lists the grape varieties as Rinolio, Pynol, and Malvasiri. Except for this latter item, these grapes are shrouded in mystery.

Early **1700's:** Mátyás Bél enumerates Bajnai (Góhér), Lisztes Fehér, Hárslevelű, Muskotály, Ökörszemű Törökszőlő, Tótfekete and Kadarka as Villány's grapes.

1882: János Jankó gives the white grapes as Fügér, Bajor, Mohácsi, Sárfehér, and Bárányfarkú, and the black grapes as Kadarka and Cigányszőlő. The same author later refers to the plantation at the Bellye Estate of western varieties, including Riesling, Tramini, Caeven, and Oporto. János Solden, the cellar master at Bóly, recalls how a lack of interest in quality led growers to cut out their Rizling and re-

place them with the commonplace Fügér (today known as Fehér Dinka). The main varieties at the Bellye Estate were Portogizi (a corrupted form of German *Portugieser*, the old local name for Oportó or Kékoportó), Kadarka, and Rizling. Some sources speculate that, in addition to Kékoportó, Kékfrankos was also introduced in Villány by German settlers in the 18th century.

By the early **20th century,** about 600 *hold* or 342 hectares of vineyard belonged to the village of Villány itself.

CURRENT VARIETIES

Rizlingszilváni

A light "annual" white; popular and affordable.

Hárslevelű

Better known from volcanic soils, e.g. from Tokaj or Somló, but also indigenous in Villány, where it impresses with a richness of taste rather than vigor. Also made in the sweet late harvest style.

Olaszrizling

The workhorse white grape in Hungary, with southern examples from Villány-Siklós being less aromatic, but milder and often more alcoholic than wines grown further north.

Rajnai Rizling

A variety best known from cooler regions, Rajnai Rizling here cannot match the rich acidity of northern versions, although in Siklós it has the spine to keep for years.

Chardonnay

Planted in smaller quantities around the village of Máriagyüd; early harvest is essential to retain acidity.

Kékoportó

Supposedly of Portuguese origins, Kékoportó is considered a second-rate grape throughout much of Europe, but it makes Villány's basic red—the leveling staple of backyard growers and star winemakers. Can be a fleeting affair due to its insufficient acidity.

Kékfrankos

Valued by many as a reliable producer; potentially full and big in southern regions like Villány. Its always dependable acidity makes it perfect for blending with softer varieties.

Zweigelt

Thoroughly discredited by socialist-era mass-production, Zweigelt nevertheless makes drinkable wine even in vineyards producing the double the average yield for Kékfrankos yields. Zweigelt from vineyards cut back to 60-80 hectoliters per hectare can be a pleasant surprise.

Merlot

Wonderfully round and supple in Villány, but not in a Kékoportó kind of way. Long maceration often results in over-extracted, rustic wines lacking elegance.

Cabernet Franc

This grape in Villány makes a superb red on a par with the best pure varietal Cabernet Franc wines of the world. Too bad it takes six to eight years to come into its own.

Cabernet Sauvignon

Potentially magnificent in Villány, as elsewhere in the world. Reprehensibly, the overwhelming majority of Villány Cabs are squandered before they could reach full maturity at four to six years of age. Spicy, big, and often ponderously tannic.

OWNERSHIP STRUCTURE

The harmful legacy of the collectivized economy will likely continue to be felt for decades in plantations with low densities and widely paced rows, originally designed to accommodate oversize tractors that have no business being in a vineyard. Even the uninitiated, when taken for a brief tour of the Kopár, will hardly fail to register the differences between a collectively cultivated tract and a privately owned plot. Today, some 60% of the region's vineyards are controlled by privately owned family wineries. Within the private sphere, enterprises producing cleaner wines for the market coexist with small individual growers, who are left to their own devices and can rarely afford to bottle their products.

WINE COMMUNITIES

The Wine Community membership of 2630 does not include every grower in the region, because people typically sign up only if they produce more than the family's consumption. While it is too early to gauge the impact of recently amended nationwide regulations categorizing wine as an excise product, it seems certain that many of the smaller parcels will fall fallow as a result of red tape.

WINE TRAIL

Villány's natural disposition to receiving visitors gave rise to the first Wine Trail Association in the country. The booming wine tourism of Villány owes much of its success to the decent facilities, the neat cellars, the kind of hospitality one would encounter in Austria, and of course the superb quality of the wines themselves. The only regrettable circumstance is the lack of distinctive regional dishes that would go particularly well with the momentous reds, but the emerging vogue for game may rectify that before long. Although Villány is a remote region—at least from Budapest—and not particularly easy to access, a visit is a must for anyone who wants to make a more than a superficial acquaintance with Hungarian wines.

VILLÁNY VINTAGES

Villány vintages regularly score higher than the Hungarian average, owing to the southern latitude and the sheltered microclimates. Below is a list of the last 13 vintages, rated in the five-star system.

1990**

The first year with substance to evaluate; bottled wines from Bock, Attila Gere, Tamás Gere, Polgár, and Tiffán, some aged in new oak. An inferior year whose wines began to decline around 1995.

JÓZSEF BOCK, VINTAGE 1948

This 45-hectare family winery owns 8 hectares in the famed Jammertal vineyard, 2.5 in the Kopár, 3 in the Feketehegy, and 2 in the Somsich. The varietal composition of red-wine grapes is led by Cabernet Sauvignon, followed by Kékoportó, Cabernet Franc, Merlot, Kékfrankos and, more recently, Pinot Noir and some Syrah for the sake of completeness. The white wines are made from Olaszrizling, Hárslevelű, and Chardonnay. The sites planted by Bock have a density of 6,000 vines per hectare. His unique wines have an unmistakable personality (enormous structure and barnyard characteristics) that sets them apart from the other excellent Villány reds. It is a dynamically growing winery, with a neat inn to put up visitors. No account of Villány could be complete without a tribute to József Bock, the almost always cheerful "Boxi" with the ear-to-ear grin, who is considered a living legend by fellow growers and aficionados alike. One of the first producers in Villány to have started bottling his own wines back in 1990, Bock earned his name with his Royal Cuvée (a blend of Cabernet Sauvignon and Pinot Noir he first made in partnership with Csaba Malatinszky) and his Bock Cuvée based on the two Cabernets. This long-standing flagship wine is now seriously challenged by Bock's own Capella Cuvée, of undisclosed composition, which is still not fully mature. The Kékoportó, traditionally released for Szent Márton's day, is one of the best-loved *primeur* wines in Hungary.

1991***

An inferior year throughout Hungary, but no worse than average in Villány. The wines turned out full-bodied despite a cool summer and heavy rains.

1992***

That's a strong three stars, for this year supplied the first wines to become sought-after items in auction halls. They had enough reserves to keep in top shape until 1996-1997 before beginning to gracefully fade. Well-kept bottles remain enjoyable in 2003.

1993****

The year when deliberate limitation of yield began in Villány. The resulting wines had unprecedented concentration and stayed on their plateau of development well into 1998.

1994***

A weak year around the country, though better than average in Villány. The wines held up until 1998.

1995****

Profiting from improved work in the vineyards, and cellar technology catching up with international standards, the wines are still very nice in 2003. The first vintage with a contemporary evaluation that still seems to stand up with the bnefit of hindsight.

1996***

A lesser year with a cool summer and autumn rains. Even at this southern location, the wines left much to be desired.

1997***

The healthiest grapes in 25 years and the possibility of choosing harvest dates practically at will raised very high expectations that many wines failed to fulfill. The initially robust reds lost power quickly; several big-name wines dried out by 2001.

1998** - ***

Are years with an even number jinxed in Villány? Increasingly conscientious yields were instrumental in the production of sound wines, although several wineries did not declare barrique treatment on their Cabernet Sauvignon labels. Wines to drink until 2005.

1999*****

Finally, a truly great year. Although rainy weeks toward the end of summer made the quality of white wines strongly dependent on protection in the vineyard, the reds ripened very well with a fine spectrum of acids. The major varieties will reach full bloom in 2005, and look set to keep in top shape for ten years after that.

2000*****

An exceptionally fine year, marked by the early completion of the vegetative period. Every variety had a chance to achieve perfect ripeness; in fact, growers had the time to wait for overripe grapes if that was what they wanted. The annual median temperature of

13.3 °C, almost 3 °C higher than the 10.5 °C average, resulted in alcohol levels in excess of the optimum, particularly in white wines. Tannin maturity, which did not keep up with the extreme sugar levels, seemed problematic at first, but the worries were soon dispelled. The wines are expected to reach their peak between 2005 and 2007, and will likely stay there for at least ten years. A few growers made absolutely world-class wines by pushing yield reduction to its sensible limits.

2001***

A forgettable year that started out fine but ended in incessant rains. Even so, low yields and meticulous plant protection permitted a few wineries to make reasonably good wines, possibly even better. A year of large quantities throughout the country, and in Villány as well.

2002****

The year started extraordinarily promisingly, but more than one grower's hopes were washed away by rain in August. Where the late-ripening grapes emerged from the rains unscathed, a very even last phase of ripening resulted in wines outclassing even the 2000's. Szekszárd has had similar experiences.

THE GROWERS

PÉTER BAJOR

A mid-size family winery with a 13.5-hectare estate in the Zuhánya, Makón and Göntér vineyards (Hárslevelű, Olaszrizling, Rajnai Rizling, Muscat Ottonel, Muscat Lunel, Kékoportó, Kékfrankos, and the Cabernets, with planting densities of 3,000-4,000 vines per hectare.) The Bajors are committed to traditional methods, complemented by modern technology. In some years, their white wines can serve as the benchmark of the traditionalist style in Hungary.

TAMÁS GERE

Tamás Gere's winery used to be the bastion of traditional fermentation and maturation methods, until barriques began to conquer ever larger chunks of this cellar as well. The

vintner, who remains known for his insistence on no-holds-barred tannin extraction, also deserves credit for his Pinot Noirs as a pioneer with this grape in Villány. A new winery in Diófás tér and the involvement of a son have provided fresh stimulus for growth.

TAMÁS GÜNZER

Tamás Günzer cultivates his own four hectares, and buys the harvest from another three. The average age of the vines is seven years; the planting density is 4,500 vines per hectare. The grape varieties include Olaszrizling, Chardonnay, Kékoportó, Kékfrankos, Blauburger, Cabernet Sauvignon, Cabernet Franc, and Merlot. The wines are matured in the 600-hectoliter capacity cellar; some spend time in new oak barrels. Guests are received at Baross Gábor u. 79. Tel.: (72) 493 163.

ZOLTÁN GÜNZER

A dynamic family winery that has caught up with the Villány wine elite. The main assets are the consistent good quality of the wines (subject of course to variation depending on

The "Millennium Quartet" of Villány's senior winemakers

205

ATTILA GERE, VINTAGE 1954

How do you start out as a forestry technician and end up ten years later as one of the country's preeminent winemakers? Attila Gere has had this unlikely career that is nevertheless a typical one in Hungary—or was, as recently as five or six years ago. As one of the key ingredients of this sweeping career, Gere grew up in a community of ambitious and hard-working people, the ethnic Donau-Schwabs who came to Hungary 250 years ago. Later, his wife Katalin provided the devoted and solid family background that is indispensable for great achievement. Last but not least, Gere has been blessed with an upbeat spirit, an optimistic view of life that seems endemic among the greats of the world of wine. Gere is an accomplished and experienced taster, but he would probably be making just as good wine if he had not tasted anything outside Villány for reference. He has expanded his estate prudently, only buying new land if the price was sensible, and choosing instead to invest more in landscaping, roads, and retaining walls—a very costly enterprise. In this way, he now owns sites that had always been ranked among the best in Villány, except that most of them were covered by fifty-year old woods when he acquired them. Gere's 42-hectare estate is geared toward the classic Bordeaux varieties. His Kopár, an emphatic blend with a distinctive label named after Villány's finest vineyard, is a large-scale red that has come to be seen as symbolic of the region's vast potential. What is the style of Gere's wines? Risking a platitude, one could say it's that quintessential Villány character. Less banally, it has to do with an inimitable charm that is invariably present, even in the weightiest, most concentrated wines. This quality in turn has been variously chalked up to a distinctive extract sweetness or lower sulfur levels, enabling quickly approachable wines. We believe this is just scratching the tip of the iceberg. What makes these dense, complex and age-worthy reds consistently true to form and gives them class is really beyond deductive, literal-minded reasoning. We can only give an inkling of this property metaphorically, by likening it to the allure of a fascinating, captivating character.

cent plantations. Apart from two hectares rated as Class II, all of Günzer's holdings are in Class I vineyards.

New investment in 2002 brought 700 hectoliters of stainless steel tanks, a new stemmer-crusher, and a worm-screw pump to the winery. The cellar has a 350 hectoliter capacity in barrels, including 72 new barriques. Günzer ages every one of his reds in wood for varying lengths of time. Annual production is 60,000-80,000 bottles.

JACKFALL BORMANUFAKTÚRA

A new kid on the Villány block, Botond Gábor Bányai is a young and ambitious winemaker just starting out with a resuscitated family winery. A sensible range of grape varieties, made into magnum-bottled wines that seem sophisticated even by Villány standards.

BÉLA JEKL (VINOLAND PLUS)

Having reached its final size in 1996, this winery currently controls 7 hectares of vines in fine vineyards, including 1 hectare in the Jammertal, 0.5 in the Ördögárok, and 4 on the Fekete-hegy. The new plantations have a density of 5,500 vines per hectare. The Jekls plan to increase the total area of the family estate to 20 hectares over the next three years.

the vintage), and sound business practices. The 15-hectare estate—8 producing, and 7 awaiting plantation in the Ördögárok—is centered on the Jammertal and Csillagvölgy vineyards, where Günzer grows Kékoportó, Kékfrankos, Merlot, Cabernet Sauvignon, and Cabernet Franc; his Kadarka plantation has not reached the bearing stage yet. He also leases lots in the Agancsos and Dobogó vineyards, and buys about 20 tons of grapes a year to supplement his own crop. His own plantations are 10 years old on average. The older lots have a planting density of 3,000 vines per hectare, compared to 5,000 in the more recent

MALATINSZKY-KÚRIA

A relatively new estate, founded seven years ago. The style of the wines has stirred controversy, but their sheer quality is always beyond reproach.

CSABA MALATINSZKY, VINTAGE 1957

Malatinszky started out as a sommelier and, although he is rarely referred to as such, became the first internationally certified exponent of the profession in Hungary. In 1993, he opened the first specialized wine shop in Budapest, and has come along in leaps and bounds ever since. Being a maverick is never easy, but it can be particularly tough in Villány. Yet Malatinszky, the undeterred outsider, wanted to work here as soon as he ascertained the region's potential, perhaps unmatched anywhere else. Committed to crafting wines for extended cellaring, he now offers a superb Chardonnay with a Californian flair, and an assortment of reds. Especially exciting are his hallmark blend of Bordeaux and Burgundy varieties dubbed Cabernoir, and his unfiltered Cabernet Sauvignon bottled sur lie–a style he has also pioneered in Hungary. Not a man who takes or asks for advice on his home turf, Malatinszky has been known to provoke resentment in the wine community, but the wines themselves are utterly convincing. They are usually not ready for drinking before their fourth year, and will take at least six to eight years to attain full maturity. Whether this is something to be criticized on objective grounds or a matter of sheer personal taste will be left for the reader to decide. As for the purity of the wines, we could do worse than recalling the words of a physician upon visiting Malatinszky's cellar: "The place is so clean I could do an operation in here…"

The cellars are located at Palkonya, where the wines are vinified using traditional techniques (25,000 bottles annually). As most of the wines are estate-grown single-vineyard items (using Olaszrizling, Blauburger, Pinot Noir, Cabernet Sauvignon, Cabernet Franc, Merlot, and Kadarka grapes), they are intended for connoisseurs of top gastronomy and other discriminating consumers.

MÁRTON MAYER

This family-owned estate is comparable to a "super second" in Bordeaux. Nowadays, Mayer cultivates eight hectares and bottles his wines himself. He owns two hectares in the Kopár, with the remaining vines dispersed in the Remete, the Várerdő near Nagyharsány, and the Hajdú at Kisharsány. He harvests his whites (Rajnai Rizling and Chardonnay) from 2.5 hectares in Siklós. The wines are pure and firm, with a personality that is forceful rather than enticing.

MONDIVIN

Owned by Jan van Lissum, Eric Sauter of Holland, and Ede Tiffán, this joint venture relies on 5 hectares in the Remete vineyard, planted exclusively with Cabernet Franc. The company released its first excellent wine onto the international market in 1993, and went fully independent in 2001.

ZOLTÁN POLGÁR

A family winery now cultivating 42 hectares in the Hunyadi, Kopár, Tüskés, Bocor, and Diászó vineyards, planted with Olaszrizling, Chardonnay, Hárslevelű, Muskotály, Kékoportó, Kadarka, Kékfrankos, Zweigelt, Merlot, and Cabernet Sauvignon. In the most recent plantations (2 ha), densities are up to 8,000 vines per hectare (the average is 4,500-5,000). The winery makes a wide selection of both white and red wines. The latter gained a niche in the higher quality category with the 1999 vintage. So far, they have far exceeded the winery's usual performance in terms of concentration and aging potential. The Polgárs are also known for their legendary hospitality, capable marketing work, and a side business renting out wine deposit vaults.

207

EDE AND ZSOLT TIFFÁN
EDE TIFFÁN, VINTAGE 1942

Tiffán is a venerated winemaker who earned his authority from his deep knowledge and experience, and kept it by means of uncompromising rigor. As the doyen of the profession in Hungary, Tiffán can rightfully regard each successful local grower in Villány as his personal disciple, and none of them would be likely to object to the distinction.

The wines are just like the man: they conquer by main force, without resorting to coy tricks or negotiation. Tiffán now relies heavily on his son Zsolt in running the family business, and he has collaborated for a decade with Jan van Lissum, making outstanding Cabernet Franc under the Mondivin label. His Cuvée Carissimae is a superbly harmonious red with the power to appease the palate and the soul. His stunningly concentrated Pinot Noir from the Várerdő vineyard is a great wine, but one in which the varietal character takes the back seat behind the powerful terroir. Finally, the "limited-edition" Grand Selection, made only in the best years, is the stuff of dreams for the Hungarian vinophile. This superlative Bordeaux-style blend relies on extremely stringent selection criteria and special barrels which lend an inimitable character to the wine. If it has not won every Hungarian competition hands down, this is only because panelists rarely give it the long bottle age and exposure to air that it needs to show to best advantage.

IMRE TIFFÁN

Imre Tiffán and his son, who has taken an active role in the winery, continue the family tradition that first defined the individual style of their wines. In recent years, the Tiffáns have been increasingly successful in communicating their commitment to quality through their wines, although their orthodoxy does not always recruit followers.

CSÁNYI WINERY
(VILLÁNYI BORÁSZAT RT.)

The leading wine facility of the region, now in family ownership, bottling wines for many retailers and controlling a fine inventory of old vintages. The Chateau Teleki line of wines has joined the old reserves in securing a place in top gastronomy. The winery cultivates some 320 hectares, including Cabernet Franc and Merlot in the Csillagvölgy and Cabernet Sauvignon in the Hársos vineyard (the planting density is 4,600-5,400 vines per hectare). Additional varieties include Zweigelt and Kékoportó. Since the winery was completely refurbished in 2001 and 2002, there is no longer anything to remind visitors of the facility's past as a socialist-era industrialized enterprise.

VYLYAN

One of the trend-setting wineries of the region, Vylyan controls 187 hectares, including more than 100 hectares of fruit-bearing vines. The density is quite high at 7,000 vines per hectare in the recent plantations, but of course lower in the older vineyards. The estate stretches across seven vineyards: the Dobogó, the Pillangó, the Mandulás, the Gombás, the Zuhánya, the Montenuovo, and the Városhegy. The winery is distinguished by its draconian limitation of yield, and heavier reliance on new oak than any other estate in the region. Of a total cellar capacity of 3,500 hectoliters, nearly 1,000 is taken up by the barriques. The majority owner is Pál Debreceni, who is responsible for the lion's share of the solid marketing work supporting the winery. István Szabó Ipacs, the talented young winemaker, is advised by Tibor Kovács of the Hétszőlő Winery in Tokaj, and by Jean-Pierre Confuron.

ALAJOS WUNDERLICH

A member of the up-and-coming generation in Villány. Area development, new cellar equipment and care are the key words for this winery as it shifts into higher gear. Recently, the estate has expanded to over 10 hectares, with sites in the Jammertal (Kékoportó and Cabernet Sauvignon) and in the Remete (Kadarka). A man of indefatigable good spirits, Wunderlich is one of Villány's ever-popular figures.

THIRD CHAPTER

Sparkling Wine
How to Taste Hungarian Wine
Wine in Entertaining
Wine and Health
The Organization of Wine

Sparkling Wine

Like Tokaj Aszú, Champagne has its legendary "inventor." Even though the precedence of Máté Laczkó Szepsy or Dom Perignon cannot be ascertained beyond the shadow of a doubt, most of us certainly like our stories to have a beginning and an end. Now, the end of the story of champagne would spell nothing short of the end of civilization as we know it. As for the beginning of that story, we cannot go far wrong if we mark it in the place and time inhabited by Dom Perignon, the distinguished monk: Hautvillers, Champagne, in the 17th century.

L ouis XIV may have indeed hailed Tokaj as "the wine of kings and the king of wines," but the same dictum is posted in Rumpoldskirchen, and who knows how many more places where good wine is grown. It seems that one had better be careful with superlatives.

Of course, respectable brand names of repute have always elicited eulogies. But just how much substance is there behind these exalted words of praise? This question is best answered by someone who has had the good fortune to spend several days in succession as a guest in Champagne or Epernay on a notable festive occasion. No drink on earth other than Champagne is able to accompany every meal for three days, including formal dinners, and then to sweeten long meetings dragging on into the night, quenching the thirst as if it were water... Needless to say, top quality is of the essence in attaining this kind of versatility. If you have pursued the above test to its logical conclusion, you will no doubt agree that Champagne is the true king of wines. If you haven't, you should probably reserve judgment until you have had the opportunity.

The story of sparkling wine thus begins in the cool-climate region of Champagne, France. By the late 1700's, Ruinart, Moët & Chandon, Veuve Clicquot, and a number of other excellent houses here were coming out with fine products. In Germany, the first sparkling wine factory was established in

Dom Perignon,
the inventor of
champagne
(1635–1715)
Törley Winery

duction and uniformity, enforced by the "great leveler" that was communist power. The state-run behemoth Hungarovin achieved an annual output of 25 million bottles, while further giant sparkling operations were set up in Balatonboglár, Izsák, and elsewhere in the country.

The political transformations of 1989/1990 reshuffled the market thoroughly, leaving the leading position to Hungarovin-Balatonboglár, acquired by Henkell-Söhnlein. In the shadow of this large company, some private cellars making excellent sparkling in smaller quantities vie with factories selling inferior products cloaked in sweetness. Treading the newly discovered old path is a sparkling wine manufactory established by Vinarium a few years ago in Budafok. The company makes four grades of sparkling under the Chateau Vincent label, relying on refined and crisp base wines sourced consistently from the same area. Even the sweet version is capable of affording an enjoyable experience due to its sound acidity. Indeed, this dynamic manufacturer has now secured a place among the top sparkling wine names in Hungary, next to Törley and François.

THE MAKING OF SPARKLE

The phrase "sparkling wine factory" is unlikely to rub anyone up the wrong way, for sparkling wine is clearly a product that is *manufactured* through a series of processes—rather than simply *grown*, *made*, or *crafted*. These last words certainly have a nicer ring to them than "manufacture" when applied to still wines. Who would expect anything other than mediocre, at best run-of-the-mill products to come out of a "wine factory?" Well, a sparkling wine factory is a different affair altogether. Let us then pay a visit.

According to a widely accepted definition, sparkling wine is a wine containing carbondioxide as a result of natural fermentation. The consensus is to accept reasonably consistent character and quality from the same brand. This is precisely where technology comes in, justifying the concept of "manufacture." While the quality of these wines should

1826, a year after the Hungarian foundation of the house of Hubert in Pozsony (today Bratislava in Slovakia), followed by the Palugyai manufactory. Further Hungarian sparkling wine factories were to emerge in 1852 (in the Józsefváros district of Pest), 1854 (in Buda), and 1876 (the Littke house in Pécs). The true career of József Törley, who had studied in Reims, began in 1882 when he relocated his champagne factory from France to Budafok in the outskirts of Hungary's capital city. Louis and César François, the two professionals Törley had brought with him, went independent just four years after their expatriation. And there is one more distinguished name to mention: that of Count Ferenc Esterházy, who established a sparkling wine manufactory in the northwestern Hungarian town of Tata in 1905. There was a time when Hungary had no fewer than 21 sparkling wine operations running, but not all of these were to remain standing. The horrendous devastation brought by World War II and the occupying Soviet forces did not spare the cellars. Some of them took the first feeble steps toward recovery when peace returned, but the nationalization campaign left no company in private hands after 1950. Then came the era of mass pro-

A dégorgement room
around
1930
(Törley archive)

not fluctuate at all, they are permitted minor changes of character. This typically happens in sparkling wines of outstanding quality known as vintage Champagne (if made in the region of the same name), or vintage sparkling. An exceptional vintage in itself is capable of supplying all the qualities that it normally takes the deliberate and clever blending to achieve. And what is blended in this process is not simply vintages, as different grape varieties and growing sites also enter the mix to complicate the picture. Here we

should mention that every sparkling wine is at its best at the time it is released by the manufacturer, which obviates the need for laying down the bottle for further maturation. The reason vintage sparkling wines are often cellared and served at a later date is that they lose their quality very slowly, and tend to go through intriguing and delightful changes with age. The recognition and appreciation of these subtle alterations take considerable skill and experience. It may be important to know that really old vintage Champagne is subject-

Bottling raw sparkling,
around 1930
(Törley archive)

211

ed to prolonged aging, for a decade or two, not in its final form as it comes stoppered with a cork, but prior to *degorgement*. To see what that and other terms might mean, let us take a look at the various steps in the making of making sparkling wine.

It all boils down to refermenting a *base wine*. Now, whether this *second fermentation* takes place in the bottle or large, pressure-tight stainless steel tanks, makes a world of difference between sparkling wines. As for the base wine serving as the raw material, it must answer the essential requirements of high acidity, lower alcohol, neutral rather than distinct aroma and taste, and, above all, a refreshing, crisp character. Of course, carbon -dioxide can only occur naturally in wine if fermentation takes place. This in turn requires sugar, in this case in the form of a *dosage* of *tirage liqueur*—the addition of what is really a pure sugar solution. You will also need a special *yeast* that is able to do the job at higher levels of alcohol, and will impart a pure, light taste to the wine.

In the next decisive step, the wine is transferred to large pressure-tight tanks or bottles where it will be refermented. Tank-fermented (Charmat or bulk process) sparkling wine can attain fairly good quality, refined and persistent effervescence, and a light fruity taste, but these presuppose decent base wines, well-chosen yeasts and rigorous discipline with the technology. For years we have found that, in Hungary, Henkell & Söhnlein's BB winery remains the uncontested champion of this genre. It is only to be regretted that their top-of-the-line tank-fermented sparkling is not available domestically through regular commercial channels.

If the wine is refermented in the bottle, in fact not parting with that bottle until drunk, then it will be labeled "méthode traditionelle" or the equivalent. This most sophisticated way of producing sparkling wine is actually the one that was perfected in Champagne itself. However, because the name Champagne is strictly protected by laws, no wine can officially be labeled "méthode champenoise," or in fact be called Champagne, unless it was made within the boundaries of that region. This

leaves the "traditional method" designation for all sparkling wines made elsewhere with the same laborious procedure. Bottle-fermented sparkling wine is distinguished by its subtlety of flavor, the refinement and persistence of its *perlage* (effervescence), and its high production cost. It is also, however, vulnerable to accidental errors slipping into the production process, which will not be noticed until the bottle is popped open for consumption. Such faulty bottles will be replaced in a restaurant, but nowhere else… Of course, the likelihood of a glitch like that happening is much smaller with the big brands, such as Moët & Chandon, Roederer, Ruinart, Mumm, or Freixenet, and in particular with their prestige cuvées.

But to come back to where we left off, let us see what happens when secondary fermentation has been completed. At this point, the bottle is transferred to special racks in a slanted position neck forward, where the painstaking labor of *remuage* or riddling—the manual process of giving the bottle a partial turn and a simultaneous tip approaching the vertical regularly over a period of time—coaxes the dead yeast cells, the by-product of fermentation, to sail down the neck of the bottle. The same result can be achieved mechanically, using the contrivance known as *gyropalette*. When the process has been completed—this may take anywhere from a few days to several weeks—the sediment is flash-frozen for easy removal together with the crown cap. This is called *degorgement*. The slightly depleted volume in the bottle is then typically replenished with a *dosage* of what is known as *liqueur d'expédition*, a solution of wine and sugar. Then the bottle is stoppered with its final cork and, after a few months of rest, it will be ready for release.

If, subsequent to degorgement, the content of the bottles is collected in large steel tanks and filtered prior to dosage and bottling, then we talk about "*classic method*" sparkling. The technique itself is known as the *transvase* process. (In Hungary, a good example for this loveliest of fizz for everyday drinking is the Hungária Grand Cuvée.) At its best, this type of sparkling wine may come close to *méthode traditionelle* wines in quality, while blending and filtering help reduce the risks of fermentation-related flaws. These wines are also not-ed for their fine *perlage*, as their carbon-diox-ide content only comes from the secondary fermentation in the bottle. They nevertheless lack that special magic that is unique to the artisanal approach, and it will be remembered that the best base wines are invariably re-served for use in *traditionelle* sparkling.

In the finished bottle, the pressure of car-bon-dioxide may be as high as six bar, requir-ing a strong bottle and very tight closure. Remarkably, certain countries grant tax breaks to sparkling wines with a pressure rat-ed below three bar, knowing that these are outside the category of luxury commodities.

As for the varieties, theoretically any grape with vigorous acids could be considered for making sparkling wine. Since fine sparkling is limited to white or rosé, black grapes can be used only if they are pressed quickly, without allowing time for the coloring substances be extracted from the grape skins. Processed in this way, Pinot Noir can yield a superb base wine, as does Chardonnay—although the latter tends to be more suitable than any other grape if used solo, without blending. Not sur-prisingly, these two international varieties provide the raw material for the most luxuri-ous of Champagne as well. For sparkling wines, it is especially true to say that the very best can be nothing but strictly dry. This truth will not be challenged by the fact that sweet products continue to lead sales around the world. At the end of the day, those who want to enjoy their bubbles to the fullest must stick to the dry versions. (Just keep in mind that there is no such thing as an expensive sweet Champagne.)

In addition to the methods described above, there are other processes of mostly lo-cal interest, such as the one that takes care of fermentation in one single step. These meth-ods do not produce appreciable quantities for the Hungarian market, nor do they represent particularly good quality. We only mention them in passing for the sake of completeness.

The know-how of selecting yeasts for refer-menting the wines makes an important contri-bution to the science of sparkling wine manufacture. In contrast, the choice of base

Years steal
Fire from the mind as vigour from the limb;
And life's enchanted cup but sparkles near the brim.
— Byron

wines to compose the cuvée depends on the cellar master's personal skill, organoleptic prowess and, above all, refinement of taste. Here, it is not so much technology anymore as it is the human factor that becomes all-impor-tant, akin to the art of blending great Cognac.

Wine is something that we may resort to even as a simple thirst quencher, but sparkling wine is more often than not enjoyed as a matter of sheer pleasure. It is a noble libation born of great knowledge and labor—some-thing we may indeed rightfully regard as the king of wines.

How to Taste Hungarian Wine

Anyone could rightfully ask what makes Hungarian wines so special that they should presuppose a unique approach, or even some background, for proper tasting. And yet perceptive and knowledgeable experts allow that a wine like Tokaji Aszú may demand some local knowledge, even some advice, before one can fully appreciate the storehouse of pleasure that it offers.

Of course, Hungarian wines made in the accepted international style will not require any special studies. In fact, tasting a Tokaji Aszú is quite a "logical" procedure in its own right. By contrast, mineral-flavored whites grown on the country's volcanic soils definitely have no chance to properly divulge their essence in the conditions that characterize a typical tasting session. Prestigious wine contests with an invited international panel, such as Vinagora or the Pannon Bormustra, regularly demonstrate the inability of the wines in this "critical" category to win recognition. The best dry Furmint and Hárslevelű wines from Tokaj or Somló, or any well-matured white from Badacsony, hardly ever appeal to the taste of acknowledged experts from around the world.

But what happens if the assessment is conducted off the conveyor belt, so to speak? At tasting events held in private, we see nothing but an expression of rapture and incredulity on the faces of seasoned wine authorities when they are confronted by a well-presented dry white, invariably matured in wood, from Árvay, Györgykovács, Inhauser, Szepsy, or Szeremley.

The solution to the riddle is a simple one: these wines need time to breathe, as any great red would, and should be tasted two or three degrees warmer than the usual temperature recommended for dry whites. The best glass for them is Riedel's Chardonnay glass, with a capacity of 20-30 cl. Whether you want to decant the wine in the classic manner or wait patiently for it to open out in the glass depends solely on the circumstances. In our experience, some of these wines show an entirely new aspect toward the end of a prolonged tasting session, when whatever wine is still left in the decanter or the glass has had time to warm up to around 20 °C. By the same token, a splendid Furmint from Györgykovács has to spend 16-24 months in wood and another two years in the bottle before it begins to resemble a fine Mersault. This is even more true for a Juhfark from the same Somló region, which will come off as a dumb rustic wine if not given the time and care it needs to unfold. All this has to do with the rich concentration of minerals that these wines invariable possess.

A series of marathon sessions tasting Tokaj, including a muster of 41 Aszús with Rudolf Knoll at the Budapest College of Wine in 1998, taught us that the aromas of this noble sweet wine are unable to sufficiently evolve in a small dessert wine glass with a volume of just about 10 cl. We find the sherry *copita* or a high quality standard tasting glass much better adapted for the purpose. When tasting sweet Tokaj, it is also a good idea to start out at the lower temperature customary for dry whites, and wait until a smaller quantity of wine has warmed up slightly in your glass. Tasting at the breakneck pace of four minutes per wine will never give you a realistic picture.

Chardonnays and Sauvignon Blancs have been hands-down winners of white wine competitions we have organized in recent years with the participation of distinguished professionals of international standing. These wines have no communication problems; they speak to everyone in a universally intelligible common tongue. This may also explain why reds tend to collect vastly more gold and grand gold medals than whites at almost every contest in Hungary, a predominantly white wine producing country.

THE BUDAPEST COLLEGE OF WINE'S CRITERIA OF EVALUATION AND PRACTICAL RULES OF TASTING

Tasting amounts to organoleptic analysis whereby we bring our vision, smell and taste to testing food or other consumable goods with the aim of forming an opinion and preparing an objective assessment. In addition to being an act of analysis, tasting is also a synthesizing operation in that it implies the comparison of the wine under review with others previously tasted. As the only standard here is the taster himself, his subjectivity and often unconscious sensory illusions get in the way of a universally valid evaluation. To make things more complicated, sensory impression is proportionate to the logarithm of stimulus concentration: it increases by arithmetical progression while the concentration of the substance increases by geometrical progression.

Therefore, we make our best efforts to ensure truth in tasting by
- screening out anatomical, biological and pathological conditions in tasters that may interfere with realistic judgment;
- expecting tasters to be in top shape physically;
- trying to consciously remove all prejudice in the interest of tasting that is truly blind.

Taking our clues from Poupen, we first examine the wine visually and then, with eyes

215

Best before tasting...
(Bouillon)

shut, we try to "see" with our nose, tongue, and palate. We do our best to proceed free of bias and influence, but filled with dedication and curiosity. Tasting in this manner is not only conducive to the purpose but it may, depending on the stature of the wines at hand, provide spiritual fulfillment comparable to visiting a concert or an exhibition of art. Since descriptions of tasting techniques will be available from any number of sources, here we choose to limit the discussion to a few aspects, both theoretical and practical, which the literature tends to treat tangentially or pass over in silence.

First, we define **taste environment** as the total "climate" of taste that various substances—foods, drinks, stimulants, possibly cosmetics and medication—have built up in the mouth of the taster prior to the tasting. The taste environment is most frequently and most intensely influenced by the wines already tasted in the lineup. It follows that no tasting can be sufficiently perceptive, detailed and precise unless the wines sampled previously in the same session had the same basic orientation of flavor. We say this as followers of the doctrine that tasting is essentially a cortical activity, in which the senses serve merely as points of entry for stimuli. What this means in practice is that you can't properly evaluate a classic great wine—say a La Tâche, Cheval Blanc, Darmagi, Schloss Johannisberg, or Caymus of the finest vintage—unless you have tasted lesser wines for context within an hour or two of the great encounter.

The notion of the taste environment directly leads to our routine of rinsing out the mouth with the first sip of the next wine in the lineup before moving on to the second mouthful for analysis. This second intake must be two or three tablespoonfuls in quantity to reach every nook and cranny of the mouth cavity. Then we spit out most of this quantity and proceed to examine the little wine retained in the mouth, even swallowing some if the number of samples does not exceed ten.

For us, **balance and harmony** are not the same. At one point we thought it would stand to reason to differentiate between these two notions, which we had till then used as interchangeable terms.

BALANCE is a trait that cannot be quantified, but is rather a matter of comparing the relative proportion of substances and characteristics that make up the wine. Thus you can use a well-known diagram (Vedel triangle, Max Deglise, etc.) to weigh components responsible for firmness or "masculine" character in a wine (acids, tannins, minerals, etc.) against components with a rounding or "feminizing" effect (alcohol, sugar, glycerin, etc.). Depending on the proportions you find, your wine may be high-acid (or excessively acidic) or heady (alcoholic), or a number of other things.

HARMONY is a word of praise that we believe should be reserved for truly superlative wines. In a harmonious wine, the separately appraised qualities are not even commensurable; they either exist or they don't. Needless to say, balance is a prerequisite for harmony, defined as the concurrence of *all* of the following conditions:

1. No single component of aroma or flavor, no matter how agreeable or delightful, sits on the other notes; all components are present in the same "organoleptic concentration."

2. The taste delivers on the promise held out by the bouquet.

3. None of the accents, be it of fruit or spice, predominates in the total ornamentation.

4. The growing location leaves no trace incompatible with the wine's varietal character.

5. Traits respectively typical of young and old wines are not simultaneously present.

Finally, we make a rigorous distinction between *material* constituents and components making up what we call the aromatics or *ornamentation* of the wine. The former include above all the acids, then tannins, and the sugar-alcohol-glycerin group. The best synopsis of the latter type of components is A.C. Noble's aroma wheel.

WHEN THE HAMMER COMES DOWN

For an auction house to feature decades-old bottles of Tokaji or Villány of unknown record, without a label (or with recent handwriting on the bottle, which amounts to the same thing), with an obviously fresh cork, and without the slightest trace of sediment—this strange custom would be inconceivable in the international wine marketplace. Hungarian auction practices are thus rather peculiar, not least because of a lack of professional auctioneers specializing in wine. More significantly, original authentic bottlings of Tokaj did not surface in domestic auctions until 2000. Unlike these items, the so-called "museum" or "museal" wines—a uniquely Hungarian wine category, itself of mysterious origins—have no documented history. This leaves the ancient device of longhand writing directly on the bottle, or that of an attached certificate, to "vouch" for the age and provenance of the wine.

A rare bottle of an aszú wine – from the ages round 1680-1700

Wine in Entertaining

To have someone as a guest means to assume responsibility for his well-being while he stays with us. (Brillat-Savarin)

One moment of celebrating the new Hungarian Ambassy in Berlin – with 100 years old Tokaji wines (Oct. 2001)

T aking our cue from the motto, we should remember that offering wine to our guests is just as much of a responsibility as entertaining itself. No private concert or literary soirée can be complete without the closing chord of fine dining. It is impossible to overestimate the importance of wine and drinks in general on such occasions. Accompanied by finger food presented on trays, the drink is clearly in the limelight. If the stress is on the food, the drinks will play a supporting role that is nevertheless vital for the success of the entire performance.

Perhaps more than any other nation, Hungarians are expected to entertain with wine. We are somewhat of an exotic spot on the world map—hopefully, less and less so as time goes by—whose wines may reach further than the fame of our scientists, artists, or the magnificent view of the Danube at Budapest. It is important for us to know

how little the world knows about us. Most foreigners will be astonished to learn that Tokaj is not just about sweet wine, indeed that dry wines are made on the banks of the Danube at all.

It will be worth our while to briefly contemplate how wine is offered and consumed in the part of the East that can be regarded as the cradle of wine, geographically as well as historically. Around the Caucasus, the central figure in the playing of host to guests is the *tamada*, a kind of toast-master appointed to deliver reiterated toasts during a protracted meal. It is enlightening to compare this institution to Károly Eötvös's 19th-century account of the people of Gyulakeszi, a small village in the Balaton-felvidék:

"Harboring the culture of the East in his soul, the simple Hungarian villager buttonholes the genteel townsfolk passing by his cellar, and invites them in with peremptory tenderness. He has just one glass but that he rinses well with wine. When he has poured a glassful, to the amazement of his guests he does not hand it over but first delivers a toast which goes something like this: 'I don't know whence my lords might come and whither you might go. But you may not pass before my cellar without coming in. All I wish is that you may walk with fortune and find your loved ones in good health when you return home.' These simple words of welcome are wrought with a peculiar elegance. They are not impertinent or inquisitive, and while certainly keeping a distance, they indicate the host's helpful and munificent disposition. Having said his toast and taken a drink himself first—which is always the host's responsibility—he rinses out the glass before he pours for the guests. He will go on mingling noble gestures with primitive ones, but the essence of the entire ceremony will remain the toast itself."

HOSTING A RECEPTION

For us, the act of offering wine must begin by providing information, a task best entrusted to menu cards. No matter how tasteful, printed brochures should never be placed next to a setting of fine Herend china. Only a listing of the food and wine to be served is acceptable; any sponsors should be relegated to the background. The information provided should be concise, objective, and free from platitude. If entertainers only knew just how many wines across Europe are touted as the "wine of kings and the king of wines," they would surely refrain from using this cliché.

Come time to contemplate the wines themselves, the first thing to determine is the number of guests invited. If it's a reception at the embassy or a garden party with hundreds of people, never think of serving great old vintages, unless you want to be lumped in with the nouveau riche. These wines are heavy, expensive, and rarely conducive to mingling and conversation. The purpose is much better served by one of Hungary's fine white or rosé wines which

can double as thirst quenchers. The entrée demands a good brand of strictly dry sparkling, say Törley, François, or Chateau Vincent. No one these days can afford the humiliation of including a semi-sweet, let alone a doux, in the selection, on the pretext that someone preferring their bubbly less than fully dry might come along. By contrast, the line-up of still white wines we offer on such occasions may contain a semi-sweet bottle, although we welcome the increasing popularity of dry versions of light aromatic wines such a Muskotály or a Tramini. Finally, we generally feature a fruity, not quite full-bodied red, even for receptions hosted in the morning hours. For standing receptions, we post the featured wines on the wall or set up a display table with a brief description, for instance, "Leányka—young, dry and fruity; Chardonnay; dry and mature" etc. The routine outlined above applies to standing receptions with a large number of invitees, where only sandwiches and finger food will be served. This selection of wines—rarely more than five or six—will be generally sufficient even if a lunch buffet of hot food is

provided. We must also mention the importance of having spittoons handy, as well as ample room for setting down glassware. When clean glassware becomes temporarily unavailable—as sooner or later will inevitably occur—it is not sacrilege to pour wine into a used glass, as long as it is not a white poured after a red.

Let us now examine Hungarian customs and the typical wine assortment for buffet receptions and large-scale sit-down dinners. Still staying with the basics, it is always vital to enable guests to find a safe place for their food. A glass clutched alongside of the plate is sure to interfere with the enjoyment of the wine. It is all the nicer to have the room to set down two or three glasses next to the plate. As a matter of course, this is never a problem for a sit-down lunch or dinner. Instead, the question here becomes whether it is acceptable to serve two wines of similar character, say two dry whites, in the same type of glass. Being believers in compromise as is any Central European, we answer the question with a resounding "Yes." This will not apply to strictly coded receptions hosted by the Prime Minister or the President of the Republic, where one should incidentally expect to be served fine food but no gastronomic revelry. The duration of these meals is rather stringently limited by a busy daily schedule, and empty glasses tend to disappear from the table almost as soon as empty plates.

If there are no time constraints, there is nothing to prevent your guests from getting a second helping of a wine already tasted. Nevertheless, it happens but very rarely at receptions hosting more than 30 guests that a waiter asked for a refill will bring a fresh glass. In fact, pouring a young Chardonnay in the same glass in which a Királyleányka has been

Zsolna jugs from the beginning of 20. century

served is nothing to frown at. Depending on the situation, you may settle for a champagne flute, a white wine glass, a red wine glass, and a glass for dessert wine for each place setting, always bearing in mind that a strict "court" etiquette demands a fresh glass for each wine on offer. At this point, opinions vary as to whether it is all right to serve wine in glasses on a tray, or whether pouring it at the table should invariably be preferred. The latter choice certainly has the advantage of offering a more intimate acquaintance with the wine by presenting the bottle rather than simply identifying the wine on the menu card. These issues of ceremony may appear conceited, but they are nothing compared to the difficulty of pleasing *bona fide* teetotal guests. Addressing this question in detail would be clearly out of place here. Suffice it to say that a good point of reference would be the code of etiquette of nations with an avowed reluctance to consume alcohol.

What we call "residential" receptions of up to 24 guests represents a special genre of entertaining from the point of view of wine. While it is conceivable to seat as many as 30-40 people at an embassy or a hotel's banquet room, an ambassador's residence tends to be more suitable for hosting 6-24 guests. The first rule to remember at such an occasion is that you cannot judiciously divide the contents of a regular bottle (0.75 liter bottle) into more than 12 glasses, especially if you watch out for any sediment (which is not a consideration to prevent you from offering the wine in the first place). This means that you will need to be ready to offer a second bottle, without opening it at the table as you would expect in a restaurant. Here, a preliminary tasting will have disqualified any "corked" bottle well in advance. After removing the cork, you decant the big reds, and reinsert the cork loosely in all other bottles. Keep the wines chilled until service as needed; you may display a sample selection on a small table. Such evenings often have the power to conjure the dearest treasures from the cellar or the wine cabinet. In Hungary, there is no accepted rule, tacit or written, for the host or a qualified server to offer a brief appreciation of the wine at hand. The word "appreciation" implies a few sentences about the producer in addition to identifying the grape variety, vintage, and growing location. As these feasts tend to be rather slow-paced, make sure to accommodate requests to retaste the wines.

Of course, formal dining is not a privilege of those who spend their lives in diplomatic circles. Any get-together of business partners, friends, or other cause for celebration may present you with similar tasks, although you can delegate most of them to experienced personnel by choosing a suitable restaurant or a hotel. If you need to host a reception in a foreign country, always use Hungarian wines as the reference when placing the order for a menu. A restaurant caring for its reputation will allow you to supply your own wines for the event, if it does not have the stock to do it for you. This option also becomes important as a tool for demonstrating the greatness of Hungarian wine. When you make your selection, try to provide a fair representation of wine styles and types rather than simply a run-down of grape varieties.

WINE GLASSES

It is imperative to use glasses capable of showing the wine served in them to its best advantage. Stemware from Riedel represents the highest standard, but it is expensive to buy, delicate to handle, and can be problematic to replace. Statistically, a hand-made Riedel glass can be used six to ten times before it will inevitably suffer one type of damage or another. Other excellent brands include Schott Zwiesel and Leonardo. Whichever product you choose, make sure your glasses have plain unadorned surfaces and a longer stem. For sparkling wine, the only proper choice is the champagne flute; reserve the type with the broader bowl for vintage sparkling as intended. Serve light wines in a flared Riesling glass with a 120-160 ml capacity. A bigger white, such as a barrique Chardonnay from Siklós, deserves a

larger goblet (200-250 ml) that is also suitable for red wine. Hungarian rosés and light, young reds demand a glass holding 120-160 ml of wine, while a mature big-scale red from Szekszárd or Villány should be served in a much larger glass (at least 300-350 ml, but 500 ml for preference). Indeed, finer restaurants in Hungary now often make it a point to present such great reds in grand cru stemware. As for sweet Tokaj, a glass holding less than 100 ml is out of the question; one with a capacity of 140-160 ml is just about ideal for the purpose. To sum up, you would be well-advised to have six types of glass on hand, using them as dictated by the assortment of wines on offer. Needless to say, a hedonistic gathering of gourmet friends will defy any rule you may care to obey or invent.

TYPES OF HUNGARIAN WINE TO GO WITH FOOD

Aperitif: Dry, possibly semi-dry sparkling. The exception to the rule is sweet Chateau Vincent, which is of sufficiently high quality to balance the faint residual sugar. Good aperitif wines include light, high-acid whites such as a crisp Királyleányka, Irsai Olivér or Sauvignon Blanc from the Mátraalja or Etyek, or a Budai Zöld or Muskotály from Szeremley in Badacsony. Dry Tokaji Szamorodni is a classic. *Salads* and other sharper-tasting *vegetable* dishes require wines that are not too hard but fairly rich in acidity, much like the aperitif group. More intensely flavored greens and vegetables will often benefit from the company of a firm Sauvignon Blanc of the latest vintage.

Soup, fish, white meats: The members of the aperitif group will be generally up to the task. Warm hors d'oeuvres on the hearty side, such as smoked fish, pâté or terrine, demand a high-alcohol Tokaji Furmint, a Szürkebarát or

Chardonnay matured in small new oak, or a nice dry rosé. Courses prepared with paprika inevitably call for a light, vigorous red along the lines of a Kadarka or Kékfrankos from Szekszárd. In fact, fish dishes with paprika or *lecsó* (pronounced "leh-cho")—a paprika-flavored stew of onions, sweet pepper (capsicum), and tomato, a sort of Hungarian ratatouille—taste best with a light red, as surely as any *pörkölt* (a paprika-based meat stew) or *gulyás* (a soupier consistency version with vegetables). White meats, especially when garnished with fruit, go really well with a semi-dry or semi-sweet fruity white, such as Hárslevelű, Furmint, or Tramini. When flavored more intensely, these meats welcome the company of Tokaji Szamorodni, dry or sweet, provided that the wine is not fortified beyond its naturally modest 11% alcohol.

Red meat and game: A big Cab or a Cabernet-based blend can be very nice, but it won't do the trick unless it is fully mature. If you don't have one ready, you will be better off with a mature classic Kékfrankos or Kadarka from any region of Hungary, or a lighter Bikavér blend from Eger or Szekszárd. If the meat is prepared sweet and spicy, or served with fruit or a fruit-based sauce, make sure that your wine is appropriately rounded with glycerin and alcohol. And one more tip: wine matured in small new oak is a great complement to smoky flavors.

Dessert: Hungary offers a wide array of sweet wines, and not just from Tokaj. The thing to keep in mind here is that the wine of choice must be sweeter than the dessert itself. *Túró*, Hungary's special fresh farmer's cheese, is strongly recommended in any one of its sweeter forms, typically flavored with raisin and lemon peel, to go with a young, 4-5 puttonyos Tokaji Aszú. (More on this in the chapter on Gastronomy.) Finally, duck liver or foie gras with Tokaji Aszú, vibrant or fully mature, is a match made in heaven

that can be the perfect starter or even a viable alternative to dessert. Finish off the meal with a digestive of Cognac or Hungarian marc called *törkölypálinka* to soothe and revitalize the stomach.

WINE AS A GIFT

Never make a gift of a single bottle of wine, unless it is a rarity and the recipient is aware of this fact. Normally, two or three bottles in a neat box is the best bet, particularly when presented along with an accessory, such a book on wine, a corkscrew, or a couple of wine glasses. If you want to treat each one of your guests to a gift, don't hand it over before they are ready to leave. On the other hand, if you want to indulge just one person with a valuable wine, present that special bottle early into the evening or the event, and invariably in public.

TRANSPORT AND STORAGE

Bottles must be kept in a horizontal position for purposes of storage and shipping, particularly for longer distances. Avoid exposure to heat or near-freezing temperatures. The proper cellar or storage temperature has no daily fluctuation, and will not vary by more than 8-9 °C over the entire year.

THE SOMMELIER

At one time, the sommelier to the Hungarian royal court used to be appointed from the ranks of the high aristocracy. Today, it would be nice to have a dedicated sommelier for at least the Parliament, who could supply the ministries and other agencies of the government with advice. At embassies and consulates abroad, a staff member with an advanced knowledge of wine by decent catering industry standards can be of great help in organizing a reception. Finding someone up-to-date in these matters should not be too daunting a challenge.

Wine and Health

Since ancient times, wine has played an important part in the life of man, fulfilling a multitude of roles: the miraculous, in ritual and sacrament, in gastronomy, and as a stimulant.

Noah planted a vineyard as soon as his Ark landed after the Flood (Genesis 7-9), thus conferring upon the grape vine the honor of being the first domesticated plant known to us. Noah also became the first "on the record" to get drunk, in which condition he was found by his sons. Jacob employed wine to deaden Esau's alertness when he coaxed his elder brother to sell his birthright to him (Genesis 27). King Solomon, in his Song of Songs, considers wine as the source of the greatest rapture second only to the kiss of lovers, and few if any latter-day poets have contested this order of priority, whatever the merits of the case. By turning water into wine for the Wedding at Kana, Jesus effectively laid the grounds for the mythic and sacral veneration of wine.

WINE AS MEDICINE: OLD BELIEFS

THE "MAGYAR CURE"

Hungary has a singular bond with wine. As the Magyar tribes arrived and settled down in the Carpathian Basin from the 8th to the 10th centuries A.D., they brought with them viticultural know-how and an advanced ethos of wine. The very ancient Hungarian word for wine, *bor*, is actually of Old Turkic derivation and originally meant a color between gray and white.

Of course, the conquering Magyars did not need to start from scratch in their new homeland. They found the remnants of a sophisticated culture of wine that the Roman colonists

223

had left behind in Pannonia, as they called the region west of the Danube. In a world of "international wines," Hungary hangs on to a colorful diversity of unique indigenous grapes and distinctive wine types that have engendered a lore of special curative powers through the ages. While studying this deep tradition, it is often quite difficult to decide whether a specific vinous therapy is really based on folk medicine or emerged as a "popularization" of indications by qualified physicians. The two types of observation, the pragmatic and the scientific, inevitably overlapped since wine until the 19th century was widely used as a medium to carry water-insoluble vegetal and herbal substances, in the form of infusion or extract. The poet József Gvadányi (1725-1801) has the following account related by the popular protagonist of his epic poem, the *Notary of Peleske*:

> The doctor ordered pills from Spain,
> But none allayed my pangs of pain.
> The Magyar cure was more benign:
> I soon got well on fine old wine.

Let us then see a few gems of this Magyar medicine, region by region.

MÓR

The sweet strong wines of Mór were expressly recommended for women in childbirth, presumably as a sedative and anesthetic. The authors of medical books in the 18th and 19th centuries claimed that an intake of wine actually eased the process of delivery itself. In the first university textbook of biology in the Hungarian language, published in 1794, Sámuel Rácz suggests that midwives on call should make a flask of warm wine part of their standard equipment. By the 19th century, this practice was not only banned, but the harmful effects of alcohol formed part of the curriculum of midwife training. Nevertheless, popular belief in the beneficial influence of wine consumed during childbirth remained entrenched for a long time.

EGER

In 1757, Simon Schultz, a Prussian physician, recommended red wine from Eger as the best treatment for gastric disorders, due to its ability to *strengthen and warm the stomach, assuage pain, and gradually restore intestinal functions to normal.* In hindsight, it makes sense that the high tannin content of dense red wines can play a role in treating enteritis.

Interestingly, Egri Bikavér would be specifically indicated against lethargy, depression, and anxiety, as a substance supposed to stimulate motivation. This observation may have some connection with the origin of the name of this famous blend. In 1552, the Ottoman forces held Eger under siege for what seemed interminable weeks, but they failed to prevail over the handful of heroic knights who defended the fortified castle against a whole army. During the protracted blockade, István Dobó, the commander, opened the vaulted cellars and ordered the women to start bringing wine to the soldiers fighting on the castle walls. The wine dyed the men's moustaches, beards and breastplates red. Disheartened by rumors that the fierce Hungarians were invincibly strong because they were drinking bull's blood, the Ottoman troops eventually gave up the siege.

TOKAJ

As recently as a couple of decades ago, Tokaji wine was featured among official "red book" prescriptions as a tonic for patients recovering from long illness. In a work on his native Zemplén County, the historian Antal Szirmay (1741-1812) writes that Tokaji cures a four-day fever, relieves headache, *"can raise a man with one foot in the grave,"* and is *"quite beneficial for procreation, particularly when taken before bedtime."* This latter comment obviously refers to the alleged aphrodisiac properties of Tokaji. Imre Thököly, the 17th-century Prince of Transylvania, is reputed to have used the famous sweet wine to cure his recurrent fevers, as did Frederic the Great, King of Prussia, who called Tokaji in a letter *"un baume pour la santé,"* a balm for health. Pope Pius I, on the advice of his doctors, drank Tokaji regularly to bolster his immune system, and George V of England also availed himself of the noble drink to hasten his recovery after a serious operation.

The unique qualities of Tokaji even fired the imagination of Paracelsus, who made a trip to Tokaj to discover and verify the actual concentration of gold that the wine was reputed to contain. Paracelsus proposed that, *"if the vegetative realm can have its king, then this wine deserves that title twofold."* The belief that not only Tokaji Aszú but the earth from Mount Tokaj were possessed of special healing powers endured for centuries after him.

VÁC

In 1735, the red wine of Vác became the subject of a medical dissertation on account of its renown as a solvent of kidney stones. although only one case was cited. The case was related to the author by a parson given to bringing his own red from Vác when invited for dinner, allegedly because his renal pains recurred every time he drank any other wine.

SZEKSZÁRD

Although growers in Eger continue to dispute Szekszárd's precedence, it is a fact of history that it was in Szekszárd that a full-bodied blended red wine first became known as *Bikavér* or "bull's blood"—so named, some say, after the Bika vineyard first mentioned in a royal charter from 1061. Franz Liszt, the world-renowned composer, was an ardent fan of Szekszárd wine, praising it for its power to stimulate the intellect and the creative imagination. He was so enthusiastic about the wine that he introduced it to Pope Pius IX, who came to regard it as "a last resort in keeping up my health and good spirits."

BADACSONY

Badacsonyi Kéknyelű and Szürkebarát have attained quite a following due to their high ratio of alcohol and glycerin, which at one time made them sought-after for treating circulation disorders.

SOMLÓ

The wine of Somló had achieved world fame, before Tokaji did, for its alleged power to promote longevity. Typically aged for a few years, an older vintage Somlói can func-

tion as natural therapy by facilitating digestion and stimulating the appetite, while it is harmonious enough not to irritate the mucous membrane of the stomach. Old pharmacopoeias often quote popular sayings on the healing prowess of Somlói: *Vinum Somlaianum Omni Tempore Sanum* ("Somlói wine is medicine any time"); *Vinum Somlaianum lac senum, pueris venum* ("Somlói wine is milk for the aged, but poison for children").

The medical historian József Antall, a Somló native better known as the first prime minister of Hungary after the democratic rebirth, offers the following account of the wine's traditionally held benefits:

1. Consume Somlói in small but regular doses to maintain sound appetite, an even nervous condition, and proper intestinal functions.
2. Effective for hemorrhoids and constipation.
3. Indicated for shivers and cold, as is or boiled as mulled wine.
4. Good tonic and hematogenic for the old, but equally restorative of anyone weakened by long illness.
5. Fresh Somlói is recommended for those suffering from hypoacidity and stomach disorders, while hyperacidity is often treated with old matured and/or sweet botrytis Somlói.
6. As an aphrodisiac, and to aid in the conception of a male offspring.
7. Often given to children during meals as a digestive, and generally to anyone not feeling well.
8. Was even used on the hill to rinse out wounds.

For centuries, the Habsburgs enforced a tradition that required kings and princes to drink a glass of Somlói before their wedding night to help ensure a male heir. The long endurance of the Habsburg dynasty may or may not have had something to do with this reputed effect of Somlói wine, but it is a fact—and one that few accounts of Hungarian wine fail to mention—that male births in the Somló area continue to exceed the national average.

THE PHYSIOLOGICAL AND PATHOLOGICAL EFFECTS OF ALCOHOL

In the countries of the European Union, 85% of the population (and 90% of men) over 15 years of age consume alcohol on a regular basis. In Hungary in the 1980's, annual per capita consumption converted to pure alcohol exceeded 11 liters, compared to 4.9 liters in 1950, catapulting the country to sixth place among the top alcohol consuming nations of the world. Whereas in France, Spain, and Italy wine accounts for 70-80% of the total alcohol consumption and liquor only for 10-20%, in Hungary spirits represent 42% of in the total. Based on the number of deaths resulting from cirrhosis of the liver in 1998, the number of alcoholics in Hungary was estimated at over 800,000. The life expectancy of alcoholics is 8-12 years shorter than the average. The following is a list of the typical conditions leading to alcohol-related fatalities, in the order of frequency:

a) cardio-vascular disease 30-50%
b) accident, suicide, violence 20%
c) other acute disease (pancreatitis) and tumors 15-25%
d) cirrhosis of the liver 5-15%

fig. I

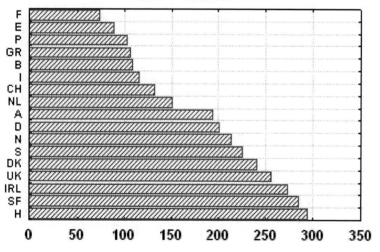

Mortality (standardized for European population) (/100 000/year)

NEW HYPOTHESES: MODERATE CONSUMPTION AND CARDIO-VASCULAR DISEASE

It would be a serious mistake to suggest that the old beliefs we listed, without any pretense to completeness, have no place in modern, scientific medicine. Over the past two decades, researchers have amassed a wealth of evidence to support the claim that a moderate intake of alcohol reduces the risk of death from ischemia, the momentary suspension of blood supply to the heart. This conclusion is based on dozens of independent research projects, including statistical comparisons between geographical and ethnic groups, case control studies, and follow-up analyses, using data from a total of 600,000 people over the course of 30 years. Adding up to over five million "man-years," this body of evidence for the prophylactic effects of alcohol seems very convincing indeed. Cumulatively, the studies have found that the risk factor of death from cardio-vascular disease is 20-80% (50% on average) lower in people who consume moderate quantities of alcohol than in the completely abstinent population. When plotted as a graph, the relation between alcohol consumption and total mortality shows a U or J shape, demonstrating that the teetotallers and the heavy drinkers are both exposed to a higher risk than those using alcohol in moderation. In contrast, the correlation between alcohol and some other diseases is positive and linear. For instance, the risk of liver disease and malignant tumors is directly proportional to alcohol consumption.

According to a comprehensive study conducted on a large population between 1978 and 2003, the intake of one to four "units" of alcohol reduces mortality to a small degree, while an intake of five units or more clearly increases the risk. Studies of the meta-analytic type have sought to discover any differences between the respective effects of beer, wine, and spirits. Some authors do not find any correlation between the type of the alcoholic drink and the preventive effect, while others attribute such beneficial influence mainly to wine, and to red wine in particular.

In summary, two things seem certain:
— In case of moderate consumption, the ben-

efits of alcohol outweigh its ever present downsides, but larger doses will demonstrate its harmful effect on practically any organ.

– The small extra advantage that wine has over other forms of alcohol has a twofold explanation. Firstly, wine drinkers consume less beer and liquor. Secondly, the flavonoids present in wine may make a beneficial contribution as anti-oxidants, and we cannot rule out dietary and psychological influences.

Indeed, it may well be the case that being a "wine drinker" weighs more in the equation than wine itself. Wine drinkers are a more auspicious type in that they generally have a better socio-economic position and tend to be more health-conscious. In this way, wine may play an important role less as a primary agent than simply as an adjunct or indicator of a healthier lifestyle. The debate is still wide open, of course.

WHAT DOES MODERATION MEAN?

Most of the authors examined intakes of one to five "units" of alcohol a day. In U.S. studies, one unit corresponds to about 12 grams of alcohol, which is comparable to 300 ml of beer, 120 ml of wine, or 40 ml of liquor of average alcohol content. Disturbingly, American and European units do not completely overlap. Instead of the 12-g American measure, an eight-gram unit of reference is recommended by the World Health Organization as well as by the British Medical Associations. This corresponds to 200 ml of beer, 80 ml of wine, or 25 ml of liquor. Basically, three European units equal two American ones; with four European units a day one stays within the limits of moderation. It is vital to keep these differences in mind when considering the various study results.

THE FRENCH PARADOX

The essence of what has come to be known as the "French paradox" is that the rate of mortality due to heart disease is much lower in France than in similarly developed European countries (fig. 1), even though the French are exposed to the same or even greater risk factors than the other European nationalities. Interestingly, the phenomenon holds strong in France despite a large intake

of saturated fats, prevalent smoking, and a generally lower level of enthusiasm for globally "trendy" exercise and active-lifestyle habits. According to French commentators, the only significant and measurable difference lies in the greater alcohol and particularly wine consumption of the French. This tendency is shown in fig. 2, as is the general advantage of Mediterranean countries.

fig. 2

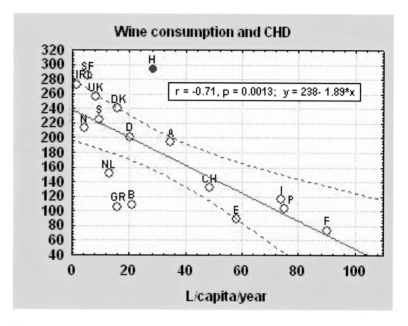

RISK FACTORS

What exactly causes ischemic heart disease remains unknown, although there are proven risk factors, particularly the high concentration of saturated fat in the blood, high blood pressure, and smoking. Each of these factors increases the risk of disease by a great margin on its own, but when they work in unison, the harmful effect is exponential.

The inverse relation between the consumption of alcohol (particularly red wine) and the occurrence of coronary heart disease was first verified in certain European countries in 1979. The term "French paradox" surfaced in 1987 in a French article that received but limited publicity, and it did not attain global currency until 1991, when *60 minutes*, the prime-time American television program, dedicated a feature to the link between red wine and a low rate of heart disease in France, despite the country's fat-rich diet. This was followed by a 1992 publication in *The Lancet*, the authoritative British medical weekly, where the theory gained support in a well-delineated scientific argument. The decade since then has seen the issue become the target of heated debate, a few elements of which we are going to discuss here.

The discovery soon made the headlines everywhere in the sensationalist media, and the wine lobby was naturally quick to respond. In 1993, Gallo of California came out with a generic red dubbed Hearty Burgundy (which had precious little in common with genuine Bourgogne). By the mid-1990's, many wineries in Napa provided a handout to go with the wine purchase that contained an article on the benefits of red wine published by one cardiologist or another in a recognized professional journal. As a matter of course, critical voices were already making themselves heard in the early days. But before looking at the detractors, let us see how the pro-wine camp attempted to explain the beneficial effect of red wine. Their main arguments concentrated partly on alcohol and partly on polyphenol-type antioxidants—flavonoids and resveratrol—naturally present in red wine.

THE ASSUMED MECHANISM OF ALCOHOL AND POLYPHENOLS

THE ALCOHOL HYPOTHESIS

Coronary heart disease typically stems from the atherosclerotic plaque that develops over decades at various points of the vascular system, hindering the free flow of blood by narrowing the cross-section of the veins. Plaque buildup has a lot to do with cholesterol, an organic steroid that circulates in human blood bound to proteins. Cholesterol-protein complexes are known as lipoproteins, and are divided into two major groups. LDL or low density lipoprotein transports the "bad" cholesterol to the cells on the periphery, while HDL or high density lipoprotein is responsible for carrying the "good" cholesterol from the periphery to the liver. In moderate doses as defined above, alcohol boosts the concentration of HDL, which is considered to be its major benefit.

Arteriosclerosis does not normally produce clinical symptoms until the plaque clogs 75% of the artery's available cross section, multiplying the chances for thrombus to develop

BENEFITS OF ALCOHOL

Boosts the level of protective HDL cholesterol (40-65% of the benefit)
Anti-coagulant: decreases fibrinogen level (20-30%)
Improves insulin sensitivity (5-10%)
Reduces stress-induced hormone reaction (0-5%)
Other anti-coagulant mechanisms (0-5%)

on the plaque surface. Full blockage results in a catastrophic impairment of the blood supply beyond the critical point, often causing death to the heart muscle (cardiac arrest) or the brain. A great many studies claim that the anti-coagulant properties of alcohol make a huge contribution to its preventive effect. Then again, the inhibited coagulatory system redoubles its function as soon as the blood alcohol level starts dropping, in what is known as the rebound effect.

FLAVONOIDS

Flavonoids are polyphenol derivatives. Although flavonoid-type antioxidants are available from a number of natural sources, including tea, garlic, onion, and apple, it is believed that flavonoids taken in the form of wine are digested and absorbed with an efficiency that is several orders of magnitude greater than with other natural vehicles. Polyphenol flavonoids taken with raw foods usually enter the digestive tract as sugar-containing glycosides, in which form their absorption and metabolism are rather limited. In fermenting red wine, these substances assume a monomeric form, and develop much better absorption and metabolic characteristics as the 10% alcoholic solution stabilizes the free cyclic compounds. Red wine has a flavonoid concentration 20 times greater than white wine, because most of these compounds are derived, through the process of maceration, from the skin and seeds of the grapes. As early as 1937, Rusznyák and Szentgyörgyi described the beneficial impact of flavonoids on vessel walls. These days, studies published everywhere elaborate on the antioxidant mechanism of flavonoids, now verified both *in vitro* and *in vivo*.

228

Researchers attribute a key role in the pathology of arteriosclerosis to atherogenic or "mutant" lipoproteins. A typical group of these mutants consists of oxidatively modified lipoproteins which, when generated continuously and in large quantities, will be absorbed by phagocytes. Once this happens, the human organism will be unable to metabolize the cholesterol ring. The cells will continue to accumulate cholesterol, eventually forming on the artery walls the deposit known as the atherosclerotic plaque. A mass of data now suggests that antioxidants are capable of blocking the mutation of lipoproteins, thereby delaying plaque formation and vessel lumen constriction of a magnitude that could cause clinical symptoms.

FLAVONOID FEATURES AND PROVEN BENEFITS

— *20 times the concentration in red wine (0.5–30g/l) than in white*
— *Group members: quercetin, catechin, epicatechin, rutin, etc.*
— *Wine-derived flavonoids have superb absorption and metabolic characteristics*
— *Effective in blocking lipoprotein oxidation, lipid synthesis in the liver, and coagulation*
— *Reduces the synthesis of atherogenic substances*
— *Enhances the secretion of vasoactive substances from the endothelium*

RESVERATROL

In addition to flavonoids, the benefit of moderate consumption owes a great deal to resveratrol, a trihydroxystilbene derivative practically unique to red wine. Discovered in 1976, resveratrol is a phytoalexin that enhances the resistance of the grape vine to gray rot. To Japanese folk medicine it has been known in the form of *kojo-kon* (Japanese knotweed, *Polygonum cuspidatum*) and used for hundreds of years in treating metabolic disorders, inflammations, and heart disease. In purified or synthetic forms, resveratrol does inhibit lipid synthesis, coagulation and allergic reactions, and it is certainly an effective antioxidant (although less capable than flavonoids). More recently, resveratrol has been shown to exhibit cancer chemopreventive activity as well.

THE RISE AND FALL OF THE RED WINE MYTH?

One camp of the medical profession insists that there is now sufficient and conclusive evidence to show that the benefits of red wine outstrip its undesirable consequences, provided that its consumption remains moderate (up to three units a day for men and two for women, preferably accompanying meals).

Others marshal counter-arguments to support their claim that we do not yet have sufficient data available to draw final conclusions, and suggest that the paradox discovered in France and other Mediterranean countries may well have more to do with lifestyle differences than with higher wine consumption. Indeed, several critics of the French paradox seek to undermine the very foundations of the doctrine. In 1993, a study of a 40-country sample found that the preventive activity of wine could only be conclusively shown in areas characterized by a typically high intake of saturated fats. There is also something to be said for the objection that official diagnostic routine in France is based on different principles, easily leading to an underestimation of the occurrence of cardio-vascular disease. Some analysts point to the real-world nonsense (as opposed to the statistical sense) of "mean" per capita consumption, demonstrating completely different graphs if abstention and heavy drinking are plotted separately. Some emphasize a perceived inverse link between cardio-vascular mortality and the share of fruits and vegetables in the diet. Advocates of the "European paradox" propose that the increased intake of vitamin E is just as good an explanation as red wine for the same set of statistical data. Others still have advanced the hypothesis that, while the link between saturated fats/cholesterol and cardio-vascular disease is a very real one, the connection between red wine consumption and lower mortality from such causes is apparent and true statistically only, without any relationship of cause and effect obtaining between the two variables.

FOR

The data available are sufficient to indicate a change of lifestyle.
Moderate consumption of red wine (with meals) is to be promoted.
People who have done so should be encouraged to continue.
Damage from excessive drinking to be emphasized.
"Civilized" drinking does not "replace" avoidance of other risks.

AGAINST

The available data is insufficient to prove beneficial effect.
The French paradox can have other explanations (of diet, lifestyle, heredity).
The benefit for cardio-vascular disease is prejudiced by the inverse influence on mortality from other causes.
Express recommendation is harmful due to the risk of contributing to alcoholism.

THE HUNGARIAN PARADOX

As we have seen, there are highly significant geographical variations in heart disease mortality; we also know that Hungary claims the leadership in that department. Of course, these variations may have a lot to do with differences of diet and nutrition. For this reason, in a study of 17 countries (Belgium, Portugal, Spain, Ireland, Greece, France, Holland, Switzerland, Italy, Austria, Germany, Sweden, Norway, Denmark, the United Kingdom, Finland, and Hungary) we compared cardio-vascular mortality data standardized for the European population as a dependent variable,

fig. 3

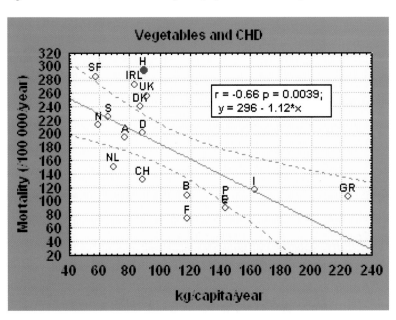

with the intake data, as the independent variable, of 13 major alimentary substances, including total fat, saturated, monounsaturated and polyunsaturated fatty acids, animal fat, cholesterol, fruits, vegetables, vitamin E, and alcoholic beverages. While there is indeed an evident negative correlation between coronary heart disease (CHD) mortality and the consumption of vegetables, Hungary is in a much more alarming predicament than it would seem from its geographical position; the Mediterranean has a significant advantage (fig. 3). Ironically, fruit consumption figures in Hungary are much lower than one would expect given the country's agricultural traditions, culture and potential. Even the Finns eat more fruit than Hungarians (fig. 4).

We have already mentioned the "European paradox," which suggests that the lower the vitamin E intake, the higher the rate of CHD mortality. The correlation certainly exists. Fig. 5 shows the gain of Mediterranean countries and the surprisingly low intake in Hungary. It remains unclear whether this low intake can be blamed exclusively on the unhealthy ratio of animal and vegetable fats in the diet, or whether traditional Hungarian cooking techniques (high heat, deep frying) also play a part by reducing the available vitamin E content of many foods (compared to the Mediterranean preference for raw vegetables and salad-oils). It is instructive to look at the representation of various food groups in the national diet compared to the average of the countries in the sample. Strikingly, the Hungarian intake of fats exceeds that average by 33%, that of saturated fats by 60%, and the consumption of spirits by nearly 80%. In contrast, the Hungarian intake of polyunsaturated fats is only 40%, vegetable consumption 60%, and vitamin E intake is barely half of the average. These dietary statistics are far from being positive, but they do not begin to explain the exceedingly high rate of CHD mortality in Hungary. This is what we may call the Hungarian paradox, a sort of negative analogy to the French phenomenon. We do not have the space in this study to even guess at the reasons behind it.

THE WINE DRINKER AS PERSONALITY

An increasingly influential argument holds that the health benefit of wine has less to do with the substance itself than with the character, disposition, and personality of the people who drink it. Already in 1819, Samuel Black, an Irish physician, observed that chest pain (angina pectoris) due to coronary sclerosis was a much rarer occurrence in France than in Ireland. He attributed the difference to climatic factors, lifestyle, national character, emotive disposition, and, above all, to the famous *savoir vivre*, the "know-how of living," of the French. As the first known iteration of the doctrine later dubbed the French paradox, Black's observation is also indirectly useful in illustrating the ways in which the Mediterranean life departs from the continental model. The authors of Californian and Danish studies (relying on samples of 10000 and almost 50000 individuals) assert that the choice of drink in itself is indicative of the individual's attitudes to life: Wine drinkers tend to be more highly qualified, smoke less, and have much more moderate drinking habits that those who prefer beer or liquor. Even in Denmark, wine drinkers follow a rather Mediterranean-type diet by consuming more vegetables, fruits, meat, greens, and olive oil. On this count, the studies make no distinction between red wine and white, adding to the question marks about the exclusive role of flavonoid activity.

Many outstanding national health professionals remain skeptical about the red wine benefit hype, for two reasons. First, they do not perceive enough evidence to justify the encouragement of alcohol consumption as a precautionary measure, especially since the certain harmful effects of alcohol outweigh its unverified preventive properties in any dosage. Second, they do not see any guarantee for avoiding excessive drinking, and they simply want to protect humanity from the ruinous consequences of alcoholism. In 1994, the World Health Organization published a press release waging war against false interpretations of red wine benefits. Some American researchers have suggested that there would be nothing wrong with recommending wine to populations where everyone could drink alcohol in moderation. Unfortunately, no such population exists.

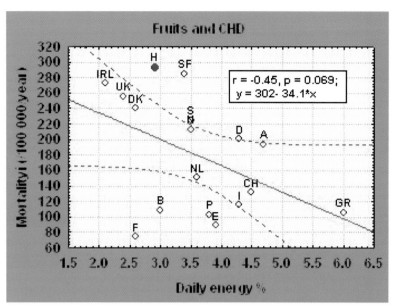

fig. 4

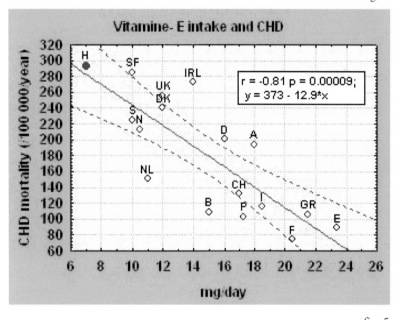

fig. 5

WINE AND LIFESTYLE

CIVILIZED DRINKING

The adjective "civilized" in this context can mean a number of things, not least moderation. There is a consensus among cultural anthropologists that in the past the consumption of alcohol—beer, wine, or spirits, depending on the region and historic period—probably reached exorbitant quantities. While it is obviously impossible to come up with a universal average figure, some calculations suggest that the daily consumption of beer or wine per capita was as high as one to three liters from the 13th through the 17th centuries. Without a doubt, this was due to a combination of factors, including the scarcity of good drinking water, the thirst-inducing properties of meats smoked or cured in salt, as well as the high energy content of alcoholic beverages.

This was also the case in Hungary, where great quantities of grapes and wine were produced from the 12th century onward—more than in any other country in Europe. Since medieval times, wine was an essential occupation and export commodity for all ranks of Hungarian society. Of course, most of the vast quantity consumed in Hungary consisted of the "light," third-rate wines that formed a daily staple of the peasantry. At least these were made from grapes one way or another, unlike some of the jug "wines" encountered today at the lower end of the market.

A statistical survey overseen by Károly Keleti between 1881 and 1883 identified a national average consumption of around 27 liters of wine and 23 liters of 35° (70-proof) *pálinka* (fruit brandy or marc) per capita. In those days, beer was practically unheard of in rural areas; urban statistics recorded an annual per capita beer consumption of 23 liters. The area distribution also offered interesting lessons, with most of the parts annexed from Hungary by the Trianon Peace Treaty in the aftermath of World War I falling into the *pálinka* zone, and much of Hungary's present-day territory being a wine belt. This distribution may go a long way to explaining the results of a 1997 survey looking at the symbols of Hungarian national identity. 74% of the people asked regarded wine as the Hungarian drink *par excellence*, whereas *pálinka* and beer accounted for 15% and 8%, respectively. Answers to further questions illustrated consumption habits tallying with sales statistics: 21% of the subjects preferred wine, 16% beer, and 13% various soda-type soft drinks. Interestingly, water and fruit juice both weighed in at 9% each, while pálinka received a mere 1.5% of the vote. All in all, alcohol-free beverages edged out alcohol by 51 to 49. The survey also revealed Transdanubia to be a more homogeneous wine area, while the people of the Great Plain and northern Hungary gave preferential treatment to beer (as if to echo the philosopher Béla Hamvas's

* Translation by Benjamin Jowett (1871).

playful train of thought about the five *genera loci* that make up the Hungarian character).

Another important aspect of moderation is mixing wine with water. The ancient Greek institution of the *symposion* (literally "drinking together") evolved around drinking wine as a major social event, typically reserved for men after dinner to discuss the affairs of the world (women were only allowed to attend as servants). The men drank the first cup neat, in praise of the Good Demon and the might of God. In the next step, overseen by the *symposiarch*, they prepared a solution in a 14-liter mixing vessel called the *crater*, in the most luxurious households chilled with snow. The mixing ratio of between one and two parts of wine to three parts of water (sometimes sea water) resulted in a drink with an alcohol content of three to eight percent. At a typical symposion, 15-20 guests consumed three craterfuls of diluted wine. The *symposiarch* remained in charge throughout the evening, ordering the procedure of various toasts, singing, and games. The ancient Romans considered undiluted wine a barbarity.

Admonitions against intemperance and diatribes depicting the punishments for excess abound throughout Hungarian history and literature. In a sermon, Péter Pázmány submitted to the audience that *"if all the wine Hungarians have drunk over their vicissitudes and plight under Ottoman rule were filled in a deep valley, and the camp of the Ottoman Emperor were driven into that valley, not one soul would come out alive but all would surely drown in that sea of wine."* Mihály Csere maintained that the intemperance of our forebears led to Hungary's fall to Ottoman servitude. *"The poor Magyar kept drinking away until the sober Ottomans overwhelmed this poor country making us drink our own blood; and yet we are slow to learn, still trying to prevail over the Emperor's troops by toasts with a raised wine cup."*

Presumably spurred on by personal experience, Plato offered these words of caution against inebriation in his famous dialogue *The Symposium: "Well, as none of the company seem disposed to drink much, I may be forgiven for saying, as a physician, that drinking deep is a bad practice, which I never follow, if I can help, and certainly do not recommend to another, least of all to any one who still feels the effects of yesterday's carouse"* (176c).*

In 1600, Moritz, the Landgrave of Hessen, founded the Order of Temperance prohibiting members to drink more than seven chalices of alcoholic beverage at one sitting. The two permitted sittings a day meant 14 chalices of drink. Multiply that by 350 ml, the capacity of a dedicated chalice from the German town of Trier, and you get a very generous tolerance limit for "temperance" in those days, although one that was very strictly enforced: transgressors had to part with their horse (their most cherished asset) or pay a fine of 300 thalers. Interestingly, the American Temperance Society, founded in Boston in 1826, banned distilled spirits but not fermented alcoholic beverages.

Impassioned denunciations of endemic drinking in Ireland used to be just as common as in Hungary. Here is a witty example from the turn of the 19th and 20th centuries, which points far beyond the issue of immoderation: *"Drink is the curse of the land,"* said the unknown Irish preacher. *"It makes you fight with your neighbour. It makes you shoot at your landlord—and it makes you miss him."*

Alcoholism as a mass infliction did not raise its head until the mid-19th century—probably simply because the average life expectancy until then had been so low that heavy drinkers died before they could develop the chronic alcoholic syndrome. In Hungary, two pre-eminent Reform Era thinkers and politicians, Ferenc Kölcsey and Lajos Kossuth, believed that consumption habits and the sanctions of excess went out of control with the abolition of most aristocratic privileges, which forced landowners to "rent out" any bar and tavern keeping rights they were allowed to keep. Ease of access, drinking on credit, and the greed of the government's revenue departments all contributed to undermining traditional rites of drinking, and thus ultimately led to extreme countermeasures such as the Prohibition in the U.S. or the stringent trade monopoly on alcohol in Finland today. It is for good reason that some experts invited to the World Health Organization conference devoted to the subject raised the issue of tightening trade regulations on alcoholic beverages in certain countries.

THE URGE TO DRINK

Traditional ways of life hardly had any occasion or event that was not linked to the consumption of wine or other forms of alcohol. At war or in peace time, before or after battle, to celebrate victory or to forget defeat, at a wedding or a funeral wake, during religious or lay holidays, at the start and at the end of work in the field or the vineyard, not to mention shopping, the signing of contracts, inauguration ceremonies and name days—drinking was an inevitable part of everyday life. Even today, the first question most of us ask of our guests is "What can I get you to drink?"

There is no denying the **social role** of alcohol in binding communities of people. For instance, co-workers spending an hour or two at their favorite place after work often drink in moderation, and in fact tend to eject the rowdy from their ranks. Such a club-like gathering is more than just a pack of men assembling at a watering hole: it is a self-reliant community of people dedicated to the ideal of solidarity, participating in a rite not altogether unlike the symposia of Antiquity.

Of course, alcohol as an anti-depressant and an **escape from reality** weighs heavily in the balance. Classic pharmacology recognizes it as a highly potent anxiolytic (anxiety-relieving agent) known for its initially euphoric power to dispel worries and relax inhibition. As a narcotic, however, alcohol is highly addictive. As habitual users need ever larger doses to feel comfortable, they will expend increasing amounts of time and energy on the daily procurement and consumption of alcohol, ultimately sustaining severe somatic and psychological damage collectively known as the alcohol syndrome.

Nowadays, some researchers are zooming in on the potential psychosocial mechanisms triggering heart disease. Using the tools of meta-analysis and evidence-based exact science, they have processed almost the entire available corpus of relevant literature, and have found that the risk of heart disease is intimately correlated with

– anxiety and depression;

– paranoid personality;

– fear of losing one's job;

233

– the experience of lacking social support.

Whether the positive effects of alcohol can be helpful in dealing with these conditions is more than open to discussion. Experience has shown that those under such psychosocial pressure rarely settle for moderate doses, and therefore have to face additional intellectual and psychological damage caused by the alcohol itself.

We cannot afford here to pursue the far-reaching implications of the fact that, in the first half of the 1990's, both total and cardio-vascular mortality rates were by far greater throughout the former Eastern Block than the European average. Total male mortality rates have been the worst in the Ukraine, followed (in descending order) by Russia, Hungary, Latvia, Estonia, Poland, Lithuania, the former Czechoslovakia, Romania, Bulgaria, Slovenia. Cardio-vascular male mortalities show a slightly different picture with again the Ukraine in the lead, followed by Latvia, Estonia, Russia, Hungary, Poland, the former Czechoslovakia, Bulgaria, Lithuania, and Romania. No exact explanation of these alarming statistics has yet been attempted. Experts tend to confine themselves to listing the usual suspects, including diet and nutrition, smoking, possible hereditary traits, obesity and lack of exercise, environmental pollution, stress, the psychosocial factors dis-

cussed above, poverty, and the yawning gap between the wealthy and the destitute in East European societies. We direct those with a deeper interest in the Hungarian psyche to recent studies that have attempted to verify a connection between the long-established "winter of our discontent" and destructive pathological addictions such as alcoholism.

MODERN RECOMMENDATIONS OF REASONABLE CONSUMPTION

As we have seen, the staunch advocate of total abstinence and the pro-health wine supporters both do their best to prove the other camp wrong. An interesting shift can be noticed in the approach taken by the official Dietary Guidelines, issued by the U.S. Department of Agriculture and the U.S. Department of Health and Human Services every five years. The 1990 edition cautiously states that *"Drinking [alcoholic beverages] has no net health benefit, is linked with many health problems [...] Their consumption is not recommended."* By 1995, the same publication points out that *"Alcoholic beverages have been used to enhance the enjoyment of meals by many societies throughout human history,"* later adding that *"Current evidence suggests that moderate drinking is associated with a lower risk for coronary heart disease in some individuals."*

The *2000 Guidelines* emphasizes that *"Drinking in moderation may lower risk for coronary heart disease, mainly among men over age 45 and women over age 55. However, there are other factors that reduce the risk of heart disease, including a healthy diet, physical activity, avoidance of smoking, and maintenance of a healthy weight.*
Moderate consumption provides little, if any, health benefit for younger people. Risk of alcohol abuse increases when drinking starts at an early age. Some studies suggest that older people may become more sensitive to the effects of alcohol as they age.

ADVICE FOR TODAY

Part of the difficulty of providing advice or opinion is that the harmful effects of alcohol are conclusively proven, while its beneficial effects are often based on conjectures, assumptions, as well as studies and experiments without sufficient breadth and depth. Today, in the age of evidence-based medicine, the

---

ACCORDING TO THE U.S. DIETARY GUIDELINES:

The beneficial effect of alcohol consumption on cardio-vascular disease may exceed the risk of damage caused by potential complications in certain population groups, including, high-risk groups; men over 40 and women over 50; people with a lower risk of alcohol syndrome.
However, no recommendation can be given for the entire population, because: consumption in moderation cannot be guaranteed on the national level; of the lack of a conclusive, prospective clinical study (whose results would be doubtful anyway due to the certainty of side effects); it is unhealthy to drink with the aim of protecting health; but "If adults choose to drink alcoholic beverages, they should consume them only in moderation."
"Some people should not drink alcoholic beverages at all. These include: Children and adolescents. Individuals of any age [...] whose family members have alcohol problems. Women who are trying to conceive or who are pregnant. [...]
Individuals who plan to drive or take part in activities that require attention or skill. [...] Individuals using prescription and over-the-counter medications."

verification and licensing of a therapy or medicine takes long runs of well-organized and monitored studies substantiated by clinical experiments, particularly if the substance is associated with serious or even just potential side effects. This is especially true for alcohol, in so far as we choose to regard it as a therapeutic agent.

In the absence of such well-corroborated test results, it remains doubtful whether a physician could rightfully encourage consumption, no matter how small. There are obvious benefits to the mutual weighing of pros and cons between the physician and the patient, and to designing advice with the specific patient in mind. However, it is much more important, and much less vague, to recommend cutting back every time the patient admits to a nebulous "moderate" use of alcohol (voluntary admissions are always misleading), not to mention higher doses.

Clearly, it would be a mistake to recommend consumption as a dubious preventive measure to an essentially abstinent person, also for the nonsense of increasing the chances of a new disease in the effort to combat an old one. This is particularly the case if the patient has plenty of room to improve on the other preventive fronts (exercise, quitting smoking, reducing cholesterol level, stabilizing blood pressure, etc.). Placing undue stress on alcohol as an effective prevention can be dangerous precisely because it can generate the illusion that this "pleasurable" defense releases the obligation of the often "unpleasant" fight with other weapons. Obviously, quitting smoking or treating hypertension has far fewer bad side effects than alcohol consumption does. If alcohol were a new medicine on the threshold of introduction, the big pharmaceutical companies would hardly go out of their way to fight for its licensing.

The ethics of the medical profession itself, the allegiance to the Hyppocratic oath, would forbid the 20-25% reduction of the chance for a disease to occur, at the risk of increasing mortality from accidents, liver disease, and cancer. Of course, it is easy to imagine a conclusive clinical study whereby two random groups of already diagnosed cardio-vascular patients would be treated to the best of our ability, with the difference that one group would be allowed a moderate intake of alcohol, and the other would not. In such a scenario, the exposure of patients to the risk of alcohol consumption could certainly be justified.

From the multitude of arguments for and against, it must be obvious that the final answer—like the perfect land for growing fine grapes according to Béla Hamvas—needs some distance and perspective. From where we stand—and considering the lifestyles, dietary habits, and addictions in Hungary—a good interim compromise would seem to consist of the reduction of alcohol intake, coupled with a shift in the structure of consumption. The "civilized" enjoyment of quality wines, in moderation and with meals, is invariably preferable to the quantity-minded approach prevalent today—of people bent on finding the quickest road to stupor, even if that road may lead through home-made "rot-gut" *pálinka* or concoctions of dubious provenance and chemical composition that one could hardly label "wine" with a clear conscience.

In summary, we can say that drinking wine in moderation is neither an omnipotent miracle cure, nor universal prophylactic, nor necessarily harmful in every one of its aspects. Prohibition or tolerance on the physician's part will have to hinge on the deliberation of risks and benefits in each specific case, and always be subject to the resignation that the final decision will be made by the none other than the "consumer." It is this decision for which I hope to have given a little guidance in this study, for all the Janus-faces of the approach I have had no choice but to adopt. It only goes to show that the classic medical doubts about alcohol, so well-known from history, are still with us—against the odds of all the science we can throw at it.

Finally, I trust that this brief examination will not be interpreted as a pamphlet promoting either extreme view—certainly not by the reader who happens to agree with Frigyes Karinthy's succinct aphorism: *"The irreplaceable significance of science lies in its relentless application to that which it does not yet know, in contrast to scatterbrained zeal which applies itself to that which it thinks it knows."*

235

The Organization of Wine

Hungary's Wine Communities make up a true and tried system, rekindled in 1994 in the wake of the political transformation, the history of which is discussed in detail in the first chapter of this book. These self-governing associations of growers—in which membership is compulsory within a given jurisdiction—operate as public bodies under the Wine Community Act, as well as according to their own autonomous rules and procedures.

At present, 550 villages number some 14,200 members, who delegate representatives to the Wine Community Councils (*Hegyközségek Nemzeti Tanácsa*) in each of the 22 official regions. In their turn, these regional organizations elect the National Council of Wine Communities. Regrettably, some 15% of the country's commercial wine production falls outside the purview of this three-tiered organization.

AS PART OF ITS TASK, THE WINE COMMUNITY

§ maintains quality standards by coordinating viticultural and enological activity;
§ assumes responsibility for guarding vineyards, and for cultivating abandoned sites;
§ sorts and synthesizes data before forwarding it to the regional Councils, and prevents tampering with the numbers in transit;
§ supports members with services and advice;
§ monitors compliance with regulations;
§ protects the interests of local growers;
§ investigates infringements of "protected origin" regulations.

AS PART OF ITS VESTED POWERS, THE WINE COMMUNITY

§ adopts and enforces locally binding professional rules at its own discretion, within the limits allowed by the wine law;

§ acts in administrative affairs assigned to its purview by law;
§ exercises reviewing and advisory rights in administrative affairs with implications for the viticulture and wine sector.

The regional Councils have the same responsibilities and entitlements, but of course on the higher regional level.

At the top of the hierarchy, the **National Council of Wine Communities**

§ supports the local Wine Communities and Regional Councils in their efforts to collect and report data;
§ designs services to facilitate the increase of Hungarian wines' share in the market;
§ may represent individual Wine Communities in matters involving quality standards and protected origin;
§ evaluates appeals of Regional Council decisions in administrative affairs;
§ collaborates with authorities and institutions fulfilling wine-related functions;
§ keeps in touch with international organizations controlling wine origin;
§ organizes wine fairs, competitions, and conferences.

An internationally accredited testing authority, the **State Wine Qualification Institute (OBI)** officially licenses the production, handling, qualification and release of products assigned to its purview by law, and may monitor those products for compliance. Operating under the auspices of the

Ministry of Agriculture, OBI uses methods of analysis which conform to EU norms.

Appointed directly by the Minister of Agriculture, the **National Wine Qualification Board (OBB)** performs organoleptic testing as well, and is solely authorized to award wines special quality status, the highest official grade. The National **Institute for Agricultural Quality Control** monitors new plantation and cultivation, oversees the production, distribution and use of propagation material, and performs official inspections in the viticulture sector.

CIVILIAN ORGANIZATIONS

It stands to reason to start with the grassroots associations of the growers themselves. It is important to remember that some of the top-notch Hungarian growers do not belong to any such group, just as there are organizations not mentioned here that nevertheless make a vital contribution to the life of Hungarian wine.

The **Tokaj Renaissance Association** – Classified Vineyards of Tokaj marshals the top growers in the country's most prestigious wine region. The members subject themselves to a Charter articulating both principles and practical constraints, including self-imposed rules of production, commitment to the highest quality, and ethical expectations. The Tokaj Renaissance fulfills a particularly indispensable role at international events. Contact: András Egyedi.

The Pannon Bormíves Céh, the **Pannon Wine Guild,** formed in 1998 to unite the winemaking elite from most influential regions in Hungary (and not just west of the Danube, as its name might suggest). The stringent stipulations embraced by the members seem all the more significant because in Hungary the actual quality of production has typically preceded appellation rules. It is imperative to approach this issue, as the Pannon Wine Guild does, from the ethical angle—certainly a fresh perspective in the world of Hungarian wine. In addition to some honorary members, the core of the Guild consists of 18 growers: János Árvay,

József Bock, Tamás Dúzsi, Mihály Figula, Tibor Gál, Attila Gere, Vince Gergely, Imre Györgykovács, Zoltán Heimann, Ottó Légli, Tamás Pók, Huba Szeremley, István Szepsy, Mátyás Szőke, Vilmos Thummerer, Ede Tiffán, Sándor Tóth, and Ferenc Vesztergombi. Each of these growers is introduced in a brief portrait in the chapter on the applicable wine region.

The **Hungarian Viniculture Public Benefit Company** has devised and implemented what are no doubt the most influential wine events in Hungary, most recently the eleventh International Wine Festival. The actual Wine Exhibition and Fair, a thrilling

Representing the Pannon Wine Guild – and Marcus del Monego

Borkollégium

markdown three-day pageant on the terraces of the Buda Royal Castle–tasting with the best growers until the early hours of morning–is only a part of this major event. The Festival itself is about much more than that, centered as it is on a series of scientific conferences and performances in music, theater,

GENERAL CATEGORIES OF HUNGARIAN WINE

Asztali bor (table wine)
Made from the must of authorized grape varieties with a sugar degree of at least 13. The finished wine must have minimum 9% alcohol.

Tájbor (country wine)
The same as above, but harvested from a growing area specified on the label. Minimum sugar degree of the must: 15.

Minőségi bor (quality wine)
Made from at least 15-degree must of grapes authorized in the given growing area, from plantations not exceeding a yield of 12 tons per hectare. The wine must exhibit the flavors and aromas typical of the location, the variety, and possibly the method of vinification.

Különleges minőségű bor (special quality wine)
Made from at least 19-degree must of ripe or overripe grapes authorized in the given growing area, from plantations not exceeding a yield of 10 tons per hectare. The wine must exhibit the flavors and aromas typical of the location, the variety, and the method of vinification, and must merit distinction due to its vintage and place of origin. Minimum alcohol: 12%.

Muzeális bor ("museum" wine–a special Hungarian category of reserve wine)
A quality or special quality wine aged at least five years, with unique aromas and flavors typical of the grape variety, the method of vinification, and maturation in cask and in the bottle. Distinguished due to its character and vintage.

Categories in terms of residual sugar content (still wines only)
száraz (dry): up to 4.0 g/l
félszáraz (semi-dry): 4.0-12 g/l
félédes (semi-sweet): 12.0-50 g/l
édes (sweet): over 50 g/l

and the arts. The HVPBC is also in charge of organizing VINAGORA, a biennial international wine competition overseen by the OIV, which in 2002 attracted wine producers from 16 different countries. We could not talk about these achievements if it were not for Zoltán Zilai, who conceived and is still running it all.

The **Hungarian Wine Academy**, the elite organization of Hungarian wine, celebrated its 10th anniversary in 2002. The members include the crème of the country's winemakers, a number of noted gastronomes, even a self-titled "gastrophilosopher," as well as artists and journalists–all dedicated to the cause of Hungarian wine. The Academy's number one duty is the election of the Winemaker of the Year.

The **Hungarian Association of Bacchic Orders of Wine** unites over thirty local wine fraternities, widely popular for their spectacular costumed processions and festivities.

The twenty-strong **Borkollégium (College of Wine)** has been meeting for 10 years for tasting sessions, producing the notes that ultimately form the backbone of the *Wine Guide.* To date, this pocket book, issued annually in English, German, and Hungarian, is the only publication listing and describing specific wines in Hungary by wine region. The Borkollégium also operates a wine course on the model of the Wine and Spirit Education Trust, and has been responsible for popularizing Slow Food in Hungary. Six years ago, the Borkollégium founded an annual award called *Bor-Élet-Út* ("Wine–the Life–the Way") to honor lifetime achievements in Hungarian wine.

The **House of Hungarian Wines** is a large-scale wine store in the Buda Castle across from the Hilton Hotel, perhaps the most wonderful spot in the city. It is the perfect place to get a taste of Hungarian wine for those who can only spare a couple of hours for this worthy pursuit.

Wine Trails have materialized in the major wine regions of Hungary, but the growers associations operating them are still learning the trade of wine tourism.

TERRA BENEDICTA

FOURTH CHAPTER - APPENDIX

Index of Growers
Some Notes on the Pronunciation of Hungarian
Glossary of Hungarian Terms

Bibliography

ALKONYI, LÁSZLÓ ET SOC.: Tokaj – a szabadság bora. 2000. Bp. Spread.

AMBRÓZY, ÁGOSTON: Tokaj-Hegyalja és néhány szellemtörténeti vonatkozása. 1932. Bp Kp. Sajtóváll.

BALASSA, M. IVÁN: Tokaj-Hegyalja szőleje és bora 1991 Tokaj-Hegyaljai Borkombinát ÁG

BALÁZS, K. SÁNDOR: Szekszárd a XXI szd. küszöbén 202 Ceba. Bp.

BODNÁR, LÁSZLÓ: A mátraaljai borvidék 2001 Szerz.k.

BROADBENT, MICHAEL: Wine tasting – German Edition: 1986. Raeber.
      Great Vintage Wine Book II. 1991. German Edition: 1994 Hallwag

CASAMAYOR, PIERRE: How to taste Wine? 2002. London, Hachette

CINDRIC, PETAR DR ET SOC. Sorte vinove loze 2000 Novi Sad

CSOMA, ZSIGMOND: Késes metszőollók Magyarországon. in: Ethnográphia 1983/1.
      Borászati munkaeszközváltás Somlón. M. Mg. Múzeum közleményei 1978-80.
      Uradalmi és... bortermelés Somlón 1993 Debrecen.

DERCZENI, D. JÁNOS: A Tokaji Bornak Termesztéséről ...etc. 1796. Kassa.

ÉGETŐ, MELINDA SZERK. Szőlőhegyi szabályzatok etc. 2001 L' Harmattan Bp.
      Hegytörvények Forrásközlései etc 2002. L' Harmattan

ENTZ, FERENC – MÁLNAY, I. TÓTH, I.: Magyarország borászata 1869 Pest.

FEYÉR, PIROSKA: A szőlő és bortermelés Magyarországon 1848-ig. 1981. Akadémia K. Bp.

FORNÁDY, ELEMÉR: A borkezelés mestersége 1948-1990. Novorg. Bp.

FRISNYÁK, SÁNDOR DR.: Tállya 1994 Tállya Község Önkormányzata

GAZDA, ALBERT-KOVÁCS, A. I.: Boremberek 2002 Bp. Litkey

HAMVAS, BÉLA: A bor filozófiája 1988. Életünk könyvek.

HARRISON, MICHAEL: Tokaji Wines a traditionin. In: W.and Sp. Review 1993 London

HULOT, MATILDE: Vins de Tokaj. 2001 Freret. Bordeaux

JABLONOWSKI, JÓZSEF: A szőlő betegségei és ellenségei. 1895. Kir. M. Tudományi Társ. Bp.

JANKÓ, JÁNOS: A Balaton melléki lakosság néprajza 1902 Bp.

JANKOVICS, MARCELL: Jelkép kalendárium 1997. Csokonai

JOHNSON, HUGH – ROBINSON, JANCIS: The World Atlas of Wine 2001 London, Beazley

KISS, ÁRPÁD DR.: Az ezerjó hazájában 1992 Albaswiss.

KNOLL, RUDOLF: Edelsüsse Weine 2000. Heyne, München

KOVÁCS, GY. ET SOC.: Hegyközség, szőlészet, borászat 1995 Agrocent Bp.

KOZMA, PÁL: A szőlő és termesztése 2001. Akadémia K. Bp.

LAPOSSA, JÓZSEF DR. – DÉKÁNY, T.: Villány. 2001. Aduprint
      Szőlőhegyek a Balaton-Felvidéken 1988. Mezőgazda Bp

LICHTNECKERT, ANDRÁS: Balatonfüred és Balatonarács története 1999 Veszprém m. Levéltár.

LIDDELL, AXEL: The Wines of Hungary 2003. London, Beazley

MAJOR, GYULA: Régi Budai Boroskönyv 1998. Szerzői k.

MERCZ, ÁRPÁD: A boroshordó. 2000 Hermesz kör. Bp.

PAP, MIKLÓS: Tokaji tanulmányok 1992 Tokaj.

PAULECZKI, FERENC DR.: Tolcsva története 1996. Tolcsva

RANDÉ, JENŐ DR.: Kóstolgató 2001 Axel Springer Bp.

ROHÁLY, GÁBOR SZERK.: Magyar Borok Könyve 2001. AKÓ. Bp.

ROHÁLY–MÉSZÁROS: Wine Guide Hungary 9. Edition 1995-2003. Bp. AKÓ

BROOK, STEPHEN: Wine People 2001 Vendome Press N.Y.

STURM, LÁSZLÓ SZERK.: Tokaj a világirodalomban 2000 Felsőmagyarország. Miskolc

SZABÓ, JÓZSEF – TÖRÖK, I.: Tokaj-hegyaljai album 1867 Pest.

SZEKFŰ, GYULA: A magyar bortermelő lelkialkata 1922 és 2002 Mundus Bp.

Szőlő és bor a kisgrafikákon. Kiáll. prosp. M.Mg. Múzeum 1972 Bp.

SZTÁRAY, ZOLTÁN: Haraszthy Ágoston 1986 Püski. New York

TAAR, FERENC: Tokaj szőlővesszein..." 1998 Kossuth

TÖTTÖS, GÁBOR DR.: A Szekszárdi szőlő és bor 1987 Szekszárd

VONYÓ, JÓZSEF SZERK.: Város a Tenkes alján. 2000 Siklós városa

WINKLER, AUGUST F.: Yquem. Die Jahrhundert Verkostung. 1999. Holzhauser. Wien.

ZILAI, JÁNOS JUN.: Bor és Mitosz. 2002. Mezőgazda K. Bp.

Index of recommended Growers

239

TÓTH ISTVÁN TRADICIONÁLIS PINCÉSZETE
3300 Eger, Kisvölgy u. 52.
Tel./Fax: 36/313 546 and 30/305 1646

VINCZE BÉLA PINCÉSZETE
3300 Eger, Váci M. u. 65.
Tel./Fax: 36/427 515

ETYEK-BUDA   p. 128-130

ETYEKI KÚRIA BORGAZDASÁG
2091 Etyek, Öreghegy, Pf. 7.
Tel.: 22/223 930 Fax: 22/223 929
E-mail: etyekikuria@hotmail.com

HERNYÁK LÁSZLÓ – ETYEKI BORUDVAR KFT
2091 Etyek, Kecske gödör, Pf. 28.
Tel.: 22/708 008 and 30/247 8994

HUNGAROVIN RT. BUDAPEST
1222 Budapest, Háros utca 2-6.
Tel.: 1/424 2500 Fax: 1/226 0429

NYAKAS PINCE
2073 Tök, Központi major
Tel.: 23/341 129 Fax: 23/341 095
E-mail cím: nyakasrt@axelero.hu

HAJÓS-BAJA   p. 113-118

BRILLIANT HOLDING KFT NEMESNÁDUDVAR
Office: 1026 Budapest, Bimbó út 212.
Tel.: 1/275 9456
Tel./Fax: 1/275 0070 and 1/275 9456
E-mail: brilliant.holding.kft@axelero.hu

SÜMEGI BORÁSZAT – KELLER KFT
6500 Baja Pf 250. Tel./Fax: 79/325 766
E-mail: kellerhu@dpg.hu

KUNSÁG   p. 113-118

HELVÉCIA RT
6034 Helvécia, Gazdaság dűlő 11.
Tel.: 76/579 034

MÁTRAALJA   p. 131-133

NÉMETH PINCE
3036 Gyöngyöstarján, Damjanich u. 4.
Tel./Fax: 37/372 027 and 20/954 2772

SZŐKE MÁTYÁS
3036 Gyöngyöstarján, Jókai tér 28.
Tel/Fax: 37/372 539
E-mail: szoke.matyas@mail.datanet.hu

SZŐLŐSKERT SZÖVETKEZET
3214 Nagyréde, Gyöngyösi út 1 .
Tel.: 37/573-500 Fax: 573-501
E-mail cím: redebor@matavnet.hu

MECSEKALJA   p. 134-136

DREYER DOMAINE VITICOLE MOHÁCS
7700 Mohács, Vaskapu 628.
Tel.: 69/329 138

EBERHARDT GYÖRGY - MOVIN KFT
7700 Mohács, József A. u. 4/a.
Tel.: 69/311 854 and 30/9026 498
Fax: 69/330 215

MÓR   p. 137-139

BOZÓKY CSALÁDI PINCÉSZET
8060 Mór, Pince u. 22.
Tel/Fax: 22/407 797

SOMLÓ   p. 142-149

FEHÉRVÁRI KÁROLY
8200 Veszprém, Egry J. u. 45/a
Tel.: 88/320 738

FEKETE BÉLA
Post: 8200 Veszprém, Látóhegy u. 3.
Tel/Fax: 88/327 407 and 20/9429 089

GYÖRGYKOVÁCS KISPINCÉSZET
Post: 8400 Ajka, Verseny u. 9.
Tel.: 88/200 116 and 30/232 3896

INHAUSER ISTVÁN,
"INDOVIN" KFT.
8483 Somlószőlős Tel.: 30/562 741

SOPRON   p. 150-155

GANGL CSALÁD PINCÉSZETE
9400 Sopron, Hunyadi J. u. 14.
Tel.: 99/329 874

IVÁNCSICS ZOLTÁN
9400 Sopron, Szegfű u. 30.
Tel.: 99/510 873

JANDL CSALÁDI PINCÉSZET
9421 Fertőrákos, Patak sor 26.
Tel.: 99/355 048

LUKA PINCÉSZET
9400 Sopron, Zerge u. 19.
Tel.: 99/316 379 and 30/352 5523

WENINGER PINCÉSZET
9494 Balf, Fő u. 23.
Tel./fax: 99/339 049
E-mail: weingut@weninger.com

SZEKSZÁRD   p. 156-164

ALISCAVIN BORÁSZATI RT
7100 Szekszárd, Epreskert u. 11.
Tel.: 74/416 955, Fax: 74/411 564
E-mail: avin@terrasoft.hu

ARANYFÜRT SZÖVETKEZET
7100 Szekszárd, Béri Balogh Ádám u. 56.
Tel.: 74/315 438, 314 4333

DÚZSI TAMÁS
7100 Szekszárd, Vadász u. 2.
Tel.: 74/319 025

HEIMANN és FIAI PINCE
2083 Solymár Hóvirág u. 31
Tel.: 26/362 188 and 20/961 7101
Cellar: 7100 Szekszárd, Sárköz u. 5163-64 hrsz.
E-mail: heimann@elender.hu

SZEKSZÁRDI MGRT LISZT PINCÉSZET
7100 Szekszárd, Rákóczi u.132.
Tel: 74/528 830 Fax: 74/528 831
E-mail: info@lisztwein.hu

TAKLER PINCE
7100 Szekszárd, Bem u. 13.
Tel.: 74/315 187
Cellar: Decs-Kútvölgy Tel.: 74/725 004

VESZTERGOMBI PINCÉSZET
7100 Szekszárd, Munkácsi M. u. 41.
Tel.: 74/ 511 846 és 74/511 847
Fax: 74/316 059
Wine-shop: Szekszárd, Béla tér 7.
Tel.: 74/410 640
E-mail:vesztergombipince@axelero.hu

VIDA PÉTER
7100 Szekszárd, Alkotmány u. 9.
Tel.: 74/317 753 and 20 911 7239

TOKAJ   p. 165-194

ÁRVAY ÉS TÁRSA PINCÉSZET
3911 Tokaj, Rákóczi u. 48.
Tel.: 47/552 155, Fax: 47/ 552 156
E-mail: tokaj.hetfurtos@axelero.hu

DEMETER ZOLTÁN PINCÉJE
3910 Tokaj, Ady Endre út 4.
Tel/Fax: 47/353 627 és 20/937 7074

KARÁDI ÉS BERGER PINCÉSZET
3932 Erdőbénye, Hunyadi u. 38.
Tel.: 20/9274 665 and 20/9609320
Fax: 1/201 2175
E-mail:zsoltberger@hotmail.hu

MEGYER RT
3950 Sárospatak, Nagy Lajos u. 12.
Cellar: Szent Erzsébet tér 26.
Tel.: 47/312 310 Fax: 47/312 320

PAJZOS RT
3950 Sárospatak, Nagy Lajos u. 12.
Tel.: 47/312 310 Fax: 47/312 320

PENDITS SZŐLŐBIRTOK ÉS PINCÉSZET
3881 Abaújszántó, Béke út 110.
Tel/Fax: 47/330 567
E-mail: Pendits@axelero.hu

SZEPSY ISTVÁN BORÁSZATA
3909 Mád, Táncsics u. 57.
Tel.: 47/348 349 Fax: 47/348 724

TOKAJ DISZNÓKŐ SZŐLŐBIRTOK
Post: 3910. Tokaj, Pf.10.
Cellar: 3931 Mezőzombor, Disznókő dűlő
Tel.: 47/569 410 és 47/369 138
E-mail: disznoko@disznoko.hu

TOKAJ HÉTSZŐLŐ RT
3910 Tokaj, Kossuth tér 15.
Tel.: 47/952 009 and 352 009 Fax: 352 219
E-mail.tokajhetszolo@axelero.hu

TOKAJ KERESKEDŐHÁZ
3980 Sátoraljaújhely, Mártírok u. 17.
Tel.: 47/321 526 Fax: 47/321 603
E-mail: tokajvin@axelero.hu

TOKAJ-OREMUS SZŐLŐBIRTOK ÉS PINCÉSZET
3934 Tolcsva, Bajcsy-Zs. u. 45.
Tel.: 47/384 505, 384 520 Fax: 47/384 504

ÚRI BOROK PINCÉSZETE Bt
3909 Mád, Kossuth u. 40/a
Tel./Fax: 47/348 601

TOLNA   p. 195-196

DANUBIANA BORKERESKEDŐ ÉS TERMELŐ BT.
7150 Bonyhád, Széchenyi tér 14.
Tel.: 74/451 212 Fax: 74/450 424
E-mail: danubor@danubiana.hu

EUROBOR KFT.
BÁTAAPÁTI KASTÉLYBOROK
7164 Bátaapáti, Hűvösvölgy u.4.
Tel/Fax: 74/409 327 and 74/409 222
E-mail: eurobor@terrasoft.hu

VILLÁNY   p. 197-208

 BOCK PINCE PANZIÓ
7773 Villány, Batthyány u. 15
Tel.: 72/492 919, Fax: 72/592 010
E-mail: bockbor@axelero.hu

CSÁNYI PINCÉSZET RT
7773 Villány, Ady fasor 2.
Tel.: 72/592 916 and 72/492 141
Fax: 74/492 009
E-mail: chateau-teleki@villanyiboraszat.hu

 GERE ATTILA
7773 Villány, Erkel Ferenc u.2.
Tel.: 72/492 195
Cellar: 72/492 839

GERE TAMÁS PINCÉJE
7773 Villány, Fáy u. 7. Tel.: 47/492 400

GÜNZER TAMÁS
7773 Villány, Déryné u. 10.
Tel.: 72/492 642

GÜNZER ZOLTÁN
7773 Villány, Oportó u. 6.
Tel./Fax: 72/492 608

JACKFALL BORMAUFAKTÚRA
7773 Villány, Hunyadi u.28/a
Fax: 1/421 5616
E-mail:info@jackfall.com

JEKL PINCÉSZET – VINOLAND PLUS Kft.
7773 Villány, Petőfi S. utca 46.

MALATINSZKY KÚRIA SZŐLŐBIRTOK
7773 Villány, Batthyány L. u. 27.
Tel./Fax: 72/493 042
E-mail: wine@malatinszky.hu

MONDIVIN KFT
7773 Villány, Teleki Zs. u. 9.

POLGÁR PINCÉSZET
7773 Villány, Hunyadi u. 19.
Tel.: 72/492 053, Tel./Fax: 72/492 194
E-mail: polgarp@axelero.hu

SZENDE PINCE
7773 Villány, Baross G.u.87.
Tel: 20/326 5767 and 72/492 396
Fax: 72/592 021

 TIFFÁN EDE ÉS ZSOLT PINCÉSZETE
7773 Villány, Teleki Zs. u. 9.
Tel.: 72/492 500 and 72/592 000
Fax: 72/592 000
E-mail: tiffan@matavnet.hu

TIFFÁN IMRE
7772 Villánykövesd, Pincesor 14-15.
Tel/Fax: 72/492 446

VYLYAN SZŐLŐBIRTOK ÉS PINCÉSZET RT.
7821 Kisharsány, Fekete hegy 092. hrsz.
Tel.: 72/579 701 Fax: 72/579 702
E-mail: vylyan@vylyan.hu

WENINGER-GERE KFT
7773 Villány, Erkel Ferenc u. 2/a
Tel.: 72/492 839

TOKAJ RENAISSANCE • LIST OF MEMBERS IN 2003

Estate: ÁRVAY PINCÉSZET
Address: 3911 Tokaj, Rákóczi u. 48.
Tel.: (36) 47 552 155
Fax: (36) 47 552156

Estate: AUREUM VINUM
Address: 3909 Mád, Árpád u. 33/B.
Tel.: (36) 47 348 780
Fax: (36) 47 348 360

Estate: BODVIN PINCÉSZET
Address: 3909 Mád, Ságvári u. 10.
Tel.: (36) 47 348 076
Fax: (36) 47 348 076

Estate: CHATEAU DERESZLA
Address: 3916 Bodrogkeresztúr, Felső u. 2.
Tel.: (36) 47 396 004
Fax: (36) 47 396 004

Estate: CHATEAU MEGYER
Address: 3950 Sárospatak, Nagy Lajos u. 12.
Tel.: (36) 47 312 310
Fax: (36) 47 312 320

Estate: CHATEAU PAJZOS
Address: 3950 Sárospatak, Nagy Lajos u. 12.
Tel.: (36) 47 312 310
Fax: (36) 47 312 320

Estate: DOBOGÓ PINCÉSZET
Address: 3910 Tokaj, Dózsa u. 1.
Tel.: (36) 47 552 147
Fax: (36) 47 552 148

Estate: DUSÓCZKY PINCÉSZET
Address: 3918 Szegi, Dusóczky-tanya
Tel.: (36) 47 309 058
Fax: (36) 47 309 058

Estate: EVINOR
Address: 3950 Sárospatak, Bercsényi u. 27.
Tel.: (36) 47 312 234
Fax: (36) 47 312 234

Estate: FÜLEKY PINCÉSZET
Address: 3916 Bodrogkeresztúr, Iskola köz 15.
Tel.: (36) 47 396 478
Fax: (36) 47 396 478

Estate: GUNDEL PINCÉSZET
Address: 3909 Mád, Árpád u. 37.
Tel.: (36) 47 348 383
Fax: (36) 47 348 383

Estate: GRÓF DEGENFELD
Address: 3915 Tarcal, Terézia kert 9.
Tel.: (36) 47 380 173
Fax: (36) 47 380 149

Estate: KIRÁLYUDVAR
Address: 3915 Tarcal, Fő u. 92.
Tel.: (36) 47 380 111
Fax: (36) 47 380 952

Estate: MONYÓK PINCÉSZET
Address: 3909 Mád, Táncsics u. 18.
Tel.: (36) 47 548 033
Fax: (36) 47 548 033

Estate: ROYAL TOKAJI WINE Co.
Address: 3909 Mád, Rákóczi u. 35.
Tel.: (36) 47 348 011
Fax: (36) 47 348 359

Estate: SZEPSY PINCÉSZET
Address: 3909 Mád, Táncsics u. 57.
Tel.: (36) 47 348 349
Fax: (36) 47 348 724

Estate: TOKAJ DISZNÓKŐ
Address: 3910 Tokaj, Pf. 10.
Tel.: (36) 47 569 410
Fax: (36) 47 369 138

Estate: TOKAJ - HÉTSZŐLŐ
Address: 3910 Tokaj, Bajcsi Zs. E. út 19. Pf. 17.
Tel.: (36) 47 352 009
Fax: (36) 47 352 141

Estate: TOKAJ PENDITS (MWB)
Address: 3881 Abaújszántó, Pf. 27.
Tel.: (36) 47 330 567
Fax: (36) 47 330 567

Estate: TOKAJ OREMUS
Address: 3934 Tolcsva, Bajcsy-Zs. u. 45.
Tel.: (36) 47 384 505
Fax: (36) 47 384 504

Estate: TÖRÖK PINCÉSZET
Address: 3909 Mád, Táncsics u. 15.
Tel.: (36) 47 363 835
Fax: (36) 47 363 835

Estate: ÚRI BOROK PINCÉSZETE
Address: 3909 Mád, Kossuth u. 40/A
Tel.: (36) 47 348 601
Fax: (36) 47 348 601

TOKAJ RENAISSANCE – 3910 TOKAJ, Kossuth tér 15., Pf. 17. – Tel./Fax: (36) 47 353 612
www.tokaji.hu – tokaji@tokaji.hu

Some Notes on the Pronunciation of Hungarian

I remember reading of a survey published by, if memory serves, some appendage or other of the United Nations that ranked the world's languages in order of grammatical complexity. The first two places were occupied by Korean and Vietnamese, and in third position was Hungarian. Indeed, when I first came to Hungary in 1997, I felt the strange sensation that I had previously read of in a book by the BBC correspondent Misha Glenny. Unlike any other capital city in Europe, Budapest provokes a peculiar feeling in the first-time visitor innocently walking round the city. For a European city, architecturally everything is fine, and the people appear quite normal; but still this sense of strangeness grows. And suddenly the reason dawns on you—not a single word makes any sense at all! If one is familiar even in passing with the three main language groups of this continent, one will not be unduly daunted by words such as *lait, latte, leche, Milch, moloko, mleko* etc. Milk. In Hungarian? *Tej*, which rhymes with 'say'.

Admittedly, things have changed even since 1997, and the tourist in Budapest will have no difficulty surviving without uttering so much as a word of the local language. But he will miss out on so much! The Hungarians are a warm and friendly people, and Hungary a sunny and colourful land—any presumptions to the contrary by those we used to call 'Westerners' are a result of misinformation, ignorance, and the imposed isolation the country has endured. Learning a small amount of the language will go a long way to dispelling these prejudices, and will increase exponentially the enjoyment and value of a visit to Hungary.

The description on paper of the pronunciation of a language, particularly one as unfamiliar to most English speakers as Hungarian, is a difficult—some might say, futile—endeavour. I seek merely to give the reader enough guidance that he might, when mentioning, say, a *cserszegi fűszeres* or *muskotály* to another wine enthusiast, make himself or herself understood. I would urge anyone planning to visit this country to purchase a self-study Hungarian book and cassette. Listening to the sounds I am about to describe is an infinitely superior method of learning them, although that is not to say that there is no merit in comparing the sounds of a foreign language with those of one's own through the medium of print.

The visitor to Hungary will find that any reasonably intelligible attempt to speak the language will be met with joy and praise, and on some occasions, astonishment, so used have the natives become to tourists assuming that English will be universally understood. So, having perhaps instilled some trepidation in my readers with the preceding lines, let us crack on. This guide to Hungarian pronunciation starts with some good news…

Hungarian has a phonetic system of spelling: how a word is pronounced is represented precisely by the way it is written. In the case of English, it is necessary for dictionaries to point out the different pronunciations of, for example *–ough* in *through, though, thought, rough, cough, bough,* and *thorough.* Seven different sounds represented by one group of letters! Imagine how this makes foreign students of English feel. In Hungarian you need only learn what sound is represented by what letter or digraph (a sound symbolised by two letters, as in English *sh* or *th*), and you can read anything.

CONSONANTS

The following consonants are pronounced more or less as they are in English:
b d f g h k l m n p r t v z

244

Just remember that *g* is always hard, as in *good* or *dog*; and *r* is trilled as in Spanish, but only very slightly, and unlike in English (*farm, forty*) it is *always* pronounced.

The following consonants all occur in English, so pronunciation is not usually problematic. The orthography will, however, simply have to be learnt. All the following, whether written with one or two letters, represent one sound, and, indeed are considered in Hungarian dictionaries to be separate letters.

c like the *ts* in 'cats'

cs like the *ch* in 'church'

j, ly both the same: like the *y* in 'yes'

ny like the first *n* in 'onion' or the Spanish 'mañana'

s like *sh* in 'sheepish'

sz like *s* in 'send'

ty a soft sound like the *t* in 'tube' or 'ritual'

zs like the *s* in 'pleasure' or the *j* in French: 'je suis juste'

The most difficult consonant for English speakers of Hungarian is

gy which is somewhat like the *d* in 'during' or 'individual'.

One must try to avoid pronouncing it as in the end of the word 'edge', this, though you will probably be understood, sounds very foreign to Hungarians.

VOWELS

This is where things get complicated. There are at least fourteen of them, and a number of those do not occur in English. Incidentally, when I say 'English', I am referring to what is known as Standard English, spoken mainly in the south-east of England, or deliberately by the educated or social climbers from other regions. I apologize to Americans and other non-standard English speakers (I myself am from the damper but more civilised North of England, where 'bath' rhymes with 'hath', not 'hearth') for this linguistic convention. Of course, the vowel sounds from English and other languages, which I give as comparisons, can only ever be approximations.

a difficult, but similar to the *o* in 'hot' or the *a* in 'what'

á long, like ah-*haa!* but open like the *a* in 'man', not 'father'

e like 'bet' or 'pen'

é like the French *mais*, or 'say' without the *y* sound

i like 'sit' or 'pin'

í longer, like 'seem' or 'cheat'

o short, as in 'nonsense' or 'politics'

ó long, as in 'fall' or 'thought'

u like the vowel sound in 'put'

ú longer, as in 'school' or 'rule'

ö like the French *le*, or German *können*

ő longer, as in French *deux* or German *schön*

ü like French *tu*, *perdu*

ű longer, like French *debut* or Scottish accented 'who' or 'you'.

Remember that in Hungarian these letters do not combine to form other sounds: all are pronounced separately, so *tea* (tea) is pronounced 'te-a'.

Lastly, double consonants are always pronounced as a longer sound. Think of the *n* sound in 'unnecessary', or the *d* in 'mad dog'. Now you can say the Hungarian verbs 'to drink' and 'to eat':

inni (in-ni) *enni* (en-ni)

When a consonant represented by a digraph is lengthened, only the first letter is doubled, as in the *sz* sound in *hosszú* (hoss-sue) which means 'long'.

Luckily, the stress *always* falls on the first syllable of a word. All syllables must be pronounced evenly with the full vowel sound. For an English speaker this requires a conscious effort, as we tend naturally to swallow or reduce the vowels in the unstressed syllables of a word. In Hungarian, the latter syllables are often the most important in a word. Speak confidently and evenly.

Now, hopefully, you can work out that *muskotály* is pronounced something like 'mush-kot-aye'. I will leave you with a few other examples (remember to stress the syllable in bold—always the first:

Tokaji aszú (**tock**-oy-ee **a**-sue)

paprika (**pop**-rick-a)

Egészségedre! (**egg**-ace-shay-ged-re — say this as quickly as possible) which means 'To your health!' or 'Cheers!'

Robert Hodgson, Budapest, June 2003

245

Glossary of Hungarian Terms

1 ha . . . . . 9,8846 roods
2,4711 acres (English)
2,4710 acres (American)

1 kat.hold . . 1,4222 acre (English)
1,4221 acre (American)

Áldomás . . . The drinking of a toast (to somebody or something)

Állami . . . . State(-owned)

Aszalás . . . . Drying

Ászkolás . . . Aging in wood

Asztali bor . . Table wine

Aszú/Aszúbor Wine made from botrytized/noble rot covered grapes

Aszúbogyó . . Shriveled berry with noble rot

Aszúsodás . . Developing of noble rot

Bakművelés . . Horned head training

Bikavér . . . . Special term for blended quality red wine in Eger and Szekszárd

Bor . . . . . Wine

Borászat . . . Winery

Borvidék . . . Wine region

Botritisz . . . Botrytis cinerea

Bujtás . . . . Layerage

Cuvée . . . . . Blend

Családi . . . . Family (adjective)

Donga . . . . Wooden stave for a cask or barrel

Döntés . . . . Graft (to a rooted stem)

Dűlő . . . . . Single vineyard

Édes . . . . . Sweet

Essencia . . . . Natural juice of collected botrytized grapes

Fehér . . . . . White

Fürt . . . . . Bunch

Gönci hordó . Name of a special Tokaj cask (136 l)

Hegyközség . . Wine Community

Hordó . . . . Barrel, cask

Karó . . . . . Stake

Kerti bor . . . Orchard wine

Minőségi bor . Quality wine

Késői szüretelésű
. . . . Late harvest

Kft (Korlátolt felelősségű társaság)
. . . . Limited liability company

Must . . . . . Must

Palack . . . . Bottle

Pince . . . . . Cellar

Puttony . . . . Hod

Sárga . . . . . Yellow

Siller . . . . . A light, non-tannic red wine (Darker than a rosé, normally with a Tavel rosé color.)

Száraz . . . . Dry

Szőlő . . . . . Grapes

Szőlőbirtok . . Wine estate/vineyard

Szőlőtermelő . Vine-grower

Szövetkezet . . Cooperative

Tájbor . . . . Country wine

Tőke . . . . . Vine

Authors

DR. GABRIELLA MÉSZÁROS
Lawyer, WSET qualified international wine academic
Grape varieties; Gastronomy

DR. ANDRÁS NAGYMAROSY
Professor and chair, Department of General and Historical Geology,
Eötvös Loránd University, Budapest
Places and Times; Sun, Wind and Rain; Wine regions — except Somló, Tokaj, and Villány

DR. GÁBOR ROHÁLY
Physician, editor of *Wine Guide Hungary*; lecturer, Weinakademie Österreich
Viticultural traditions; Somló; Tokaj; Villány; Section III.

DR. LAJOS SZOLLÁR
Physician; Director of Institute of Pathology and Dean of General Medical School,
Semmelweis University of Medicine, Budapest
Wine and Health

DR. SÁNDOR TÓTH
Oenologist, estate owner
A concise history of Hungarian wine

Photography

TIBOR DÉKÁNY • 14, 17, 85, 95, 96, 97, 98, 103, 106, 107, 108, 109, 111, 113, 116, 117, 122, 123, 124, 125, 126, 128, 130, 131, 133, 134, 136, 137, 139, 140, 144, 146, 159, 160, 162, 164, 166, 167, 170, 172, 173, 174, 180, 186, 191, 194, 195, 196, 200, 203, 204, 206,

ZOLTÁN KOMÁROMI • 67, 69, 216, 219, 232,

ATTILA MÉSZÁROS • 68, 69, 70, 71, 72, 73, 74, 75, 77, 78, 79, 80, 81, 82, 83, 214

GÁBOR ROHÁLY • 15, 16, 23, 24, 26, 33, 93, 99, 102, 127, 142, 143, 147, 148, 150, 152, 153, 156, 161, 168, 175, 177, 178, 179, 181, 182, 183, 184, 185, 188, 190, 198, 205, 207, 215, 218, 231, 238

ZOLTÁN SZABÓ • 87, 88, 89, 90, 91, 101, 104, 105 p.

The different meals shown in the chapter „Gastronomy" were composed by KÁLMÁN KALLA (Chef of Restaurant Gundel in Budapest). The recipes in English are available on the following site: **www.ako.hu**

BORKOLLÉGIUM

Copyright:

AKÓ KIADÓ, BUDAPEST

Responsible editor:

GÁBOR ROHÁLY

PRINTINGHOUSE DÜRER, GYULA
Director: ANDRÁS MEGYIK

Wine districts in Hungary

I Dunáninneni district

- I/I Pozsonyvidéki region
- I/2 Nyitra, Bars, Felső-Komárom region
- I/3 Hont, Nógrád, Vácz region
- I/4 Pest, Kőbánya, Hatvan region
- I/5 Dunáninneni kerti szőlők region

II Dunántúli district

- II/I Fertőmelléke region
- II/2 Győr vidéke region
- II/3 Neszmély, Esztergom region
- II/4 Buda vidéke region
- II/5 Fehér, Veszprém, Tolna region
- II/6 Somlyó region
- II/7 Balaton melléke region
- II/8 Zala, Vas, Sopron region
- II/9 Villány, Pécs region
- II/10 Szegszárd region
- II/11 Belső-Somogy, Tolna region

III Tiszáninneni district

- III/I Eger, Visonta region
- III/2 Miskolcz vidéke region
- III/3 Torna, Abaúj-Gömör region
- III/4 Tokaj, Hegyalja region
- III/5 Felső-Zemplén, Ung, Felső-Beregh region
- III/6 Alsó-Beregh, Ugocsa region
- III/7 Tiszáninneni kerti szőlők region

IV Tiszántúli district

- IV/I Szathmár, Kővár-vidéke region
- IV/2 Érmellék region
- IV/3 Ménes, Magyarát region
- IV/4 Temes és Krassó felső vidéke region
- IV/5 Temes és Krassó alsó vidéke region
- IV/6 Tiszántúli kerti szőlők region